Cross-National Encounters

The Personal Impact of an
Exchange Program for Broadcasters

Herbert C. Kelman & Raphael S. Ezekiel

With the collaboration of
Rose B. Kelman

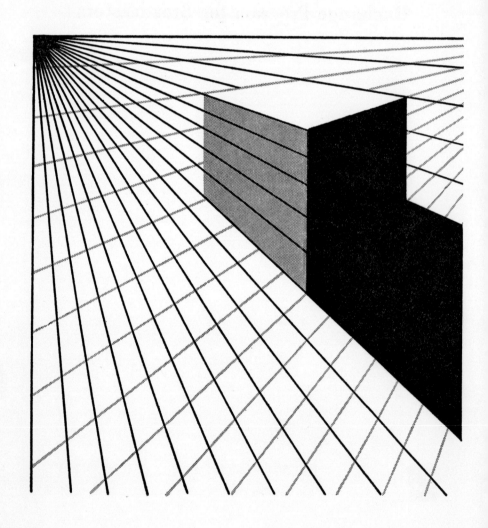

CROSS-NATIONAL ENCOUNTERS

Jossey-Bass Inc., Publishers

615 Montgomery Street · San Francisco · 1970

CROSS-NATIONAL ENCOUNTERS
The Personal Impact of an Exchange Program for Broadcasters
Herbert C. Kelman and Raphael S. Ezekiel

Library of Congress Catalog Card Number 76-110630

Standard Book Number SBN 87589-055-5

Manufactured in the United States of America
Composed and printed by York Composition Company, Inc.
Bound by Chas. H. Bohn & Co., Inc.

JACKET DESIGN BY WILLI BAUM, SAN FRANCISCO

FIRST EDITION

Code 7007

The Jossey-Bass
Behavioral Science Series

General Editors

WILLIAM E. HENRY
University of Chicago

NEVITT SANFORD
Wright Institute, Berkeley

To

Daniel Katz & M. Brewster Smith

teachers, colleagues, and friends

Preface

Cross-National Encounters presents the results of an intensive evaluation study of a multinational seminar for broadcasting specialists from sixteen countries who spent four months studying, exchanging ideas, and traveling in the United States. The seminar took place at Brandeis University, under the auspices of the Communication Research Center (later known as the Morse Center for the Study of Communication), during the summer of 1962. It was sponsored by the Bureau of Educational and Cultural Affairs, United States Department of State. The inclusion of an evaluation study was built into the plan of the seminar from the beginning, and Herbert Kelman agreed to undertake this study in the fall of 1961 at the request of the directors of the Brandeis center and of the research staff of the Bureau of Educational and Cultural Affairs. Data were collected in the spring and summer of 1962 and in the spring and summer of 1963. Raphael Ezekiel joined the project in the fall of 1964. The analysis and the writing of this book were mostly done at the University of Michigan, where Kelman worked (in the Department of Psychology and the Center for Research on Conflict Resolution) between 1962 and 1969, and where Ezekiel has been since 1964.

The authors first met in Accra in the summer of 1963. The Kelmans were traveling through several countries to conduct the follow-up interviews for the study reported here, and they had just arrived the night before to begin the Ghanaian part of the journey. Ezekiel had come with Brewster Smith to interview American Peace Corps volunteers in Ghana as part of a study of the impact of the Peace Corps experience on its young participants. It is hard to recapture the optimistic mood of those days. Whatever our general criticisms of American foreign policy may have been at the time, we were enthusiastic about the Kennedy administration's new emphasis on international cooperation and exchange—as exemplified by the formation of the Peace Corps and the upgrading of the Bureau of Educational and Cultural Affairs within the State Department —and we welcomed the opportunity to undertake research related to these governmental programs.

The delays that often characterize academic research and publication have placed us in an anomalous position. Research that we undertook in one mood is being published in an era marked by a very different mood. Today, efforts at international cooperation and exchange by the United States government seem to us overshadowed and altered in meaning by the overall posture of America in the international system. However, our distress about the state of our own society and its policies and our greater pessimism about the role of international exchange in the current context do not in any way limit the validity and relevance of the findings reported in this book. What we have learned from the present case about the impact of international exchanges, the conditions for enhancing their effectiveness, and the satisfaction of their participants is applicable to a wide variety of international programs, whether they be sponsored by governmental or private agencies and whether they be conducted under national or international auspices. *Cross-National Encounters* is thus relevant to individuals charged with policy formation in the field of cross-national education and with the organization and conduct of international exchange programs, conferences, workshops, and professional tours. At the same time, the findings have relevance to social scientists interested in the multidimensional assessment of attitudes toward such complex entities as foreign countries and in the nature of attitude change—in general or specifically in the context of cross-national encounters.

This study could not have been carried out without the enthusiasm, the openness to new ideas, and the active support of the men in charge of the object of our evaluation—the Brandeis Multi-National Communications Specialists Seminar. We express our deep appreciation, therefore, to Louis G. Cowan, director of the Communication Research Center at the time this research was carried out, and to Henry Morgenthau, III, associate director of the center at that time and director of the seminar itself. We also appreciate the help and cooperation we received at all times from Constance Kanter and other members of the seminar administrative and academic staff.

We are grateful to the Bureau of Educational and Cultural Affairs, United States Department of State, for their financial support of the study; to Kenneth Cooper, the Chief of Research Programs at the bureau at the time the study was initiated, for his personal interest in the project, his encouragement at every stage, and his readiness to facilitate the process; and to James Moss, associate and then successor to Cooper, for his consistent support and friendship.

Financial support from the National Institute of Mental Health enabled us to undertake additional analyses of the data obtained in this study, to explore some of the broader theoretical issues of attitude measurement and attitude change, and to bring the present volume to completion. This work was carried out as part of a research program on social influence and behavior change supported by United States Public Health Service Research Grants MH-07280 and MH-17669. The generous and broadgauged support of this research program by the National Institute of Mental Health over a period of years is gratefully acknowledged.

Many individuals contributed to this research. We cannot name them all, but we particularly express our thanks to several whose contributions were extensive. Victoria Steinitz played a central role in the development of research instruments, collection of data, and initital data analysis. John M. Darley participated in the construction of questionnaires. Amy and Andrew Billingsley conducted many of the interviews with seminar participants. Marvin Hoffman took charge of group observations and conducted staff interviews. Stephen Leff assisted with administrative arrangements and group observations. Reuben Baron played a major role in the development of coding schemes for both interviews and questionnaires. Allan Levett took responsibility for the coding of questionnaire responses. Catherine Hoch not only handled much of the coding of interview and questionnaire responses but also gave her devoted attention to numerous administrative and secretarial tasks. John DeLamater commented on an earlier version of the manuscript. Elizabeth Musgrave typed and proofread most of the manuscript. Carolyn Boykoff took part in the final processing of the manuscript and in the reading of proof. Rose Kelman's contributions to the study and to the book at all stages—in planning the research, developing the instruments, making the administrative arrangements, collecting and analyzing the data, drafting the manuscript, reading the proofs, and preparing the index—were so extensive and indispensable that they could be properly acknowledged only by listing her name on the title page.

Finally, we take this opportunity to thank the participants in the seminar, who gave us many of their free hours and their well-considered thoughts while they were in the United States and then added to these their personal warmth and hospitality when we interviewed them in their home countries. Special thanks are due to members of the comparison group, who graciously consented to fill out lengthy questionnaires on two separate occasions and—after completing these chores—still treated us as friends when we finally met them and interviewed them in person.

Some of the findings of the study were reported earlier in articles published in the *Journal of Social Issues*[1] and the *Journal of Applied Behavioral Science*.[2] We thank the editors of these journals for permission to reprint portions of these articles in this book. We also thank Holt, Rinehart, and Winston for permission to use several quotations from *International Behavior: A Social-Psychological Analysis*.

Cambridge   HERBERT C. KELMAN
Ann Arbor   RAPHAEL S. EZEKIEL
February 1970

[1] H. C. Kelman, with V. Steinitz, "The Reactions of Participants in a Foreign Specialists' Seminar to Their American Experience." *Journal of Social Issues,* 1963, *19*(3), pp. 61–114.

[2] H. C. Kelman, "The Effects of Participation in a Foreign Specialists' Seminar on Images of the Host Country and the Professional Field." *Journal of Applied Behavioral Science,* 1965, *1,* pp. 149–166.

Contents

Cross-National Encounters

The Personal Impact of an
Exchange Program for Broadcasters

*The use of traveling is to
regulate imagination by reality
and, instead of thinking how
things may be, to see them as
they are*
Samuel Johnson

1

International Exchange

Since the end of World War II, the scope and rate of educational and cultural exchange across national boundaries have shown a marked increase. In particular, large numbers of students, scholars, and specialists in various areas have gone abroad to obtain special training, to familiarize themselves with activities in other countries that are relevant to their own fields of interest, or to exchange ideas and experiences with colleagues from other parts of the world.

Professional and educational exchange activities are carried out by a variety of private organizations. These include various professional organizations, whose primary concern is the advancement of their respective fields through developing and improving mechanisms for training, communication, and collaboration. They also include organizations concerned with international cooperation and exchange, either as ends in themselves or as means toward the improvement of international relations and the reduction of international tensions.

Exchange activities are also carried out, in the United States as well as in many other countries, under the auspices of various governmental agencies. Such activities may be related—either directly or in-directly—to specific foreign policy goals of a government or to its broader foreign policy orientations. For example, a government may foster such activities in the interest of reducing international tensions and creating an amicable climate for international relations. It may be interested in transforming the hostile, suspicious, or indifferent attitudes that other peoples have toward it into favorable ones, or at least to increase their understanding and correct their misconceptions of its policies and of its country in general. It may initiate exchange activities in order to assist in the development of other nations, which in turn may be linked to a num-ber of different foreign policy goals. Finally, a government may view par-ticipation in international exchange activities, in their own right, as an integral part of the conduct of foreign affairs, consistent with the general increase in the rate of international contact and communication during the past two decades.[1]

Granting that international exchanges may have great intrinsic merit and may contribute to various goals of individuals, organizations, and governments, do they have any bearing on fundamental questions of war and peace? Proponents of such activities often argue that they con-tribute to creating the conditions for peace by increasing international understanding and improving mutual attitudes. There is no clear-cut evi-dence that international exchange in fact produces more favorable atti-tudes. But even if it did, "is it reasonable to suppose that favorable atti-tudes developed through personal contact can overcome the realities of a conflict of interest? If conflicts between nations are based primarily on in-compatible goals rather than on lack of understanding, it is doubtful that increased understanding can contribute greatly to their resolution."[2] De-spite these limitations, international cooperation and exchange are likely to contribute, at least indirectly and in the long run, to creating the con-ditions for peace. The paper just cited distinguishes "four types of effects of international cooperation and exchange that may have an impact on the relations between two nations and may reduce the likelihood that con-flict between them will take violent forms: (1) an increased openness, among key individuals in each nation, in their attitudes toward the other

[1] For a discussion of the role of educational and cultural exchanges in the foreign policy process in the United States and in several other countries, see P. H. Coombs, *The Fourth Dimension of Foreign Policy: Educational and Cultural Affairs* (New York: Harper and Row, 1964). Philip Coombs was the first Assistant Secretary of State for Educational and Cultural Affairs—a post newly created by President John F. Kennedy—at the time the study reported in this book was initiated.

[2] H. C. Kelman, "Social-Psychological Approaches to the Study of Inter-national Relations: The Question of Relevance," in H. C. Kelman (Ed.), *Inter-national Behavior: A Social-Psychological Analysis* (New York: Holt, Rinehart and Winston, 1965), p. 573.

nation; (2) a reduction in the level of tension between the two nations; (3) an increased commitment to an internationalist ideology; and (4) a development of a network of relationships cutting across national boundaries."[3] Let us examine each of these effects briefly.

POLITICAL IMPLICATIONS

1. Participants in international exchanges and other types of international cooperative ventures, as we have already noted,

> . . . do not universally and necessarily come away from these experiences with wholly favorable attitudes toward the other nation or nations involved. Yet the indications are that such experiences can and usually do produce some very important attitude changes —provided the experiences themselves are personally and professionally satisfying to the participants. These are not necessarily changes in general favorableness toward the host country, but rather changes in the cognitive structure—for example, in the complexity and differentiation—of images of the host country. . . . Such changes are probably more meaningful in the long run than total approval of the country would be. They indicate a greater richness and refinement of images and a greater understanding of the other society in its own terms. Moreover, participants in such activities are likely to develop personal ties to the other country and to certain individuals within it, and thus a sense of personal involvement in its fate.[4]

Though this increased understanding and involvement may not overcome real conflicts of interest between the nations, it may create a greater openness in individuals' attitudes toward the other nation.

A continuing pattern of cooperation and exchange between two nations, drawing in many individuals who occupy leadership positions within their own societies, should create a *"predisposition within each nation to trust the other nation, to perceive it as nonthreatening, and to be responsive to it. . . .* Thus, while it would be naive to assume that a pattern of cooperation and exchange is a sufficient condition for peace between two nations, such a pattern should decrease the likelihood that the nations will resort to violence in resolving their conflicts. If conflicts arise between nations whose citizens have a history of close and friendly contact, there should be less of a tendency to perceive threatening intent in the other and to formulate the issue in black-and-white terms, and a greater readiness to communicate with one another and to seek accommodation."[5]

2. If two nations *are* in conflict with each other, but are, at the

[3] *Ibid.*
[4] *Ibid.*
[5] *Ibid.*, pp. 573–574.

same time, involved in mutual exchanges and other forms of cooperative activity, the level of tension that marks their overall relationship is likely to be reduced:

> They are more likely to engage in at least some interactions that are free of hostility and mutual threat, and that provide opportunities for communication and for the discovery of common values and interests. Needless to say, these more positive interactions will not cause the basic conflict between the two nations to vanish and will not persuade them to abandon the pursuit of incompatible goals. They can, however, contribute to the creation of an *atmosphere in which these basic conflicts can be negotiated more effectively and political settlements can be achieved.* . . . Positive interactions between two nations in areas outside of those on which their conflict centers, by reducing the level of tension, may help to build up some degree of mutual trust and thus at least make it somewhat more likely that serious negotiations on the issues in conflict will get under way. Moreover, the establishment of cooperative relationships in some domains may help to counteract tendencies toward complete polarization of the conflicting nations and may thus make it easier to find ways of "fractionating" the conflicts between them.[6]

3. Participants in international exchanges and cooperative ventures —provided these exchanges are intrinsically useful and satisfying to them —can be expected to become more world-minded and committed to an internationalist ideology. As the rate of international exchange and cooperation increases, ideological changes in these directions are likely to become more widespread, thus strengthening the ideological underpinnings to a peaceful world order.

> Such changes in the belief systems of individuals, in and of themselves, are not likely to produce major changes at the institutional level . . . . [But] international exchange and cooperation may contribute to the development and strengthening of international political institutions by increasing the *ideological readiness for them among influential segments of the participating nations,* even though the major force toward the development of such institutions is likely to come from functional requirements rather than from an abstract commitment to an internationalist ideology.[7]

4. Perhaps the most important political implication of international exchange and cooperation is that they contribute

> . . . to the development of human networks that cut across national boundaries. Participation in such activities, if they are successful, is

---

[6] *Ibid.,* p. 574. For a discussion of the values of fractionating conflicts, see R. Fisher, "Fractionating Conflict," in R. Fisher (Ed.), *International Conflict and Behavioral Science* (New York: Basic Books, 1964), pp. 91–109.

[7] Kelman, pp. 574–575.

likely to lead to the establishment of ongoing relationships around common professional concerns among individuals representing different nationalities. These relationships have functional significance for the individuals in the sense that they are directly relevant to their professional interests and the effective performance of their professional roles. Thus, individuals and groups from different countries become committed to international cooperation not as an abstract value, but as a concrete vehicle for carrying out personally important activities and pursuing their immediate and long-range goals. They become involved in a network of interdependent individuals and groups, without reference to national differences, and are likely to develop a sense of loyalty to it. What is crucial here is that this loyalty cut across national lines; it need not be antagonistic to or competitive with national loyalty, but simply independent of it.

Insofar as international exchange and cooperation contribute to the development of such cross-cutting loyalties, they help to create the conditions for peace . . . . The development of *networks, based on professional and other interests, that cut across national boundaries* can contribute to the stability and integration of the international system. It would do so, not by eliminating conflicts, but by counteracting tendencies toward complete polarization—toward subordinating all relationships to a single basic conflict along national lines.[8]

EVALUATING EFFECTS

Various kinds of social research can help us assess whether international exchange programs do indeed contribute to the achievement of the specific and long-range goals that have just been outlined, and they can also help us delineate the conditions that would maximize the effectiveness of such programs. One relevant type of research is evaluation research, involving the systematic study of specific programs and their impact on the participants in them. Such research would allow us not only to conclude whether the program under study achieved the goals of the organizations that sponsored it and of the individuals who participated in it, but also to develop recommendations for enhancing the effectiveness of similar programs in the future.

Evaluation research, in itself, cannot tell us whether international exchange in general or the particular program under study contributes to the long-range goals of creating the conditions for peace; but it can help us check out some of the assumptions on which the presumed long-range effects depend, by providing detailed information about the actual nature of the exchange experience. Moreover, insofar as evaluation research can help enhance the effectiveness of international exchanges, it is relevant to

---

[8] *Ibid.*, pp. 575–576. For a discussion of the role of cross-cutting ties in intergroup conflict, see L. A. Coser, *The Functions of Social Conflict* (New York: Free Press, 1956).

these long-range goals, since their achievement is predicated on exchange experiences that are successful and personally and professionally satisfying to the participants.

This book is based on a detailed evaluation study of a specific exchange program: a multinational seminar for communications specialists, sponsored by the Bureau of Educational and Cultural Affairs, U.S. Department of State, and conducted at Brandeis University in the summer of 1962. A plan for thorough evaluation was built into the design of this seminar from the beginning. The conditions for such evaluation research were particularly favorable. First, initiative for the evaluation came from the directors of the seminar themselves. Since the seminar represented a new venture, they were eager to obtain specific information that might contribute to the improvement of future seminars of this sort. They regarded the evaluation as an integral part of the seminar, at least equal in importance to the program activities themselves. Second, the staff of the Bureau of Educational and Cultural Affairs was, at the time of the study, interested in initiating systematic and intensive research on exchange activities. Although strongly committed to the values of international exchange, they wanted to know more about the specific aspects of such experiences that are most valuable and about the possibilities of further improvements in projects they were sponsoring. Third, the special nature of the Brandeis project facilitated evaluation research, since its administration—starting with the selection of participants—was more centralized than is usually the case.

The book focuses on our findings about the reactions of participants to the exchange experience and about the impact that this experience had on them. Although our conclusions and recommendations are specific to the seminar being evaluated, we point to problems that are germane to cultural and educational exchange programs in general. The findings should thus be of interest to specialists in the field of cross-national education and exchange. At the same time, the book should be relevant to the concerns of many social scientists. Not only does it portray one attempt to translate research findings into their concrete policy implications, but it also reports a study of adjustment and attitude change in an inherently interesting situation—that of an extended gathering, in a foreign country, of a multinational group of specialists.

PERSONAL IMPACT OF THE EXPERIENCE

This study is one of many investigations of international exchange carried out in the postwar years.[9] For theoretical as well as practical rea-

[9] For examples and reviews, see the following references: R. Morris, *The*

sons the social scientist has found the phenomenon of the sojourner abroad arresting. The sojourner is caught up in an experience that touches on some rather central problems in social psychology, yet an experience with which almost anyone can empathize. Most of us have had the experience, to however small an extent, of suddenly realizing that we are far from the myriad of objects and acts and words (our own and those of others) in terms of which we are accustomed to deal with the world. It is an eerie and unsettling experience to discover how different one can seem to others when he is in a new setting, though he "hasn't changed at all" and "is still the same person." We become more aware of the extent to which identity does in fact depend on acts of commerce between the person and the environment. We become more aware that the self not only can *seem* different to onlookers in new environments, but, treated differently by them, can indeed *become* different.

The sojourner in another land confronts these issues head on. He has left his homeland as an individual, but immediately upon arrival in the new country he is turned into a representative of his nation. People perceive him and act toward him, by and large, in terms of his nationality, which is a new cognitive category for him. The social scientist finds much of interest in looking at some of the variables that help to determine the nature of this experience, at the processes by which it is shaped, and at the personal changes it produces.

Many reasons support a sojourner's decision to go to a given foreign country. He may, as in some former times and places, be a youth from a wealthy family who seeks to acquire culture, polish, and adventure on some traditional circuit of travel. He may, as in the case of most programs that have been studied, be a student who seeks new educational and living experiences in a foreign and often more developed country. He may, as in the present case, be a professional who seeks further training and experience in his field.

There are also many reasons, some of which have been outlined earlier in this chapter, for a host country's decision to seek out sojourners. In the postwar years, in particular, public and private agencies in various countries have been interested in spreading skills and training, and in

Two Way Mirror (Minneapolis: University of Minnesota Press, 1960); C. Selltiz, J. R. Christ, J. Havel, and S. W. Cook, *Attitudes and Social Relations of Foreign Students in the United States* (Minneapolis: University of Minnesota Press, 1963); M. B. Smith (Ed.), "Attitudes and Adjustment in Cross-Cultural Contact: Recent Studies of Foreign Students," *Journal of Social Issues,* 1956, *12* (1); G. V. Coelho (Ed.), "Impacts of Studying Abroad," *Journal of Social Issues,* 1962, *18* (1); S. Lundstedt (Ed.), "Human Factors in Cross-Cultural Adjustment," *Journal of Social Issues,* 1963, *19* (3); I. de S. Pool, "Effects of Cross-National Contact on National and International Images," in Kelman, pp. 106–129; and A. L. Mishler, "Personal Contact in International Exchanges," in Kelman, pp. 550–561.

developing more detailed knowledge about their countries and perhaps more favorable attitudes toward them among foreign nationals.

To what extent do sojourners in fact acquire new knowledge, attitudes, and skills? The earlier studies of international exchanges suggest some answers,[10] which will be amplified by our findings. Thus, it is often the case, as in the present study, that the sojourner's attitude will not become markedly more favorable to the host nation, but that his conceptions of that nation will become considerably more complex. One of the strengths of the present study is the inclusion of a control group, which, for practical reasons, has been impossible in most of the earlier research. Use of a control group allows us to show that the increase in complexity of the seminar participants' conceptions of America was not matched by a similar group of specialists who did not come to America.

What accounts for the sojourner's development of more complex conceptions of the host society? The literature suggests involvement in rather intensive interactions with members of that society as a major variable. And what, in turn, determines the likelihood that a sojourner will have frequent, intensive, far-reaching interactions with Americans? Several relevant findings from the previous literature were confirmed in the current study. We shall see that a facilitative factor in interactions is that the sojourner come from a culture that is accorded a fair degree of status in America, or one that possesses a considerable degree of cultural kinship with America. We shall also see that outcomes are related to the role that the sojourner plays at home and the goals he has set for himself in the present encounter. Here we shall introduce a new distinction that has a bearing on the outcome—a distinction between those who are and see themselves as accomplished professionals and those who see themselves, to a greater or lesser extent, as akin to apprentices. Earlier studies have also contrasted groups differing in level of professional advancement, such as professionals and students, or graduate students and undergraduates. However, these distinctions have generally coincided with differences in age and in professional commitment. It is not surprising, therefore, that the professionally less advanced (younger, less committed) individuals in these studies tended to have more intensive contact with Americans and to learn more about America. In our study we shall note a reverse finding, related to the marked differences in the agenda of our two groups. We shall see that the professionally less advanced group is caught up in a more rigorous agenda. As apprentices, they are much more concerned about acquiring specific professional skills; they are intense and task-oriented in a way that precludes many of the interpersonal experiences of those who are professionally more accomplished.

[10] These comments draw heavily on the review by Mishler.

Finally, we shall conclude, as does much of the literature—at least by implication—that there are many ways to profit from participation in a cross-cultural exchange. Even when mistakes occur, the experience has such intrinsic merit and offers such diverse opportunities that participants often find a way to turn even a disappointing program to advantage. Thus, our professionally accomplished group, as we shall demonstrate, suffered some personal disappointments during the early parts of the sojourn, being forced to take more passive roles than suited their perceived capacities and their expectations. Nevertheless, they emerged from the experience having gained as much as or more than the professionally less advanced group. The apprentices gained technical knowledge, and were grateful for it. The professionally advanced group, on the other hand, was able to use its considerably more varied agenda to generate interesting new goals to be pursued during those portions of the sojourn that offered them insufficient professional stimulation.

PLAN OF THE BOOK

After describing the seminar (Chapter Two) and the design of the evaluation study (Chapter Three), we shall present three sets of findings yielded by our research:

The first series of chapters is devoted to the reactions of the seminar participants to their experiences. Chapter Four discusses their reactions to the university phase of the seminar, and Chapter Six to the travel phase. Chapter Seven presents their retrospective reactions to the seminar as a whole, obtained shortly before their departure from the United States and again about a year after their return home. This section of the book also includes a brief discussion of the seminar staff's reactions to the university phase of the program (Chapter Five). In all of these chapters, and particularly in Chapters Four and Six, we present specific recommendations for future seminars, based on the reactions of the participants and on our interpretation of them.

Chapters Eight to Twelve focus on the impact of the experience on the participants' attitudes and images. In Chapter Eight we consider their views of what the sojourn has meant to them personally. Chapter Nine describes their views of America and American broadcasting in the light of their experiences. Chapter Ten provides some basis for assessing the extent to which the American sojourn had actually affected participants' attitudes by comparing their responses in an interview held about a year after their return home with those of a control group. Finally, the findings presented in Chapters Eleven and Twelve, unlike those in the preceding chapters, are based on written questionnaires rather than intensive personal interviews. Though they lack the richness and detail of the interview data, they provide us with direct and controlled evidence of attitude changes attributable to participation in the seminar, since identical questionnaires were administered both before the seminar and about a year later, both to participants and to the control group. Chapter Eleven describes changes in the cognitive structure of participants' images of America and American broadcasting, and Chapter Twelve presents changes in the content and the affective component of various images.

Chapters Thirteen and Fourteen present analyses of the reactions to the sojourn among different subgroups of participants and the impact it had upon them. Specifically, Chapter Thirteen compares two subgroups selected on the basis of their questionnaire responses: those who had shown a considerable increase in the differentiation of their images of America and American broadcasting, and those who had shown no such increase. By comparing these two groups, we can gain some insight into the process out of which such cognitive changes may emerge. Chapter Fourteen compares two subgroups selected on the basis of a demographic dimension, to which important differences in prior experiences, in expectations, and in personal agenda for the sojourn are likely to be linked: European versus non-European origin. By comparing these two groups, we can learn something about different styles of reaction to a sojourn experience, differences which may have both theoretical and operational implications.

The fifteenth and final chapter brings together the major implications of our findings for improving the conduct of international exchange programs, for assessing their outcomes, and for understanding the psychological processes they set into motion.

2

The Seminar

The seminar on which our study focuses was conducted by the Communication Research Center at Brandeis University in the summer of 1962, under a grant from the State Department's Bureau of Educational and Cultural Affairs. The Communication Research Center came into being about a year before the seminar convened; prior to the seminar, it had a permanent staff of four, including the Director and Associate Director. The seminar represented the Center's first major project.

As originally conceived, the seminar was designed to deal with the mass media of communication in general, but gradually its primary emphasis was narrowed down to the broadcasting media, and particularly to their use for educational purposes. The plan was to bring to the United States, for a four-month period, specialists in broadcasting and related fields from a number of different countries. The countries were to be selected so that different degrees of experience with television would be represented in the seminar.

GOALS

In order to develop criteria and measures for evaluating the seminar (to be described in Chapter Three), the research staff had to ascertain the goals that the organizations sponsoring and conducting the seminar were hoping to achieve. Procedures could then be devised to assess the ex-

11

tent to which these goals were in fact met. Thus, in January 1962, we held a meeting with several members of the Bureau's Program Research and Evaluation Staff to learn about their goals and expectations for the seminar and about the impact they hoped it would have on the participants. In February 1962 a similar meeting was held with the organizers of the seminar at the Communication Research Center.

Our discussion with the staff of the sponsoring agency revealed several interrelated goals that they hoped this seminar would achieve; some of these goals were specific to the present seminar, whereas others applied to the whole range of their activities. Our informants expressed the hope that seminar participants would come away with a greater awareness of the educational possibilities of the mass media, of the importance of concentrating on quality productions, and of ways of strengthening the media so that they can resist external pressures. They regarded it as essential to communicate to participants from countries in which television was in the initial or planning stage that the United States does not have "the answer"—that it would be desirable not to imitate American procedures, but to develop television in their own way, in line with the needs of their own societies. As for the relationship between the United States and the countries represented in the seminar, the sponsoring agency hoped that seminar participants would come away with the feeling that communication represents a universal endeavor in which their countries are associated with the United States, and that the seminar is the first step in a continuing process of learning from one another. A related goal mentioned was the increase in exchange of program materials between the United States and the countries represented in the seminar.

The sponsoring agency also hoped that the seminar participants would become aware of the pluralism that characterizes mass communications in the United States and of the revolution going on in this field. To this end, they wanted to acquaint the participants with the whole range of broadcasting activities—educational as well as commercial, successes as well as failures—and to give them an opportunity to make their own comparisons. Similarly, with respect to American society in general, our informants stressed the importance of avoiding a propaganda effort, and of exposing seminar participants to a wide range of experiences. They expressed the hope that participants would come away with a sharper, clearer view of the forces underlying American society, and a better understanding and knowledge of America as a country and people. Such an understanding would not necessarily result in wholly favorable attitudes toward the United States, but ideally would be reflected in the objective quality of subsequent reporting about this country.

The organizers of the seminar at the Center expressed similar goals, although they placed somewhat greater emphasis on the potential contributions of the seminar to the professional advancement of the participants and to the development of the mass media in the participants' own countries. On the first point, they expressed the hope that the seminar would broaden the participants' background and increase their skills. These skills may relate, for example, to the use of television for educational purposes, or to the training of others, depending on the level of development of television in a given participant's country. On the second point, they expressed the hope that the seminar would increase participants' sensitivity to the potentials as well as the limitations of the mass media; that it would provide them with a better basis for comparison in judging the quality of mass communications; and that it would help them in working out their own ways of improving the process of communication in their respective countries, particularly as it relates to education and to national development in general.

Another goal mentioned by the organizers of the seminar was that the participants would come away with a more international view of broadcasting, based on the experience of working together on common problems, as well as an interest in continued association with their American counterparts. They hoped that channels of communication opened as a result of the seminar would also allow American broadcasters to learn about methods and materials developed by their colleagues abroad. Specifically, they mentioned that they would like to obtain various materials (such as tapes or scripts) from the participants to add to the resources of the Communication Research Center. Finally, they shared with the sponsoring agency the hope that participants would acquire a clearer view of American mass media and of American culture and society in general.

The general goals of the sponsors and organizers—which we can presume to be similar to the goals of other exchange programs of this type—can be summarized as follows: (1) to provide the participants with a professionally useful experience, yielding new information, new ideas, and new contacts that can enhance their professional work and their capacity to contribute to the solution of problems in their own countries; (2) to open up channels of communication and exchange between the participants and their colleagues in America and in other countries, which can be continued and developed after they return to their home countries; and (3) to provide the participants with first-hand knowledge of American mass media, as well as of American society and American life in general.

With respect to the third goal, both the sponsors and the organizers of this seminar stressed the importance of giving the participants a complete and objective picture of American mass media and American life, including not only accomplishments, but also problems, difficulties, and shortcomings. The hope was that the participants would leave with a fuller, richer, more detailed, and more differentiated picture of American mass media and American institutions, and that they would gain a more intimate understanding of American society and of the way in which the mass media fit into its general institutional structure and cultural patterns. Ideally, they would become more fully aware of the range of activities and points of view in American broadcasting and American life in general. But this increased awareness does not mean that they would change their attitudes in the direction of an uncritical acceptance of American patterns and procedures.

We agree that the development of wholly favorable attitudes toward the host country is neither a realistic expectation, nor even a desirable goal for exchange programs. Such programs can be considered successful if—in addition to meeting the professional needs of the participants and establishing better channels of communication—they help the participants to refine their views of those areas of American society that are of special concern to them.

SELECTION OF PARTICIPANTS

The list of countries from which participants were to be selected was drawn up so as to represent different levels of experience with television. It included countries with extensive experience in television and its use for educational purposes, countries in which television had been introduced only recently or was about to be introduced, and countries in which television was in the planning stage. Furthermore, in most of the countries on the list, English was either the dominant language or widely spoken among the educated segments of the population.

The criteria for selecting participants within each country called for individuals "on the policy-making and creative level who are engaged in television itself or are in education, radio, government information ministries, or journalism, and are currently preparing themselves for important positions in the field of television." The intention was to select participants who were at the highest possible levels within their own organizations, so that they would be in a good position to implement whatever they learned at the seminar. Preference was to be given to individuals concerned with the educational side of broadcasting, but this emphasis was by no means exclusive. Finally, for the participants from non-English-speaking countries, the criteria included an excellent command of English, although several of the individuals actually selected did not fully meet this criterion.

A distinctive feature of the seminar was the procedure for selecting participants. The director of the Seminar (Associate Director of the Communication Research Center), together with the Chief of the Foreign Specialists Branch of the Bureau of Educational and Cultural Affairs, personally visited fifteen countries, including most of those from which participants were finally selected. In each country, they consulted with leading figures in broadcasting, educational, and governmental agencies that had some relevance to the concerns of the seminar; they interviewed prospective participants to determine their interest and suitability; and they worked out, with officials of the American Embassy, arrangements for the processing of nominations that would assure their conformity with the professional requirements of the seminar.

On the basis of these various consultations, a procedure for nominating seminar participants was developed in each country, and a selection panel was set up to take charge of this task. The composition of these panels varied from country to country, but in most cases the nominations were handled completely by nationals of the country in question. They might have included, for example, the director of the country's broadcasting system, a representative from the ministry of education or information, and important officials from other relevant agencies who had had the opportunity of discussing the purposes of the seminar and the criteria for selection with the seminar's director. In most cases, an official from the American Embassy—usually the Cultural Affairs Officer or Public Affairs Officer—was attached to the panel to provide liaison with the Embassy. The names of nominees selected by each panel, together with biographical information about them, were then submitted to the Communication Research Center and the Bureau of Educational and Cultural Affairs for final approval.

These selection procedures eventuated in a group of twenty-eight participants, coming from sixteen different countries, thirteen of which had been personally visited. The countries represented and the number of participants from each are listed in Table 1. About one third of the participants were professionally concerned with educational broadcasting, most of them with the production of television or radio programs for schools. A somewhat smaller number were concerned with broadcasting in the area of news and current events; and about one third were concerned with the production of a variety of other types of programs, or with administrative and supervisory tasks in the program divisions of their respective broadcasting systems. The distribution of the participants among these different areas of specialization is presented in Table 2.

After the selection procedure for a given participant had been completed, he received a formal invitation from the United States Ambassador in his own country. Another formal letter of invitation was sent

Table 1

COUNTRIES REPRESENTED IN THE SEMINAR

Countries	Number of Participants
Australia	1
Japan	2
Philippines	2
Thailand	2
Iran	1
Israel	2
Cyprus	1
Kenya	2[a]
Rhodesia	2[a]
Nigeria	3
Ghana	2
Italy	1
Yugoslavia	2
Sweden	2
United Kingdom	2
Jamaica	1
Total	28

[a] One African and one Briton.

by the president of the sponsoring university. The director of the seminar personally wrote to each participant, giving him information about the program. Each participant also received four books on various aspects of American society and culture. Finally, the director of the evaluation study sent a detailed letter to each participant, soliciting his cooperation in the research, and enclosing the first questionnaire (to be described in Chapter Three).

FIRST PHASE: THE UNIVERSITY

Most of the participants arrived in the United States just before the opening of the seminar on June 9, 1962. They spent the first six weeks of their sojourn at Brandeis University. Three of the participants (all Europeans) were accompanied by their wives from the beginning; a fourth wife arrived about a month later. All participants were housed in dormitory rooms. They were given the option of sharing a room or taking a

Table 2

AREAS OF SPECIALIZATION OF SEMINAR PARTICIPANTS

Areas of Specialization		*Number*
Educational (instructional) broadcasting		9
Employed by broadcasting system	6	
Employed by school system	3	
News broadcasting		4
Programs[a] on current events, documentaries, talks		3
Programs,[a] general		10
Primarily concerned with administration	6	
Primarily concerned with production	4	
Government		2
Ministry of Education	1[b]	
Ministry of Information	1[c]	
Total		28

[a] Most of the broadcasting systems represented divide their regular broadcasting activities into two divisions, one concerned with "news," and the other with "programs." The latter division includes special features, documentaries, talks, discussions, cultural programs, music, entertainment, and programs addressed to special populations (for example, women's programs). In this table, current events programs, documentaries, and talks are separated from the rest since, in some analyses to follow, specialists in these types of programs are grouped together with news specialists, with whom they have much in common.

[b] In subsequent analyses, this participant is grouped with educational broadcasters.

[c] In subsequent analyses, this participant is grouped with specialists concerned with administration of general programs.

single room, and about three-quarters of the participants chose the latter alternative. Small charges for these rooms were deducted from the $15 per diem allowance that each participant received. The participants took most of their meals at the university cafeteria; payments for these meals were made on the basis of a flat rate per day, deducted from the $15 allowance. The per diem allowance was more than adequate for the period spent at the university, but—as we shall see later—some of the participants found it insufficient for the travel period.

The program of the seminar during the university phase was divided into two major parts: professional activities and academic activities. A central feature of the *professional activities* was a series of professional seminars. Four such seminars were scheduled for each of the six weeks the participants spent at the university. During the first week, the

seminars were designed to give participants general background information about the structure and function of American mass media, with
special emphasis on the role of the broadcasting media within this wider
context. During subsequent weeks, the seminars were conducted by invited
speakers, most of whom were outstanding specialists in their various fields.
The speakers included producers and writers of television and radio programs, administrators of commercial and educational broadcasting systems, specialists on educational broadcasting media from a variety of
organizations (within universities, school systems, foundations, governmental and international organizations), and an occasional critic and
journalist. The seminars dealt with the operations of educational broadcasting in the United States; with the uses of broadcasting media for various specific instructional purposes (such as the teaching of science or
languages); with research on educational television and programmed instruction; and with a variety of activities in the United States in the fields
of news and documentaries, cultural and dramatic programs, and entertainment. Typically, a speaker would come for a single day and spend
several hours with the participants, starting with a lecture or demonstration before lunch and continuing with further discussion after lunch. The
speakers usually described their own activities and the philosophies that
governed them, and presented samples of their work. In two cases, the
same topic extended over a two-day period, and the seminars were combined with opportunities for detailed observations of the activities under
discussion. Both of these two-day sessions dealt with the activities of local
organizations in the educational broadcasting field and could thus combine lectures and film showings with visits to facilities, demonstrations,
and discussions with various staff members of the organizations.

The two local organizations that participated in the two-day seminars were among a number of local agencies and businesses whose facilities
the participants were able to visit and part of whose activities they were
able to observe. These organizations included educational and commercial
television stations; newspaper offices; a communication training program,
a center for producing programs in language instruction by television and
for training teachers in the use of these programs, and other educational
facilities at universities in the area; and a company producing audiovisual
equipment. In addition, some field trips outside the Boston area were
arranged, which included a visit to the offices of the *New York Times,* to
the headquarters of a large manufacturer of electronic and television
equipment in New Jersey, to an educational television station in Philadelphia, and to a small university radio station in New Hampshire.

In addition to the invited speakers who made presentations at the
professional seminars, a number of prominent visitors were brought in to

speak to the group and participate in informal discussions. These additional addresses and discussions were generally held in the evening. Some of these guests were specialists in broadcasting or other areas of communication, and thus rounded out the professional part of the program. Others came from the fields of education, social welfare, race relations, politics, and the arts, thus contributing to the second major part of the program—the so-called academic activties.

The term *academic activities* was used to refer to activities not directly concerned with communication media, but rather, activities focused on providing general information about American society and American institutions. The major activity in this area consisted of a series of seminars led by members of the university faculty and covering various aspects of American society. Four weekly seminars dealt, respectively, with American courts and civil rights (including discussions of civil liberties and constitutional guarantees); American government and politics (including discussions of the party system and of the relationship between Congress and the Presidency); trends in American philosophy (especially social criticism and social thought); and American social structure (with emphasis on race, religion, and social class). The last two of the four seminars met simultaneously, so that participants had to choose between them. Although the participants were told that attendance at these seminars was optional, the large majority seemed to feel that it was expected and did attend on a regular basis.

A number of social activities were also planned during the six-week period at the university. Participants attended several cultural and entertainment events, including music, art, and film festivals; they visited some places of historical significance; and they were invited to dinners at the homes of university officials and in connection with visits to broadcasting or newspaper facilities. The two main social events arranged for the group were an outing and boat ride on the Fourth of July, and a weekend of private hospitality with families in a small New England town.

Participants' contributions to the seminar. At the beginning of the seminar, the participants were asked to prepare descriptions and analyses of the broadcasting structures of their respective countries. These papers generally turned out to be comprehensive, well-documented reports, and were reproduced and distributed among the participants, though they did not serve as bases for group discussion.

Opportunities for informal exchange among participants were numerous, since they lived together and spent most of their free time with each other. Planned and scheduled occasions for exchange, however, were limited to a series of presentations of samples of their work (in the form of tapes or films) that the participants had brought with them at the request of the organizers of the seminar. Most of the presentations were film showings; there was less interest in sound materials, some of which, moreover, were in languages not understood by many of the participants.

No detailed arrangements for the presentation of these materials had been made in the program originally prepared for the seminar. The scheduling for these presentations was left to a committee of the participants which was formed, with the encouragement of the directors, during the second week of the seminar. The committee scheduled presentations during whatever open times were available in the program, generally in the late afternoon or early evening. Some of these presentations were replaced, however, by a guest speaker or some other activity that was newly scheduled or had to be rescheduled for one or another reason. Often the presentations came at the end of a full day of seminars and addresses. Moreover, because of the lack of certain technical facilities, it was not possible to show some of the materials or to show them to their best advantage. For these various reasons, the "viewing and listening sessions," as they came to be called, were infrequent and not well attended.

In addition to arranging the schedule of "viewing and listening sessions," the participants' committee took it upon itself to deal with other matters of common concern to the seminar and to serve as liaison between the participants and the directorate. Thus, the committee made recommendations, both to the participants and to the directorate, about certain procedural details and about arrangements for the travel period.

Some of the participants were interviewed by representatives of the local press or on local radio stations. In addition, several participants took part, as a group, in a television program in which they discuss their own countries and their experiences in the United States.

SECOND PHASE: TRAVEL

After six weeks at the university, the participants embarked on a two-month trip throughout the United States. They left together by bus for Tanglewood, Massachusetts, where they attended concerts of the Boston Symphony Orchestra and visited at the home of Mrs. Serge Koussevitzky. From there they went to Hyde Park, New York, where they had lunch with Mrs. Franklin D. Roosevelt. The bus then took them to New York City, where the group dispersed and each participant followed his individual itinerary.

Itineraries were personally arranged for each participant to meet his special needs and interests. Each participant met with members of the seminar administrative staff and volunteer assistants to work out his travel plans. Many participants had specific ideas about places they wanted to visit for professional or personal reasons. All of the participants had ideas about the types of facilities they wanted to see and experiences they wanted to have. The staff, in consultation with educational and broadcasting specialists, attempted to locate sites that would meet these various requirements. Cooperation of the pertinent officials in the various organizations was solicited, and letters were sent off introducing the visitor and giving the approximate dates on which he could be expected. In each community, an individual or an agency—such as a State Department reception center, a university international center, or a local hospitality group—was designated as the primary contact for participants who would be visiting there. The hosts were apprised of each visitor's plans and were asked to facilitate his sojourn in their respective communities. Transportation and hotel accommodations were arranged through a private travel agency.

Some participants traveled alone; others traveled in pairs, for all or part of the time. In several cases, the two participants from the same country traveled together for most of the period. Several participants (all European) rented or borrowed automobiles for all or part of the trip; included in this category were three of the participants who traveled with their wives.

Each participant devoted a major portion of his two-month travel to various professional activities, including visits to broadcasting stations and to other organizations concerned with various aspects of the field of broadcasting or of education. Some participants spent extensive periods of time in a single station, observing it in detail or directly participating in its activities. Most participants, however, paid only short visits to a number of different facilities in various parts of the United States. Each trip also included visits to other sites of special interest to the individual participant, and visits of general interest designed to acquaint him with America and American life. Hospitality was organized by local agencies in many of the cities visited. In addition, many of the participants had their own contacts in various places, or established new contacts spontaneously.

Each participant's itinerary included New York City (with visits to the large broadcasting networks); Washington, D.C. (with visits to some major governmental agencies); Los Angeles; and San Francisco. Additional stops varied from individual to individual, but most participants had at least some exposure to communities in the Midwest and the South.

The participants were able to arrange—and, if necessary, rearrange —their travel plans within a specified travel allowance. In addition, as has already been mentioned, they received a $15 per diem allowance for housing, meals, and miscellaneous expenses.

FINAL PHASE: RETURN TO THE UNIVERSITY

At the end of their two-month travel period the participants returned to the university for a final series of seminars and discussions. The total time scheduled for this final phase was two and a half weeks. Several participants had to leave the United States before the beginning of this final phase because of other obligations, but the large majority participated in it for at least part of the time. After the first week, however, participants began to depart on a staggered basis, in keeping with their individual plans, so that group membership shrank from day to day.

For this final phase, the participants stayed at the university guest house, a former country estate in an isolated, wooded area. The participants all had their sleeping accommodations in this building and took their meals there. Meetings and discussions were also all scheduled there, with the exception of a few visits to broadcasting, educational, and other organizations in the Boston area. In general, the living arrangements made for a relaxed and informal atmosphere during this final period.

During the first week of this final phase, each of the four academic seminars convened for one session to review its domain in the light of the participants' travel experiences. In addition, several guests from the fields of communication, education, and civil rights came to address the group and participated in informal discussion. In comparison with the first six weeks, however, the number of scheduled activities was considerably reduced. There was a fair amount of unscheduled time, some of which the participants spent in informal discussion and evaluation of their experiences. This phase of the seminar, then, was largely a period in which participants tried to pull together the information they had gathered during their travels and from the contacts they had made, and in which they prepared themselves for departure.

During this period, at the request of the local educational television station, one of the participants from the United Kingdom produced a program entitled "American TV: An Outside View." In this program, which appeared on television while the final phase of the seminar was still in progress, several of the participants discussed their observations and impressions of American television.

The director of the seminar also arranged a meeting with the participants to discuss means of increasing international exchange of programs and staff. On the basis of this meeting, several participants drew up a memorandum, which was then circulated among all participants after they returned to their home countries. This memorandum reviewed some of the difficulties involved in the exchange of programs and made some recommendations for overcoming them; it recommended possible arrangements for the exchange of personnel, particularly between emerging, inexperienced organizations and highly developed ones; and it expressed appreciation to the directors of the seminar for giving the participants the opportunity to get to know the United States and each other and to make personal contacts that they greatly cherished.

3

Evaluation Study

The evaluation study was an integral part of the total planning of the seminar from the very beginning, and the research program developed parallel to the seminar itself. The research staff maintained close liaison with the organizers of the seminar and had their full cooperation at every stage of the research effort.

PURPOSE

The evaluation study had two major interrelated purposes. The first was to obtain evidence of the *effectiveness of the seminar* in achieving its goals. These goals, as seen by the sponsors and the organizers of the seminar, have already been described in Chapter Two.

In evaluating the effectiveness of the seminar in achieving these goals, the present study relied, in part, on the participants' own formulations. The participants were able to relate how useful they found the experience professionally, what effect it had or was likely to have on their professional activities, and how they thought it may have changed their views. This kind of information can be obtained in the course of the seminar, particularly toward the end, when the participants have an overview of the whole experience and anticipate returning home. It can also be obtained after the participants have been back home for some time. Their reactions at that point are of special value because, by then, they are likely not only to have a better perspective on their experience, but also to be in a position to evaluate its actual impact on their professional activities in their customary settings.

The present study did not rely entirely, however, on the participants' own formulations for evaluating the seminar. It also tried to establish whether participation in the seminar had, in fact, produced changes in relevant attitudes—specifically, in the participants' conceptions of their professional roles, in their ideas about the function of broadcasting in their own countries, and in their views of American mass media and other aspects of American society. With respect to the last point, our interest was not in finding whether attitudes had become more favorable, but whether they had changed qualitatively, that is, whether they had become richer and more differentiated.

Certain types of information that would be highly pertinent to an evaluation of impact were not collected in the present study. For example, we did not undertake objective analyses of the participants' professional activities after their return home or of the impact their trip actually had on their respective organizations. Thus—largely because of practical limitations—we did not use various techniques that could have been used in the evaluation of effectiveness, such as content analysis of programs or articles prepared by participants after their return, or interviews with their personal and professional associates, or before- and after-observations of the organizational units within which they carry out their professional activities. Effectiveness in this study was assessed entirely through attitude changes observed in the participants and through their own reports on their activities and orientations.

The second purpose of the evaluation study was to discover the *specific features of the seminar that were most successful, and those that created problems and difficulties.* Such information should be very useful for planning future seminars, and could provide some basis for deciding which features should be maintained or even expanded, and which need improvement. The best source of information for this purpose are the participants themselves, who can evaluate different arrangements and activities in the light of their own expectations and needs. Although relevant information can be obtained from the participants retrospectively, their reactions during the course of the seminar are especially important. Events that they are evaluating are still fresh in their minds then, and their reactions are likely to be specific and concrete. Reactions obtained while the seminar is in progress can also be related to our direct observations of the seminar itself.

In short, the evaluation study was designed to answer two policy questions: (1) Was the seminar successful in producing the effect that it was intended to produce? (2) What specific arrangements and procedures are likely to enhance the effectiveness of this and similar seminars? An analysis of the relationship between the participants' reactions to different aspects of the seminar and the effects it has on them should be particularly instructive. The most useful conclusions of an evaluation study are likely to refer not to the overall success of the program, but to the effects of certain specific procedures and arrangements on certain kinds of participants, given their particular needs and expectations. This kind of information has the greatest relevance for future planning, since it can aid in the proper matching of participants and programs.

To the extent that the study allows us to relate the participants' reactions to different aspects of the seminar to our findings on impact and attitude change, it can also partially overcome one of its inherent limitations. This limitation derives from the fact that the study deals, essentially, with a single case—one seminar. We can only speculate whether the strengths and weaknesses of the seminar are unique to the particular situation or can be generalized to other, similar exchange programs. By studying both the program and its impact, however, it is possible to learn something about the conditions under which certain effects are achieved. This kind of information is relevant not only to the evaluation of this particular case, but also to the development of propositions that might apply to exchange programs in general.

DESIGN

To meet the purposes that have been described, the evaluation study was designed to yield two types of information: (1) information about the participants' role in the seminar and their reactions to it, obtained *while the seminar was in progress;* and (2) information about the impact of the seminar on the participants and about the kinds of changes it produced in their attitudes, obtained at various points, but particularly some months *after the participants' return to their home countries.* The first type of information was obtained through intensive interviews inquiring into the participants' reactions to their experiences during the time they were taking place, and through some observations of these experiences. The second type of information is based on before- and after-questionnaires and on detailed follow-up interviews, administered to the participants and an appropriate comparison group.

Interviews with the participants. While the seminar was in progress, each participant was interviewed intensively on four separate occasions. The interviews were conducted by five skilled interviewers, trained either in social work or social psychology. Before each interview, the interviewers met to review the questions and to make sure that they were aware of the purpose behind each question and the information it was designed to elicit. The interviews were all structured, but respondents were encouraged to reply in their own words and in as much detail as they were willing to provide. Interviewers were encouraged to probe further if an answer was not sufficiently clear, or if the information a question had been designed to elicit was not given in the first response. Furthermore, the interviewers were free to make occasional changes in the wording or order of questions, in the interest of rapport, continuity, or comprehension, and to omit questions that already had been answered in earlier contexts. Interviewers took notes that came as close to a verbatim record as possible; they also noted down their own probes and any changes in wording or order that they had introduced. Each interview lasted between two and six hours, with the modal time being approximately three hours.

With very few exceptions, the same interviewer conducted the first, second, and fourth interview with a given participant. For the third interview, however, which was conducted during the travel period, there was a fair amount of switching among interviewers. This was a necessary adjustment to the complexities involved in scheduling interviews at approximately the same time with respondents dispersed over different parts of the country. This adjustment had benefit, in that a different interviewer was sometimes in a better position to obtain fuller information on topics that had already been covered, but only sparsely, in earlier interviews. Interviews with all but one of the participants were conducted in English.

The timing and content of the four interviews were as follows:

The initial interview was conducted within a few days after the participants' arrival at the university. It dealt with their preparation for the trip; their reactions to the selection procedure and to the arrangements for the trip; their expectations regarding the seminar and its various components, and regarding their own activities and contributions to the seminar; their previous contact with America and Americans; and their initial feelings and impressions upon arrival in America.

The second interview was conducted during the fifth week of the sojourn, that is, just as the first phase of the seminar was drawing to a close. In this interview, participants were asked to give their general evaluations of the seminar and of the extent to which it met their expectations, was geared to their background and interests, and was conducive to the achievement of their goals. They were then asked to react to: the composition of the group and the contributions of their fellow-participants; various specific aspects of the program (including the academic seminars, the professional seminars, the informal discussions, and the social activities) ; and the living arrangements at the university.

Questions about their plans for the trip through the United States were
also raised. Finally, the interview inquired into the participants' feelings at
the moment, and into new impressions of American broadcasting and of
America in general that they might have gained during the preceding
weeks.

The third interview was conducted in the field, during the second
month of the travel period, and focused on the participants' experiences
during their travels. The respondents were asked to evaluate their experiences and to indicate the extent to which the trip met their expectations, interests, and needs. This interview went into considerable detail on
the participants' impressions of American broadcasting and broadcasters.
Moreover, participants were asked about the contacts they had with
Americans during their travels; about their observations regarding differences (regional, religious, ethnic, socioeconomic) within the American
population and the role that these play in American society; and about
the new insights that they had gained into American life.

The fourth interview was conducted within a few days before each
participant's departure from the United States.[1] In this interview, the
respondents were asked to evaluate their own experiences and activities
from the point of view of what they had accomplished, what they found
particularly enjoyable or difficult, and what, in retrospect, they would
have liked to have done differently. They were then asked to evaluate the
seminar and to discuss features of it that they would like to see preserved
and features that they would like to see changed. Additional questions
focused on the participants' expectations for the future, particularly the
way their experiences in the United States were likely to affect their situations back home; on their introspections about the changes in views and
perspectives that they had undergone in the course of their sojourn; and
on their feelings about leaving and returning home.

Taken together, then, the four interviews provided detailed information on the participants' reactions, feelings, and impressions, at a
time when they were still immersed in the experiences they were discussing. For analysis of the interview data, coding categories were developed
to capture the content of the responses in the interviews and to provide
ratings on some of the dimensions in which we were particularly interested.

Observations of the seminar in progress.   In order to gain some

---

[1] We were unable to obtain this fourth interview from one of the participants, who left unexpectedly toward the end of the travel period because of ill-
ness. In two cases, the fourth interview was obtained immediately after the third
interview because these participants (as expected) had to depart before the formal
completion of the seminar.

direct impression of the progress of the seminar, the nature of the activities offered, the different roles the participants were taking, and the kind of life they were leading, members of the research staff used whatever opportunities for direct observation were available during the university phases of the seminar.

During the first six-week period, most of the scheduled group sessions were observed formally by a trained observer. These observations yielded running accounts of each meeting, ratings on a number of dimensions of group behavior and atmosphere for each meeting, and weekly ratings for each individual on his behavior in the group along a number of dimensions. The weekly ratings of individual behavior were made on such dimensions as leadership, involvement, hostility, and nurturance. A complete list of the dimensions used by the group observer and of their definitions can be found in Appendix A.

In addition, both during the first six weeks and during the final two weeks at the university, informal observations were made of group meetings, various other activities, and of the participants' daily life. In order to obtain a fuller picture of the nature of the experiences to which the participants were reacting, we also conducted interviews with seminar staff members. These interviews yielded information about what the staff were trying to accomplish, what they felt was actually taking place, and how satisfied they were with the outcome.

Before- and after-questionnaires. A special "Questionnaire for Specialists in Broadcasting" was developed for purposes of this study. This questionnaire (which is reproduced in full in Appendix B) included several precoded questions, for which respondents selected one of a number of answer-choices. Most of the questions, however, were open-ended, requiring the respondent to reply in his own words. The questionnaire covered four substantive areas:

1. Views of American broadcasting: Questions 2, 4, 5, 6, 7, and 10. Questions 5 and 6 involved comparisons between the functions of television in the United States and the respondent's own country, and are thus also germane to area 3 below. Although all of these questions may provide some indirect information about the respondent's views of American institutions in general, Question 10 is particularly revealing, for it concerns an aspect of American mass media that is likely to be especially salient for a visitor from abroad—their coverage of information about his own country.

2. Views of America and Americans in general: Questions 9, 10, 11, 12, and 15. In addition, Question 13—though focusing on the respondent's presentation of his own country—is indirectly related to this area, since it concerns the relationship between the respondent's country and America,

and taps his views of what Americans ought to know in order to gain a correct picture of his country. Answers to this question may thus provide information about the respondent's image of America and Americans in relation to his own country. Question 14 was intended primarily as a bridge to Question 15 and was not coded. Question 9 was intended in part as a bridge to Question 10; it was hoped that it might also yield some information about the respondent's views of American institutions, but since this information was not gained, the responses were not coded.

3. Views of broadcasting in the respondent's own country: Questions 1, 3, 5, 6, and 8.

4. Views of the respondent's own professional role: Questions 16, 17, 18, 19, and 20.

The questionnaire was administered to the seminar participants on two occasions: before their arrival in the United States, and approximately nine months to a year after their return to their home countries. The purpose of these two administrations was to note changes in response over the intervening period—a period which included the four-month seminar in the United States and a sufficiently long time back home to have given respondents some perspective on their experience in the United States and some opportunity to integrate it into their regular professional lives. Completion of the second questionnaire after a delay of nine or more months gave us some assurance that we would be dealing with relatively stable changes, representative of the longer-term impact of the experience. If the second questionnaire had been administered at the end of the American visit, it might have captured in part the more transitory immediate impact of the experience while the person was still completely caught up in it.

The before-questionnaire was mailed to the participants in the spring of 1962, shortly after they had been notified of their participation in the seminar. A detailed letter, explaining the purposes of the study, accompanied the questionnaire. The participants were asked to complete and return the questionnaires before their departure for the United States, and most of them did so. Several participants did not complete the questionnaires until immediately after their arrival in the United States; this delay tended to occur in cases where the selection process had been protracted, so that the questionnaire was relatively late in reaching the participant.

The after-questionnaires were mailed to the participants in the spring of 1963. The covering letter to each participant also explained that a member of the research team would be coming to interview him during the summer, and asked him to have the questionnaire completed by that time. Several questionnaires were not ready by the time of the interview, and were returned by mail in the fall of 1963. All participants, however, completed both the before- and the after-questionnaires.

The interpretation of changes from the before- to the after-questionnaire would remain highly ambiguous in the absence of a comparison group. Although the visit to America intervened between the two questionnaire administrations, one cannot at all be certain that this visit accounts for whatever changes might be observed. Attitude changes might result from other intervening events which have little or nothing to do with the American trip: for example, changes in the individual's professional activities, or in the field of broadcasting in his country, or in the world situation. Even his image of America might undergo changes in the course of a year that are based on new information about the country, quite independent of his trip. This possibility is particularly likely for broadcasters who are exposed to much new information in the course of their regular activities.

In order to control for these alternate possibilities, it was necessary to select a comparison group of individuals who were as similar as possible to the participants, but who did not take part in the seminar. The members of the comparison group completed the same two questionnaires as the participants, in 1962 and 1963. By comparing the participants' responses to those of the comparison group, we can identify those changes in the participants that can be ascribed to their American experience. There should be no systematic differences between the two groups in changes resulting from extraneous events (that is, events not connected with the seminar). If there *are* any differences between the groups, we can conclude that they are caused by the one systematic factor that distinguishes the two—participation versus nonparticipation in the seminar under study.

The selection of an appropriate comparison group in this type of situation is an extremely difficult task. Ideally, from the point of view of research design, one would ask each participating country to nominate twice the number of candidates than can actually be invited. One would then select, on a random basis, half of the candidates for participation in the seminar, and half for the comparison group. For practical reasons, however, such a procedure is usually impossible. In the present study, this procedure was approximated for about half of the participating countries. In those countries, *alternate* participants were nominated, who—for one reason or another—were not the first choices for participation, but who met all the qualifications necessary for participation. These alternates were then asked to become members of the comparison group. In about half of the countries, however, no alternates were nominated. In those cases, we invited broadcasters from each country involved who were known to the director of the seminar and whom he considered to meet all the criteria for participation.

The first questionnaire was sent out in the spring of 1962 to forty-six broadcasters in the sixteen participating countries who were not coming to the seminar, with a covering letter explaining the purpose of the study and the need for a comparison group. Questionnaires were returned by twenty-three of these individuals. In the spring of 1963, the second questionnaire was mailed to the comparison group. As in the case of the participants, the covering letter explained that a member of the research team would be coming to interview the respondent and asked him to have his questionnaire ready at that time. All comparison-group members completed the second questionnaire. Two members of the comparison group, however, had visited the United States in the period intervening between the two questionnaires, and therefore had to be omitted from the group. Thus, a comparison group of twenty-one members was left, which means that seven of the participants did not have a matching control. Ten of the twenty-one controls had visited the United States on an earlier occasion, as had nine of the twenty-eight participants. This difference, however, is not statistically significant.

This procedure for selecting comparison-group members did not yield anything resembling a pure control group. Like the participants, the members of the comparison group were almost all in the field of broadcasting. In some cases, the match between a particular participant and his control was very good: they were both in the same type of position, doing similar work, at approximately the same level. Sometimes the match was too good, in a sense: participant and control were both working in the same office, the one serving as deputy to the other, a situation which raises the possibility that the participant may have communicated much of his experience in America to the control and thereby influenced the latter's attitudes. Thus, if we find *no difference* between the two, it may be not because the seminar had no impact on either of them, but because it had an impact on *both!* In yet other cases, the match between participant and control was rather poor: they were both broadcasters from the same country, but one may have been a producer of instructional broadcasts, the other a manager of a commercial station.

On the whole, one certainly cannot claim that the comparison group and the participant group represent either randomly selected or precisely matched samples. What can be said, however, is that the comparison group consists of individuals all of whom *could* have been participants—that is, all of whom fully met the qualifications for participation in the seminar—but who in fact were not participants. On this crucial dimension, then, the two groups are clearly comparable.

Follow-up interviews. In the late spring and summer of 1963, intensive personal interviews were conducted with the participants and the members of the comparison group. These interviews took place in the respondents' home countries, and were carried out by three of the five original interviewers. The interviewing style and the form of the questions were similar to those employed in the earlier interviews. The post-return interviews with seminar participants were also similar in length to the earlier interviews; the interviews with controls were somewhat shorter.

Post-return interviews were obtained from all twenty-eight of the seminar participants. Of the twenty-one members of the comparison group, four were out of the country at the time the interviewer arrived. It was thus possible to obtain only seventeen of the twenty-one interviews (although all twenty-one comparison-group members completed the after-questionnaire). This left us with eleven participants for whom we did not have a matching control ready to be interviewed. In ten of these eleven cases, however, we were able to locate a matching control on the scene—that is, a broadcaster from the same community, with a position and background similar to that of the seminar participant, who was willing to be interviewed. Thus, for purposes of comparing responses of the post-return interview, we have matching controls for twenty-seven of the participants; for seventeen of these controls we also have before- and after-questionnaires, whereas for the other ten we have the interviews only.[2] In addition, there were four controls for whom we had questionnaire data only.

The post-return interviews explored further some of the areas covered in the questionnaires. They focused, in particular, on changes in the respondents' professional roles and activities, on their views about changes and needed changes in the field of broadcasting in their own countries, on their involvement in and plans for international exchanges and their views of the value of such exchanges, on their impressions of American society, and on their perceptions of changes in their images of

---

[2] We would have been able to obtain our full complement of matching controls were it not for one unforeseen circumstance. One of the members of the original comparison group expected to be out of his country at the time the interviewer was scheduled to arrive there. He therefore made arrangements to meet with the interviewer in another country at a later time. At the last minute, however, he was forced to change his plans and could not keep the appointment. By that time, it was too late to locate a substitute control of the same nationality since the interviewer had already passed through the country in question. Thus we were left with matching controls on the post-return interview for only twenty-seven of the twenty-eight cases. We did, however, conduct an *extra* control interview in one of the countries, so that we actually have a total of twenty-eight control interviews, of which twenty-seven are matched by nationality. In Chapter Ten, which reports the relevant data, all twenty-eight control interviews will be used as a matter of convenience, since we are thus enabled to compare groups of equal size.

their own countries and in their plans for the future. Thus, it was possible to see whether participants reported any significant changes in their activities, ideas, and plans after their return to their home countries. By conducting interviews with a comparison group at the same time, it was possible to determine whether any changes observed in the participants could legitimately be attributed to their participation in the seminar. In addition, the interviews with the participants specifically inquired into their perceptions of the impact that participation in the seminar had had on their activities, ideas, and plans. They were also asked to discuss in retrospect the usefulness of the seminar and of its various specific features.

4

Participants' Reactions to the University Phase

The primary purpose of the analysis of participants' reactions to their experiences at the university is to identify some of the problems and successful features of the seminar. The data are based almost entirely on the second interview, conducted during the fifth week of the seminar—that is, just as the sojourn at the university was drawing to a close—although we shall, on occasion, draw on data from earlier or later interviews. The analysis will emphasize *criticisms* raised by the participants. Even when such criticisms represent only minority points of view, they may give some insight into problems that can be avoided and improvements that can be introduced. Features of the seminar that are criticized by some participants may be highly valued by others, in which case it is important to know which participants make the criticisms and for what reasons. This kind of information can be extremely useful in the proper matching of participants and programs.

One cannot infer, from the mere presence of criticisms, that a participant was generally dissatisfied with the seminar. While statements of satisfaction are always difficult to interpret, indications are that most participants in the seminar were generally satisfied, even though they may have made specific criticisms and suggestions for improvement. In particular, it must be kept in mind that the participants viewed the seminar as a pilot project and the evaluation as an attempt to find ways of improving future projects. They were, therefore, predisposed to offer criticisms.

When asked to give an overall evaluation of the initial portion of the seminar, seven participants expressed themselves as very satisfied, fifteen as quite satisfied, four as somewhat satisfied, and two as not very satisfied. We also asked participants to estimate the proportion of the program that was directly relevant to their interests, and the proportion that was at least indirectly relevant. Eleven participants indicated that 75 per cent of the program or more was directly relevant, and an additional four found 75 per cent or more at least indirectly relevant. Twenty-four respondents felt that 50 per cent or more of the program was directly relevant. On the whole, it would seem that the level of satisfaction was rather high; a large majority of participants were at least "quite satisfied" and found something of direct relevance to their interests in at least half of the program.

Before we examine participants' reactions to specific aspects of the experience, it would be useful to highlight those features of the university phase that they were especially prone to single out for praise or criticism. To this end, we examined the portions of the interviews in which respondents spontaneously brought up features of the seminar that they liked or disliked, that they considered successes or failures, or that were sources of satisfaction or of dissatisfaction and disappointment. We found that the following features were spontaneously mentioned in highly positive terms (as especially well-planned, as especially valuable or enjoyable, or as surpassing expectations): the opportunity to listen to some of the professional speakers (mentioned by thirteen respondents) and to learn about American broadcasting (16), and the high quality of the speakers (8); the visits to mass media facilities (14); the academic seminars (16); and the week-end visit with an American family in New Hampshire (21).

The following features were spontaneously brought up in critical terms (as especially poorly planned, inconvenient, or disappointing): the relative lack of depth in the professional part of the seminar (9); the heterogeneity of group composition (8); the tendency to overschedule activities, thus limiting opportunities for absorbing materials and for recreation (16); the inefficient handling of certain administrative details, usually of a minor nature (13); the geographical isolation of the university, coupled with inadequate provision of transportation (21); and the inadequate provision for entertainment and for leisure-time activities (8).

These points should be kept in mind as we review participants' reactions to specific parts of the experience, because they represent features spontaneously singled out for praise or criticism by at least a quarter of the participants. They do not cover all the points that will be discussed in the sections that follow, some of which emerged only in response to direct questions and some of which were raised only by a small subgroup of the participants. Several of the most interesting points, in fact, are not in the above lists. Though we consider them, nonetheless, important enough to discuss, they must be viewed within the perspective of the features mentioned spontaneously and frequently.

PROFESSIONAL ACTIVITIES

Professional seminars. In Chapter Two, we described the professional seminars, which consisted mainly of talks and demonstrations by invited speakers and which served as the major focus for the professional activities arranged for the participants. The participants were generally impressed with the quality of the invited speakers (as we have already seen) and were pleased with the information presented. A number of the participants spontaneously praised the professional seminars for the high quality of the speakers. There were no indications that the participants objected to the idea of having experts brought in, and of being exposed to lectures and demonstrations. Many participants apparently found this situation consistent with their view of themselves as learners. Even those who did not view themselves primarily as learners—those, for example, who came from countries with highly developed television systems—seemed content that the seminars were essentially set up to convey information to them, and pleased that outstanding individuals were brought in to discuss and illustrate their own work. Thirteen participants appreciated the opportunity to learn about the patterns of mass communication in America. Fourteen specifically praised the seminars for the amount of information that was presented, which, they felt, would help them in their own work by providing new program or production ideas.

The extent to which participants were actively engaged in the professional seminars varied from session to session. Our group observer reported that their interest and involvement fluctuated, depending on speaker and topic. Some sessions were too general to meet the specialized interests of many of the participants; some were too specialized to be of interest to those in other areas. On the other hand, in some sessions there was widespread participation, and in others, though only a few participants made active contributions, the overall level of interest was manifestly high. Participants' contributions most often took the form of introducing examples from the experiences of their respective countries and of drawing parallels between their own broadcasting situations and the situation in America.

Although most of the participants were satisfied with the general structure of the professional seminars and with the definition of their own roles within these seminars, there were some criticisms of the focus of the individual seminars and the way they were organized into a total program. The participants appreciated the visiting speakers, but some feeling was expressed that the speakers were too numerous, with not enough time for each and not enough continuity between them. Several participants criticized the professional seminars for their repetitiveness—the fact that there were too many speakers or too much overlap between speakers. Thus, one participant indicated that he found most of the professional seminars stimulating,

> . . . but some did go over the same ground. The individuals were generally good, but there were just too many of them. One was subject to sit for an hour and a half to listen to the same speech but from a different personality.

Another participant said, in this connection:

> I think the planning was well done. The documentation was adequate, but the things included in the courses were a bit too much. We could have done with less of the talks. There was lots of repetition. Repetition, I know, has advantages of stamping impressions on one's mind, but if that mind is already fatigued, then it will be annoyed, rather than helped.

What a given participant considers repetitive depends on his particular interests. Thus, a participant whose own work was in the area of news broadcasting told us:

> I was impressed with the number and variety of speakers and lecturers, although I thought there was a duplication of some of the . . . educational television programs. As soon as it had been established what educational television was, one almost anticipated everything else. I personally don't think that the instructional programs provide much material for discussion.

In response to specific questions about the professional seminars, four of the participants criticized them for a lack of depth and an excess of generalities. We have already seen that nine individuals spontaneously expressed disappointment in the relative lack of depth of these seminars. Continuity was also a problem, which one participant saw as directly related to the large number of invited speakers:

I think we had too many people; 80 per cent of the material for the seminars came from visiting speakers. It is hard to get a coherent system of knowledge or ideas from such a jumble of presentations.

In short, the gist of these criticisms seems to be that the organization of the professional seminars made for an inherently interesting, but somewhat superficial and not fully integrated kind of learning experience. Since most speakers had only a limited amount of time and did not know in detail the content of previous sessions, they tended to start out with general statements about the background and context of their work, and then to proceed with a description and a presentation of samples of their own activities. Thus, in their general nature, the introductory statements tended to be repetitive. A number of participants preferred more detailed discussions of more limited areas, focusing on specific issues and concrete problems. Moreover, there was only limited opportunity for the different presentations to build on each other, and some participants felt that the information gathered from these discrete presentations did not add up to an organized framework. There was no deliberate attempt to integrate the material or to point up relationships.

The limitations of the professional seminars in terms of the depth of learning that they made possible were by no means of universal concern to the participants. Some participants, apparently, were pleased with the opportunity for meeting various representatives of American broadcasting, observing their personalities, and comparing their approaches and their stands on general issues in the field. However, participants who were primarily interested in content found this way of organizing the professional seminars somewhat disappointing.

Participants' reactions to the professional seminars on the depth dimension depend, to a very large extent, on their particular professional interests. Thus, participants who work in the area of instructional broadcasting may ask for more specificity and detail for seminars that deal with instructional television, but may consider other seminars unduly repetitive. On the other hand, participants who work in news broadcasting may consider seminars dealing with instructional television needlessly detailed and time-consuming. In short, participants seem to like detailed seminars in their own specialties, but prefer general ones outside of their own field. By the same token, participants prefer fewer seminars in areas outside their specialty and are more likely to find these repetitive. Although they may also prefer a smaller number of speakers in their own area, in order to allow for more detail and depth, they are considerably less likely to find these seminars repetitive. They are usually better attuned to the differences in the presentations of speakers in their own area and more interested in nuances that escape the nonspecialist.

The question of relevance to the participants' professional interests leads us to a final, but possibly central, criticism of the professional seminars. Organizing the professional seminars into a series of talks by invited speakers limited the possibilities of a *problem-centered* approach. Each speaker came for only a relatively brief period. There was little opportunity for the participants to take up the issues raised by the speaker, to bring in their own relevant experiences, and to focus on specific problems that were of professional concern to them. The absence of an organizing framework for the professional seminars and the limited continuity between them, again, precluded an orientation toward specific common problems. The participants had a good opportunity to learn about the range of activities in American broadcasting, but little opportunity to relate this information to their own situations and to delve into its implications for matters of common concern.

This point of view was expressed by seven of the participants, who criticized the professional seminars for offering insufficient opportunity to discuss the participants' own problems and situations, and for their overemphasis on American broadcasting. Thus, one participant said:

> Even during the discussion periods we did not talk much about *our own work*. We listened mostly to the American experts. People asked questions, but they were mostly about American programs.

Another participant made a related point, when he said that the seminars were not organized in such a way as "to let the participants contribute. You just question the speaker and get an answer." Finally, the remarks of a third participant can be cited in this connection:

> I didn't expect the professional seminars to be a regular classroom. . . . I thought we would sit in a room and discuss problems of one country or another.

Exchange among participants. As mentioned in Chapter Two, planned and scheduled occasions for exchange among participants were limited to a series of presentations of samples of the work that the participants had brought with them. At the time of the interview, about half of the participants had presented such programs or were still planning to do so.

A number of participants seemed to feel that these presentations did not have an important enough place in the overall program of the seminar and that they were not arranged in such a way as to be of maximum benefit to the participants. They represented a peripheral activity, not fully integrated into the rest of the professional program. As a result, there was less interest in these activities and attendance was low. One participant remarked, for example:

> We had already watched so much other material, and our material was not related to that, so that they were not worked into a whole presentation. This was felt to be a burden to some people, so the attendance was small.

The peripheral status of these presentations is illustrated in another participant's answer to the question: "Did you present any special program to the group?"

> We had one on tap the other night, but due to some misconception or bad communication, no one came to view it. We have been trying to get another program on, but we haven't been able to yet.

Another participant, whose work is in the field of radio, told us in response to the same question:

> Yesterday I was to present one, but the people failed to come . . . so we canceled the program. It was to be the first sound program. All the others were television programs and school broadcasting.

Some participants mentioned practical difficulties that interfered with the showing of programs they had brought, or with the optimal integration between the showing of a film and discussion of it. The major obstacle (mentioned by five participants) was the lack of the necessary technical facilities for showing certain programs. They may have been particularly concerned about such difficulties because these presentations represented the only structured opportunities for discussing their own work in the context of the program.

It seems clear from various comments made by participants that they would have wanted the presentations of their own work to be upgraded and more fully integrated into the overall program. Moreover, a number of participants indicated that they were not interested in simply seeing each other's work, but would have preferred more opportunities for *discussion* of the work following the presentations. Such discussions would have made it possible for the person giving the presentation to hear the reactions of other participants to his work; and for the others to raise questions about why and how things were done in a certain way, and to relate the work to their own relevant experiences. In other words, indications are that participants wanted more opportunities for exchange among themselves—including presentations of their own work, but not restricted to this activity—to be built into the total program. Thus, one participant said:

> I would have liked to have seen more coming together to exchange ideas, to talk about our respective countries.

Several participants pointed out that opportunities for exchange could have been maximized if they had been planned more deliberately and included as part of the formal program:

> The people in the seminar should have an opportunity to defend their work, to make presentations like those that the guests made. There should not be just a brief showing of their films.

> I would have liked for everyone here to be given a time for a short talk—not just to show a film, but to lecture on what has been done in their country in radio and television.

> I thought that it would be a multinational seminar, that there would be more discussion of each participant's country's broadcasting. But, these discussions are mainly operated by the Fellows on their free time outside of the seminar. . . . I think we should have more time to include this in the seminar schedule.

One participant seemed to feel that the problem was not merely one of providing more time for exchanges in the schedule, but also one of providing a framework within which such exchanges can be carried out:

> Some framework should have been worked out so the members could have made more of a contribution to the seminar from their own experience. . . . We were given an opportunity to plan some programs ourselves, but we had no particular framework for it. It is not enough to tell people to spontaneously share their experiences. People are a bit shy, and they need a framework within which to make their contributions.

The disappointment with the limited amount of opportunity for exchange among participants probably had three interrelated sources. First, some participants seemed to feel that their own potential contributions were not sufficiently utilized. Thus, one participant, when asked how the others reacted to the special program that he had presented, replied:

> In the main, they were very well interested in it. There could have been more of an informal discussion. I thought I would do more talking about my particular experiences. I came *prepared* to offer a great amount.

A second reason for disappointment was that some participants would have liked to obtain more systematic information about activities in other countries. One participant said, for example:

> Discussion groups, with each country telling what they are doing in each country, would have been helpful. Actually it seems that one should have discussions in which the ideas of the various countries would be aired, they should be jotted down by someone, and a pamphlet should be gotten out as to what the other countries are doing,

so that we could take something away from here on the other countries, rather than just information about America.

The same participant pointed to a third source of disappointment—the limited opportunity to benefit from the reactions of others to one's own work:

> One thing I thought would happen that didn't happen is that I thought all the people attending would be given time to tell the others what they themselves are doing in their country. I suppose the Seminar thought that these kinds of things would be done privately and informally. As it was, people with film shows could say what they are doing in their country; but if you don't have a film show, you're finished. There is not much time spent saying what you have been doing and how one could improve what he has been doing. There is not much opportunity to air what you have been doing, to have people criticize you, and point out ways of improving these things.

At least by implication, this and other remarks about the opportunities for exchange among participants bring us back to a point that was stressed in the preceding section: Some participants would have preferred a more problem-oriented approach, a greater focusing on specific issues directly related to their professional activities.

Effects of group composition. The nature of the professional experience is partly a function of the composition of the group. As has already been pointed out, the group was heterogeneous with respect to level of development of television in the countries represented, with respect to the primary professional interests of the participants, and with respect to types of professional positions held by the participants. The general reaction to the diversity of the group was favorable, although, as noted, eight participants spontaneously remarked that the composition of the group was too heterogeneous. When asked specifically about the multinational composition of the group, thirteen indicated that they considered it beneficial, while fourteen expressed mixed feelings about this feature of the seminar.

One of the benefits ascribed to the multinational character of the seminar (by eleven respondents) was that it promoted a better understanding and appreciation of countries with different cultural and political institutions. One participant, for example, pointed out that it gave him an opportunity to learn about the opinions held in other countries. "Every day you get an image of the whole world," he added. A larger number (eighteen respondents) considered the multinational composition beneficial because it made possible an interchange of professional skills and ideas. Participants' views differed precisely with respect to the specific professional gains they were able to derive from the diversity of the group.

Some seemed to feel that the diversity did indeed enhance their professional gains, whereas others felt that it diminished their gains. Thus, fourteen participants indicated that the multinational composition of the group had adverse effects because it produced diversity of professional interests, backgrounds, or positions. However, their reactions were not entirely unfavorable, for some of these same individuals also saw value in the interchange of professional skills and ideas made possible by the multinational composition.

Participants from countries with relatively limited experience in the field of broadcasting were more likely to see professional value in multinational composition. Thus, out of sixteen respondents who particularly valued certain technically superior presentations by fellow-participants working in highly advanced broadcasting systems, eleven were non-European in origin. On the other hand, the participants who expressed mixed feelings about the value of the multinational character of the seminar and those who noted adverse effects of professional diversity were more likely to be European in origin and to come from countries with considerable experience in broadcasting. Presumably, these individuals felt that they had less to learn from a group representing different levels of development.

This pattern had exceptions, however. One participant from a highly advanced broadcasting system, for example, when asked how much he benefited from the contributions of the other participants, replied:

> Quite a lot. I have not learned much technically, but the seminar has thrown light on the members as people, and their problems—the problems they are having with educational television, for example. I have learned about the setting in which they operate.

It seems reasonable to assume that this respondent (and probably others) valued the diversity because it gave him insights that he would be able to apply if, in the future, he were called upon to advise colleagues in countries with newly developing television systems. Thus, he was oriented not only to improving his own work, but also to improving his ability to assist others.

Several respondents felt that they would have preferred greater homogeneity in the level of professional knowledge or the general level of sophistication of the participants. A somewhat larger number expressed a preference for greater homogeneity in the professional interests of the participants. Thus, when asked what he thinks of the make-up of the group, a participant in the field of educational broadcasting answered:

> It is very good, but it would be better if all of them were in the same field. I can discuss professional things with some of them—

we have the same vocabulary. With others, I can only talk about general things.

A participant from the field of news broadcasting answered as follows:

Perhaps the whole group should have been people from school television. Perhaps that was the idea. Perhaps it would be better if all were from exactly the same interests. Some of us are newsmen, but the chorus is more concentrated on school television. You could make a separate seminar for the school people and for the news people, and more would be gained.

Some participants, although concerned about the heterogeneity of interests, did not propose a more homogeneous composition. Rather, they suggested an alternative solution: breaking the total group into subgroups for certain activities, in line with the particular professional interests of the participants. Thus, one participant commented:

I think maybe one would achieve better results if one put all the people who were not in broadcasting in one group, and all the people in broadcasting in another group and then brought the two groups together from time to time.

Another participant suggested the following:

I think there should have been room in the organization for smaller groups, or pairing off of those with related interests. They could get together with a visiting staff member or a member of the directorate. . . . If a portion of the group with similar interests could have got together for a bread-and-butter session about getting things on the air, it would have been quite helpful. But there is no use taking the whole group through that kind of session, and the larger sessions had to confine themselves to discussions in generalities.

In sum, it would appear that at least some of the seminar participants felt that the heterogeneity in professional interests made it difficult to focus on specific problems. This difficulty can be resolved either by limiting the selection of participants in terms of more specific interest areas around which the seminar could then focus; or by subdividing the seminar into special interest groups.

ACADEMIC ACTIVITIES

The major academic activity, as described in Chapter Two, consisted of four series of weekly seminars dealing with various aspects of American society. In general, participants expressed a high degree of satisfaction with these academic seminars. Many of them, as we have seen, mentioned them spontaneously as especially positive aspects of the experience. Nineteen respondents described them in wholly positive terms;

another seven regarded them as useful, though professionally irrelevant; and only two felt they were essentially useless. Ten respondents, in fact, indicated that the value of the academic seminars surpassed their original expectations. The *initial* expectations for the academic seminars tended to be lower than those for the professional seminars—perhaps because participants were not entirely clear about their role and nature. In the final analysis, however, the participants as a group were at least as positive about the academic seminars as they were about the professional ones.

It is particularly instructive to examine which participants showed the greatest satisfaction with the academic seminars. In terms of professional interests, it turns out that five out of the seven participants in the field of news and current events were wholly satisfied with the academic seminars, and the remaining two considered them useful, though not professionally relevant. On the other hand, of the ten participants in the educational field, only four were wholly satisfied, four considered the seminars useful though professionally irrelevant, and two considered them both useless and irrelevant. The most reasonable interpretation of this finding seems to be that a participant's satisfaction with the academic seminars is related to the extent to which they fit in with his professional needs. Much of the content of the academic seminars—particularly the information about American political and legal institutions—was of direct interest to the participants in the news field. On the other hand, it had little relevance to the specific professional concerns of participants in educational broadcasting. Most of them found the academic seminars of some general interest and value. As one participant commented: "These things are not necessary to my work, but they did help me to understand America." It is understandable, however, that their level of satisfaction was not as high as that of the representatives from the news field, and that they felt that the academic seminars occupied too much time and received too much emphasis in the total program. One of the educational broadcasters said, for example:

> I felt that rather than listen to how justice was administered here and about the Negro problem, I would have preferred to go out and watch actual production in a television studio.

Another factor that seems to be related to the level of satisfaction with the academic seminars is the relevance of the participants' general background to the content of these seminars. It is not surprising that participants of European origin were somewhat more likely to single out the academic seminars for praise than non-Europeans, since their general cultural and educational background provided more immediate points of contact with the material presented. A related factor here seems to be language facility. Participants who were dissatisfied with *their own roles* in the academic seminars cited language problems most often as the reason for their concern. Language difficulty was more of a barrier in the academic seminars than in the professional ones, presumably because the latter were more directly tied to the participants' day-to-day activities.

The most frequent basis for praise of the academic seminars was that they provided participants the opportunity to learn about America (mentioned by twenty respondents). One participant, for example, in answer to the question "How much useful, new information do you feel you acquired from these seminars?" replied:

> Well, in some fields more and in some less. But even in those where there was no new information, I got a new light on some things. Really, I can't say enough in praise of these academic seminars. I think they were first-rate. If you are going to do broadcasting to a people, you should know something about their politics, their philosophy and so forth, and this seminar has given us a very good chance to learn this about America. I think, in fact, that I know more about America now than I do about my own country.

The function of the academic seminars was generally perceived as that of providing background information about America—a function that most of the participants considered valid and important. In this context, then, they judged the effectiveness of the seminars. Some of the participants saw the increased understanding of American society provided by the academic seminars as particularly useful preparation for their travel period. Another source of praise of the seminars was the high competence of the speakers (mentioned by twelve respondents). Six respondents praised them for their effectiveness of teaching. Six were particularly pleased with the frankness and objectivity with which information about America was presented. None of the participants expressed any feeling that the seminars were being used, in any way, for propaganda.

Critics of the academic seminars fell into two categories: those concerned with their method or manner of presentation; and those concerned with their content. Nine participants brought up criticisms related to the methods that were used, specifically: there should have been more use of audiovisual aids; written outlines or resumes of the lectures should have been prepared; there should have been a greater use of concrete examples and case histories in the course of the lectures, and less recourse to statistics and broad generalizations; the lectures were often too fast and too complicated; and there was not enough opportunity for discussion. Not surprisingly, the participants who had some language difficulty were the most likely to be critical of the way in which the seminars were conducted. One of them commented:

I could understand 70 or 80 per cent of the lectures in the professional seminars, but the academic seminars are very difficult. I could understand the general problems, but I could not understand special subjects. I do not know technical terms. . . . I cannot help hesitating to ask questions. . . . If before the lecture some outline or chart or illustration was given out, we could understand more.

One participant suggested that it would have been valuable to use a comparative approach, to bring in related experiences from other countries. Although he was the only person to bring up this point, it may be worth quoting him because of the relevance of his remarks to our earlier discussion of professional exchange among participants:

I think it would have been better if several members of the group had been specifically requested to prepare short statements or a paper on aspects of their own country. For example, the operation of the courts or the parliamentary system. . . . I think it would have been better if we could have had a more comparative perspective. Also, we could have had more discussion. . . . It would have been well if we could have drawn out what some of the participants had to offer. They would have got a sense of doing something for the group, and also the group would have benefited from their experience and point of view.

Criticisms related to the content of the academic seminars were raised by eight participants. A number of people felt that material that could easily be obtained from written sources available in their own countries should have been kept to a minimum. Some people would have liked to see more emphasis on certain specific areas that were of special interest to them, such as foreign policy or literature and the arts. In some cases, these preferences reflected an interest in those aspects of American society that were more germane to the participant's specific professional concerns. Thus, one educational broadcaster told us that he would have preferred academic seminars with less emphasis on political issues, and more emphasis on such topics as parent-child relationships and the role of children in American society. Needless to say, participants in the news field were satisfied with the political emphasis.

There was some feeling that too much emphasis was being placed on race relations in America. Some participants viewed this as a special American problem of little interest to them. The point was also made that, in emphasizing race relations, the seminar was satisfying the interests of the African participants, at the expense of the participants from other parts of the world. However, it is difficult to separate reactions on this topic from reactions specific to the seminar on American social structure. The leader of this seminar devoted a large proportion of his time to problems of race, and presented his point of view in a manner that antagonized many of the participants. In view of the special circumstances under which the race issue was introduced, it would be hazardous to generalize too much from this particular experience. There is no reason to conclude that participants would be disinterested in an objective presentation of race relations within the context of American society. As a matter of fact, it can be assumed that at least some of the participants would view with suspicion any attempt to play down this topic.

PERSONAL AND SOCIAL EXPERIENCES

Advance information and preparation. Our interviews revealed a number of areas in which some of the participants would have preferred to have more advance information and preparation. A very brief review of these points may help to alert us to potential problems that should be anticipated.

One area in which participants wanted to have fairly detailed advance information was the nature and purpose of the seminar. They wanted to know about the activities that were planned, the different subdivisions of the seminar, their own role within it, the reason why they were selected, and the criteria used in composing the group. Without this information, they found it difficult to make the necessary preparations, and they experienced some discomfort, since they did not know what to expect and what was expected of them. Many participants felt that they had a very good idea of the seminar before they came, but some indicated that they did not have enough advance information or that information from different sources seemed to be different in some respects. Nine felt that information about the purposes of the seminar was insufficient or unclear; thirteen felt that information about the content of the seminar was not entirely adequate.

Some participants would have liked more advance information about certain practical arrangements. They indicated that they might have done things differently had they had the necessary information on which to base a decision. Thus, for example, one participant might have brought his wife, had he known this was feasible. Another might have made arrangements for a car, had he known more about the transportation situation.

Finally, some participants found certain of the procedures and requirements relating to travel to the United States and entry into the country unpleasant and arbitrary. They would probably have been less disturbed if they had been prepared for these details in advance and given some explanation of their rationale.

Use of free time. There was a general feeling that the seminar schedule did not leave enough free time for the participants. Sixteen of our respondents, as we have already noted, felt that the schedule was generally too crowded, making it difficult for participants to absorb all the experiences they were exposed to. One participant told us, for example:

> . . . between lunches and cocktails and speeches—I must say it is interesting, but you cannot always absorb everything. One thing I feel might have been taken into consideration is that some people come from countries with a different tempo of life. It takes some time to get used to this high pressure.

Seven participants felt that the distribution of scheduled activities, and not necessarily the total amount, was the issue. Thus, one participant commented:

> . . . it could have been better sorted out. Some days we were overworked, and some days were too lax.

A number of reasons for wanting more free time were mentioned by participants. Five indicated that they would have wanted more free time for informal exchange among the participants themselves. Five mentioned that they would have wanted more free time for independent work or study. As one respondent pointed out:

> . . . we were very busy, so I couldn't read the books or materials that were given by some lecturers. Day and night we have some schedule. I want to have some leisure to research materials and books. I want some consideration for someone like me with poor English ability.

Nine participants indicated that they would have wanted more free time for leisure activities. On the other hand, it appears that leisure activities were limited, not so much by lack of free time, as by lack of opportunities. Thus, twenty-one participants gave some indication that the location of the university made it difficult for them to use their free time to best advantage. Since the university was far from town and transportation was not always readily available, they did not have easy access to recreational and cultural activities that they might have been interested in. Some participants mentioned that the arrangement of contracting for all meals at the university also tended to limit their freedom of movement, since it created a financial incentive for remaining on campus for all meals. Finally, some participants would have liked to have certain additional facilities at the university available during their free periods. For example, they pointed out that the library was usually closed by the time their schedule allowed them to get there.

Social activities. As noted in Chapter Two, one of the main social events arranged for the group was a weekend of private hospitality with families in a small New Hampshire town. Even though some participants originally had misgivings about this outing, it turned out to be the most successful social activity. Almost all of the participants (twenty-six out of the twenty-eight) reacted very favorably to this experience. They appreciated the opportunity to relax for a weekend, to meet Americans outside of their own professional field, and to get inside an American home. For example, one participant spontaneously mentioned this visit as the most noteworthy thing that had happened to him during the first few weeks of the seminar. He added:

> Maybe that's the only time we'll get inside an American home. It was very enjoyable. We were really inside, *en famille*. There was no need to probe for what was really happening; we could actually see.

Another participant described this visit as his most enjoyable experience:

> I could spend two days in a private house and live with children and in the household, and enjoy their music, food, sightseeing, boating, a very beautiful place on the lakeside.

Most participants also appreciated the other social activities that were planned. A number of them mentioned that they felt people were being very kind and considerate in their attempts to arrange these activities. Nevertheless, twelve participants felt that not enough social activities—at least of a certain kind—had been planned. The younger members of the group were particularly prone to raise this criticism. (Of the twelve participants who felt that not enough social activities had been planned, eight were below the median age—that is, between the ages of twenty-five and forty; and four were above the median age—between the ages of forty-one and fifty-four.) Eight respondents indicated that they would have wanted more opportunities to go to theatres, concerts, or other cultural events. Eight participants indicated that they would have liked more opportunities to meet people from the area, aside from professional colleagues, perhaps in informal social gatherings. Five individuals mentioned that they would have liked more organized entertainment for the group, such as parties for the participants and some compatible people from the area.

The participants' feeling that not enough social activities were planned can be understood more clearly in conjunction with the related criticism, raised by fourteen respondents, that there were not enough opportunities for *spontaneous* social activities. It is apparent that the feeling that not enough social activities were planned does not reflect a wish for additional organized activities involving the entire group. Rather, it reflects a desire for a larger number of opportunities to engage in a variety of leisure-time activities, including activities selected spontaneously by individual participants. If given access to the necessary facilities, many of the participants would have been quite capable of arranging their own social activities, as they did during the travel period. Because of the distance of the campus from most of the activities in which they were interested, however, participants were limited in the arrangements they could make on their own. Thus, it would seem that the needs of most participants would have been satisfied, not by a larger number of organized activities, but by the facilitation of spontaneously selected activities—for example, through arranging transportation, making available tickets for various events, and providing opportunities for informal contacts with Americans.

It must be kept in mind that not all people are equally comfortable about establishing social contacts or arranging their own entertainment. Both personality factors and cultural factors are likely to effect variations here. Participants with a limited command of English would have special problems, as would women, especially from non-Western countries. For these participants some of the organized social activities may be less burdensome and hence more attractive. In line with this, we did find great variability in the way in which participants reacted to the organized social activities. Some enjoyed them greatly. Others would probably have preferred to have a variety of types of social activities available, from which they could have selected those that were most congenial to them. Such an arrangement would have had the added advantage of conducting most of the social and recreational activities with smaller subgroups, which would allow for a smoother and more personal operation.

Personal relations. As might be expected in a multinational seminar, there were some differences in attitudes and values among the participants. On the whole, these differences did not seem to create much friction within the group. Only four respondents felt that the participants did not function as a congenial group. The remainder were evenly split between twelve who described the group as very congenial and twelve who described it as moderately congenial. Those who noted some friction within the group most often attributed it to personal idiosyncrasies of some of the members (eight), to conflictiing ideologies (five), or to lack of common interests (four).

Some participants considered the differences in attitudes and values within the group as a valuable feature of the experience. One mentioned, for example, that there were

> . . . recognized differences. These, I feel, have a political background. But it's just as well to expose one's viewpoint to the other.

I think it was good. They got to know that there were other views. Whether they changed does not interest me.

In a very few cases, however, participants were sensitive to differences between themselves and others—perhaps in political or religious views—and felt that these affected their personal relationships.

Occasionally, a participant expressed the feeling that others in the group were in a more advantaged position. To a large extent, this was related to differences in language facility. Thus, one respondent commented:

> . . . some people are not so good in English. They hesitate to ask questions because their English is poor, and if they are preparing their questions, other people speak up in the meantime. It sometimes happens to me. I find it difficult to intervene. Some people speak very little or nothing at all. If you are better in English and the questions are not so important—it is easy to ask questions. Another man may have something more important to ask—but he may not have a chance to speak. Knowledge of English is very important.

Occasionally, the feeling was expressed that some of the participants were accorded preferential treatment. Thus, a participant from an Asian country told us that

> . . . sometimes treatment by members of the staff was not the same. I think the staff was partial towards some members of the seminar— those from Europe and those who, perhaps, speak English better and feel freer to talk. . . . Sometimes when there was not enough for the whole group, they got special preference. One time there was not enough tickets; so they got the tickets and some others did not get them. Then there were some other things, like books and invitations by the staff. . . . I think things like that should be more equal. If they did not have enough for everybody, they should not give to anybody. This might be all right in America, but I think when you deal with a foreign people it is more difficult, because foreigners are liable to consider that discrimination.

These comments serve to remind us very clearly of the sensitivities that participants—especially from non-European countries—bring to the situation. They often feel that their own countries are undervalued by Americans and by Europeans, and are especially sensitive to any act that would confirm this expectation.

The complexity of the reactions that may arise in a multinational setting is demonstrated by another criticism that was raised by some participants. They expressed the feeling that the interests and problems of the African participants tended to play a disproportionately large role in the seminar. This is yet another indication that concern with national status

is likely to be an important issue in this kind of situation, and that participants will feel resentful if, subjectively, they experience a status deprivation.

A person may experience a sense of status deprivation not only if
he feels that his nation has somehow been slighted, but also if he feels that
he personally has not been accorded the status that is due him. This may
explain, in part, why seven of the participants commented on the youth-
fulness of some of the members of the staff. Some of the comments seemed
to convey the feeling that this represented a lack of recognition of the importance of the participants' positions.

RECOMMENDATIONS

From this analysis of participant reactions we can formulate a
series of recommendations for multinational seminars that might be organized in the future. These recommendations represent our view of the implications of the findings and, inevitably, are influenced by our own values
and opinions.

1. Recommendations concerning professional activities:

*A certain degree of homogeneity of group composition—in terms
of a focal problem with which all participants are professionally concerned
—would seem to be desirable.* Such a focal problem should not simply
be one in which all participants have an intellectual interest (such as the
mass media of communication), but one directly related to their specific
professional activities. As long as, at some level, there is such *a shared
problem on which all participants can come together,* there can and
should be divergences in background, experience, and professional role.
The arrangement proposed by the organizers of the present seminar, for
example, which calls for the inclusion of two types of participants in
future seminars—representatives from broadcasting systems who are concerned with educational programs, and representatives from ministries of
education and other agencies that set policy for educational broadcasting
(see Chapter Five)—would be completely consistent with this recommendation. Although these two groups are engaged in rather different activities, they do have common problems that are of direct professional
concern to them and that can serve as the focal point for the seminar.

*Opportunities for alternative activities should be built into the
seminar program,* so that wherever there are divergent interests, subgroups can be formed around specific issues and can operate separately.
There is no reason to assume that all participants will engage in all of the
organized activities. In the course of some of the general discussions, held
at the beginning of the seminar, various specific problems, of special concern to some of the participants, may suggest themselves. The program

should be so structured that there is room in it for small work-groups to form around such problems. For many other purposes, the group can continue to meet as a whole.

The organizing principle for the seminar should, ideally, be in terms of problems, rather than entirely in terms of speakers. That is, there should be some organized framework, defined in terms of general issues in the focal area of concern, that provides continuity for the whole program. Individual speakers should be scheduled in line with this framework, and should know how and where they fit into it. Participants too should have advance information about this organizing framework. A problem-oriented organization of this sort implies that the primary basis for planning professional activities is the relevance to the professional concerns of the participants. Thus, in a seminar for broadcasting specialists, the central content would not be simply coverage of what goes on in American broadcasting. Naturally, in the course of the seminar, participants would have the opportunity to learn about American broadcasting activities, an area of great interest to them. These activities, however, should represent special cases of general, shared problems, to which the participants can readily connect in terms of their own interests and experiences. To maintain the focus of the professional seminars around the professional concerns of the participants, and avoid their preemption by information about America, there may even be some virtue in separating out the discussion of American mass media per se and devoting a special academic seminar to this subject. Such a seminar could be broadened to include information, presented by the participants, about parallel activities in their respective countries.

In emphasizing problem-orientation, the value of introducing to the participants outstanding American personalities in their own field should not be neglected, since such contact does seem to be a valued part of the experience for most of the participants. Invited speakers can fit within the problem-oriented framework, as long as they are selected in terms of their relevance to the focal problems. Also, certain outstanding personalities can be invited for special sessions outside of the general organizing framework, for example, for special evening meetings.

The approach recommended here presupposes that there will be fewer invited speakers, with more time for each, and with greater opportunities for following up on each speaker's presentation. Each speaker would serve as a starting point for discussion and exchange. This more intensive interaction with each speaker would make it possible to go beyond questions and answers, and to explore concrete issues in greater depth. At the same time, it would make it more possible for participants to bring in their own relevant experiences, and thus provide *opportunities for ex-*

change among the participants themselves. They would be able to learn more adequately about each other's situations, and to benefit from the reactions of others.

A logical extension of the idea of bringing invited speakers to the seminar for longer periods of time is the possibility of including several Americans as regular participants in the seminar. They would be specialists whose central professional concerns are the same as those of the other participants. Ideally, these American specialists would remain with the seminar during the entire period that foreign visitors are resident at the university. A possible compromise might be to have these American participants come for a period of one or two weeks. The essence of this recommendation, however, is that these Americans would not come as invited speakers, but as regular participants, who have a direct professional interest in the focal problems of the seminar, and who see themselves as involved in an exchange activity, rather than simply in information-giving. Although this recommendation is not derived directly from the comments of our respondents, we feel that it has an unusual potential for creating a favorable climate for cultural and educational exchange.

A possible concrete arrangement for combining some of the recommendations made above might take some such form as this: The professional seminars would be organized in terms of a central problem for each week. If the seminar did not include American participants for the total period, as suggested above, then at least an attempt would be made to include some Americans as regular participants during the entire week devoted to a particular problem. The first part of the week would be spent in exploration and formulation of the problem by the participants (including the Americans). In the course of these explorations, different participants would be called upon to make specific presentations, to lead discussions, or to give relevant demonstrations. During the latter part of each week, an American expert in the area under discussion would be invited to speak, to give demonstrations, to participate in discussions, and to serve as a resource person to the group. This particular format is presented here merely as an example of one possible way of organizing the seminar so as to maximize some of the desirable features we have discussed.

Our recommendations are based on the assumption that the specific professional concerns of the participants must provide the basic context of a satisfactory and effective exchange experience. We would emphasize problem-orientation, therefore, as the organizing principle for the typical exchange program. Other desiderata that should be applicable to a wide range of exchange programs are opportunities for participants (a) to make personal contributions to the program and to bring in relevant experiences from their own countries, and (b) to work and talk with American colleagues as equal partners on shared professional problems.

2. Recommendations concerning academic activities:

It is apparent from the reactions of the participants that the combination of academic seminars with the more specific professional activities is very worthwhile, and we recommend that it be maintained in future programs. In planning such academic seminars, several considerations should be kept in mind.

Some participants in a specialists' program may be interested in a variety of general topics. For many, however, the attractiveness of academic seminars is likely to be a direct function of the relevance of these seminars to their particular professional concerns. Thus, specialists in news broadcasting are more likely to be interested in political topics, whereas specialists in instructional broadcasting are more likely to be interested in family relations. *In devising an academic program, one should, therefore, take into account explicitly the particular professional interests that the participants represent.* It is probably safe to assume that the majority of almost any group of specialists will have some interest in the political and legal structure of the United States. Very likely, a review of general intellectual trends within the United States will also be of interest at least to a subgroup of the participants. It would seem reasonable, therefore, to include such seminars in the program. Additional academic offerings, however, should be planned with deliberate attention to the composition of the group and to the aspects of American life that are most directly germane to their professional specialties.

Within the limits set by practical considerations, it would be a good idea to structure the academic program in such a way that participants can choose from a series of seminars those that are of greatest interest to them. One method might be to arrange several academic seminars; during the first week, have each seminar leader give a general lecture in which he summarizes his major points; and then let each participant choose one or two seminars, dealing with those topics into which he wants to delve more deeply.

Since the academic seminars often involve concepts and terms that are outside of the participants' fields of specialization, language problems are likely to become especially acute. *If, therefore, there are participants whose facility in English is limited, some attempts should be made to take this into account in the planning of the academic seminars.* For example, it might be helpful to prepare written outlines and summaries. If necessary funds could be made available, simultaneous translation would be most useful here.

The value of the academic seminars derives not only from the specific information that is communicated, but also from the opportunity to interact and exchange ideas with some American intellectuals—which was a major reason why the organizers of the seminar under study were especially eager to hold it on the university campus. *In view of this, it would be valuable if the leaders of the academic seminars could be integrated into the general program.* For example, they should be encouraged to spend time in informal contacts with the participants, to be present at some of the meals, or to invite the participants to their homes. The combination of interaction in the course of the seminars with such informal contacts outside of the seminars is likely to enhance the value of both.

    3. Recommendations concerning personal and social aspects of the experience:

    In communicating with participants in advance of a seminar, it is important to keep in mind that they are coming into a strange and ambiguous situation, which requires both practical and psychological preparation on their part. They should be given as much information as possible to facilitate this process of preparation. In particular, the following kinds of information should be provided: (1) a clear and consistent description of the purpose and structure of the seminar, which will tell participants what to expect and what is expected of them; (2) any information about possible alternative arrangements, which would help them in planning and allow them to choose in line with their own preferences; and (3) any information that might help them anticipate problematic, unpleasant, or seemingly arbitrary situations.

    In arranging the schedule, free time should not simply be equated with unscheduled time, but rather should be planned deliberately, with specific attention to the overall program in which the participants are engaged. Free time should be scheduled in relation to the general flow of activities; it should be introduced at points at which participants are likely to need time for absorbing new material, for reflection, or for relaxation. Only under very special circumstances should free time that has been set aside for these purposes be usurped by new additions to the program. Moreover, free time should be scheduled in such a way that it can be used to maximum advantage. For example, if participants have some free time in town during the afternoon, it would usually be a good idea to avoid scheduling activities for that evening, so that they can take the fullest advantage of their trip into town.

    In arranging facilities, the daily pattern of activities in which the participants will be engaged should be taken into account. Thus, availability of transportation, meals, library services, and recreational facilities should all be arranged in such a way that participants can use their free time to maximum advantage.

In planning social and recreational activities, it is important to keep in mind that organized activities for the group as a whole, although often valuable and favorably received by many participants, should be supplemented with other kinds of opportunities. Wherever possible, activities should be organized in such a way that participants can choose between different alternatives and can be formed into smaller subgroups. A more individualized arrangement of this sort would both take into account their diversified interests, and allow for a more congenial atmosphere. Moreover, quite apart from any organized activities, it is important to help participants in making their own arrangements for social and recreational activities. It would be necessary to acquaint them with the available possibilities and then facilitate their participation in whatever activities they choose. In some cases, such help would simply mean giving information, purchasing tickets, and arranging transportation. In other cases, a greater degree of assistance may be required. The important point is to acquaint participants with the range of opportunities available and to make sure that they are able to take advantage of them.

Above all, it is important to provide opportunities for the participants to interact with Americans on an informal, personal basis. Informal gatherings, to which members of the community are invited, can be arranged at the university. This would allow participants to meet Americans from various walks of life, and possibly to arrange subsequent contacts with them. Also, some gatherings in private homes can be arranged, to which participants, along with members of the community, can be invited. Ideally, these would be relatively small gatherings, including only several participants at a time. Finally, private hospitality for individual participants in American homes should be encouraged as much as possible. For some participants, such invitations may develop spontaneously out of their informal contacts with Americans; for others, they may have to be specially arranged.

In the selection and briefing of staff, special attention should be paid to the national and personal sensitivities that participants are likely to bring to the situation. Thus, for example, it is important to be aware of the possibility that individual participants, who are identified with a minority point of view, might sometimes feel or in fact be rejected by others in the group. Though such reactions cannot always be prevented, organizers must ensure, insofar as possible, that these participants not be completely isolated from the rest of the group. Similarly, it is essential to avoid any implication of preferential treatment for some national groups as compared to others. Although it may not be possible to forestall the arousal of national sensitivities entirely, the staff should be prepared for such sensitive reactions when they do occur and at least make sure that administrative arrangements do not contribute to their occurrence. Finally, it is important to keep in mind that the participants in specialists' programs are mature people in responsible positions in their own countries, and that they must be accorded the status to which they feel entitled.

5

Staff Reactions to the University Phase

At the end of the six-week period at the university, members of the research team held interviews with the directors of the seminar, the instructors of the four academic seminars, and members of the administrative staff. The purpose of these interviews was to find out how they reacted to the first phase of the seminar: to what extent they felt that it achieved its goals; what they saw as its high points and its problems, its successes and its failures; and what ideas it gave them for future seminars of this sort.

The reactions of the directors are of primary importance here, since they had a better overview of the entire program than the other staff members and since they were in the best position to implement changes in future programs. The directors were generally satisfied with the success of the seminar. They were particularly pleased with the level of interest and support shown by the invited speakers. They thought that the blend between professional and academic activities was a very desirable feature of the seminar, which should be maintained and improved in future seminars. They were pleased with the quality of the participants and their contributions and with the way they got along with each other, and felt

61

that combining participants from developing and industrialized countries was a worthwhile practice, to be maintained. They were well aware of a number of problems that had arisen, including the inadequate integration of academic and professional seminars, the failure to incorporate participants' own presentations into the overall program, the limited technical facilities for presenting some of the materials the participants had brought, the occasional language difficulties, the scarcity of unscheduled time, the inadequate transportation facilities, and the limited administrative personnel. Some of these concerns—especially those relating to personnel and transportation—were echoed by members of the administrative staff, who also brought up a number of other problems relating to the details of living arrangements at the university.

On the whole, the perceptions of the seminar directors seemed to match those of the participants fairly closely. Like the participants (or at least a sizeable segment of the participants), they listed among the highlights of the seminar the inclusion of academic seminars; the high quality of some of the professional speakers; and the visits to broadcasting, educational, and other facilities. They also showed awareness of some of the problems that seemed particularly salient to many of the participants: the relative lack of depth and of opportunity for contributions by participants in the professional seminars; the tendency to overschedule the time; the inadequacy of transportation, especially in view of the isolation of the campus; and the presence of certain inconveniences relating to administrative details. They did not seem to be aware of the dissatisfactions that a number of the participants expressed about leisure-time activities, nor did they seem to be as cognizant of the problems arising from the heterogeneous group composition that were stressed by a vocal subgroup of the participants. It may be that on these issues participants felt less free to communicate their disappointments to the directorate.

PROFESSIONAL SEMINARS

The seminar directors were pleased with the quality of the outside speakers who were brought in for various professional seminars. They felt that the participants were also satisfied with this part of the program and that they "got much out of it, even if they couldn't absorb it all. It will take effect later." They indicated that those lecturers who accompanied their presentations with film demonstrations of their work were particularly effective and well received.

Although satisfied with most of the individual sessions, the seminar directors did express some criticisms of the overall design of the professional part of the program. They felt that it needed a clearer structure, that too many sessions were scheduled, that there was some overlap and repetitiousness among speakers—points that were also made, as we have seen in the preceding chapter, by a number of the participants. Thus, one director told the interviewer:

> I think perhaps the professional seminars could have a clearer design. We tried that, but it broke down a little. . . . A clearer design, less redundancy, a few less people. During the introductory period, or through some kind of control while the program is going on, it could be more carefully coordinated.

One of the suggestions made for improving coordination and enhancing the relationship between the different sessions in future seminars was the institution of an advance planning meeting of the various professional speakers, which would allow them to divide the domain among them and to work out their contributions in full knowledge of the overall design.

Visits to facilities and direct involvement in some of their activities were seen by the directors as very useful parts of the experience, which they would want to expand in future seminars. For example, one director said:

> I think the field trips and the laboratory experiences—like working with the local educational TV staff—these were good, and more of them should be planned. Those kinds of laboratory experiences are very valuable.

The purpose of these visits, as seen by the directors, was not to provide technical training for the participants, but to give them an opportunity for more thorough and detailed observation of procedures used in the United States.

The directors were aware of the fact that opportunities for participants to make contributions to the professional seminars were limited, and they indicated that "in the future it would be desirable to integrate their own programs . . . more thoroughly into the whole program." They were also aware that "the technical facilities for showing films were less than adequate [and] equipment for presentation of program material should be improved."

We have already noted that the directors were pleased with the group composition and were less concerned about the problems caused by heterogeneity that several of the participants (though a distinct minority) stressed. They did feel that diversity of background posed some problems for the professional seminars, but concluded that these were small compared to the positive values of a diverse group. Thus, one director said:

> Some of the people who knew a great deal about what was said had to sit through things they weren't interested in. I don't think there was much of that though. The advantages outweighed the dis-

advantages of diversity. . . . Language was a factor. Those whose English wasn't as good got a little less out of it. . . . Those who were more developed could talk with more shorthand or at a different level. This was some disadvantage to those who don't know the technical side of television. But, on balance, the pluses outweighed the minuses. Some of the individuals might have preferred a more sophisticated and esoteric discussion.

Very similar sentiments were expressed by the other director, when asked about the effects of diversity on the professional experience of the participants:

On the whole it was very good. This kind of diverse background was mutually exciting. They got a lot from each other. The idea of having two from each country . . . was good. . . . In the professional seminars, most of them got something on their own level. Some of them probably felt a bit left out. Particularly if the lack of development was also coupled with a language problem. . . . In some cases, those on the most sophisticated level may have been somewhat bored and found some redundancy. On the whole, getting people from different levels and different backgrounds was a good idea.

These sentiments, while not universal, certainly seemed to be shared by a majority of the participants.

ACADEMIC SEMINARS

The directors felt that it was indeed important to include the academic seminars in the overall design of the program, that they provided the participants with insights and background information about the United States that they could not have obtained in any other way, and that they were both stimulating and useful for the participants. Thus, one of the directors evaluated the academic seminars in these terms:

Part of the purpose was to look below the surface. And this I believe we accomplished. In some of the conversations I had with participants, one told me that if he hadn't had the academic seminars he wouldn't have understood the technical details. Another told me that while we have a complicated system of democracy he had a feeling that it worked. A third told me that he felt that his attitude toward his own country had changed. . . . So, the seminar even helps them re-look at their own country. Someone told me that one of the big surprises was the candor with which we conducted the seminar.

The directors felt that, although the contents of the different seminars were fine, it would have been good to relate them to each other more effectively, and also to integrate them more fully with the professional

seminars. They would have liked to see more leadership on the part of
the participants themselves; and also a greater degree of involvement of
the instructors of the academic seminars in the total program, with more
opportunities for informal interaction with the participants.

The directors also pointed out that the spirit of inquiry and academic freedom that prevailed in the academic seminars provided effective demonstration that the program did not have a manipulative intent.

> We were able to be candid and present all of the less pleasant
> aspects of the society clearly. . . . This brought a fair amount of ac-
> ceptance, enabling the participants to understand the U.S. better.
> . . . They realized that [the mass] media are not instruments of the
> government as means of propaganda.

From all indications, the participants shared this impression.

The instructors of the academic seminars varied in their evaluations of their respective seminars and of the extent to which they had been
able to achieve the goals they had set for themselves. On the whole, however, they tended to feel that they were at least moderately successful. The
instructor who was least certain about his success felt that the participants'
initial level of information about the United States was lower than he had
anticipated, and that the materials he had asked them to read were probably less than ideal, and were, in any event, generally left unread. In view
of the diversity in language facility and educational background, he felt,
it would have been better to use specially prepared materials, including
graphic aids. It is interesting to read excerpts from the group observer's
final summary of this particular seminar:

> The most striking aspect of this seminar was the shift that took place
> after the first session toward a heavy emphasis on factual material.
> [The instructor] felt that the necessity of providing this material be-
> came obvious very early, and that a more broad, interpretive ap-
> proach was out of the question until this foundation was con-
> structed. He did in fact return, in his last session, to the attempt to
> draw some general deductions. . . . The defect in his method was
> that at points the factual material became far too detailed for the
> needs of the participants and they lost interest.
>
> The emphasis on details and factual information led to a
> great deal of participation of one kind in the seminar, namely the
> asking of very specific informational questions. The exception to this
> was, again, the last seminar, where more general statements set the
> tone for the participants' broader remarks.
>
> This concentration on factual information allowed [the in-
> structor] to cover a great deal of material. . . . He was admirably
> well-acquainted with the material he covered, but was not as success-

ful in choosing the most suitable material in terms of level and degree of detail. However, the group generally reacted favorably to him, and it was clear that he was personally satisfied with the job he was doing.

The group observer's final summary of the seminar that was judged most successful by the majority of the participants is also instructive:

> This seminar began on an uncomfortable footing, possibly due to [the instructor's] own discomfort. . . . The manner he adopted was one of . . . functioning on a very elementary level. Somewhere along the line, his presentation and the group reaction to it changed; . . . possibly it became apparent that they were really intrinsically interested in the subject matter. The atmosphere became one of greater comfort, which facilitated the free exchange of ideas.
>
>   One component of this change in atmosphere was the decline in hostile behavior on the part of the members. This was illustrated in the last session when he was subjected to a series of questions which had completely undermined another leader's seminar. He handled himself so well that he received support and praise from the group. One of the keys to this was his emphasis on objectivity. True, the subject matter he dealt with made this stance easier for him than for some of the other seminar leaders, but he was extremely careful to differentiate between fact and personal opinion.
>
>   His whole approach was a fairly informal one, which was fairly permissive of interruptions by the participants. Despite this "loose" approach, he covered a surprising amount of ground . . . without overburdening the Fellows with technical materials. The sessions also benefited from the degree of preparation invested in them by the seminar leader. This was not true of all the seminar groups. . . . The degree of preparation was also reflected in the material which he distributed to the members.
>
>   . . . The level of the sessions was upgraded after the early sessions, and this change benefited the seminar in terms of interest level and reactions to the leader. The last session ended with prolonged and loud applause, which seemed to reflect the genuine feelings of admiration which the participants held for him and what he had accomplished. The general consensus among the participants was that his seminar had been the most successful of all.

These two instructors structured their sessions differently: the first placed his emphasis on the transmission of factual information, while the second took a more interpretive approach. In line with these different orientations, participation in the first seminar was mostly of the question-and-answer variety, while the second facilitated a freer exchange of ideas. Participants' reactions to the second seminar were clearly more enthusiastic, but they also found the first seminar to be of value. Both of these instructors agreed that the academic seminars were a useful part of the total program. Thus, the first told the interviewer:

I think this is an important part of the program. I think this was proved conclusively. They need the factual information. This is absolutely necessary if they are to get a feeling for the American political system. . . . I think it is essential to discuss American national character, because it is on everyone's mind. It was not useful for some. In some cases, ideological bias prevented communication. It just served to confirm their bias. . . . This could be overcome by individual meetings between teachers and students informally. . . . This would be kind of a tutorial in conjunction with the actual lectures.

The second instructor spoke of his own seminar in these terms:

Insofar as it succeeded it was useful, because they are in the area of communications. The subject matter is essential in understanding the trends in human relations. It has professional importance to them in terms of interpreting the U.S. to people back home. It permits a better interpretation of U.S. news. But the seminar can also be justified in terms of understanding what they see here.

DIRECTORS' RECOMMENDATIONS

Out of the interviews with the two directors, several recommendations for future seminars—made by one or both of the respondents— emerged. These can be summarized as follows:

Selection. In selecting participants, it would be good to extend the geographic range to include, for example, representatives from Latin America, France, Poland, and Russia. As for areas of specialization, one director favored broadening the composition to include representatives from the newspaper field and other communication fields, whereas the other favored an even greater emphasis on educational broadcasting than prevailed in the present seminar. Another suggestion involved the selection of a "team" from each country, including one representative from the broadcasting system and one individual with policy-making responsibilities in the area of educational broadcasting. Furthermore, it was recommended that the final responsibility for selection in each country be left to a selection committee made up of nationals of that country.

Preparation. More advance preparation of participants would be desirable, to give them a better sense of what to expect from the seminar.

Timing. Future seminars, particularly if they are to emphasize educational broadcasting, should be scheduled at a time when schools are in session. It would be desirable to reduce the overall length of the seminar, since it is difficult for most potential participants to take off four months. It would be best to design a less crowded program for the seminar, leaving the participants more unscheduled time for themselves and for spontaneously developed activities.

Professional seminars. The professional seminars should be designed more clearly and individual sessions coordinated more effectively. To this end, it would be useful to arrange a planning session for the various lecturers before the seminar begins. More lectures and demonstrations in the field of educational radio should be included, in line with the importance of radio in many of the countries represented.

Other professional activities. Visits to and affiliations with broadcasting facilities should be expanded, and more laboratory experiences should be provided for the participants. Audiovisual materials, teaching aids, bibliographic materials, and the like should be made available, both for demonstration purposes, and for the participants to take back with them when they leave. Greater opportunities for active participation in the seminar should be created. To this end, it is important to provide more adequate facilities for the presentation of program materials that the participants bring with them.

Academic activities. Better integration between academic and professional seminars would be desirable. A greater amount of interaction of the academic faculty with seminar participants should be encouraged. More efforts should be made to bring in American Negroes as speakers in the academic (as well as the professional) part of the program.

Administrative arrangements. More funds are needed for administrative staff during the university phase of the seminar. Planning for the travel period should be set into motion at an earlier point.

Some of these recommendations are quite specific to the situation under study (and some of these were, in fact, implemented the following year). Some of the more general recommendations are similar to the ones presented in the preceding chapter on the basis of interviews with the participants. Both the specific and the general points, however, suggest the kinds of issues that might arise in any exchange program, regardless of its form or purpose, and that must be kept in mind in the planning of such programs.

6

Participants' Reactions to the Travel Phase

The participants' general evaluation of the second phase of their sojourn was very favorable. In the third interview, which was conducted in the field during the second month of the travel period, eighteen participants indicated that they were very satisfied with this portion of the trip; seven were quite satisfied and three somewhat satisfied. (The comparable figures for the second interview, referring to the university phase, were seven very satisfied, fifteen quite satisfied, four somewhat satisfied, and two not too satisfied.)

The high evaluation of the travel period was also manifested in later interviews. Thus, in the fourth interview—just before leaving the United States—eight participants singled out the travel period as the most valuable part of the seminar; eighteen indicated that they gained more from the travel period than from their stay at the university. When asked about experiences that they found particularly meaningful or valuable during the total four-month stay, seventeen respondents cited the travel period. Specific experiences characteristic of the travel phase were also brought up many times: first-hand exposure to American life (mentioned by 22 respondents); interpersonal experiences in relation to Americans, such as meeting Americans in their homes (seventeen); observations of local broadcasting facilities (sixteen); exposure to new program ideas (eleven); and observations of the physical environment (eleven).

Some months after the participants had returned home, the travel period still stood out in their memories. Among the features of the visit that exceeded their expectations, seventeen respondents mentioned the opportunity to travel throughout the United States. Seventeen respondents also mentioned the travel period as one of the most satisfying aspects of the experience; and many mentioned either the travel period as such or certain components of it among the most useful aspects of the experience.

Returning to the third interview, we note that the specific experiences cited as having been especially important or enjoyable—as representing highlights of the trip—covered a wide range for most participants. Thus, twenty-two mentioned some professionally relevant experiences (for example, visits to broadcasting stations); twenty-one mentioned interpersonal experiences (such as meeting "average" Americans); and twenty-one mentioned certain aspects of the physical environment (such as scenic or architectural wonders).

In describing their most important accomplishments during the trip, seventeen said that they had learned more about the pattern of mass communication in America; thirteen, that they had learned more about America in general; and seven, that they had acquired specific new professional skills, experience, or knowledge by working at a broadcasting station. Not all participants, to be sure, were able to accomplish all that they had hoped to. Seven mentioned that they were not able to observe all the mass media facilities that they had planned to observe, and nine said that they were not able to meet all the people whom they had planned to meet.

PROFESSIONAL ACTIVITIES

A major portion of the two months of travel, as we have already noted, was devoted to various professional activities, including visits to broadcasting stations and to organizations in the field of broadcasting and related fields. Typically, participants paid short visits to a number of different facilities across the country, although sometimes they stayed at a single station for an extended period of time.

All but one of the participants had an opportunity to observe at one or more stations, and only two participants found this experience unsatisfactory. Half of the participants made very few comments or suggestions to the staff at the facilities they visited. The other half made many comments or suggestions and all indicated that these were well received. Only six participants actually had an opportunity to work at a station, and all of them found this experience satisfactory. Another nine participants indicated some disappointment in the fact that they did not have a chance to work at a station. We shall return to this point later.

In general, most participants expressed high satisfaction with the professional side of the trip. Eleven were wholly satisfied, while seventeen gave a mixed evaluation—being satisfied in some respects and dissatisfied in others.

Various reasons for satisfaction with the professional experience were brought up. Many participants were pleased because they were able to obtain a good picture of the great variety of approaches to broadcasting in America and of the range of activities in the field (mentioned by eighteen respondents). Many appreciated the fact that they met fellow-professionals who were very helpful to them (eighteen). Fifteen respondents mentioned that they learned many new things about broadcasting techniques that would be helpful to them after they returned home. Eleven told us that they obtained new ideas for programs. A number of participants indicated that they benefited more from discussions with the broadcasters in the field than they did from the ones they met at the university. Although the latter were generally more impressive, the men in the field were more concrete and participants could talk to them about specific problems that they were facing. Thus, in comparing the broadcasters he met in the field to those he met at the university, one participant remarked:

> Experience-wise they might be inferior. Those people who came to speak to us were producers and directors. But the people at the stations had more time to talk with me personally about communications and the problems that we confront. We have exchanged more ideas.

Another respondent, who was attached to a station for a while, commented:

> They explain their program as they operate [it]. They show and talk about broadcasting in general, and at their stations in particular. They were able to answer specific questions and specific problems that I brought up.

The last comment reflects another source of satisfaction, which was mentioned by fifteen of the participants: the opportunity to work at a station or to observe its operations in detail. How profitable the participants found such opportunities can be illustrated with a comment from a program director who had paid a brief visit to the United States at an earlier point:

> I have learned about television production on the whole. And specifically I have learned what are some of the facilities that are needed for television programming and what some of the equipment and techniques are. The last time I was here I just visited stations. This time I actually worked in one and I got to know the people better and also some of the techniques. I saw how it actually works. I will be able to use some of this information when I go back to my own country. I also got some pretty good ideas about what is expected of us when we establish our own television system.

The opportunity for such direct involvement in an on-going operation seems to us to be one of the most important sources of satisfaction with the trip. Most of the participants who had this opportunity expressed very high satisfaction with their professional experience as a whole. (The results are even clearer when we look at the relationship in the other direction: nine out of the eleven participants who expressed unqualified satisfaction with their professional experience had this opportunity for direct involvement, as compared to six out of the remaining seventeen participants.) This may very well have been the high point of their trip, at least as far as its professional side was concerned.

Although the general level of satisfaction with the professional experiences in the field was high, it seemed to vary systematically with the participant's area of specialization. Satisfaction was highest among the people in news broadcasting and almost equally high among those in general programming, but was clearly lowest among the people in educational broadcasting: only one of the eleven participants who expressed unqualified satisfaction with the professional experience was in the educational area. We can understand this relationship better if we look at some of the specific criticisms raised about the professional side of the trip. These criticisms fell into two major categories: the complaint that certain relevant people or facilities were inaccessible; and the feeling that the experiences were not sufficiently intensive.

As for the first criticism, nine respondents mentioned that they were unable to meet some of the people they wanted to see or to spend enough time with them. None of the news broadcasters raised this point; by contrast, the issue came up in seven out of the ten interviews with educational broadcasters. Five of the people in the educational field registered the related complaint that they would have wanted more opportunities to see school facilities. The nature of the problem can be seen in the following quotation:

The main problem has been that for anyone like myself—interested in educational television and interested in mass communication—there are simply not enough professional people available to see during the summer. They are away or are on vacation. It seems quite important that when you organize a seminar such as this you can't assess the value of educational television when the schools are closed during July and August. These are the two months *not* to be touring the States with the idea of carrying out research in educational television. I haven't wasted my time, but we did miss the opportunity to go into the schools. Also, there is a counter-advantage. Where individuals were available, people had the time to give me. They were not under the pressure of programs. On the whole, the disadvantages, however, outweighed the advantages.

Another eductional broadcaster made a similar point:

Though I have talked to people in projects often, I do not talk with the top people. All the big shots are away on vacation. I wanted to see how the school television programs were received, but I couldn't because the schools were not in session. In Washington, some clerk took me around. I could see that I was interfering with them. I would get shunted to other people. They were very nice, but it would be better if we could get to see the right people.

It would seem, then, that inaccessibility of relevant people and facilities was, at least in part, a practical difficulty resulting from the timing of the trip. The same issue came up at another point, when respondents were asked whether the various places they visited were appropriate and rewarding. The most frequently cited source of dissatisfaction was that certain facilities or operations could not be observed because activities were curtailed during the summer (mentioned by six respondents) and that the people whom the participant wanted to see were away on summer vacations (five). This problem, of course, did not affect the educational broadcasters alone. As it happened, however, it constituted a real limitation for them, and apparently none at all for the news broadcasters.

The reason for inaccessibility was not always that the relevant people were out of town, but often that they were simply too busy to spend much time with the participants. Many participants mentioned how busy the people in the field were, and expressed their own reluctance to intrude upon them. Some respondents did not at all complain about this situation, but accepted it as being in the nature of things. Thus, one respondent, when asked whether he had observed all that he had wanted to in the field, replied as follows:

Not all—but I don't say this with a feeling of disappointment. You can't stay too long in any one place. You become a nuisance for the people who are showing you around.

A number of participants were so sensitive about taking up too much time that they set their own limits and did not always return to a facility they had visited, even when the person in charge had indicated his willingness to see them again. It seems to us that this kind of problem is most likely to arise when the situation is structured as the typical courtesy tour for a visitor. When a visitor is attached to a facility for a somewhat longer period and more integrated into its ongoing activities, access to the relevant people would probably present less of a problem.

This leads us to the second major type of criticism the participants had of the professional experiences in the field. Eleven of the respondents made one or more of the following points: that they saw too many stations and could not stay long enough at any one of them to absorb sufficient detail; that they saw only the facilities at the stations they visited and not enough of their actual operations; or that they were unable to work at a station even though they would have liked to. (The last point was made by eight respondents, although in another context it was made by nine.) In short, these respondents criticized their professional experience on the trip because it did not provide them enough opportunity for a deep and detailed exploration of their professional concerns. The nature of these criticisms can best be illustrated by several quotations. One participant commented:

> I and most of my colleagues have found that during this trip there comes a time when you think: if I have to see one more television station I'll scream. You feel that you just cannot take any more. They are all so much the same. It would be better if there was more specialization in our trips. If, for example, in one place we went to see the station, and in another place we went to be attached for a period of time, and in a third place we went to talk with the management. This would break up some of the monotony.

A participant from the educational field said:

> Everywhere I go I'm shown the facilities. This doesn't interest me because I am not a technical person. I wanted to know about the actual programming, the administration, and the receiving in the schools. . . . I would like mainly to spend two or three weeks in one place so that I could work in one place. . . . I wanted to stay in a place where production was going on.

Finally, another participant, again from the educational field, responded as follows:

> I think our itinerary has been good. It has been so helpful, but I feel that if I could have had more time with one professor or director, then I could go more deeply into the professional side. But these people are very busy. They would see us for one or two hours, but that's all. And then I think our poor English would bother them.

We have seen many stations and people. We got the ideas of those people and stations; but for professional study, if we could stay longer at some institutions, universities or stations, it may be more helpful. This is not good for sightseeing, but it is better for professional purposes.

These criticisms are reminiscent of parallel points that were made with regard to the professional seminars (see Chapter Four). The participants were not entirely satisfied with experiences that consisted largely of being shown facilities, without enough opportunity to see these facilities in operation and to learn more about the actual processes and problems of program production. They tended to feel that this type of experience was too repetitive. They missed the opportunity to go more deeply into some of the procedures, to gain a detailed knowledge of operations, and to focus on specific problems of mutual professional concern. A number of participants expressed the desire to have been attached to a single station for a longer period of time, so that they could have had closer contact with its actual operations. Some would have been interested in actually working on the staff for a while. Others would have liked to have been attached to a producer and to have observed his activities in detail. In any event, this would have meant visiting fewer stations, but spending a longer time with a deeper involvement in one or more of them. As we have already noted, those participants who did have this type of opportunity were highly satisfied with the professional side of their trip.

This type of criticism, again, was made most frequently by the participants in the field of educational broadcasting. It was raised by six out of the ten participants in the educational field, and by only one out of the seven in news broadcasting. This is probably related in part to the fact, already discussed, that people and facilities relevant to the interests of educational broadcasters were less accessible during the summer. But there may be another reason why educational broadcasters were particularly prone to raise this type of criticism: It seems that they brought more specific professional goals and expectations to their American visit, and that a more specific type of professional experience was needed to meet their particular requirements. The people in general programming—most of whom were in top administrative positions—had an interest in seeing many facilities, observing their range of activities, and making comparisons between them. The people in the news field, as we have already noted, had some professional interest in almost any information about America; it was all grist for their professional mills. The satisfaction of the educational broadcasters, however, depended to a larger extent on their opportunity to observe detailed operations and to focus on specific problems of direct professional concern.

SOCIAL ACTIVITIES

The social side of the travel period seemed to work out extremely well. All of the participants indicated that they had an adequate opportunity to meet Americans, and twenty-seven out of the twenty-eight found it easy to get to know the people they met. All of the participants had an opportunity to visit private homes; in fact, eighteen of them mentioned that they had many opportunities to do so. In general, the level of satisfaction with this aspect of the trip was very high: twenty-three respondents expressed unqualified satisfaction, while five had mixed reactions.

Hospitality was organized by local agencies in the various cities visited by the participants. Most participants also met many people through arrangements made by the university. In addition, many of the participants made social contacts on their own: fourteen reported that they had themselves arranged many social contacts ahead of time; seventeen were apparently able to establish many new contacts spontaneously.

The organized hospitality was particularly successful. It was singled out for praise by twenty-one of the respondents. For example, one participant from an Asian country told us:

> In every city, besides the people of the stations and the universities, I had a chance to meet some families. I think that these experiences were very precious for me. People are much more frank and open here than we are in my country, and more so than Europeans. I like Europe, but they are not so open. I visited various families and found those families were very good families.

Another respondent said that he had numerous opportunities to meet Americans. He added:

> I have happily accepted hospitality everywhere I went, and I have met it everywhere. My hand is aching from the bread and butter letters that I have been writing.

Although the overall reactions to the organized hospitality were highly favorable, there was some variation in the reactions the participants had to their experiences in different cities. In general, the participants seemed to evaluate the private (nongovernmental) hospitality centers somewhat more positively. One factor that seemed to make a difference for some of the participants was the relative popularity of a city as a destination for foreign visitors. Thus, one participant, who had rather few contacts of his own and who also had some language difficulty, was particularly grateful that he had been advised to go to Seattle and Portland:

> The people there were very glad to see me and I enjoyed it very

much. I don't think that they often have foreign visitors. It was a good idea to go there.

Since it was difficult for this participant to make his own social arrangements, it was probably particularly wise for him to go to communities that were less inundated with foreign visitors and where he was able to receive more personal attention.

A few participants made some general criticisms of the organized hospitality. Occasionally, a participant would feel that too much was planned in a particular community, so that he found his schedule too exhausting. Some mentioned that they would have liked more privacy, or the opportunity to arrange their own schedules. A different type of criticism was raised by one participant, who would have liked a wider range of contacts. He mentioned, for example, that he experienced difficulty in meeting American Negroes and wondered why the hospitality committees failed to arrange such meetings.

Only two of the participants gave any indication that they had unpleasant experiences in the course of the hospitality visits. One felt that his hosts were often patronizing; the other felt that she had to "sing for her supper" by performing as a foreigner. These two types of experiences represent rather common dangers in international contacts, particularly when these are contacts between an American, for example, and an African or an Asian. It is quite easy for people who offer hospitality to become patronizing, to play the benefactor, and both to exploit and offend the visitor by questioning him about his "primitive" country and its quaint customs. What is really encouraging is that only two of our respondents reported such experiences. Most of the participants reported quite the opposite kind of experiences. They felt that their hosts were genuinely interested in them, and they enjoyed the opportunity for frank discussion. Although a few of the participants were a little disturbed at the lack of information about their countries that they encountered, others were rather surprised that the extent of information was so great. Moreover, most of them felt that their hosts were truly interested in learning more. Participants were most likely to come away from their encounters with American families impressed with the openness and frankness that they found.

ARRANGEMENTS FOR TRAVEL

During the interviews in the field, respondents mentioned a number of problems that they had encountered (eleven indicated that they had encountered some serious problems or difficulties) and offered some suggestions for making the travel experience smoother and more convenient in certain respects. Although most of the points are obvious once they are mentioned, listing the problems and suggestions that were brought up most frequently should help identify areas in which difficulties tend to arise, and details that should be considered in the planning of individual trips.

Itinerary and schedule. Sixteen participants were not entirely satisfied with all aspects of their itineraries. The most frequent reasons for dissatisfaction were related to the time allotted to various places and to the timing of stops. Thus, five respondents felt that on some stops they did not have enough time for the activities that had been arranged for them; six felt that so many commitments had been arranged for them that they did not have enough time for spontaneous activities. Four respondents mentioned that the schedule did not allow them to use their time to maximal advantage. In this connection, a number of participants indicated that one-day stops were usually not very valuable. This type of arrangement turned out to be very tiring, and did not give them enough time to do anything. It was also mentioned that it would be best to avoid scheduling arrival in a new city on the weekend. The weekend is usually a good time for social activities, but the maximal use of this time requires earlier arrival so that the necessary arrangements can be made.

Twenty-two of the participants made some changes in their itineraries as they went along; eighteen of them reported no difficulty in making these changes. Three participants would have liked to make changes but found it impossible.

Financial details. A number of participants indicated that they were not clear about the exact amount of their travel allowance and the regulations governing the use of these funds. Since most of the participants were traveling on a tight budget, it was important for them to have precise information on funds available, so that they could guide themselves accordingly. For the same reason, some participants indicated that they would have liked to have exact information on baggage allowance and charges for excess baggage. Eight participants found the per diem allowance inadequate. Some suggested that a special allowance for intracity transportation would have been helpful.

Another financial problem that arose quite frequently (it was raised by ten respondents) was the difficulty in cashing checks. This problem seemed to be only partly the result of lacking information about the proper procedures to follow; for instance, in many cities a lack of facilities where a nonresident could cash a check provided difficulties. Participants suggested that it would be a good idea to make specific arrangements with banks in different cities that would honor the checks, and to provide each individual with a list of these banks.

Transportation. Seventeen respondents found the transportation arrangements adequate, seven found them inadequate, and four gave mixed reactions. More specifically, a number of participants complained about long bus trips, which they found tiring, especially when the trip was scheduled at night, or when it took them through dull countryside, so that they could gain no compensatory pleasure from looking out the window. They would have preferred to use a different means of transportation in those cases, even though it would have been more expensive. Some participants mentioned that they would have liked to have information on the use of cars for transportation—for example, information about the possible values of going by car as compared to other modes of transportation, and the possible arrangements for renting a car. They felt that they might have preferred to do part of the trip by car, if they had had the necessary information ahead of time. It has already been noted that a number of participants did go by car for all or at least part of the way.

Accommodations. Twelve respondents found their hotel accommodations adequate, six found them inadequate, and ten gave mixed reactions. In some cases, participants were so dissatisfied with the hotels into which they had been booked that they found it necessary to move elsewhere. Dissatisfaction was sometimes based on the lack of personal comforts, such as private baths or air conditioning (mentioned by six respondents), or on the feeling that the hotel was unattractive and perhaps not quite in keeping with the individual's own status (mentioned or implied by ten respondents). Three individuals were dissatisfied because the locations of some of the hotels were inconvenient, away from the center of town and from the facilities that they were planning to visit. As a result, they could not use their stays to maximum advantage. The implication was clear that these participants, if given a choice, would have selected better and more centrally located hotels, despite the greater expense this would have entailed.

Local arrangements. Sometimes, a problem arose when participants were not met on arrival in a particular city, despite their expectation to the contrary, and thus were not prepared for handling the situation by themselves. This problem was especially troublesome for women, and was at the core of at least one of the few cases in which an African participant had a really unpleasant personal experience in the South. In describing his visit to a city in the upper South, one African participant related the following incident:

> There I met with your problem of discrimination. . . . At first, the man who was supposed to meet me got a letter stating the wrong time. I was there two hours before he expected to pick me up. So I was not met at the airport. But then I tried to get a taxi into town and I couldn't ride in it because the other people in it were white.

So I had to hire a car and that cost me eight dollars in order to get into town. When I got into town they wouldn't let me stay at the hotel. Then I finally found a Negro hotel and went there to spend the night. Then the man who came to pick me up was looking all over for me and he finally found me. They said they were worried about what had happened to me . . . . Then they moved me out to the college and everything went well after that.

Clearly, this was a case in which it was especially important to assure proper coordination, and, at the same time, to give the participant enough information so that he could handle any eventualities that might arise.

Useful information. Some participants mentioned that they would have appreciated some advance information on cultural activities and other events that were taking place in the cities they were visiting. It would have been useful not only to be alerted to what was going on before arriving in a city, but also to have tickets for such events. Participants would also have appreciated information about the travel plans of their fellow-participants. Usually, the participants who visited the same city at the same time would meet each other, because they were staying at the same hotel or going to the same television station. Sometimes, however, they did not meet, or met only accidentally after they had both been in town for a few days.

RECOMMENDATIONS

1. Recommendations concerning professional activities:

Our two major recommendations for maximizing the value of the professional experience during the travel period are continuous with our recommendations for the period of residence at the university.

In general, the plan for the travel period should permit longer visits to fewer places. The visits should be worked out with the understanding that the participant will have an opportunity to be close to the day-to-day operations of the facility and to observe them in detail. If interested, he should be able to take the role of a temporary staff member, participating directly in the ongoing activities. Or he may be given access to the facilities and allowed to study daily activities, perhaps by attaching himself to his own professional counterpart in the organization as the latter carries out his regular tasks. Managers of the host facilities should be oriented ahead of time about the interests of their visitors and the nature of the involvement they desire.

It is important to understand clearly the difference between the role of the professional colleague and the role of the sightseer. For certain purposes, the latter may be the most appropriate role for a visitor; however, if the travel period is to be a meaningful professional experience for the participant, then it must provide at least some opportunities for direct involvement in specific professional activities. Thus it is necessary to have a sufficiently long and close association with one or more facilities, so that the participant can exchange ideas and experiences with American colleagues on specific common problems, and so that he can gain some detailed information that is directly relevant to his professional activities at home.

In arranging the trip for a given participant, it is not enough to place on his itinerary facilities that appear relevant to his interests, even if considerable time is scheduled at these facilities. It is also necessary to match, as specifically as possible, the kinds of professional experiences that are made available to him with his particular professional needs. In other words, *it is important to select facilities that will allow him to carry out those activities and partake of those experiences that he is interested in.* Such precise matching is more important to some participants than it is to others. In our study, for example, we have seen that the educational broadcasters seemed to have more specific professional needs and thus required more deliberate planning. Although it may sometimes be quite difficult to arrange a satisfactory matching, it is important to keep this in mind as a goal to be approximated. The main question to be asked, in arranging the trip, is not so much what the participant wants to *see,* but what he wants to *do.* Professional facilities should be selected and oriented in such a way as to provide each participant with the maximum opportunity to do what he wants to do.

2. Recommendations concerning social activities:

Organized hospitality programs seem, in general, to be a very successful feature of the travel period. It would certainly seem worthwhile to maintain this feature, in some form, in future seminars for foreign specialists.

Although it is highly desirable to make these social opportunities available to the participants, and although there is every indication that they are generally appreciated, they should not be turned into obligations for the participant. On occasion, a participant may find himself involved in a whole set of social activities that were planned for him and that he would rather have avoided, for one reason or another. He may find the schedule too exhausting at this particular juncture of his trip, or he may prefer to have more privacy, or he may want to arrange his own activities. Under such circumstances, it would be unfortunate if the individual found himself caught up in a whirl of activities because others have committed him to them. To some extent, this situation can be anticipated and prevented through prior planning. It would be a good idea to raise this issue with the participants before they start on their trip, to find out how much of this type of activity they would want and in which cities; in some cities, for example, they may have their own contacts, or they may plan to concentrate on professional activities. Since these problems cannot all be anticipated during the planning phase, however, it is also necessary to alert local organizations to the possibility that for some people at some times a heavy social program may be too much. *They should be sure to structure the hospitality program as a set of opportunities that they are happy to make available, but that the visitor is not obligated to utilize.*

In planning itineraries, it would be well to consider the inclusion of communities that are smaller and less frequented by foreign visitors (provided, of course, that they have something of general as well as of professional interest to offer to the participant). Such communities may be in a better position to give the visitor more personal attention, which would be particularly important for those participants who do not have wide contacts of their own and who for one or another reason (such as language) have difficulty in making their own social arrangements. By the same token, when such individuals visit cities that *are* inundated by foreign visitors, special attention should be paid to planning their social activities ahead of time, so that they will not find themselves completely isolated.

3. Recommendations concerning arrangements for the travel period:

In preparing a cross-country trip for a foreign visitor, it is important to keep in mind some of the practical problems that might arise in the course of such a trip. Although problems centering around financial arrangements, transportation, or accommodations may be peripheral to the basic purpose of the trip, they may have a decisive effect on the way the person feels about the experience as a whole and how much value he feels he has derived from it.

Whenever one or another type of arrangement for the travel period has to be decided upon, it is important to ask the participant for his preferences—to present him with the alternatives available and allow him to make the choice. One must keep in mind that these decisions usually involve competing values, and there should be no blanket assumption that one value will always predominate for every participant. For example, most visitors travel on a limited budget and would prefer, wherever possible, to spend as little money as possible. Yet, one cannot assume that everyone would therefore prefer to have the least expensive accommodations available. Some participants might prefer to pay more money and stay at a better hotel because considerations of status, comfort, or convenience happen to be more important to them in this particular case. The same would hold true in selecting the mode of transportation. In this connection, it is valuable to *give participants enough general information so as to increase the range of alternatives known to them.* For example, the alternative of traveling by car might not occur to many participants, unless this possibility—together with its advantages and disadvantages— is called to their attention.

In drawing up an itinerary that will meet the needs of the individual participant, it is not enough to arrange for time in all of the places that he wants to visit. Rather, one must think very specifically in terms of the activities in which he wants to engage. When one adopts that point of view, it soon becomes evident that the problem is more than just setting aside time. For example, a one-day stop may satisfy the requirement of placing a particular city on the itinerary, but it gives the individual very little opportunity to do what he might want to do, unless he has a very specific purpose in making this stop and all of his activities there are arranged in advance.

It is impossible to avoid all difficulties and inconveniences, such as might for instance arise from the failure to connect with the local contact person. It goes without saying that such difficulties should be avoided through proper coordination wherever possible (and particularly where they might lead to great embarrassment). *It is also important, however, to try to anticipate some of the difficulties that might arise, despite careful planning, and to prepare the visitor for dealing with them.* Thus, for example, the experience of the African participant who was not met at the airport as anticipated would have been less unpleasant if this eventuality had been foreseen and he had known how to deal with it. In short, it is better to anticipate difficulties and prepare for them than to deny the possibility of their occurrence.

It is important to consider the various possible ways in which a visitor's experience in a given place can be enriched and to try to make these additional opportunities available to him. Generally, this would involve giving him as much information as possible (for example, information about ongoing activities in the cities he plans to visit, and information about his fellow-participants who will be there at the same time), so that he will have a greater range of choices when he arrives in a particular place. Often, it should also be possible to make facilitative arrangements so that the individual can take advantage of the opportunities that are available.

7

Retrospective
Reactions

Chapters Four and Six described the reactions of the participants to the
two major phases of their experience while they were in progress, and
presented a series of recommendations based on these findings. We now
turn to the participants' retrospective reactions to the seminar as a whole
and to its two major phases. These data were obtained at two points, each
of which provided a different perspective, instructive in its own right:
(1) immediately prior to the participants' departure from the United
States (the fourth interview)—thus at a point at which the total experience had come to an end, but was still very fresh in their memories; and
(2) some nine months to a year after their return home (the post-return
interview)—thus at a point at which they had gained some distance from
the experience and had an opportunity to assess its impact on their activities in their regular environment.

Our purpose in the present chapter is to give a brief overview of
these findings in order to see how the total experience appears to the
participants in retrospect; to ascertain whether these findings are consistent with the more detailed findings about the university phase and the

travel phase, obtained while these were still in progress; and to examine whether our main conclusions and recommendations need to be changed or qualified in the light of the participants' retrospective reactions.

PREDEPARTURE REACTIONS

Perceived goals. After the seminar concluded, we asked the participants to review and evaluate the goals that it had hoped to accomplish and to estimate the extent to which the organizers of the seminar had actually been able to achieve these goals.

Participants recognized three main goals for the seminar. Most frequently mentioned was the desire to create an understanding of American broadcasting, especially of American television: nineteen participants indicated that the organizers of the seminar had wanted specialists in other countries to become well acquainted with the accomplishments and the problems of that enterprise. The second major goal again involved a presentation of America to outsiders, this time a presentation of America as a society and as a culture: thirteen participants stated that a major intent had been to provide them with a survey of American philosophical, political, and economic ideas. Only two participants, however, felt that there had been an endeavor to "win friends and influence people" for America. The third major goal perceived by the respondents was of a different nature. Eleven participants suggested that a major intent had been simply to provide a context in which an exchange of experiences and ideas between persons who were working in different professional situations would be possible.

Were these goals achieved? Only one participant felt that they had not been achieved at all, and the majority felt that they had been fully achieved. Were the goals satisfactory to the participants? The answer was a qualified "yes." Ten participants felt that some goals were more acceptable than others. Several participants suggested that some of the goals were inappropriate for the kind of group that had been gathered together; several suggested that certain goals were unrealistic; several suggested that staff goals were incompatible with participants' goals. Seventeen participants, however, approved fully of the seminar's goals as they perceived them.

Participants' reactions about goals are illustrated by the following responses of five participants to the question, "What, in your opinion, were the main things that the organizers of the seminar were hoping to accomplish?":

> It is difficult for me to say. They had in mind (1) to show us American radio, and (2) to understand the American people. This was part of the international relations program. It was not *strictly* a

radio and television seminar. Yet, I would hesitate to say propagandize. . . .

1. I think, in my opinion, they were out to give us an inside picture of production in the United States.
2. I think that they were very keen to give us as much experience with American television as possible.
3. I think they were trying to give us an overall picture of America as a country.
4. They were trying to equip us with the knowledge and know-how of production methods, programming methods in communication in general.
[*To what extent do you think they were able to achieve each of these goals?*] I think they have achieved satisfactorily all of these goals. Although the know-how would have been needed more so that one would have had practical experience—more practice . . . .

First, they wanted to give a picture of American doctrines, peoples and problems. Second, they wanted to introduce us to the idea of educational television. Third, they wanted us to exchange ideas, in this field of work.
[*To what extent do you think they were able to achieve each of these goals?*] I think they were successful on the first and the second. I think on the third they were not successful. We did not exchange ideas very well. I think there should be more organized discussion seminars among the participants. It is not possible to leave it to the members themselves. It should be more organized and a definite part of the program . . . .

I described in an earlier passage what I achieved and those were the goals of the seminar except for professional training. Perhaps, the seminar was organized for "top executives," who needed no training. They were to be given a chance to discuss and get to know the system under which American radio and television function and to get them to benefit from the introduction of a multinational aspect and to give them an insight into American life. [*Are you talking about the goals for top executives?*] Yes. [*To what extent do you think they were able to achieve each of these goals?*] These aims, they achieved quite satisfactorily except there wasn't enough give and take between the participants. The viewing of films should be better organized. We have dissected and analyzed *ad nauseam* the American system, but we hardly ever got much about the other countries . . . .

I think the understanding between countries should be—could be the most accomplished thing the organizers get from the seminar. [*Is that what you think they were hoping to accomplish?*] I don't know, but I hope they were hoping to accomplish that! [*To what extent do you think they were able to achieve this understanding?*] . . . you cannot say . . . you can get people all together and they can understand each other, but I think there are still some more ways that you can get these people to understand each other more. [*Can you give me an example?*] We didn't once have a chance to talk individually about what is in our mind. Particularly, when we came back from the tour. But we never had a chance. Even if you have to spend a whole day, you should let people exchange ideas and talk one by one. And if, before going out touring the country, you let us talk one by one, then we can learn more from each other.

It is interesting that one logical possibility was scarcely represented among the goals suggested by our respondents: Only four participants mentioned that one of the goals of the seminar was to enable Americans to learn from their colleagues from abroad and to exchange ideas with them. The participants seemed to have accepted the tacit understanding that they had been invited to America to learn from Americans about American broadcasting and American institutions, and to exchange ideas with each other, but not to bring knowledge to or exchange ideas with their American counterparts. As we have already suggested in Chapter Four, a seminar with the goal of mutual exchange built explicitly into its structure might make for a professionally more involving experience.

Suggested changes for the university phase. What changes would the participants suggest for the program at the university? Did they feel that there were any things of consequence that should have been done differently? All participants answered "yes" to the latter question. Their suggested changes referred largely to matters of scheduling, choice of speakers and topics, mode of interaction, and facilities.

There was a common feeling that scheduling had been too intense and that too much time had been spent at the university. Fifteen participants wanted to reduce the length of the university period. Two of them would have shortened the academic seminars; two would have shortened the professional seminars; and eleven would have shortened both sets. Five participants felt that the schedule should be rearranged so that there would be more time to relax, to read the materials that had been distributed, to go into the city and move about among the people. At an even more concrete level, three participants suggested that there should not have been discussions following the noon meal. The following quotation can serve to illustrate this general concern:

One suggestion. During the first few weeks, the schedule was a bit too packed. Although one can sympathize with the organizers—being so far away from town and left with no activity—it would have left some void. However, at the same time, some discussions in the evening dragged on and on and on and were very tiring. If the discussion could be stopped a bit earlier in the evening perhaps it would be better. One can sympathize with the organizers for wanting to keep active.

The choice of speakers and topics is inevitably a problem for so mixed a group. Seven participants felt that there should have been fewer professional speakers. Two felt that there had been too much time spent on the single topic of American race relations; others felt that not enough time was spent on certain other topics in which they had a special interest. Some respondents felt that there should be more speakers representing cultural fields other than the mass media and mass media other than television, or that there should be permanent lecturers, or that lecturers should be selected in terms of their capacity for effective communication.

Mode of interaction and participation was a major issue that underlay many suggestions. Six participants asked that opportunities be built into the program for participants to discuss their own experiences, for example, to compare programs that they had produced and explore some of the problems these have presented. Seven made suggestions that reflected a desire for improved communication, making active participation in discussions more feasible—for example, that openness on the part of participants be encouraged; that there be small group discussions; that non-English speakers be encouraged to participate; that there be more chances to talk to lecturers. Several other suggestions called for opportunities for more active involvement on the part of participants in practicum-type experiences. Thus, three persons asked that a strong link be built with the educational broadcasting station near the university. For example, the participant cited in the last quotation responded as follows, when asked what features of the Brandeis program should be strengthened:

> The attachments to the working stations. Although the lectures are good, the working is more important. This is the general impression I have received from talking with many people.

A second participant told the interviewer:

> I would recommend attachment to local broadcasting services . . . for the stay. It would be very difficult. It would involve more organization with the local stations, but I don't see why the participants couldn't have worked at the local stations. They could have both attended lectures and worked at the local stations. That would have made the six weeks worthwhile . . . .

Another respondent commented that participants might be asked to produce their own programs as laboratory exercises—which, incidentally, strikes us as a rather promising idea.

Finally, a fair number of comments were made about facilities. Few respondents went so far as the one who suggested that the participants ought really to be lodged in Boston and only commute to the university. Nevertheless, quite a few participants did suggest that there ought to be opportunities to attend cultural events and to see the Boston area, and that there ought to be better transportation facilities. They also would have liked more radios, television sets, and tape recorders, and better facilities for showing films. They would have liked better rooms, and a few people would have liked a more mature administrative staff. One respondent, for example, recommended the following improvements:

> Better rooms. Better possibilities to get in and out—perhaps a car for every member or daily tours by student drivers. Each member must have an opportunity to go places and not have to spend each night in his room.

A number of the concerns about the university phase of the seminar are well illustrated in the comments of an African participant. When asked what he felt should have been done differently at Brandeis, he replied:

> I think we should have been organized in a better way. Meanwhile, with nearly all the countries here, unless one spoke with people one does not know what is going on in [their countries]. There is no time planned. There should be a write-up about television in different countries. I myself would have loved to hear a report about what is going on in different countries. That was ignored too much. There was too much about what America could offer and not what other countries could offer. There should have been days when other people could speak their mind . . . I would have allocated days for people to speak . . . Yes, I would have put it down in the schedule. But it wasn't done and it wasn't clear to the committee.

Further along in the interview, he again discussed the theme of possible improvements at Brandeis:

> I think there should be recreation activities. I think these should be considered important. There is nothing here like a game or a swimming pool or anything. There is not even a dance place. We are left to rot. We don't have easy access to any television set except one. We cannot switch from one station to another. Why not have television in every room? They have it in hotels for the same price. We are asked in the interviews, how do we like television, but we haven't seen any. There is only one crooked set which broke down. [*What features should be strengthened?*] Recreation and discussion periods. Everyone should be made to speak and this can be done by breaking up into small groups. We could discuss certain subjects. Some person in the group could take down notes. Instead of a mass group we could discuss the same subjects in the small groups. As it is we would

get some talkative woman who talked the whole time. [*What features should be added?*] Practical work on the spot. [*What features should be dropped?*] Serious talks immediately after a heavy meal. There is too much after dinner discussion. One's head is swimming at that point, and one wants to go to bed.

Suggested changes for the travel phase. Suggestions concerning the travel period were mostly aimed at expanding the opportunities for profitable and involving professional activity. Five respondents suggested that the schedule be arranged in such a fashion that a participant might spend a considerable amount of time at two or three stations. Thus, in discussing possible improvements for the travel phase, one respondent recommended

> . . . longer attachment to the stations for practical work. Then if the person concerned wants to see more of the United States he can spend short times going to Disneyland, Grand Canyon, and so on. This is better than entering the television station from one door and coming out the other.

Another participant commented in a similar vein:

> The travel period was very good. Only one thing has to be better. I always have to go back to my first point: if it is a specialists' seminar, then it would be very good to find TV stations to prepare for people—to give them an opportunity to work with the people for two weeks, to be a member of the crew. They should discuss planning of the program, be behind the camera man, be a member of the crew. Each station should take one or two of the participants for a two-week period. This time should be definitely set. The person would be expected at a definite date. They should send materials a month ahead of time, so that the person would prepare himself for this two-week period. This is much more valuable than just talking about general things—being asked what happened in your country and so on. I arranged this for myself for one week in [one of the cities I visited].

Eight respondents noted that the visits ought not to come at a time when a number of the logical hosts would be on vacation. For example, one participant suggested in this connection that

> . . . the seminar should start toward the end of July or August and run for about five or six weeks and then start the tour. Most universities or colleges are on vacation. We couldn't see all the people. If we start in September, maybe the officers and people will be more active. For example, we can watch demonstrations. But in the summer there is no school television.

A few respondents suggested that work or training opportunities might well be arranged before the travel period is actually begun. Preparations for the participant's arrival at various places ought also to be better worked out, several noted, since at some places he was hardly expected. Finally, twelve respondents recommended that the directorate provide more detailed suggestions as to where participants ought to go and what they ought to see; there should be explicit information, for example, about the educational TV stations that are to be found in each state. The following comment illustrates this point:

> I think that very soon after arrival, the members of the seminar should be handed a document which lists the various kinds of activities in the states that are possible to see with recommendations about the best places to go and suggestions about the length of time one should stay there in order to make the best use of these facilities. For example, there should be a list of where you can find visual aids in museum libraries, schools and stations around the country. Such a document would have made the task of the travel organizers much easier.

A second block of suggestions concerned travel comfort. Small sets of respondents recommended that better hotels should be provided, that automobile travel be easier to arrange and more commonly employed, that the cashing of checks be facilitated, and that fewer appointments be set up at each step of the tour.

Exchange among participants. We have already seen that respondents spontaneously suggested increased opportunities for exchange of ideas and for active participation in discussions for the university phase of the seminar. Several questions focused specifically on this and related issues.

Half of the respondents felt that the opportunities for exchange of ideas among participants (which many respondents perceived as a major goal for the seminar) had been sufficient; half felt that they had not been sufficient. To improve exchange in future seminars, eleven respondents suggested that participants be given a greater opportunity to address the group and present their own ideas, experiences, and problems. Eight felt that the overall structure of the program be so designed that discussions among participants have a more integral place in it—that such discussions, in other words, be more deliberately planned.

Only a quarter of the respondents felt that the seminar had utilized the individual talents of the various participants to the fullest. Half felt that a moderate degree of utilization had been achieved, and another quarter felt that only a low degree had been achieved. This situation might be improved, they said, by having participants lead discussions on various broadcasting topics, and by incorporating individual showings of the par-

ticipants' own work into the formal program of the seminar and providing
more time for them.

As far as their *own* potential contributions were concerned, a
third of the participants felt that these had not been adequately employed
at the university. Most participants felt, however, that during the travel
period adequate use of their particular talents had been made. This may
help to explain, in part, why eighteen participants considered the travel
period to have been more useful to them than the stay at the university.
Four others reported that they had gained more at the university, whereas
five respondents said that they had gained about equally during both
phases.

A lengthy quotation from one of the Europeans may illustrate
some of the modal responses:

> [*Do you feel that the seminar provided sufficient opportunity for the
> exchange of ideas among participants?*] Very little—or better: not
> enough. [*What recommendations would you make for improving this
> exchange in future seminars?*] The speakers—from America or from
> other countries—should speak about a specific problem and then
> everyone should discuss how this problem is handled in his country.
> They should bring in their own experiences with respect to a specific
> problem. You can't do this when you discuss only general problems.
> For example, how do we handle unhappy endings in children's pro-
> grams? How should we approach this problem? This is a problem
> all over the world, and people handle it in different ways. This is
> one example—there are many others. If you talk about such prob-
> lems, you can exchange ideas, see how people work and so on. You
> can't do it if all that happens is that they show movies they made.
> There is a problem about Westerns, cowboy movies. That's a prob-
> lem all over the world. It would be very interesting to discuss it. To
> show some Westerns and discuss just that. It needs a good moder-
> ator, to draw out discussion. *This* kind of seminar would be an ex-
> cellent opportunity for people all over the world.
> [*Do you feel that the individual talents of the participants in the
> seminar were utilized to their fullest extent?*] No, because it was not
> enough specialized. They were used, but not enough. [*What about
> your own participation: do you feel that adequate use was made of
> your potential contributions?*] Whenever I took part in discussion, it
> was because I felt it would be useful. But I wasn't invited to do that
> and I am not so sure they were satisfied with what I said. I am the
> kind of person who doesn't like to be silent, I like to feel free. But
> I wasn't invited to speak about things—except in a general way:
> "Who has some questions?" Maybe some of my statements are
> wrong, because I am speaking from my custom in our country. If
> we have money or time to have a program, we would use it in the
> best way to increase the knowledge and experience of the people. I
> have been moderator of conferences. I try to talk to people individ-

ually, to encourage each one to use the discussion, to bring up his questions, so that each individual would get the most out of it. [*Were there any contributions that you felt you could have profitably made, but that you were unable to make?*] I think all of us would have been able to do more than we did. We should have discussed the central questions, not just lectures and then general questions.

General focus of the seminar. In general, participants felt that the seminar had been sufficiently matched to their particular interests. There were a few complaints: that there had been too much educational television; that there had not been enough opportunity to observe the actual utilization of TV programs in school; that material was not covered at a high enough level. Twenty of the participants believed that the organizers had demonstrated an adequate understanding of their particular needs and of the situations in their respective home countries. Fifteen felt that they had been given a reasonably well-balanced picture on most topics; eight felt that there had been some distortion—for example, in the coverage of the race question.

All but one participant said that a similar seminar should be held in the future. All but one were satisfied with the current seminar sponsorship, but ten would have liked to see a shift in its geographical base. Ten felt that the same kinds of participants should be included in a future seminar; sixteen called for a change in composition. The latter felt, for example, that it would be desirable to increase specialization (mentioned by nine respondents) or to restrict participation to people with direct experience in broadcasting (four). Nineteen participants felt that there should be changes in the roster of countries included, but this suggestion generally turned out to mean that they wanted even more countries placed on the next list.

POST-RETURN REACTIONS

In their post-return interviews, participants continued to be enthusiastic about the experience as a whole. All twenty-eight said that it had been worthwhile and enjoyable. Only five felt that they had accomplished less than they had hoped to, whereas seven thought that they had accomplished even more than they had anticipated. Twenty-two respondents had found more aspects of the sojourn satisfying than dissatisfying; the remaining six had found satisfactions and dissatisfactions to be about equal.

Before we summarize the reactions of the group as a whole, it may be useful to provide some concrete illustrations of the kinds of dissatisfactions, satisfactions, and suggestions for change that emerged from the post-return interviews. We shall again utilize, for this purpose, an extensive quotation by a single participant, a European:

[*When you think back over your stay in America, how do you feel about it?*] Enormously grateful for having had the opportunity to go there. A sense of gratitude is the overriding feeling. Coupled with that is the broadening of one's horizon, one's thinking and experience, which this has given me. American problems—American achievements—fall into a picture, which I now understand at least in part. Before I was so grossly underinformed about America that my whole thinking about America was false and wrong . . .
[*In general, do you feel that you accomplished what you wanted to by your trip?*] Yes, I do. I think more than I had hoped for. How much of that was purely professional and how much horizon-broadening, I wouldn't want to define. But, overall, it was more valuable than I had anticipated.
[*In what ways did the trip fall short of your expectations?*] It didn't fall short of them at all. [*In what ways did it exceed your expectations?*] In the number of really worthwhile people one was able to meet, listen to and talk with—and the quality of these people. Secondly, in the great freedom one was given in the travel, and the scope which was possible as regards travel. The organization of the travel side was extraordinarily good . . .
[*At this point, as you think back to the Brandeis seminar, which parts did you find particularly useful?*] I found both professional and academic seminars enormously useful and valuable. I enjoyed them immensely and learned a great deal—more academically than professionally. I went there deeply suspicious of the academic seminars, but I was disarmed within a couple of days. There was a little too much depth perhaps on the American legal system, but on reflection it was important. In the light of subsequent events in the South, it really helps to be able to understand the problems and complexities of the American legal system.
[*From your present perspective, what improvements would you be able to suggest?*] The seminar was too long. It could have accomplished quite easily in a month what took us six weeks. Each seminar was very valuable, but the whole thing could have been streamlined. We would have done better not to have *lived* at Brandeis, but to have lived more in America. I was frightfully frustrated in not being able to get out. Waltham is no picnic, while Cambridge is a very rewarding place . . . Being confined to the monastic existence of Brandeis, it was very frustrating . . .
[*What about the selection and composition, could that be improved?*] I think the group was a little too big. One carefully chosen person from each of fifteen countries would have been ideal. Making quite sure in advance that each participant had a reasonably comparable professional background and experience and interests. There were some people who had never even been in radio—they tended to ask questions that in their naiveté irritated others in the course. We were held up by questions that should have been an automatic

part of everyone's equipment. I am *not* talking about the African delegates, most of whom were very good and all of whom had experience in broadcasting. One other thing: during the seminar period I would have liked to live and work in a station for a week or a fortnight. Not just to observe, but actually be attached in a working capacity. It would be best to start the seminar with such an experience for each participant. Then we could all come back and pool these experiences in the seminar . . .

[*Do you expect to come back to the U.S. at some future time?*] I hope to. I would very much like to, and if an opportunity became available, I would grasp it with both hands . . .

Having seen the pattern of reactions as they coalesce in the response of a single individual, let us turn to a review of the dissatisfactions, satisfactions, and suggestions for change as they distributed themselves over the entire group.

Dissatisfactions. When asked what things they wished they had done differently, seven participants told us that they wished they had visited fewer places, and six that they wished they had stayed at a single station for an extended period. Five wished that they had placed more emphasis on professional activities. Others wished that their English had been better, or that they could have traveled longer, or that they could have gone by car, or that they could have met more "average Americans."

Disappointments with conditions outside of one's self focused on a number of different aspects of the sojourn. Six respondents cited poor planning or organization of one or another feature of the seminar or the trip. Five were disappointed at being unable to visit relevant facilities because of summer schedules. Five found some or all of the professional seminars, and three found some or all of the academic seminars, disappointing. Other disappointments concerned insufficient opportunity to exchange information between participants, lack of certain technical facilities at the university, and lack of opportunity to work at or affiliate with a broadcasting station.

Three items were cited by five or more people as the least satisfying aspects of the experience: the fatigue induced by an over-filled agenda of travel, attendance at certain seminars or lectures that were least relevant to the participant's own professional interests, and the geographical location of the seminar.

Satisfactions. What were some of the ways in which the sojourn exceeded the participants' expectations? For seventeen participants, it was by affording them an opportunity to travel throughout the United States. Apparently it had not been possible to anticipate from abroad the impact that such a journey would have. America's continental scope, its incredible variety, and the rugged beauty of its Western lands traditionally exceed the expectations of American travelers as well. Twelve participants were pleased beyond expectation by the opportunity to meet many people. Eight were excited by the opportunities to learn about people from other countries. Others were pleasantly surprised by the hospitality and friendliness of the Americans whom they met, and by the opportunities to learn about educational television, and by the opportunities to learn about communication media in America. It is interesting that rather few participants cited professional experiences—such as those to which the last two items refer—among the ways in which the sojourn exceeded expectations. Understandably, the places visited and the people met represent the most vivid memories after the passage of a year. There is also the likelihood, however, that for many participants the relatively passive nature of their professional involvement prevented it from becoming a high point of the experience.

What aspects of the experience were most satisfying? Once again, travel was a first choice. Seventeen people cited the travel period as the most satisfying aspect, as against four who cited the period at the university. Nine participants spoke of the exchange of ideas with other people, and five spoke of the seminars that were particularly relevant to their own special interests. Four spoke of visits to broadcasting facilities, and two of the opportunity to work at a station. Eight cited the chance to "travel around the country and meet average Americans"; six referred to the hospitality and friendliness of the people; and four referred to the chance to see the beauty of the American terrain. Here, professional experiences did take their place side by side with the pleasures of travel and interpersonal encounters, although the latter still predominated.

What parts of the sojourn had they found particularly useful after their return? Twelve nominated the academic seminars in general. Eleven nominated specific seminars and lectures that were related to their particular interests. Nine spoke of the opportunity to observe broadcasting or educational facilities; eight of the professional seminars in general; and eight of the exchange of information and ideas with other participants. Finally, eight respondents simply mentioned the travel period.

Suggested changes. The participants had many improvements to suggest from their post-return perspective. Eight mentioned that it would be useful to clarify the aims of the seminar. Twelve suggested that selection procedures be changed to insure greater homogeneity.

Many comments referred to improvements in the professional part of the seminar. Thus, six respondents made general statements to that effect. Others were more specific: six called for more opportunities to be attached to a station and work with American counterparts; five asked that more opportunities be provided to observe facilities; five suggested that the timing of the seminar be coordinated with the availability of relevant facilities (such as school television). The desire for more active professional participation is reflected in a number of suggestions: five participants proposed that the experience be organized more in the nature of a workshop or a laboratory; five suggested that participants be given the opportunity to form into interest groups or discussion groups; four called for more opportunity for professional exchange among participants.

Other suggestions included an overall reduction in the length of the seminar (mentioned by eight respondents); a reduction in the amount of time given to lectures and seminars (nine); and an increase in the amount of time available for rest, for reflection, or for travel (four). Four participants suggested that staff take a more intensive role in working out more individualized travel plans, and four others suggested that the seminar be held in a different location.

It is interesting that, whereas six respondents said that they would recommend participation in a similar seminar to anyone who had the chance to attend, twenty-one would recommend participation to some people but not to others. There was no consensus about the type of person for whom participation was seen as particularly appropriate. Thus, nine would recommend attendance by specialists in educational broadcasting, but not by general broadcasters; on the other hand, three would recommend attendance by those in general broadcasting but not by those in educational broadcasting. Five would recommend attendance by working broadcasters (for example, in production work), in contrast to those in policy or administrative posts, whereas four would make precisely the opposite recommendation.

CONCLUSION

As one reviews these retrospective reactions of the participants, several points stand out. Regarding the composition of the group, about half of the participants mentioned, in some fashion, that they would prefer greater homogeneity. Most often this preference seemed to be related to a desire for a more specialized focus to the seminar. This point did come out in the earlier interviews, although it seems to be stressed a bit more in retrospect. Our earlier recommendation on this point (Chapter Four) appears valid in the light of the additional information.

With regard to the university phase of the experience, several points stressed in both retrospective interviews echo points that also emerged sharply in the second interview: (1) It would be desirable to resist the tendency to overschedule the seminar; the number of lectures and seminars ought to be reduced and more time left for rest, reflection, and individual pursuits (see Chapter Four). (2) It may be desirable to reduce the overall length of the university phase; in the post-return interview, we were particularly likely to hear the suggestion that the seminar as a whole ought to be shorter—perhaps because some participants were more cognizant of problems that had arisen during their four months abroad or of the difficulties in catching up after such an extended absence from the office. (3) It may be desirable to center the seminar in a less isolated setting, or at least it would be necessary to find more adequate means of transportation so that participants would feel less confined and cut off and would be better able to take advantage of the cultural offerings of a large city (see Chapter Four).

What really stands out, however, in respondents' retrospective reactions to the university phase of the seminar, is their desire for a professional experience that would allow for a greater degree of involvement and active participation, and for a fuller utilization of the participants' own talents. Thus, they suggested more opportunities for presentations on the part of participants, in which they can report on their personal experiences, discuss their own programs and the problems associated with them, and get the reactions of other participants based on their own relevant experiences. They suggested more planned discussions among participants, perhaps in the context of specially formed interest groups, in which they can exchange ideas on problems of common concern; these should be incorporated as integral parts of the overall program. They suggested more opportunities for participants to show samples of their own work, again integrated into the overall design of the seminar. Another type of active participation that a number of the participants stressed is involvement in practicum-, workshop-, or laboratory-type experiences, perhaps through more intensive affiliation with a local broadcasting facility. All of these points came up in our earlier interviews, but they emerged more clearly and more emphatically when the participants reflected on their experience in retrospect than they did while the experience was still in progress. Our recommendations regarding opportunities for more active participation (Chapter Four) appear even more valid on the basis of these retrospective reactions than they did before, and they deserve to be underlined.

With regard to the travel phase of the seminar, respondents stressed the importance of working out plans for the professional side of the trip more explicitly so that benefits accruing from these experiences can be maximized. Specifically, this implies more deliberate selection of the facilities to be visited and taking steps to assure that they will be prepared for the visitor when he arrives. Of obvious importance here is timing the trip so that the facilities most relevant to participants' interests will in fact be available; problems had arisen for some of our respondents because of summer vacations. Another point, brought up in both retrospective interviews, is the desirability of arranging for more intensive experiences by visiting fewer places, with more time devoted to each. All of the above points echo similar points raised in the interviews conducted in the course of the travel period itself (see Chapter Six). One point that was raised in the earlier interview but received considerably more emphasis in retrospect—and especially on the post-return interview—is the desirability of providing more opportunities for affiliation with a broadcasting station. A subgroup of the participants felt that attachment to a facility, with direct involvement in and detailed observations of its ongoing activities, would greatly enhance the professional value of the experience; and they seemed to feel this more strongly the farther removed in time they were from the experience.

In short, what emerges more sharply out of the retrospective interviews than out of the "in-progress" interviews is the desire for a greater degree of active involvement in professional activities, a greater opportunity for exchange of ideas and experiences with fellow-professionals (other participants as well as American broadcasters), and a greater scope for making personal contributions and utilizing one's own talents. Perhaps it is professional experiences of this sort that stand out in one's memory as time passes, far more than professional experiences of a more passive kind. That is not to say that the latter experiences are not useful; they may be interesting, informative, and enriching, and they may leave a lasting impact on the person's fund of knowledge and level of understanding. Certainly, we have every reason to believe that our respondents appreciated what they were able to observe and hear about American broadcasting during their visit; much of it they found useful on returning home, and some they were even able to apply to their own situations. What stood out in their memories, however, were not these professional experiences, but the trip throughout the United States—the places they were able to see and admire and the people with whom they were able to make genuine human contacts.

8

Personal Significance

The preceding chapters have dealt with the participants' reactions to the way in which the seminar had been organized and executed. We now begin a series of chapters concerned with the impact of the seminar on the participants. Chapter Nine will deal with its impact on their images of America and American broadcasting. Chapters Ten through Twelve will present relevant comparisons between participants and controls. In the present chapter we are concerned with the personal significance of the sojourn for the participant, as reported by him in the fourth and in the post-return interviews—the two retrospective interviews that were also used in the preceding chapter. Did he enjoy the sojourn? Did he feel that he had accomplished something? What aspects of the experience were most meaningful for him? In what way does he see himself as having changed as a result of the experience? These are the kinds of questions to which we shall address ourselves.

Our point of reference in this chapter is the individual participant, rather than the seminar. What we want to find out is what this experience meant to him. In Chapters Four, Six, and Seven, the participants served, in essence, as expert informants about the seminar. They gave us information relevant to the evaluation of the seminar that only they, as participants, were able to supply. Now, however, the participant himself and his subjective reactions are our objects of study.

Before turning to some of the specific meanings that the sojourn had for the participants, let us examine their responses to certain general questions about the experience. The participants were strong in their general approval of the sojourn. At the time of the fourth interview, all but two were positive in their evaluations; at the time of the post-return interview, all twenty-eight said that the trip was both worthwhile and enjoyable. In reporting their experiences in that interview, twenty-two participants made it apparent that they had found more aspects of the trip satisfying than dissatisfying; the remaining six reported about equal numbers of satisfactions and dissatisfactions.

Had they been able to achieve their original goals? Had they accomplished all that they had hoped to accomplish? Before leaving America, ten participants said that they had achieved all of their original goals, and eleven said that they had achieved most of them. This left five who said they had achieved some of them and only one who felt that he had achieved few. After returning home, five felt that they had accomplished less than they had set out to, and seven felt that they had achieved more than they had expected. They felt that these original goals, which they had largely attained, were reasonable and appropriate. Only seven suggested that they would have changed them.

Had the trip created any special problems? Eighteen said that this had not occurred. For seven respondents problems had arisen, usually just because they had been away from their homelands and their offices, but sometimes because they had specifically been in America. Thus, several men said they now felt a sense of frustration; they had gained new ideas in America, but could not carry them out. Another man noted that normal problems had simply piled up on his desk while he was away; and another told us that, because of his absence, he had missed the chance to participate in the development of a new program.

As we shall show, the experience had been significant in a number of professional and nonprofessional ways. Yet one wonders: taken as a whole, in which of these two broad ways was it more significant? The answer seems to depend upon the way one phrases the question. The accomplishments that seemed most important were those made in professional areas. The experiences that seemed most meaningful or enjoyable were those that fell in nonprofessional areas. These data can be seen more clearly in Table 3. The most appropriate way to summarize this table is to say that both areas were of considerable importance to the respondent, and the succeeding sections of this chapter will explore them in some detail.

Table 3

PROFESSIONAL AND NONPROFESSIONAL SIGNIFICANCE OF THE SOJOURN

Number of Respondents Citing:

	Professional Area	*Nonprofes-sional Area*	*Total N*[a]
As locus of most meaningful or enjoy-able experiences	11	16	27
As locus of most important accomplish-ments	19	8	27

[a] As noted in Chapter Three, one of the twenty-eight participants left unexpectedly before the completion of the seminar and there was no opportunity, therefore, to schedule her fourth interview.

At the end of the sojourn, participants were asked whether they had experienced significant changes in their ways of looking at things. Twenty-one reported altered perspectives about America. Thirteen said that they had acquired a new vision of the potentialities of the mass media. Five said that they had achieved a fuller realization of their communality with people from other countries. In the post-return interview, twelve participants reported that, directly or indirectly, the trip had led to changes in the plans they had for the future.

According to their own reports, then, the sojourn did have important meanings for many of the participants. Let us turn to some of the more specific ways in which such a trip can have meaning for those who participate in it. In the sections that follow we shall look at the experience in terms of its effects—from the participant's point of view—on (1) his professional knowledge, insight, and activities; (2) his knowledge about the profession as practiced in America; (3) his knowledge of America as a whole; (4) his sense of enjoyment in a foreign setting; (5) his orientation to international exchange and contact; and (6) his perspective on his own country.

PROFESSIONAL KNOWLEDGE

Much effort in arranging the seminar was devoted to shaping an experience in which the participant could enlarge his professional competence. We have seen in previous chapters that much of the appreciation and the criticism earned by the seminar was a function of the perceived opportunities for professional learning. It is not surprising, then, to find that this learning was one of the most significant features of the experience for the participant. This significance is illustrated most clearly in six points, each of which was made by about half of the participants. When asked (in the fourth interview) to list their important accomplishments, fourteen noted that they had increased their overall professional experience, and eleven noted that they had gained a greater appreciation of the value of educational television. When asked to list initial goals that had been accomplished, fifteen pointed out that they had learned about educational television. When asked to list meaningful or enjoyable experiences, sixteen included the opportunities that they had had to observe local facilities, and eleven referred to their exposure to new program ideas. Finally, thirteen reported in another section of the interview that they had gained new perspectives on the potentialities of the mass media.

There were of course other sections in the interviews in which smaller numbers brought up professional learning as a valued experience. Thus, four men cited their period of work at a station as a highly meaningful experience; five cited those seminars that were related to their professional interests as especially satisfying aspects of the experience. The high consensus on the benefits listed above, however, is particularly impressive.

The extent to which this professional learning can be personally significant is indicated in the remarks of an African who had been asked about his most important accomplishments:

> For me the most important thing is that for the first time I had an introduction to television. All I know up to now about television I learned here. This was new to me and I learned so much. I learned not only what television is, but I learned from experience what television can do. . . . All of this was new to me because I am new in broadcasting.

This kind of response is not limited to those who are new to broadcasting, however. Let us consider the response of a well-established educational broadcaster to the same question:

> I think there was a shift in my attitude to the possible value of straight instructional courses on television at the adult or near adult level. I think now that there is more value to these programs than I thought before. I am also more aware of the potential market of this kind of thing. It is more relevant to my country than I thought before. I have also reinforced my belief that educational television can have a job to do on a small scale. The concept of a university station I find quite meaningful and I can see its potential even more. . . .

As we see, for this man professional learning did not take the form of instructing him in the way things might be done, but of stimulating him to think about the implications for the home situation of the activities he saw carried out in the American context.

In the final analysis, the value of professional learnings depends on their relevance to the person's own professional situation and to the performance of his professional role. Do we have any evidence that the participants as a group saw such relevance, as the two cited above clearly did?

In the fourth interview, respondents were asked whether they had gained new perspectives on their professional roles. Thirteen said that they had, and thirteen said that they had not. Again, they were asked whether they had gained new perspectives on the way broadcasting should be run in their own countries. Twelve said they had; fourteen said they had not. Some of the specific new views that they had gained were: that broadcasting should be more dynamic, that it should strive harder to reach more people and to meet their needs better, and that it should place more emphasis on educational activities. Half of the respondents reported that their views on the future of educational television in their own countries had changed; they unanimously saw it as having very important potential. Finally, many participants were strengthened in the view that commercial control of broadcasting may have deleterious effects.

Participants were queried again in the post-return interview about the professional relevance of their experience. Had the sojourn affected their *views* of broadcasting at home? Only three said that it had not. What kinds of views had been affected? Sixteen said that they now felt that the use of broadcasting media in educational pursuits should be extended. Seven said that they felt more confirmed in the advocacy of public, noncommercial control of the media. Four felt confirmed in their advocacy of an emphasis on radio. Four wanted to extend public service broadcasting. Three wished to emphasize the development of television.

Participants were asked whether their professional *activities* had been affected by the sojourn. Ten said that there had been a large-scale effect. Fifteen referred to a moderate effect. Three reported no effect. What were some of these effects? For five participants, it was a change in position or responsibility. For thirteen, it was that they could now contribute to the development of educational television. For sixteen, it was that their own professional skills had been enlarged. For eleven, it was that they could apply specific programs or methods modeled on American broadcasting.

Had they been able to apply specific ideas or procedures acquired in America to their present professional activities? Seven had not tried to. Eight had tried to and had been successful. Four had tried with mixed success; one, without success. Eight had tried and did not yet know how things would work out. The innovations with which they had concerned themselves had included: the extension of instructional or educational broadcasting; changes in program style (such as the style of news presentation); the introduction of new types of programs (such as audience participation, quizzes, interviews); changes of a technical nature; and the increased use of international exchange of personnel or programs. These and several other attempts at innovation are shown in detail in Table 4.

Table 4

ATTEMPTS TO APPLY AMERICAN IDEAS AND PROCEDURES IN
PARTICIPANTS' OWN BROADCASTING SYSTEMS

	Number of Participants Who Devised:		
Innovations	*Successful Efforts*	*Unsuccessful Efforts*	*Trial Efforts*
Extension of instructional or educational broadcasting	4	0	8
Changes in program style or content	3	2	1
Introduction of new types of programs	3	0	3
Changes of a technical nature	3	0	2
Increased use of international exchange of personnel or programs	2	0	1
Introduction of programs specifically modeled after American programs	0	1	1
Increased use of indigenous personnel or materials	0	0	2
Allocation of more time and channels for public service programs	1	0	2
Introduction of research into audience reactions	0	0	1

KNOWLEDGE ABOUT THE PROFESSION IN AMERICA

A number of people found the experience significant partly because of the opportunity to find out about the way their profession functioned in America. Several interview items were answered in this vein by

large numbers of participants. When asked about some of their most
meaningful and enjoyable experiences, seventeen participants cited the
travel period (which included visits to many professional facilities) ; eleven
specifically cited the observations of local broadcasting facilities that they
had been able to make. When asked about their important accomplishments,
eleven respondents included the acquisition of greater knowledge about
television in America. When asked to list initial goals that had been accomplished, thirteen mentioned that they had learned about the problems
that confronted their counterparts in America. Finally, when asked if they
had acquired all the knowledge about American broadcasting that they
had hoped to acquire, fifteen said "yes," and twelve said that they had
attained a reasonable degree of familiarity.

We can illustrate these sentiments by referring to the interview
with an Asian. He had been asked what experiences he would single out as
having been most meaningful to him. He cited the two-month trip, and was
asked what in particular was most meaningful about the trip. He replied:

> The tour to educational television stations and to audiovisual facil-
> ities and to universities. The excellent instructional material library
> in Los Angeles. Each station in the country has a unique character;
> this is very interesting to me. For instance, the educational television
> station in Seattle is attached to the university. It is trying to extend
> programs to rural populations. In Albuquerque, the station has the
> best programs for schools. In San Francisco and New Orleans, there
> are the best community stations.

This man took back to his home country a highly differentiated picture
of the many specific ways in which communications are being employed in
America. One may assume that this image will be one of his most concrete memories. Its anchorage in professional details with which he is
especially concerned distinguishes it from the images of America as a
nation.

KNOWLEDGE OF AMERICA

The evidence that participants attached importance to learning
about America is quite conclusive. Asked (in the fourth interview) to list
some of their most meaningful or enjoyable experiences, twenty-two participants spoke of the first-hand exposure to American life, and seventeen
made references to interpersonal experiences with Americans. The importance of learning about America probably lies behind the response of
six persons who referred to the academic seminars, and is also implicit
(along with the desire to learn about the profession in the U.S.) in the
responses of the seventeen who referred to the travel period in general.

Further along in the interview, twenty-one respondents reported that the new perspectives that they had gained included new insights about America, its institutions, and its people. Twenty-four respondents said that the acquisition of first-hand knowledge about America had been one of their original goals that had been accomplished. In the post-return interview, when asked how the trip exceeded expectations, seventeen referred to the opportunity to travel in America and twelve to the opportunity to meet people. Asked about the most satisfying aspects of the trip, seventeen referred to the travel period, and eight to the opportunity to travel and meet average Americans.

One set of data suggests that learning about America may have had a rather global meaning for some of the respondents and a more differentiated one for others. When they were asked to cite important accomplishments of the trip, twenty-two participants gave responses that we have coded as "gaining a greater understanding of the American way of life, of American values." Considerably smaller numbers of participants gave responses that were less diffuse and more concrete and analytic; for example, only eight respondents spoke of gaining greater knowledge about the institutional structure of America, and only six spoke of gaining greater knowledge about the American educational system. Thus, although learning about America was a highly significant aspect of the experience for almost every respondent, the content covered by that phrase may have varied greatly from one respondent to another.

Several quotations may help to illustrate this point. One respondent described his most meaningful experiences as follows:

> At first, the insight into American politics, that is, academic seminars at the university and travel around the country and making my own investigations. Second, specifically, the opportunity through the academic seminars to study the Negro problem, particularly in the South.

Next, a European answered the same question about meaningful experiences in these words:

> The American way of life. After a week of being here, I thought I understood many things about America. I had written some letters to directors of journals and magazines. The directors after receiving the letters answered that the letters could be published as short articles. But after four months in America, I am not sure that I understand America. The American society, the American way of life are the things of most importance that I have found. Therefore this question doesn't make any sense. I came here to learn about America and not about television. The most important thing was the whole experience. If you like, I can single out one or two to make

you happy, but I don't think it makes any sense. It is the whole four months that is meaningful.

Or, to cite another European:

I have not had the opportunity [previously] to get experience about American society by myself. Everything I knew was through literature, music, radio, articles in newspapers. [*This is before you came?*] Yes. Writers write books in their own way. American movie producers express American life in their own Hollywood way. Our journalists write mostly about economic and political questions. I have some image. But now that I spent four months here, I could see things with my own eyes. Now my image is clearer than before. Having the opportunity to be introduced to your country, I was able to see life more plastic than before—more sculptured. [*In greater detail?*] Yes. It's like putting two photos next to each other. You get a three-dimensional image. I tried to see America with American eyes. . . .

Finally, the African whom we previously quoted, who saw learning about television as his most important accomplishment, spoke of his most meaningful experiences in these terms:

My stay at Brandeis before the journey began and my going around the country. Two experiences stand out in my mind: my New Orleans stop and then Washington and Philadelphia too. The first place, New Orleans, this was the first time I came across Negroes. I stayed with a Negro family. I shared their life and studied their problems and thinking and so on. I talked with Urban League people. In Philadelphia, I was impressed by staying with a mixed group —white and black staying together, trying to understand each other. I stayed at Fellowship House there. It was like New Orleans showed me the problem and Philadelphia showed me one solution to the problem. I enjoyed Washington because of the places I visited and the people I met—the historical places and the government of the United States, the Senate. [*And what was most meaningful at Brandeis?*] The introduction to the whole life of America. This was a key experience. I felt as I went around that the stay at Brandeis had opened my eyes to what to see—the government, the racial problem, and so on. It was a very good introduction. Without it one would be in trouble. One wouldn't know what to expect. I think it was very good and well organized.

ENJOYMENT OF A FOREIGN SETTING

Travel is more than a chore and an education. A sojourn in a foreign country is an opportunity to move among new people and to enjoy the savor of new sights. These pleasures are not always available, of course. It may happen that one's private agenda during a sojourn leaves no time for any but highly specific professional contacts; that one's biases regarding a nation prevent any but formal contacts; that one's personal defensiveness prevents any but uneasy contacts; or that one's lack of familiarity with the language or the culture prevents any but superficial contacts. Fortunately, these problems seem not to have existed for most of our participants. Seventeen said that their most meaningful times included interpersonal experiences with Americans, and eleven cited, in this context, their observations of the physical environment.

The following quotation presents a European's discussion of his most enjoyable experiences:

> The human contacts, I would say. Talking with people. These have ranged from a Negro waiter in a New Orleans restaurant to a producer at a party in Chicago. Then the sheer physical experience of being in certain parts of the U.S. has been enjoyable. Arizona, San Francisco, and Charleston particularly stand out in my mind. Then the exploratory aspects of travel—finding off-beat places that Americans don't even know about. For example, in Georgetown, Colorado, there is a silver mining town where I went because I had been referred to the local editor of the paper there. . . .

Another European described his most enjoyable experiences as follows:

> Since I am fresh from the trip today, the most enjoyable was the trip, and during the trip there were so many things that were enjoyable. [*Can you mention a couple?*] Some places in some states were very enjoyable because they were very beautiful. They were tourist attractions to look at beautiful things. I especially remember the trip between San Francisco and San Luis Obispo. We followed the coastline. . . . Then we enjoyed an unexpected meeting with cowboys in Colorado. We talked about Western romance and what is wrong with Westerns today. We stayed with them in their poor house. We met them in a bar in a hotel. They said, "Come up and see what we are doing. We work sixteen hours a day—it is not so romantic." We went out and rode horses. . . .

ORIENTATION TO INTERNATIONAL EXCHANGE

Participation in this instance of international exchange expectably affected attitudes toward exchange programs. The impact appeared greater to the participants after they had been home for a year, as shown in Table 5. The difference in pattern of response between the fourth interview and the post-return interview may simply reflect a difference in the context in which the respective questions were asked within each of the interviews; but there is a more interesting alternative possibility. Most participants may have had positive feelings at both points of time. In the fourth interview, however, they were still in America and still within the context of an exchange experience. Being favorably disposed to such experiences may then have seemed a very natural attitude and one that they

Table 5

CHANGES IN THE EVALUATION OF INTERNATIONAL EXCHANGE

Number Who Say That Their Feelings:

Questions	Have Not Changed	Have Become More Negative	Have Become More Positive
Fourth interview: Have your views about the value of international exchange changed . . . since you have been here?	18	1	6
Post-return interview: Were your views on the value of international exchanges affected in any way by your experiences in America?	7	2	18

had always held. In the post-return interview, on the other hand, the question was answered after the respondent had been back home for some months, during which he might have become aware that—at least in a small sense—he had become different as a result of his experience. Participation in this exchange experience had become an important part of his personal and professional identity, as he moved among those who had not had the experience. This may have made the value of exchange programs more salient than it was when he moved among those who shared this claim to distinction, and may have made him more aware that he had indeed become more positive in his view.

Participants were asked in the fourth interview to list some of the possible benefits of international exchange. Eight pointed out that it could promote international understanding; seven, that it led to mutually beneficial exchange of professional information; and one, that it led to the formation of personal friendships.

They were then asked what their own potential contributions to exchange might be. Thirteen said that it would lie in professional areas; eight, in nonprofessional areas. More specifically, eight said that they could communicate their own professional knowledge; three said that they could use their positions to promote exchange; three, that they could take a personal interest in foreign visitors; four, that they could present documentaries about their own countries.

Participants were also asked, more generally, about the effect of their experience on the professional and personal contacts that they had made. On the professional side, twenty-two participants reported in the post-return interview that they had established contacts with American individuals or organizations while in America; of these, seven reported establishing many such contacts. The greatest number of these contacts were with American networks; others were with foundations, universities, and seminar personnel. They were also asked whether they had been able to make professional contacts with persons from countries other than America. Three had made many such contacts, and ten had made some. Most of these contacts were with other seminar participants.

How important were the professional and personal contacts to the participants? Twelve of them listed, among their important accomplishments, the establishment of relations with fellow professionals; six listed the opening of relations with people outside their profession. Seven listed as one of their most meaningful and enjoyable experiences the establishment of contact with fellow participants in the seminar. Five mentioned at another point, as already noted, that they had come to realize more fully their communality with people from other countries and to experience greater ease in interacting with them.

Before departure, most participants said that they were going to try to keep up their contacts with the Americans whom they had met and with the other seminar participants. Their success in this endeavor was checked in the post-return interview. They seemed to have done surprisingly well at keeping in touch with the Americans, if not with their fellow-participants. Ten had kept up relatively intense relations with Americans—for example, by exchanging long letters. All but one of the others had at least exchanged Christmas cards. Contact with other participants had been less sustained. Three had kept up some sort of meaningful relation; thirteen had maintained perfunctory communications; and ten, none at all.

PERSPECTIVE ON HOME COUNTRY

Our respondents, in their retrospective reactions, confirmed the traditional wisdom that one never appreciates home until he leaves it and that foreign travel is the best way to gain an understanding of one's own country. All but four participants acknowledged in the fourth interview that they had gained a new perspective on the home country; all but two made this acknowledgment in the post-return interview.

Participants from the more Western nations tended to deplore conservatism, bureaucracy, and lack of adventurousness; those from less-developed countries deplored ignorance, the slow pace of educational expansion, and the inadequate enthusiasm for work. As aspects that they had learned to appreciate more, both groups tended to select the commonly accepted distinctive good features of their own national cultures. Thus, there were references to the fine social welfare systems of some of the more advanced states; to patterns of interpersonal relations that are closer than in America and that assume that "a man is not lost in society, [and] people will listen to him"; to the more easygoing way of life of the traditional cultures; to the greater capacity of a people to laugh at themselves; and to the potential of some states for future development.

When asked whether he had gained a new perspective on his own country, one European participant, for example, replied:

> Oh yes. That most markedly. . . . It has made me realize what is good in my country—socialized medicine, government intervention, the traditions of my country. These are on the *positive* side. The architecture, the historical events, also as a nation—its strength in all that—how mature it is in a slightly old-fashioned way. Old in relation to America. The defects are that they are very slow in accepting new ideas, new thoughts; they do not jump into things. It's tempered by caution. By sitting on a fence. It is not too bad. It needs to be more adventurous. . . . This is the first time I have been such a long time away from it. It is very important. It has given me a broader perspective. It has broadened me, too.

And an African said, in response to the same question:

> I wish that we had more facilities. It has only shown me how much is to be done in my country, not only in communications but in many fields, and what a short time there is to do it in. . . . I think I like our way of life better. Life in America is dull and people try artificially to make it exciting. [*Is there anything about your country that you now appreciate less than you used to?*] Ignorance . . . ignorance is all around. I think it is more magnified now because I am so determined to play a bigger part in it by trying to do something about it. I feel it more now than before.

9

America and American
Broadcasting

We now turn to the participants' views of America and American broadcasting, as these were revealed in the various interviews.[1] We shall draw especially on their responses to the third interview, which was carried out during the travel period and which probed into this area in some detail; and also on their responses to the post-return interview, which gives us some indication of participants' attitudes at a point at which they had already gained some distance from their experience in the United States.

We must keep in mind that the participants were hardly uninformed about America at the time of their arrival. Nine had visited the United States on a previous occasion. Seventeen told us, in the first inter-

[1] The reader is reminded that the Seminar took place in 1962, and the interviews were conducted in 1962 and 1963. The participants' views about American broadcasting and particularly about American society were obviously influenced by events of those years. We certainly cannot assume that participants in a comparable seminar today would end up with images similar *in their specific content* to those described here. The present data can, however, tell us something about the *nature and structure* of the images that this kind of exchange experience can effect.

view, that they had close American friends. All but six of the participants had had occasion to inform themselves—for professional or other reasons —about America before this visit; of these, fourteen felt that they were quite well-informed. Only four participants reported little previous contact with Americans. Thus, the participants' experiences on this visit were by no means their first encounter with America, and one can certainly not assume that the views they expressed were entirely a product of these experiences. This trip did, however, represent their longest and fullest exposure to America and its mass media, and it is interesting to see what attitudes they expressed while they were in the midst of this intensive contact and after they had gone through it. We shall see in the next three chapters that this exposure did, in fact, produce changes in their attitudes. For the moment we shall examine only what these attitudes were.

AMERICAN BROADCASTERS

We shall start our review with the participants' views of American broadcasters. They met quite a few broadcasters during the first phase of their sojourn, including those who came to the university to give lectures and demonstrations, and those who staffed the various broadcasting facilities they visited. The number and range of broadcasters whom they met, however, was greatly extended during the travel period. In particular, they had the opportunity to meet men in small local stations, both commercial and educational—a type of broadcaster with whom they had had relatively little contact at the university.

The participants reported in the third interview that they had been able to establish close contacts with American broadcasters. Thus, sixteen indicated that they had a relatively close social relationship with at least some of their professional counterparts; for example, they had been guests at their houses. The professional relationship had been sufficiently deep to allow most participants to acquire a good deal of understanding about the problems, activities, and interests of American broadcasters. Most of them indicated that they now felt closer to their American counterparts than they had before.

Their general feeling was that American broadcasters were similar to the ones in their own countries. Many participants echoed the words of this respondent:

> I think people who work in broadcasting are the same the whole world over. I found this to be the case. American ones aren't very different. There is a great sort of masonry among broadcasters. They talk the same language, they have the same interests.

Or, to quote another respondent, from an African country:

> Well, we are friendly to each other. Broadcasting is a sort of frater-
> nity. We call each other by our first names. . . . The differences
> . . . are not very much.

Nevertheless, some participants did point to differences, often in the facilities and financial means available to the two groups, and sometimes in
their relative competence. Thus, according to one respondent, American
broadcasters

> . . . are very professional, with lots of experience, very skillful and
> capable. This is more so than in my country. Even the technical
> people are very intelligent. One can rely on them to handle every-
> thing, including the cutting, the lights, and so on. This takes much
> time and experience. . . . You have more means, more facilities
> and money. We must keep many people because of the union and
> complicated problems. An American broadcaster thinks he can be
> fired tomorrow if he's not good. Ours is very different.

The participants' evaluation of American broadcasters was largely
favorable, though not outstandingly so. Our coders inferred, from the
respondents' remarks, that nineteen out of the twenty-eight participants
judged American broadcasters to be "fairly good," that six felt they "compared favorably with the best broadcasters in the world," and that three
regarded them as "rather mediocre." A major source of criticism of American broadcasters was the feeling that they did not meet their responsibilities to their audiences adequately, usually because of commercial considerations and pressures from sponsors. Twenty respondents brought up
some criticism in this area, even though most of them felt (in response to
a direct question) that, in general, American broadcasters were meeting
their responsibilities fairly well. Two examples will suffice:

> To the extent that they put out some first-class news programs and
> documentaries and other types of public affairs programs, they are
> meeting *part* of their responsibilities, but the proportion of these
> programs is not very high to give broadcasting any cause for satis-
> faction. There is too much emphasis on programs to find a ready
> sponsor.

> I think that in the matter of technique their sense of responsibility
> to their work assignment is very good. They are all quite responsible
> to their employers. But their sense of responsibility to the audience
> is another question. They say that they don't like the way American
> television is being run. All of them condemn it—yet they go on doing
> it. I say, why not change it? When you press that point they come at
> you with the most disarming, discouraging, exasperating statements.
> They say, of course, the shareholders must have their dividend.

Some respondents pointed out that, given the pressures under
which they worked, American broadcasters were meeting their responsi-

bilities fairly well. Many made distinctions between different groups of broadcasters, pointing out that there was less commercial influence among broadcasters in the large networks as compared to those in local stations, among news broadcasters as compared to the "producers who are closer to sponsors," among the men in production as compared to those in management, among the staff of educational stations as compared to those in commercial stations. One participant responded quite sharply to the question about responsibilities cited above:

> What responsibilities? They don't think they have any. Their responsibility is to their sponsors and to the people who pay them. It is only in educational TV that you find people with a sense of responsibility to their audiences.

Another participant stressed a different distinction:

> On the whole I would say that American broadcasters are a nice breed of people. They are intelligent and they feel their responsibilities. The broadcasters are fine. But when it comes to management you don't feel that you are speaking the same language. The producers and program managers—we speak the same language. But the station managers might well be managers of banks. They might well be managers of any commercial enterprise. The professionals are different. You could switch places with them.

Twenty participants felt that the conditions under which American broadcasters worked, although sometimes very good, were sometimes also poor. The reasons most frequently cited for poor conditions were excessive constraints by the pressure of advertisers (thirteen cases) and the insufficiency of government control in the interest of public welfare (eight cases). Thus, again, criticisms focused on the commercial control of broadcasting and the feeling that it led, on the one hand, to insufficient freedom to produce controversial and high-quality programs, and on the other hand, to too much freedom to ignore the public interest.

Further information about participants' views of American broadcasters was obtained in the post-return interview. Evaluations of American broadcasters were still high, perhaps higher than in the earlier interview. In eighteen cases, they impressed the coders as being more favorable than unfavorable, in seven about equally favorable and unfavorable, and in only one more unfavorable than favorable. Favorable points cited most frequently included the high degree of technical skill and competence of American broadcasters (nineteen cases) and their enthusiasm, interest, and industriousness (thirteen cases). On the negative side, the limited effectiveness of educational broadcasters, because of their poorer conditions, was often cited. Thus, one participant replied to a question about the professional competence of broadcasters in the following words:

Their competence is enormously high everywhere. The technical people are absolutely out of this world—unbelievable, first-rate. The program people and production staff too: the competence is enormously high. They are really good at their jobs. Competition is high and the best person gets the job. Another thing that was very nice is that all the ones I met—both in educational and in commercial broadcasting—seemed to love their jobs; they liked what they were doing. [*What about their working conditions?*] Most of them work hard. Aside from that, the working conditions are very good in commercial stations, but bad in educational stations. They have to improvise a lot. It's encouraging that they get things done under these conditions, but the things they do are not always good. [*What about their opportunities for rewards and advancement?*] Again, they are completely different in the commercial and educational fields. In the commercial field it *can* be enormous. In the educational field, most of the people are idealists. They are not starving, but you can't compare it to the bigger commercial outfits.

The distinction between commercial and educational stations is obviously a frequent feature in the responses we obtained.

Many respondents, as in the third interview, described the conditions under which American broadcasters worked in mixed terms. On the one hand, they indicated that American broadcasters had good opportunities for rewards and advancement and were able to work under favorable financial and technical conditions. On the other hand, they felt that the competitiveness and fast pace of work in American TV and the commercial element created excessive pressures for the broadcaster. As a result, despite his very high level of competence, the quality of his work sometimes suffered.

The following two quotations illustrate participants' views about the pressures stemming from the competitive atmosphere in American TV. Their similarity is particularly striking since the two respondents came from extremely different parts of the world:

I was very impressed with [American broadcasters] as professional workers: they are very clever professionally. And they work very hard—harder than in our country. It is of course a hard competition in the U.S., and they have had TV for many years. The people working in it are the best ones in the world. On the other hand, they are not always working with the best materials. If they had better scripts, the results would be even better. But as professional producers, directors, photographers—they are excellent. And they work so hard—we were surprised. They are higher paid than we are in our country. On the average they work harder than we do—more hours. I am speaking of the program people, not the technical people. I don't know about them, but they have unions with strict rules. The program people work on a hard tempo. They don't have good time to make their programs—to prepare them, rehearse them. . . .

It must be difficult to reach the top. You have to be very clever. There is a hard competition and only people with nerves succeed.

What I saw of American broadcasters—my impression was that they were very hard-working people. So much was expected of them that I wondered whether they had time to polish their work well before it was broadcast. For example, at one station, one man was doing two programs each day, seven days a week. I can't understand how anyone can be creative with such a schedule. As a result, I was not impressed with some of his productions and I didn't blame him for it. In cases where people have the time to devote to their work, they produce marvelous programs. [*What about their professional competence?*] They are very good. I was highly impressed. [*What about their opportunities for rewards and advancement?*] Very good too.

The following two quotations illustrate participants' views about the pressures stemming from the commerical element in American broadcasting:

At the program level, I found [American broadcasters] efficient and enthusiastic—which is all you would ask. At the executive level I must compare them unfavorably with our broadcasting executives— not because they wouldn't like to indulge their sense of dedication, but because they can't, due to the profit motive which rules the industry. I found a lot of people who were disgusted with it. The program people have a real sense of dedication which is in sharp contrast with the profit-oriented society in which they must operate.

Americans in general, right from the start of my experience in the States, impressed me with their efficiency and well-organized ways of working. The same is true of broadcasters. They work hard and efficiently. . . . They are very competent. It is a pity that the conditions under which they work—working merely for selling products —don't give them much chance for really creative work, in a permanent sense—creating things that will have some permanent artistic value. [*What about their opportunities for rewards and advancement?*] I would say they are very good for the good broadcasters.

In sum, it appears that most participants had a sense of colleagueship and of identity in interests and values vis-à-vis their American counterparts. They had generally high regard for them, and certainly evaluated them more favorably than unfavorably. They did have criticisms, particularly about the way in which American broadcasters met their responsibilities toward their audiences. They tended to ascribe the shortcomings of their American colleagues in this area to the conditions under which they worked, which in turn were related to the structure of American broadcasting. Let us turn, therefore, to the participants' views of American broadcasting itself.

AMERICAN BROADCASTING

On the basis of participants' responses to a number of questions in the third interview, our coders concluded that the vast majority (twenty-five out of the twenty-eight) had a mixed opinion of American TV—that they were favorably impressed by some aspects of it, and unfavorably by others. Among the features that impressed many respondents favorably was the quality of some of the educational television programs, of the documentaries and experimental programs produced by the major networks, and of the technical equipment used. Features that they found particularly problematic or disappointing were the lack of balance in programming (for example, the limited commitment to educational programs relative to commercial ones); the inadequacy of funds available for educational television; the surprisingly poor technical facilities with which some stations (the small local stations, especially in the educational field) had to work; and the unexpectedly low quality of some news programs and the tendency to interrupt these by editorializing and commercials. It seems that the participants perceived the major successes of American TV to be in the high quality of some of its outstanding products, and its major problems in the tendency to invest only a small proportion of its resources in these high-quality products. Thus, American TV has proven its potential for quality programming, but is not set up so as to maximize this potential.

Almost all participants felt that most American broadcasters were aware of the major problems of American television, but were not doing much to solve them. Eleven of the respondents indicated that the situation called for a greater degree of government regulation of broadcasting in the public interest. A number of others pointed to the need for creating higher standards of program quality, but only a few mentioned mechanisms for achieving this end, such as pressure by local publics or by broadcasters, self-policing by networks, or increased selectivity of financial support by foundations or government.

Clearly, many participants felt that private ownership was an important source of the major problems experienced by American television. Thus, twenty-four of the twenty-eight respondents indicated that commercial considerations interfered with the development of high-quality programming. They do so, in the eyes of the respondents, both by frustrating efforts to improve the general level of public taste, and by leading to a neglect of specialized audiences interested in high-quality programs. Again, twenty-four respondents perceived a basic conflict between the requirement of making a profit and the provision of public service.

The participants were by no means entirely negative in their evaluation of private ownership of broadcasting facilities, although some did express themselves quite negatively, as in the following remark:

> I think that broadcasting power and influence are too profound to be in the hands of private business. The development of Telstar reinforces my view that this is not good.

Only ten participants, however, saw no advantage at all in private ownership; six felt that it had some advantage for America though not for their own countries; and another ten saw some advantages in private ownership in general. The advantages mentioned most often were that private ownership makes for competition between stations, and that it provides greater freedom in choosing and organizing programs. The following three quotations can serve as examples:

> One basic advantage of private ownership is this: a higher degree of freedom in organizing the programs. Another advantage is supplied by the competition existing between the various networks.

> When they are privately owned they have competition among the networks. I think that that is good. . . . I think that privately owned [broadcasting] makes for more freedom than the public organization. They can have a variety of opinions. . . . In our country, we always have to be very careful to be in the middle, so that we have criticisms from both the right and left wing. Here you can express the greatest variety of opinion. But we need not worry about private finances. Here you are always worried. We collect money each month from our audiences.

> Viewers have the opportunity to choose and I think that is very good. In my country we have only one company. . . . I think it is a good idea to have competition, but the basic problem remains—how to have good quality.

Private ownership does not imply complete absence of controls. Some respondents pointed to the existence of the FCC and indicated that it should be given more power or encouraged to use more effectively the power it already has. One respondent, who saw some advantages in private ownership of the media, added:

> Even though they are privately owned, there should be some controls. Not necessarily government controls. The problem of giving people what they want to see should be changed to giving people what they should see, not what they want to see.

Another source of data on the participants' views of American broadcasting is their answers to a question about the applicability of the approaches of American broadcasting to the situations in their own countries. The majority felt that American approaches had some, but only some, applicability to their own situations. In particular, they felt that the manner of handling public affairs programs and some of the features of educational television could be profitably adopted. Here are several answers to the question about the extent to which American approaches are applicable:

> Very little extent as far as commercial broadcasting is concerned. . . . We can learn a lot from your educational broadcasting. . . . Certain of the program ideas I have picked up. In the field of language teaching I have learned quite a bit.

> In vast areas of broadcasting, [they are] not applicable at all. . . . The main areas of overlap with our system are the cultural affairs and educational broadcasting. . . . The use of TV for direct instruction . . . we will have something to learn from the U.S. in this field.

> In general, I don't think so very much. . . . There are some . . . how they do news and documentaries.

Reasons given for lack of applicability, or limited applicability, were the differences in structure and financing of broadcasting in the two countries; the low quality of American programs; and the lack of requisite experience or facilities for using certain American approaches in the home country.

Participants were also asked about features of American broadcasting that they felt should be avoided in their own countries. About half of them mentioned commercials in general and the interruption of news programs by commercials in particular. In answer to a related question, more than half of the participants thought that America could profitably adopt some of the features of broadcasting as practiced in their own countries. Most frequently mentioned were the limited role of advertising, and the use of radio for high-level public service and educational programs.

With regard to radio, almost all participants felt that it functioned differently in their own countries than it did in America. Seventeen noted that in America radio played a rather insignificant role. For example:

> People seem to listen to it only in cars. They listen only to pop records and news. That is the cheapest way to use radio.

> You have only music and advertisements and a bit of news and baseball. Radio can do so much more than that. . . . You should have more talks on radio about other people.

> It is a pity that radio is dead here. There are certain things it could

do but doesn't. . . . They should bring more real programs, talks, discussion, etc. One could get tired of watching TV. Discussions on radio could be as interesting as television.

I think it is not considered to be as up-to-date as TV is. Everybody goes out for TV. If you have extra money, you can buy a radio and put it in the kitchen. I noticed that radio plays a big part in cars where TV couldn't be.

In their own countries, most participants felt that radio would and should remain an important force in its own right. They mentioned, among the many advantages of radio, that it is more economical to produce, transmit, and receive radio programs; and that the equipment, staffing, production, and programming required by radio are simpler and more flexible. In many countries, radio will be needed for some time to reach large segments of the nation; in others, certain cultural and informational programs can be produced more cheaply and at least as effectively on radio as on television.

AMERICA AND AMERICANS

Interviews held during the travel period revealed that most participants had developed favorable, if complex, evaluations of America and Americans. Thus, for example, on the basis of a number of questions, our coders judged the opinions of Americans held by the participants to be generally favorable in twenty-three out of the twenty-eight cases. For fifteen of the twenty-three, however, they noted that opinions—although generally favorable—were critical in some specific respects. The major disappointment about America mentioned most frequently was America's handling of the Negro problem. Features of America that were most often mentioned in answer to the question, "What has pleased you most?" were the democratic atmosphere of America (for example, the general openness and tolerance for differences of opinion), the sociability of Americans (such as their informality and ease of making friends), and the beauty of the country.

Most of the new insights that participants had gained during the travel period tended to concern either qualities of the American people or the institutional structure of America (that it, its political and economic system). A number of participants reported that they had gained a better understanding of the underlying character and philosophy of America as a country. Others spoke of their increased understanding of the importance of diversity and variety in America—of the role, for example, that regional differences played.

Several questions specifically addressed themselves to various differences within American society, since we were interested in finding out to what extent participants had become aware and knowledgeable about such differences. In reply to some of these questions, twenty of the twenty-eight respondents mentioned some regional differences that had struck them during their travels; of these, fifteen reported that these differences represented new discoveries for them, rather than mere confirmations of things they had already known. Among the differences most frequently mentioned were differences in social customs (for example, in the role of tradition in Boston as compared to Chicago); in the tempo of life (for example, the less hurried and businesslike approach to life on the West Coast as compared to the East Coast); in the ease of making acquaintances; and in the climate. Fifteen respondents felt that such regional differences played an important role in American society, having an impact primarily on domestic policy.

Other differences within the American population that some participants spontaneously cited as being important to an understanding of American society included racial and ethnic differences (mentioned by nine respondents), socioeconomic differences (five), and religious differences (three). In response to direct questions, fourteen respondents felt that religious differences played an important role in American society, twenty-three felt that racial and ethnic differences played an important role, and fourteen that socioeconomic differences played such a role. Eighteen respondents indicated that these various differences—especially on the racial-ethnic and socioeconomic dimensions—were related to the way in which broadcasting has developed in America.

In sum, the field interview revealed a favorable, though not wholly uncritical, attitude toward America and Americans, and an increased awareness and understanding of the complexity and diversity of American society. Further data were obtained from the post-return interview, which explored participants' views of America after they had been back home for some months. One source of information about participants' views of America was a pair of questions in which they were asked to think back to their visit and describe those expectations about America and Americans that had been strongly confirmed by their own experiences, and those that had been disconfirmed. Sixteen of the respondents mentioned more confirmations than disconfirmations; eight mentioned about an equal number of each. It is interesting to read some examples of expectations that had been confirmed, since they reveal some of the salient impressions of America and Americans that these visitors carried away with them. The following three quotations are taken from interviews with European participants:

> I expected to come to a country in which it was very easy to live and easy to be together with people and talk to people—an unconventional country. And that was true. It was very easy to talk to

people. They were very frank. You could criticize America as much as you wanted and they didn't kill you. It was easy to reach people, to talk to them. It was a kind of informality that became formal. . . .

First, that America is not a country but a continent. I expected it, but it was really emphasized. Secondly, the warmth of Americans. That didn't vary anywhere—here one can really talk about them as a nation. The tempo of life—certainly in the cities—was as hectic as I expected it to be.

Their go-getting nature and their capacity for quick action to meet a situation was confirmed. Their variety was certainly confirmed. . . . Their tremendous openness and affability—that was certainly confirmed. What impressions I formed of American political life were confirmed. . . . There is greater concern and involvement than one finds here [in his home country], coupled also with greater cynicism. . . . The capacity for ruthlessness in the course of innovation, of "progress," strikes one more forcefully when one is there. . . .

The next two quotations come from interviews with Africans:

The general friendliness of the people. The high level of development of the economy and public services. A much more efficient organization of activity. These are all things that one associated with an industrial society.

That Americans generally have much more than we have in this country, and perhaps in many other countries. They have the basic necessities which many people in this country lack. That America is a highly developed country, a technical civilization. That Americans were friendly, and much more informal in their intercourse with other people, with strangers.

Of even greater interest than the confirmations are the disconfirmations, for they point to what we can presume to be new discoveries and new learnings that were derived from the visitors' first-hand exposure to American life. First, let us look at two responses by African participants when asked about expectations that had been disconfirmed:

The general belief that every American is a millionaire. Because people here have contacts with rich businessmen, officials, and politicians.

The Hollywood glamorous type of life. Especially when I went to L.A. and found that it was just like any other big city. . . . I was expecting big mansions, but they had just ordinary dwellings.

Next are some quotations by participants of European origin (though some of them resided outside of Europe):

The country was more beautiful than I had expected. On balance, I did not find that the much-flaunted American efficiency was quite as efficient as I had expected it to be. . . . Despite the tempo, the end result was not as efficient as people overseas would picture it. I suspect that in part this comes from the social pattern in America where people are reticent to stand forth as leaders. In many instances, there were people who I think would have taken over, but they didn't step forward because it countervenes the social norms. People were reluctant to take leadership. The herd instinct was much stronger than I expected. I was extremely surprised that privacy was not respected anywhere in the United States. The attempt to destroy privacy rather than encourage it—for example, hedges between houses in the suburbs are cut down rather than allowed to grow. I felt anyone who let it grow would be regarded as an outcast. I did not anticipate finding this at all. I was shocked more than anything by the American undertaking business. I heard about it but never thought it was operated on this scale. It struck me that here in particular was the herd instinct. People wouldn't stand up against this pattern even though they don't like it. It indicates a sort of subservience to customs which I hadn't expected to find—a lack of independence of thought. I found that very surprising.

I had expected the American way of life to be quite uniform. What was disconfirmed is that there isn't just one American way of life. The variety is so great. You can find your own group. You can find a framework in which you don't have to conform. There is conformism of course, living like the Joneses—but it's not half as bad as I had expected it to be. . . .

The notion that they are always in a rush, tearing from A to B, was not confirmed. . . . Their capacity for self-criticism was to some extent rather unexpected—criticisms of their own institutions, way of life, and so on. . . . The physical beauty of the country, the landscape was much greater than I had been led to expect. I was surprised by some of the implications of the cult of youth. . . . The notion that Americans were always efficient received a crude shock —including, I must say, at the seminar. One other thing I wasn't quite prepared for is the amount of wastefulness in America. . . .

Some observations clearly came up repeatedly, but there were also some interesting differences in the impressions of different respondents. Thus, one of the three participants cited above was surprised by the high degree of conformity in America, the other by the fact that conformism was not as extreme as expected. Both, of course, may be right, since their initial expectations may have differed and since one was focusing on a general pattern and the other on possible deviations from such a pattern. One man's disconfirmation may also be another man's confirmation, as can be seen in the differing assessments of the pace and tempo of American life.

Another pair of questions on the post-return interview provided further information about the participants' views, as well as information about their evaluations, of America and Americans: "What has disappointed you most about America and Americans?" and "What has pleased you most about America and Americans?" The participants' generally favorable evaluation is evidenced by our coders' judgment that twenty-five out of the twenty-eight respondents had found more things about America and its people to be pleasing than to be disappointing. The remaining three mentioned pleasing and disappointing features in about equal proportion.

The most frequently mentioned features of America and Americans that impressed participants favorably included the high living standard and technological advances of America; the generosity and hospitality of Americans; and the friendliness and informality of Americans. A smaller number of respondents mentioned the ability of Americans to voice opposition and to criticize themselves and their institutions; and the physical beauty of the country. Several more idiosyncratic responses are of special interest. One African participant said:

> What has impressed me was the fact that throughout the country people regretted, resented, and even actively fought against [segregation] . . .

Two participants commented as follows:

> The most exhilarating thing [about Americans] is their tremendous optimism. The easiest way to think of this is to ask what one tended to think of one's self in America. I often thought of myself as a real cynic, which I was in America. At times, of course, this optimism is slightly irritating. One feels its foundation is unjustified.

> I was pleased by the vastness, the wide openness, the variations both in climate and scenery and in people. The incredible efficiency in communication, for example, the airlines—efficiency coupled with the simplicity with which they are run. Enormous technical efficiency. The vitality of the entertainment world—absolutely unique in the world. These things delighted me. . . .

One respondent, after mentioning some positive features of America and Americans, added the following remark:

> In the 1960's, for a person who is fairly progressive to become convinced that America is really a nice country and the people are nice is something very important. It makes a big difference. You have something to lean upon. It is terribly important for you to be able to like America, to feel that it is a country in which you can believe. There is not this feeling of hopelessness.

The most frequently mentioned disappointment in America concerned the extent and severity of the racial problem. Thus, the African quoted above, who was impressed with the struggle against segregation in America, also stated that what disappointed him most was "the fact that these racial troubles exist." Another African criticized Americans for

> . . . their failure to extend health service to those of its citizens who are not wealthy or self-sufficient. Their failure to achieve a solution to their racial problems.

A smaller number expressed disappointment in the inefficiency and poor organization that they had encountered; and in the emphasis on material values. With respect to the last point, one respondent expressed his

> . . . disappointment in the American record in the field of art in general—art, in any serious form. . . . Then, my overall impression of America—I feel something does not satisfy me, but I haven't been able to put it into words. There is something lacking—a sort of basic human essential or element that has been lost, maybe because of automation, the mechanized way of life, maybe living away from nature. Nature has its way of taking its revenge, redressing what it loses. There is a dry pragmatism that you meet with all the time. . . .

The majority of participants had presented one or more programs about America after their return. Their orientation seemed to be one of broadening their listeners' perspective about America, rather than attempting to support either a negative or a positive view of America. The kinds of information that they had presented—or were planning or expecting to present in future programs—dealt with the country (its size, variety, and landscape); with places and personalities of special (historical or touristic) interest; with the racial situation; with social and economic institutions; and with the lives of average Americans. The major themes of the presentations they had given or were planning to give were the diversity and heterogeneity of America; the complexity of America and its problems (for example, in race relations or politics); the inaccuracy of popular images of America and Americans (as conveyed, for example, by Hollywood movies); the progress and advances in improving race relations; and the generosity, hospitality, and industriousness of Americans. Some of these themes emerge clearly from the following sample responses:

> The kind of information I would present is, first of all, the vastness of the place. The hardworking nature of the people. . . . The American achievements in the field of science, technology, education, and industry. That is something which is worthy of emulation. Another aspect of American life which I would stress is the great

effort being made by all Americans to weld together into a people of different nations and races. I think there is an opportunity there for a unique achievement for the American people, and I would stress it. . . . Another thing: the human side. . . . The American people by and large are good-natured, kind-hearted people—and they enjoy a good laugh, like the African people, which is different from the British, who are a bit phlegmatic.

America is a new society, taken from a lot of nations. . . . First, I stressed that I can't give the whole image about the country and the people. . . . It is very difficult to tell that America is this kind of country or that kind of country. . . . People say that all Americans are capitalists and so on. But if you look at people you see that they are different—not all are the same. Many want peace. . . . I tried to stress that people at the other end of the earth are just like people here. They are hard-working. Some are rich, some poor; there is some unemployment, but they have insurance, help of the government. I tried to say it is a big country, with many problems. . . .

I would stress the importance that is given to the role of education in the U.S. The diversity of forms of education. The easy availability. In particular, I would dwell on life on the campus—I would stress this very alive give-and-take that goes on among students. It seemed to me that there was a real search—a search for knowledge. As for the racial issue, I would try to present the problem in its right context—the historical development of the problem, how it came about; what the problem is right now; why there are so many vested interests against desegregation; the clash between the state and federal authority; the difficulty the President is facing in trying to make a decision, which is mainly political. I would say that in the moral sphere most people are desegregationists. . . .

It is impossible to generalize about American life, how very varied it is. . . . When you leave New York and Boston you really feel that you are in America. That's where the differences really start. . . . One of the things that make America so attractive, that give flavor to it, is that it is still a country of immigrants. . . .

A point that comes up repeatedly in these remarks is that America is diverse, heterogeneous, and complex. It was stressed again when participants were asked whether or not "one can speak of an American attitude or point of view." Only three respondents were willing to speak, without qualification, of a general American point of view; eleven felt that there was a general point of view, but that one had to keep in mind America's complexity and diversity; and twelve felt that the complexity and diversity of America were so great that one could not possibly speak of a single point of view. Some of the negative answers to the question about an American point of view took these forms:

No, there is no firm American attitude. On the Eastern seaboard, there is a sense of enthusiasm, a liberal outlook which is in sharp contrast with the reactionary attitude in the South. I found that the isolationism talked of in the Midwest does exist. As to the West Coast—anti-intellectualism would be wrong—there seems to be, though, a relatively careless attitude toward politics. In short, there is *no* American attitude.

I am convinced you can't. There is the official attitude from Washington, shared perhaps by a million Americans. And then the average American. And the attitudes are very different indeed. I don't think one can speak of *an* American attitude. It varies with the part of the country one comes from, the intellectual level, the amount of travel. I came back convinced with what I already believed: that one cannot speak of America as a country. It's a continent. . . .

You can speak of an "official" American attitude . . . but you cannot talk of an American viewpoint as you travel across the States. There are at least three or four dozen different viewpoints. While there is an official view, the majority of Americans are not necessarily in possession of it.

In answer to this question and subsequent ones, many participants distinguished subgroups within the American population—groups differing in level of education, ethnic background, socioeconomic status, political preference, and regional origin—who diverged in their basic points of view.

Many participants, although stressing the complexity and diversity of America, were willing to mention attitudes that at least came close to constituting a general American point of view. Most frequently mentioned were the belief in freedom and democratic values, and the preoccupation with communism. These points are contained, in some form, in each of the following quotations:

One is repeatedly brought up against . . . the American conception of freedom. . . . It seems sometimes naive and overoptimistic in its assessment of the virtues of humankind: that laissez-faire attitudes will bring the best to the top. Every weakness, of course, has its counterpart in strength. You have these extraordinary contradictions. There is this strong feeling on the one hand that no one can knock you around, tell you how to conduct your affairs. On the other hand, you have this strong streak of conformism—which is anti-individualistic and results in . . . strains. . . . I think this rather naive conception of freedom is also the thing which leads to an oversimplified classification of political attitudes into black and white—an oversimplified attitude to the problem of living with the Russians, and so on. Then, the conception of progress, I think, is a bit distorted in America. There is a willingness to innovate, which is marvelous. But it is often allied with insufficient thought about the validity of the innovation. Again, there is this magnificent belief that anything is possible. Problems are regarded as challenges to action. And, although no doubt there are subtleties of social stratification, there is still, I think, for the visitor a very strong feeling that one is being judged for what one is, and not for the label one bears. And that is a splendid characteristic too.

Americans seem to have an obsession with thinking about the Cold War. Who is against us. They can't be without a stand. Now, as for economic matters—each person has to be for himself. The state shouldn't do too much, or else people will get flabby. . . . The individual's rights are important. Due process is emphasized. There seems to be a healthy acceptance of individual rights. The government cannot grow greater than the law.

I could mention several American attitudes. American pride in feeling a free nation—you meet this everywhere: people saying "We are a free people in a free country." Together with this, you have freedom of enterprise. There must be several other freedoms. They like to feel free to discuss political issues. This same sense of freedom makes them hate communism and socialism. [Socialism] seems to be as bad as communism—I suppose because it means state interference in economics. There is an attitude towards helping other nations. Speaking very, very generally, I would say I came away with the feeling that the American nation is a very conformist nation. There is no room for the rebel, the nonconformist.

Other components of a general American point of view mentioned, though with less frequency, were a certain internationalism of outlook; an awareness of America's importance in world affairs; a respect for hard work; and—as can be seen in the above quotations—a tendency toward conformity.

Responses to the post-return interview confirmed, in essence, the conclusions we drew from the third interview. Participants' images of America varied greatly, although certain common themes emerged again and again. Some of these were positive in tone, some were negative, and some cannot really be placed on a favorable-unfavorable dimension. On the whole, the participants' view of America and of Americans was clearly more positive than negative, but it was by no means wholly noncritical. The point that came up most frequently and most emphatically was the participants' awareness of the complexity and diversity of America. Not only were they cognizant of these characteristics of America and its population, but they often spoke knowledgeably about the kinds of differences that did exist and evaluated different patterns differentially.

10

Post-Return Attitudes: Participants Versus Controls

All participants and their controls were interviewed in their home countries in the late spring or summer following the participants' American sojourn. This chapter compares responses of the twenty-eight participants and the twenty-eight controls in this post-return interview.[1] It reports all interview items for which there is a difference of five or more (that is, of at least 18 per cent) between the number of participants and the number of controls who respond in a given way.

The major group differences that the items suggest are twofold. First, the participants emerged on several items as having attained a more differentiated conception of America. Second, the controls seemed more ready to denigrate their own country in relation to America.

[1] The composition of the control group used in this chapter is described in the final section of Chapter Three, including footnote 2.

The participant spoke of American diversity and complexity. He said that there was no such thing as a single American point of view. He spoke of things that reflected an insider's knowledge of Americans—the life of the average American, the generosity and friendliness of Americans, American devotion to equality, the zealousness and enthusiasm of American broadcasters. He was aware of the salience of economic status in American life.

The control spoke of his country's limitations, its dependence on the United States. He said that the national media needed improved programs, more trained personnel, and more technical advice and broadcasting equipment. He was optimistic about the benefits of exchange. He thought American broadcasters were more efficient than those at home. He was willing to rely on official U.S. information sources to learn about the United States. His view of America was dominated by the U.S. aid program. He had come to feel less favorably about his home country during the past year.

The control's image was dominated by the relations between the two countries. He had a more idealized image of America, centered on what America could do for his country. The participant had acquired a more differentiated and specific view; he saw the United States and American broadcasting in their own terms and with greater realism about the benefits one might expect from association with the United States. He had established a more individualized relation to the United States that went beyond the general relations between the nations.

PERCEPTIONS OF AMERICA AND AMERICANS

As might be expected, the participants' picture of America a year after the seminar was quite different from that of the controls. The nature of this difference fully supports the conclusions of Chapter Nine. The discriminating interview items relevant to perceptions of America can be found in Table 6.

As may be seen, some differences reflected the immediacy of experience from which the participant could speak. He could present a program about his own experiences in America—a program that might well have more impact than more formal instructional or documentary programs. Moreover, he was not as likely to be dependent upon official American sources for materials for his programs; he knew how to obtain information through private American networks, through personal contacts, and through foundations and universities, in addition to such sources as the American Embassy and USIS. But we gain more insight into the effects of the sojourn if we ask what differences there were between the groups in terms of the information that might be presented in a program.

In the first place, the participant was more likely to feel that he could present a program about the lives of average Americans. This is an important result of his immediate contact. Both groups were able to pre-

Table 6

PERCEPTIONS OF AMERICA AND AMERICANS:
COMPARISON OF PARTICIPANTS AND CONTROLS

Items that Discriminate	Number of Respondents to Whom Each Item Applies	
	Participants	Controls
The kinds of programs about America that the respondent has presented or plans to present include		
personal reports on his experiences in America	15	1
instructional programs	6	12
documentaries	17	21
Information that he has presented or would be likely to present in broadcasts includes descriptions of the lives of average Americans	10	5
Major themes that he has presented or would be likely to present in broadcasts about America include		
the generosity and hospitality of Americans (kindness, openness, friendliness)	6	0
the diversity and heterogeneity of American institutions and people	10	4
the complexity of America and its problems (racial, political, and so on)	9	4
The sources from which he would obtain material about U.S. for broadcasts include official American sources in his own country	14	24
When asked which groups of Americans have different (nonmodal) views of his own country, he mentions those who have had direct contact with the country	10	16

Table 6 (Continued)

PERCEPTIONS OF AMERICA AND AMERICANS:
COMPARISON OF PARTICIPANTS AND CONTROLS

Items that Discriminate	*Number of Respondents to Whom Each Item Applies*	
	Participants	*Controls*
When asked whether there is such a thing as an "American attitude or point of view" he replies that[a]		
there is no such thing as an American point of view	1	0
one cannot speak of a single American point of view because of America's complexity and diversity	11	3
there is a general point of view but that one must be aware of America's complexity and diversity	11	15
there is a general American point of view	3	7
He feels that one component of the American point of view is a belief in democratic values (equality, freedom of the press, and so on)	12	5
When asked which American groups differ from each other in basic point of view, he cites socioeconomic groups (for example, social classes)	9	2

[a] The replies that follow are mutually exclusive; that is, each response was coded in terms of one and only one of these four categories. Two participants and three controls did not respond to this question.

pare programs giving coverage of the country, of special places and people, of institutions, or of the racial situation. Helpful as programming of that sort may be, there is much to be said for the additional ability to describe, from intimacy of contact, the everyday life of the average man. Unlike controls, participants were enabled to speak on their home broadcasting systems in terms that allowed America to emerge as a country occupied by understandable, nonmythical people, ordinary individuals engaged in pursuits recognizable to the listening audience. One European participant, for example, described part of a report he had prepared in the following words:

> I also wrote my impression about life in an American typical family, about the relations between the members of a family—that is, the father, mother, and the grown children. . . . I started with one impression of life in an American family. It started on a Saturday afternoon in the summer. They were going on a trip with the family. . . . The family enters and the husband makes a couple of jokes. They are very good people—he is a dear man. He helps his wife in the kitchen. He is a man of 55 years. His wife was always "honey, dear." His son came from college and drove a truck and delivered pop. He didn't wear shoes or a shirt. He was drinking orange juice, and the others were swimming. I wanted to say to the people that the evaluation of the man was through his activity—that is, he could live very good in his parents' house, but the father wanted his son to earn a living by his own labors. [*How was this report received?*] The people told me it was very interesting. It was fresh to the people.

One does not find this kind of homey detail in the interviews of the controls. To some, such programming did not seem to have occurred as a salient possibility. Thus, a control from the same country as the participant quoted above described his programming about the United States as follows:

> In all our transmissions we have points of emphasis. [For America,] it is the life of a highly civilized country and we speak about housing, TV, cars, and other things that make up this high level of civilization. When we broadcast about Africa, we emphasize music. We speak about things characteristic for the given country. [*For America, then, you spoke about technical progress?*] About the *result* of technical progress. About technical progress we spoke on the program regarding the St. Lawrence River.

Other controls recognized the value of talking in terms of immediate experiences and everyday life, but hesitated to approach America in these terms because they had not had the necessary firsthand contact. An Asian control, asked what information he might present on a program about America, said:

> The United States is a very big country. There are so many states united. Only one state is as big as our country. I would like to introduce the American citizen—both urban and rural—because life in America is what is most misunderstood. Some of the programs or films are too serious—like *Death of a Salesman,* or *Place in the Sun.* Others are nonsense. Even today, many people think Americans are

still fighting Indians. Some believe that America is fantastic—you can get anything there. Others think that America is going to the end; that it is the last phase of capitalism. Both are wrong. [*What would you present?*] I think family life is the core to understanding. I would get one family to show to our audience. Of course, it would be very difficult to find the right family—but I think it is possible. I myself don't know what is in the United States. I like Dvořak's Fifth Symphony and so I think I would like America!

Only among the participants did we find a group who felt that a major theme to be presented in programs was the kindliness, the openness, and the friendliness of Americans. A comment made by an African, and already quoted in part in the preceding chapter, is worth repeating in this connection:

> . . . Another thing: the human side. Barring the occasional racial eruption which takes place, the American people by and large are good-natured, kind-hearted people—and they enjoy a good laugh, like the African people, which is different from the British, who are a bit phlegmatic.

The participants' awareness of the complexity and diversity of America, stressed so much in the preceding chapter, emerges clearly in the comparison with the controls. When a participant presented a program about America, he was more likely to highlight, as one of its major themes, the complicated, diverse, pluralistic reality of America. He was less likely to present a simplistic picture, to accept a single-minded interpretation, to analyze along a single dimension. America to him was a diverse and heterogeneous land of varied people and complex problems that did not yield to quick solutions. Two quotations by African participants speaking on the problems of race relations in America illustrate this point nicely:

> In this country people have stereotyped ideas about what happens in America. The idea was to either confirm or blow up stereotypes about America. . . . On the race question, people here think it is either black or white. I found there were many shades of gray in between. . . . There are extreme positions on both sides—but there are many who hold positions between these extremes. One hears more about the atrocities that are perpetrated against American Negroes, because this is sensation. But one hears little about how little American Negroes are doing for themselves—which I found annoying. And opinions on the race question are not as clearly demarcated as they appear on the outside.

> . . . They [members of the respondent's own society] didn't know that there were some white Americans who contribute to the eradication of discrimination in the States. They thought whites and blacks were in conflict. . . . [*What were the main points you tried to make in the program?*] What the *real* position is. How the Negroes are

reacting to new developments. [*What new developments?*] Well, in the past the Negroes supported the NAACP, but now there are dynamic young men who are coming to talk to them and educate them—for example, from CORE. . . . Also about the formation of the Black Muslims—their role. I compared it to the Ku Klux Klan. . . . I also mentioned my incident [of discrimination] in Raleigh; also how the Kennedy administration appeared to be very much concerned with racial discrimination. . . .

Controls were less likely to be so sensitive to the complexity of American realities. For example, the following comments by an African control are noticeably more dogmatic and less firmly anchored in concrete events than the two preceding quotations:

Well, we think that the average American does not fully demonstrate his belief in racial equality. Well, let me put it this way. Although the American seems to go all out in helping colonial, developing countries, we think they are not doing enough at home for the colored people. On a given colonial issue, Americans will say on colonialism, "Down with certain issues," but back home, they preach something different.

A closely related point of difference between participants and controls arose in their responses to a question about the existence of an "American attitude or point of view." For the participants, the perception of American complexity was so salient that many found it difficult to speak seriously about such a thing as *an* American point of view. They considered it impossible to give a simple answer when asked, "How do Americans feel about this or that issue?" Thus, one participant told the interviewer that one could not speak of an American point of view because "you are the most diversified people in the world." An African responded to the same question as follows:

It is extremely difficult. I thought one could [speak of an American point of view] before I went to the United States. Except for one thing, as I said: American attitudes toward Communism. That's pretty general, although even there you can pick out the university people. No matter what they believe, at least they have reasons for their attitudes. It's extremely difficult to generalize—which I wish a large number of Americans would realize about this country.

And a European commented:

It is very difficult to tell. I think newsmen all over the world—yours and others—try to establish something like that. But I think there are many components which make up the American point of view, the American way of life. Different people speak quite differently—each has his own point of view. Many are different from the official point of view. We can speak of the official American point of view—but not everyone holds that point of view . . .

By contrast, controls were much more likely to reply affirmatively when asked whether one could speak of a single characteristic American attitude or point of view. If we examine some of these responses, we find that they describe the unidimensional America that often comes across in major communication media and in official pronouncements, rather than the complex America of personal experience. The replies of four controls to the question about the existence of an American point of view may serve to illustrate this point:

Well, there is a distinct American attitude or point of view. I firmly believe there is. There are typically American attitudes. Well, I should imagine, their power and wealth rather gives them a feeling of superiority. This is obvious in international relations. This is just an opinion of mine. I think their openness in certain fields—for example, in space probes—is commendable.

Yes. One thing is that those of us who have not been to America get the impression that Americans see everything as "anti-Communist" or "anti-Castro." We also have the impression that Americans are lavish in their way of spending money, but this may be due to their standard of living. That is an image of America that we have. All of this is connected with what I said. Americans like to live well and to see Africa in a few weeks.

Americans seem so afraid of Communism. They dread it. [Why?] It is born out of fear. It is a way of life that contradicts their democratic life. They are scared of anything that threatens their way of existence. I think the *average* American takes things *so* easy, that is, their personal comforts are provided for, they have automation, a higher standard of living. The average American gets anything and everything within his reach. Not by manual labor. It is different in other parts of the world.

Yes, I think so. [*Could you mention some of the major components of this attitude or point of view?*] The Western point of view in general can be described as anti-Communist. There is a general tendency, in expressing an opinion or taking an action, to do it because otherwise the Communists may gain an advantage. There is a general attitude that American influence must be felt in [this country]. That is, [this country] is viewed as a key country and so American influence must be felt here to be felt on the continent. There is a general feeling about religious efforts being made in America—there is a feeling of mission in the field of religion which people here think exists in America. That's all.

Participants and controls differed in terms of the groups within

American society that they identified as having different points of view. They were equally likely to mention groups varying in education, region, and race, but the participants were more likely than the controls to mention socioeconomic groups as differing in point of view. Perhaps the controls had a greater tendency to see America in terms of the stereotype of "the rich nation" (as illustrated in some of the above quotations), and were thus less cognizant of socioeconomic differences within America and of differences in point of view built upon these.

Finally, when asked about the components of what might be termed an American point of view, participants were more likely than controls to include the belief in democratic values. For example, an African respondent described as a component of an American point of view:

> . . . the people's own background of a constitution, which I like, and which people speak very favorably of. Some Americans who were very simple said to me: "The Constitution says. . . ." They didn't know much about the content of the Constitution, but they knew it was there and were committed to it. . . .

Several other quotations relevant to this point can be found in the preceding chapter.

PERCEPTIONS OF AMERICAN BROADCASTERS

The respondents were asked a number of questions about American broadcasters. Most coding categories yielded similar frequencies for participants and controls. Participants, however, were much more likely to mention enthusiasm and zealousness about their work among the characteristics of American broadcasters. Such comments were made by thirteen participants and by only three controls. Thus, an African noted that "my impression was that they were very hard-working people," and an Asian commented, "I can't think of any differences [between broadcasters in America and my country] except perhaps they work harder."

On the other hand, familiarity seemed to have dimmed illusions about great disparities of talent. Only five participants, compared to eleven controls, believed that broadcasters in their home countries differed greatly from American broadcasters in terms of competence. The more differentiated view of the participants is exemplified in the following response by a European participant, when asked to compare American broadcasters to those in his own country:

> That varied enormously. On the one hand, there were people . . . who were first rate. Very good minds. Integrity about their jobs. They knew what they wanted to do. Intelligent. It was a pleasure to talk to them. But then you have people—even some who came to lecture to us—who are dull technicians. Absolutely nothing. I met

several such. It varies greatly. At BBC [which this respondent had visited], while not everyone is as good as for example the WGBH people, you wouldn't find people like some of the ones I met—who have no integrity, no aesthetic interests, no real motivation behind their work. Then, of course, you have normal people, quite good and nice, whom you can meet anywhere. . . . [*What about the professional competence of American broadcasters?*] Their competence is enormously high. . . . They are really good at their jobs. Competition is high and the best person gets the job. Another thing that was very nice is that all the ones I met—both in educational and in commercial broadcasting—seemed to love their jobs—they liked what they were doing. . . . Most of them work hard . . .

Or, as another European participant put it, simply:

Well I met people in America who are a damn sight better and a damn sight worse. In other words, I think they have the best and the worst.

A European control, on the other hand, told the interviewer:

I don't know many American broadcasters personally. I must judge only their work. I think the American broadcasters sometimes—in comparison to our broadcasters—very often are more technically prepared. They arrive to the profession after a more organized experience. . . . They have more specific training. . . .

VIEWS ON INTERNATIONAL EXCHANGE

Table 7 presents those discriminating items that deal with views on international exchange. Both groups felt that other countries could help in the development of broadcasting in the home country by exchanging programs, personnel, and ideas; controls also suggested the exchange of broadcasting equipment. Both groups believed that exchange could lead to real increases in technical skill (an item accepted by eighteen participants and sixteen controls), but the participants were considerably more dubious about the training value of exposure to ideas and practices in other countries with an eye to adapting these to the home country. Apparently they had learned that it was difficult to make such adaptations, or perhaps, in some instances, that it was better to avoid the ideas and practices of others even if they could be readily adapted. Participants were also more dubious than controls about the training value of increasing broadcasters' knowledge of media in other countries—again, perhaps, because they considered as remote the possibility of adapting these to their own situations.

The somewhat limited endorsement of international exchange that these items suggest seems to appear elsewhere as well. When asked what kinds of exchange would be valuable, the participants were less likely to

Table 7

Views on International Exchange:
Comparison of Participants and Controls

Items that Discriminate	Number of Respondents to Whom Each Item Applies	
	Participants	Controls
Respondent feels that other countries could help the development of broadcasting in his country by supplying equipment	3	9
Contributions that international exchange could make to training of broadcasters in own country include		
increasing their knowledge of broadcasting or communication media in other countries	5	12
exposing them to ideas and practices in other countries that they can adapt to own situation	6	17
Valuable forms of international exchange for broadcasters include		
exchange of personnel between networks	10	16
exchange of information about developments in communication media	15	8
Respondent's current professional contacts with America include		
American broadcasting networks and educational networks	16	10
directors of the seminar	8	0
professional literature	9	4
Respondent's current professional contacts with other countries (aside from America)		
are nil	7	1
are with networks	11	19
are with other Seminar participants	6	0

cite exchange of personnel; they appeared more satisfied with the simple exchange of information about developments in the communication media.

Some of the professional contacts participants made in America had survived the year. They reported more current professional contacts than controls with Americans in the broadcasting and educational networks, and, of course, with the seminar directors. Given these American contacts, the participants may have had less need for connections with foreigners in third countries. In any case, controls reported more professional contacts with third-country nationals. The only category of third-country contact in which participants inevitably showed greater numbers was that of contact with other members of the seminar.

VIEWS ON BROADCASTING

Most respondents expected many new developments in broadcasting in their own countries. Most were fairly well satisfied with the directions that those developments were taking. Controls, however, were more likely to hope that the country would be seeing an increase in the number of trained personnel; ten controls mentioned this, as compared to three participants. Controls were also more likely to say that they hoped to see an improvement in the quality of programs; twelve controls made this point, compared to only five participants. Perhaps this means that participants felt less apologetic about the quality of programs at home after seeing American programs.

Nineteen controls said that their ideas about broadcasting had not changed during the year; only thirteen participants admitted to such static views. The new views that were cited were rather similar, with two exceptions. Participants became more convinced about the importance of emphasizing the development of TV. They became also more convinced, however, that—despite the development of TV—the emphasis on radio should continue or be even more pronounced in their countries. This may well be a product of their experience in America where—in the view of many participants—radio had been allowed to decline in vigor with the advent of TV.

OTHER COMPARISONS

Job changes. Two-thirds of each group reported a change in position or responsibilities. Twelve participants, but only seven controls, attributed these changes to the recognition of their own abilities. The two groups were otherwise similar in reported job satisfaction, in expectations of change, and in innovativeness on the job.

Views of the home country.   There was no difference in the number of participants and controls who reported gaining a clearer view of the role of their own countries; or who reported gaining a more differentiated view; or who reported, simply, gaining a more favorable view. Controls were, however, more likely than participants to report that they had become less favorably inclined toward their own countries in the course of the year (two participants as compared to nine controls gave such a response). Instead, participants were more likely to report no change at all (eight versus three). Thus, it appears that the experience in America kept some participants, who might otherwise have done so, from developing a more negative view of their home countries. It is possible that participation in the seminar had somehow insulated them against developing a sense of disaffection from the home country. Perhaps they brought home a higher morale and more energy; perhaps they learned to judge the home country from a greater distance and with more compassion and patience; perhaps they were buoyed by new skills or prestige.

Interest in future visits.   Respondents were asked whether they wished to visit America in the future. The greater interest of the participants is shown in Table 8. The participants also thought it more likely that they could make another trip, although this time they would prefer to come—or probably have to come—on an individual basis.

Table 8

INTEREST IN FUTURE VISITS TO THE UNITED STATES:
COMPARISON OF PARTICIPANTS AND CONTROLS

Items that Discriminate	Number of Respondents to Whom Each Item Applies	
	Participants	Controls
Respondent's desire to visit the U.S. is		
moderate	11	16
strong	16	10
He thinks a visit unlikely	5	10
He would like to visit		
on an individual professional basis	21	12
as part of an organized exchange program	5	13

11

Images of America and the Profession: I. Changes in Cognitive Structure

In Chapter Three we described the "Questionnaire for Specialists in Broadcasting" (see Appendix B), which was administered to the participants and to a comparison group before the beginning of the seminar and again approximately nine months to a year after the completion of the seminar. These questionnaires are our primary source of information about changes attributable to participation in the seminar. In the present chapter we shall discuss the most clearcut and the most interesting changes documented by the questionnaires—changes in the cognitive structures of the images of America and of American mass media held by our respondents. In the next chapter we shall turn to additional changes—in the content and the degree of favorableness—of respondents' views of America, of the field of broadcasting, and of their own professional roles. Before presenting these data, however, we must give a more detailed account than we have done so far of the purposes of the questionnaire and of the ways in which it was used.

PURPOSE OF THE QUESTIONNAIRE

The present seminar—in keeping with the goals of other similar exchange programs—aimed, among other things, to provide the participants with a professionally useful experience, yielding new information, new ideas, and new contacts that could enhance their professional work. At the same time, it was designed to provide the participants with first-hand knowledge of American mass media, as well as of American society and American life in general. To the extent that these goals were fulfilled, one would expect some changes in the participants' images of and attitudes toward their professional field—that is, their views both of the broadcasting media in their own countries, and of their own professional roles. Similarly, one would expect some changes in images of and attitudes toward America, particularly American broadcasting media. The purpose of the questionnaire in the present study was to assess whether such changes did indeed occur. By comparing answers that participants gave before the seminar with those they gave after the seminar, we can gain some idea of the extent to which the intervening period produced the expected changes. By comparing these changes to changes manifested by the control group over the same period of time, we can determine whether the changes observed among participants can in fact be attributed to their experience in America.

In developing questions that would tap the respondents' images of America, we placed our emphasis on American mass media. Thus, a large proportion of the questions dealt specifically with American broadcasting—its functions, contributions, and problems. Even those questions that focused on America and Americans in general were linked, insofar as possible, to the respondents' professional concerns with the mass media. For example, Questions 11 and 12, which asked the respondent to describe the impressions that Americans had of his own country, were linked to questions on the coverage of information about his country by the American mass media. Question 15, which was designed to tap the aspects of the U.S. that the respondent considered important, was framed in terms of the coverage of information about the U.S. by his country's mass media.

There were two reasons for this emphasis. First, given the focus of the seminar and the professional concerns of the participants, changes in the view of American mass media were of more direct and obvious relevance than changes in the view of any other aspect of American life. Individual participants may have shown changes in one or another area, in keeping with their *particular* interests and experiences; for the group as a whole, however, it was most reasonable to expect changes with regard to the mass media, since this represented the area of interest and experience shared by all participants. Moreover, changes in this area were likely to have continuing and far-reaching effects, since they tied in with the participants' professional activities. Thus, questions relating to the American mass media were of particular interest for an evaluation of the effectiveness of the seminar in achieving its goals.

The second reason for the emphasis on the mass media related to the maintenance of rapport with the respondents. We felt that respondents might resent the use of too many questions that focused directly on their images of and attitudes toward America. They might feel "put on the spot" by questions about America posed by American researchers; and they might interpret these questions as evidence that the seminar was primarily a "public relations" device, designed to create a favorable image of the host country. Questions that were clearly related to the respondents' professional concerns, however, would not elicit such resentment. Consequently, the questionnaire emphasized American broadcasting media; and phrased even the more general questions in ways that related them to the respondents' professional concerns.

Nevertheless, the questionnaire did provide information about the respondents' views of America in general and about changes in these views. For one thing, their views of American mass media certainly reflected, at least to some degree, their general views of American society and its institutions. The mass media are, after all, a key institution in the society, and, moreover, the one to which they had the greatest exposure. For another thing, the general questions, despite their indirect nature, provided rather meaningful contexts for assessing the respondents' images of America. Thus, Question 15 asked the respondent what he, as a broadcaster, would want to communicate about America to his own countrymen. Questions 11 and 12 explored the respondent's perception of what impressions Americans had of his country—a highly salient dimension for evaluating the nationals of another country. A respondent's perception of Americans on this dimension was likely to determine his general attitude toward them; and his answers to these questions were likely to reflect this general attitude.

Question 12 exemplifies another basic assumption underlying our whole approach to the assessment of images and attitudes about American broadcasting and America and Americans in general. Our primary interest was not at all in assessing the degree to which the participants' images and attitudes became more *favorable* as a result of their American experience. Rather, we were concerned with the *cognitive structure* of these images and attitudes. There is no particular reason to expect that a sojourn in a foreign country, even under the best of circumstances, will produce an increase in overall favorableness toward that country. To be sure, there is the likelihood that the person's attitude will become warmer and more personal, if he has had satisfying experiences and formed meaningful interpersonal relationships with nationals of the host country. Yet, he need not become more favorable on the whole toward the country and its institutions. Those who start out with negative attitudes may find confirming evidence for them; those who start out with positive attitudes may have little room for change in the favorable direction; and those who start out neutral may find some things they like and others they dislike. It would be unrealistic to expect marked changes on this dimension to result from international exchange programs. Nor is the uncritical acceptance of all features of the host country even a desirable goal for international exchanges.

Both realistic and desirable, however, as outcomes of such programs, are qualitative changes in the cognitive structure of images of the host country. Thus, the organizers and sponsors of the present seminar were particularly interested in the extent to which participants would gain a fuller, richer, more detailed, and more refined picture of American mass media and American society in general (see Chapter Two). Such a change would imply an increased awareness of the range of activities and points of view in American broadcasting and American life; a deeper understanding of patterns and problems from the inside; and an increased ability to respond differentially to different segments of American society and different aspects of American life (including the mass media). Development of a global undifferentiated positive attitude would be as antithetical to this type of goal as the development of a global undifferentiated negative attitude.

In line with the assumptions that have just been outlined, we made special efforts to capture the *complexity* and *differentiation* of images and attitudes, both in the formulation of questions and in the coding of responses (to be discussed below). We did not ignore the dimension of favorableness toward America and American broadcasting, but we regarded it as of secondary importance. This approach to attitude measurement also has some methodological advantages, especially in a situation such as the present one. The favorable-unfavorable dimension is often subject to distortion and presents difficulties in interpretation. At best it gives only a limited picture of a person's attitude toward an object, which must be supplemented by assessment of the cognitive dimensions of the attitude.

In addition to tapping images of America, including American broadcasting, the questionnaire explored the respondents' images of and attitudes toward their professional field. These parts of the questionnaire included, first of all, questions about the broadcasting media in the respondent's own country—the role of the media in society, their specific functions, their contributions, and their problems. It was assumed that participation in the seminar, exposure to American mass media, and exchange of ideas with colleagues from around the world, might produce changes in a person's images in this area. He might, for example, become aware of certain new possibilities for the development of broadcasting in his country, or of certain new problems that needed to be solved, or of certain new approaches that could be applied. He might become more or less satisfied with the status of the media in his country. And, again, changes in the cognitive structure of his attitudes might take place; for instance, he might develop a more complex and differentiated view of the role that the broadcasting media in his country could perform. These were the kinds of changes the questionnaire was designed to tap.

Similarly, participation in the seminar might produce changes in the person's attitude toward his own professional role and toward his activities within the field of broadcasting. The questionnaire thus included items designed to explore the respondent's definition of his professional role, his assessment of the importance of different aspects of his job, his satisfactions and dissatisfactions with his professional life, and his hopes and expectations for the future. These are all areas that may very well be affected by the kinds of experiences that the seminar provided for its participants.

It can be assumed that an effective seminar would probably produce some changes in the participants' professional images—their images both of their field and of their own roles within it. It is very difficult, however, to specify what form these changes ought to take. They are likely to be quite different for different individuals—depending on such factors as the person's professional position and the level of development of broadcasting in his own country. Perhaps the only general statement that can be made is that the person ought, ideally, to come away with a richer and more differentiated view of his professional field, reflecting new insights derived from exchange of ideas and exposure to new patterns.

CODING OF RESPONSES

Precoded questions. Those questions in which respondents were merely asked to choose from among a set of predetermined responses presented no special coding problems, since the coding categories were already built into each question. For the more complex precoded questions (1, 2, 16, and 20), however, composite indices were developed, based on a combination of the various subparts of each question and a comparison of the before- and after-questionnaires.

Thus, for Question 1, two indices were developed: an index of the overall amount of change (from the first to the second questionnaire) in the respondent's view of the *actual* pattern of activities for TV in his country; and an index of the overall amount of change in the respondent's view of the *ideal* pattern of activities for TV in his country. Indices for Question 2 were similar to those based on Question 1, except that they dealt with the respondent's views of TV in America. In addition, for each questionnaire, a special index was computed to provide a comparison between answers to Questions 1 and 2. This index represented the *extent of difference* in the patterns of activities that the respondent attributed to TV in his own country and in the U.S. By comparing the value of this index on the second questionnaire with that on the first questionnaire, we can determine whether and to what degree the respondent, a year later, saw American TV as more different from (or more similar to) TV in his own country than he did before.

For Question 16, an index of the overall amount of change in the respondent's evaluation of the activities associated with his job was constructed. For Question 20, indices of change in the respondent's definition of his professional role were developed.

Open-ended questions. For those questions to which respondents answered in their own words, coding categories had to be developed to permit analysis of the material. The categories were based on a combination of two considerations: the kinds of information that a particular question was designed to yield; and the kinds of information that it actually yielded, as revealed by an examination of a sample of responses.

Two types of codes were developed: (1) *Content codes,* that is, lists of content categories to which responses to a given question could be assigned. For example, the content code for Question 3 consisted of a list of "areas in which others can benefit from experiences of respondent's own country." For a given respondent, more than one area could apply (that is, content codes were "multiple codes"). For example, his answer might suggest that others could learn something from the pattern of ownership of the broadcasting system in his country, and from its approach to programming. In this case, the coder would check both of these categories on the list of ten categories that this particular code happened to employ. (2) *Rating scales,* that is, orderings of positions on a particular dimension in terms of which responses to a given question could be assessed. For example, the coders were asked to rate answers to Question 3 in terms of the "extent of perceived contribution of respondent's own country." In this case, a four-point scale was used ranging from "no contribution" (respondent feels that his own country has nothing to contribute, from its experiences, to broadcasters in other countries) to "major contribution." Rating scales were "single codes," that is, only one category could be checked for each respondent, and the coder had to select the one that seemed to apply most closely.

For most questions, several codes were developed to capture the relevant information. Typically, these would include both a content code and a rating scale, as in Question 3—the example used in the preceding paragraph. Some of the content codes were, moreover, combined with rating scales. Thus, in the content code for Question 3, the coders were asked first to check the content areas mentioned by the respondent and then, for each area checked, to rate, on a three-point scale, the strength of emphasis it received in his response.

For some of the questions, more than one content code was used. For example, for the analysis of Questions 7 and 8, three lists were developed: areas in which TV (in America, or in the home country) faces problems; causes of problems faced by TV; and proposed solutions for these problems. For some of the questions, more than one rating scale was developed. For example, each respondent's remarks about the typical American in response to Question 11 were rated on three dimensions: the degree to which the typical American was pictured as well informed or ignorant about the respondent's own country, as sympathetic to the respondent's own country, and as prepared to accept that country on an equal basis. Finally, some rating scales were designed to capture a more pervasive quality, characteristic of responses to several questions. Thus, for example, coders were asked to rate the respondent's general attitude toward American TV on a five-point scale (from extremely favorable to extremely unfavorable); these ratings were based on responses to Questions 4, 6, and 7.

Altogether, thirty-three codes were developed for the analysis of the open-ended questions (exclusive of the complexity-differentiation ratings to be described in the next section). All of the questionnaires were coded by a "primary coder," who was "blind" in the sense that he did not know whether any given questionnaire that he was working on had been completed by a seminar participant or a comparison group member, nor whether it had been filled out before the seminar or after. In order to increase coding reliability, the following procedure was used:

For eight of the codes, *all* of the questionnaires were analyzed by a "check-coder" in addition to the primary coder. In cases of disagreement between the two coders, final judgments were arrived at by bringing in a third coder and/or by conference.

For the other twenty-five codes, *ten* questionnaires were analyzed by a check-coder, whose judgments were then compared with those of the primary coder. Disagreements were resolved by conference between the two coders. For eighteen codes, the agreement between the two was so high that it was possible to use the primary coder's judgments on the remaining eighty-eight questionnaires without further review. For five codes, agreement was quite high, but the conferences between the two coders had produced a slight revision in coding criteria; the primary coder therefore reviewed his original judgments on the remaining eighty-eight questionnaires in the light of the revised criteria. Finally, for two codes there was enough disagreement to warrant check-coding on all of the remaining questionnaires; the primary coder and the check-coder then proceeded to compare all of their judgments and, in cases of disagreement, to arrive at final judgments through conference.

Complexity-differentiation ratings. In view of our special interest in the cognitive structure of images and attitudes, we tried to capture in our coding scheme not only the specific content of responses, but also their *structure* or *style.* Specifically, we wanted to assess the degree to which different responses revealed a complex and differentiated image of the object under discussion—whether it be American broadcasting, American society in general, or broadcasting in the respondent's own country. Our expectation was that participation in a successful seminar should, on the whole, produce an increase in the degree of complexity and differentiation of these images.

Two simple three-point rating-scales were constructed and applied to responses to all open-ended questions concerned with American broadcasting, America and Americans in general, and broadcasting in the respondent's own country (Questions 3, 4, 6, 7, 8, 11, 12, 13, and 15b). The first scale called for a rating of *range of response.* The rating criteria for this dimension were defined quite objectively: ratings depended on the number of distinct points a respondent made in response to a given question. For example, in answering Question 3, respondents could mention various areas in which others might benefit from broadcasting experiences of their own countries. If a respondent mentioned just one distinct area, he received a rating of 1 (narrow range); if he mentioned two distinct areas, he received a rating of 2 (moderate range); and if he mentioned three or more areas, a rating of 3 (broad range).

The second scale called for a rating of *depth of response* and required somewhat more subjective judgments. Two criteria were taken into consideration in making these judgments: the elaborateness of the response, and the importance of the points mentioned. Thus, however many or few areas might be mentioned in a response to Question 3, the discussion of each area could vary in its elaborateness: it might range from a mere mention of the area, to a detailed exposition of it. Similarly, the areas mentioned could vary in their importance: they could refer to central features of the broadcasting system, its organization, and its role in society (for example, the sponsorship of TV in the country; the use of TV as a means of combatting illiteracy or creating national unity); or they could refer to relatively minor features (for example, the type of lighting effects used; the use of canned versus live programs). The combination of the two criteria yielded one of three ratings: if a respondent merely mentioned the areas, or if he discussed "unimportant" areas with little detail, he received a rating of 1 (superficial coverage of content areas); if he discussed moderately important areas with little detail, or unimportant areas with considerable detail, he received a rating of 2 (moderately detailed and elaborate coverage); and if he discussed important or moderately important areas with considerable detail, he received a rating of 3 (very detailed and elaborate discussion). Despite the obviously subjective nature of these judgments, the consensus among the coders was amazingly high.

In order to increase reliability, all ratings of range and depth were done independently by three coders. The primary coder, as has already been mentioned, did the ratings "blind." The check-coders knew in each case whether they were coding a before- or an after-questionnaire, belonging to a participant or to a control. They did not, however, code the before- and after-questionnaires of the same respondent in close proximity to each other. Thus, biases that might have arisen from the coders' expectations of change were minimized.

In cases of disagreement among the coders, the following procedure was used to arrive at the final rating: If two out of the three coders agreed on the rating, their judgment prevailed. In the rare cases in which all three coders disagreed with each other, the middle rating (which also represents the average of the three ratings) served as the final score.

The level of agreement among the coders was very high. In the majority of cases, all three coders independently gave the same rating. Only on several occasions did all three raters disagree. In those cases in which two out of the three raters agreed and their judgment prevailed, we decided that it would be important to check on the distribution of the "winning" pairs. If it were to turn out that the two check-coders constituted the winning pair in a disproportionately large number of cases, it would give cause for concern, since there was at least some possibility of bias in their ratings (which had not been done "blind"). Accordingly, twelve of the eighteen complexity-differentiation codes (the twelve that entered into the major index used in this study, to be described below) were analyzed in detail, to determine how the final scores were arrived at. The results indicate very clearly that the two check-coders did not dominate the final ratings. As a matter of fact, the primary coder tended to be in the winning pair more often than either of the other two. We feel quite reassured, therefore, that the complexity-differentiation scores are not only reliable, but also relatively unaffected by obvious sources of coder bias.

INTERPRETATION OF RESULTS

In interpreting the results of the questionnaire study, we must be fully aware of the limitations of these data. First, as has already been pointed out (Chapter Three), the comparison group is not only incomplete, but also provides less than a perfect match for the seminar participants. Secondly, there were many gaps in respondents' answers to the questionnaires. Many respondents, for example, failed to answer some of the questions about America or American broadcasting because they felt that they lacked the necessary information. Moreover, if a respondent failed to answer a given question on *one* of the questionnaires, we could not use his answer to the same question on the second questionnaire either, since our concern was with the assessment of change. Thus, most of our analyses are based on fewer than the total number of cases. Thirdly, there was considerable variation in the fullness with which individual questions were answered. While some responses were very rich, others were quite sparse. Some respondents had obvious difficulties in the use of English; others were unaccustomed to this type of questionnaire procedure. On the whole, the questionnaires did not offer the opportunities for communicating the intent of questions, for eliciting full responses, and for following these up and exploring them further, that were present in the personal interviews. Understandably, therefore, the questionnaire responses were less rich and complete and often did not do justice to the views of the respondent.

Yet, at the same time, the questionnaire data make a very unique and important contribution to the overall design of the evaluation study. This was the only part of the study in which identical questions were presented both before and after the seminar, and both to the participants and to the comparison group. Thus, it was the only part of the study that met the conditions of an experimental design permitting us to conclude whether or not the seminar did in fact produce attitude change. This is not to say that other parts of the study provided no information about change. The interviews conducted while the participants were in the United States called for their own formulations of changes they were experiencing at the time. The follow-up interviews, obtained a year later, were especially rich sources of information about change, and there was the added advantage that comparable interviews with members of the comparison group were conducted at the same time. While these follow-up interviews did provide data about change, and even permitted comparison, we did not have controlled before-interviews against which these data could be measured. The comparison group was not interviewed before at all, and while the participants were interviewed shortly after their arrival in the United States, most of the questions in that interview differed from those on the follow-up interview. Thus, if we want to know whether participants' responses *to the same stimuli* in 1963 differed from their responses in 1962, and if we want to have some assurance that observed differences were not due to extraneous factors, we must turn to the questionnaire data.

Given both the unique values of the questionnaire data and their limitations, what use can be made of them? We would argue that they must be used in conjunction with the much fuller and richer interview data. They can indicate—on the basis of fairly sound experimental evidence—whether we are justified in concluding that the seminar did indeed produce some measurable changes. We must turn to the interview data, however, in order to learn just what these changes were. This we have done in the preceding chapters, which examined the nature of the changes by analyzing what the seminar participants (wherever possible, in contrast to comparison group members) said about their professional roles, about broadcasting in their home countries and in America, and about American society in general; and how they themselves described their American experience and the effect it has had upon them. In short, the questionnaire data in the present study can tell us, with some assurance, whether the seminar had any measurable impact, and the interview data can inform us about the nature of that impact.

With this perspective in mind, let us now review the data bearing on changes in the cognitive structure—specifically in the degree of differentiation—of respondents' images of America and American mass media. In Chapter Twelve we shall review various other changes in attitude documented by the questionnaire results.

DIFFERENTIATION OF IMAGES

As has already been indicated in our discussion of the rationale and purpose of the questionnaire, our major interest was in exploring changes in the cognitive structure of respondents' images of American broadcasting and America in general. It seemed to us reasonable to expect that participation in a four-month seminar would produce more complex and differentiated images of the host country. Moreover, such changes represent a significant and widely shared criterion for evaluating the success of international exchange programs.

Index of change in differentiation. A preliminary inspection of our data revealed that it was indeed on the dimensions of cognitive structure that the most consistent changes seemed to occur. In view of this finding, taken together with our special interest in these dimensions, we decided to construct an overall index of change in differentiation of the image of America. To construct this index, we used *all* of the codes that had been designed to capture the complexity and differentiation of the respondents' images of one or another aspect of American life. The index includes codes that refer specifically to American broadcasting, as well as codes that refer to America and Americans more generally. Since the two sets of codes tended to produce similar results, and since it could be assumed that for our respondents American broadcasting was a highly salient feature of American life in general, it seemed reasonable to combine the two and thus provide a stabler measure. In all, the following fifteen codes entered into the index (see Appendix B for the questionnaire items on which these codes are based):

(1) The score for the extent to which the respondent perceived differences between the patterns of activities of TV in his own country and in the United States, based on comparison of responses to Question 1 and Question 2 (see section on precoded questions above). This score was derived as follows: For each activity on Question 1, the respondent would receive a score of 3 if he checked it as a "major activity," a score of 2 if he checked it as a "minor activity," and a score of 1 if he checked it as "hardly ever done." The same procedure was followed for each activity on Question 2. For each of the activities, then, the discrepancy between the score on Question 1 and the score on Question 2 was computed (disregarding sign); for example, if "providing specific information" was checked as a "major activity" (score 3) for the respondent's own TV system and as "hardly ever done" (score 1) for American TV, he would receive a discrepancy score of 2 for this activity. The discrepancy scores for all thirteen of the listed activities were then summed to yield a total score for the extent of difference in the patterns of activities attributed to the two TV systems. The potential range of the scores was from 0 to 26; the actual range from 0 to 18. It was assumed that an increase on this score—that is, an increased perception of differences—from the before-questionnaire to the after-questionnaire would be an indication of a more highly differentiated image of American TV: As a person comes to see American TV in greater detail and in its own terms, he is more likely to become

aware of its unique features and hence of the specific ways in which it differs from the TV system to which he himself is accustomed.[1]

(2) The rating of range of response to Question 4, which called for discussion of experiences in broadcasting in the United States. Criteria for this and all other ratings of range of response were described above, in the section on complexity-differentiation ratings. In all cases, the potential and actual range of scores was from 1 to 3.

(3) The rating of depth of response to Question 4. Again, criteria for this and all other ratings of depth of response were described in the section on complexity-differentiation ratings. The potential and actual range of scores for all ratings of depth was from 1 to 3.

(4) The rating of range of response to Question 6, which called for discussion of the differences in function between TV in the respondent's own country and TV in the United States. It was assumed that a wider-ranging response to this question reflected a more differentiated image of American TV.

(5) The rating of depth of response to Question 6. Again, it was assumed that a more detailed and elaborate response to Question 6 reflected a more highly differentiated image.

(6) The rating of range of response to Question 7, which called for discussion of problems facing American TV, the major causes of these problems, and possible measures that might alleviate them.

(7) The rating of depth of response to Question 7.

(8) The rating of range of response to Question 11, which called for discussion of the impressions Americans have of the respondent's own country. This question was designed to yield some information on the respondent's image of the "typical American."

(9) The rating of depth of response to Question 11.

(10) A score for the extent to which the respondent's answer to Question 12 indicated specific knowledge and differentiation of American

---

[1] It is possible to place a different interpretation on an increase in awareness of differences between the two systems. It could reflect a disenchantment with American TV, resulting in a tendency to reject it. Such rejection could take the form of exaggerating the differences between American TV and TV in the respondent's own country, with the implication that American TV was either inferior or irrelevant to his own system. If that were true, an increase in extent of difference would be a sign of global rejection rather than of an increase in differentiation of the image. We doubt very much, however, that this interpretation applies in the present case. An examination of other codes provided no evidence that the individuals who showed increased awareness of differences also became less favorable to American TV; if anything, the trend was in the opposite direction. In support of our assumption, we found that individuals who showed an increased awareness of differences also tended to be high on the overall index of change in differentiation.

society. Question 12 asked the respondent whether he could think of groups of Americans whose impressions of his country differed from those he had just attributed to the "typical American" in his answer to Question 11. It was assumed that the more such groups he was able to mention, the more differentiated his image of American society—that is, the greater his awareness of subsegments of American society, each with its own unique characteristics. We also felt, however, that the *nature* of the groups mentioned would have to be considered in assigning this score. Thus, a respondent could answer Question 12 by mentioning groups of Americans who have had some direct contact with his own country—for example, "people who have visited my country," "American diplomats," or "American missionaries in my country." This kind of answer does not provide evidence for a very differentiated image of American society; it acknowledges that there are differences between different groups, but the specific ones mentioned do not represent important groupings in terms of which the American population is stratified. They are essentially logical categories that anyone (even in the absence of any knowledge about America) could have listed on the assumption that those who have had direct contact with a country will have different impressions from those who have had no such contact. A listing of such groups, then, can be taken to indicate a relatively low degree of differentiation. Again, a respondent might answer Question 12 by mentioning groups that do reflect important bases for the stratification of the American population—such as "educated Americans" or "immigrants"—but that may still represent logical categories for answering the question. For example, it does not necessarily take a knowledge of American society to suggest that educated Americans will have different impressions of foreign countries than uneducated ones; or that immigrants will have different impressions than native-born Americans. The listing of such groups, then, can be taken to indicate a medium degree of differentiation. Finally, a respondent might answer Question 12 by mentioning groups that represent important bases for the stratification of American society—such as groups defined in terms of regional differences, religious differences, ethnic differences, or occupational differences —and that cannot be expected to differ in their impressions of the respondent's country merely on logical grounds. The listing of such groups would reflect some detailed knowledge of American society and can be taken to indicate a relatively high degree of differentiation. Using these criteria, answers to Question 12 were scored as follows: A score of 0 was assigned if the respondent indicated that he could think of no groups of Americans differing in their impressions; a score of 1, if he mentioned only "low" groups (as defined above) ; a score of 2 if he mentioned only "medium" groups, or only medium and low groups; a score of 3 if he mentioned one "high" group; and a score of 4 if he mentioned two or more high groups.

(11) The rating of range of response to Question 12. This rating was based, not on the number of groups mentioned, but on the respondent's description of the *ways* in which the impressions of these groups differed from those of the typical American.

(12) The rating of depth of response to Question 12, again based on the description of the ways in which impressions differed.

(13) The rating of range of response to Question 15b, which asked the respondent to discuss the kind of information that might be included in a feature program about the United States.

(14) The rating of depth of response to Question 15b.

(15) An overall rating of the respondent's degree of knowledgeability about the American scene, based on his responses to Questions 4, 7, 11, and 15b. This rating represents, essentially, the extent to which the respondent described the American scene in specific, concrete, factual terms, rather than in vague, abstract, stereotyped terms. To a large extent, this rating was based on the number of significant facts that the respondent included in his answers. Examples of "significant facts" would be the names and functions of specific broadcasting programs, organizations, and regulatory agencies; specific statements about major social problems in the United States, such as the extent of poverty, the assimilation of various ethnic groups, or the relations between the races; specific features of the American political system and its functions; specific features of various geographical regions in the United States, such as their level of industrialization and urbanization; and concrete statements about American history and culture. In addition to the number of facts mentioned, the rating also took into account the quality of the responses. The ratings were done on a four-point scale. A rating of 1 represented responses given in vague, overly abstract, oversimplified, stereotyped terms, showing little or no knowledge of America. Such a rating was assigned to respondents who mentioned no significant facts. A rating of 2 represented responses in terms of broad generalities, which showed some knowledge of America but not a very thorough one (assigned to respondents who mentioned one significant fact together with such general points as "commercialism in broadcasting"). A rating of 3 represented responses in terms of broad generalities, which did however evidence a good basic knowledge of America (assigned to respondents who mentioned two or three significant facts). Finally, a rating of 4 represented responses given in specific, concrete, factual terms (assigned to respondents who mentioned four or more significant facts).

Results for individual codes. Before turning to a discussion of the overall index of change in differentiation, which was based on the fifteen codes that have just been described, let us examine the results obtained with each of the fifteen individual codes. These findings are summarized in Table 9, which presents—for each of the fifteen codes—the mean before-score, mean after-score, and mean change-score for both the participants and the controls. Looking first at the participants, we see that in twelve out of the fifteen comparisons, the after-score is higher than the before-score (indicating greater differentiation), in two it is identical with the before-score, and in only one comparison it is lower. According to the sign-test (which is a very conservative statistical test) this pattern is significant at better than the .01 level of confidence. By contrast, for the controls, the after-score is higher than the before-score in only five cases, identical in two, and lower in eight. This pattern does not depart significantly from chance.

The most revelant basis for evaluating the results presented in Table 9 is a comparison of the mean change scores obtained by participants and controls on each of the fifteen codes. Such a comparison reveals that, in twelve of the fifteen cases, the mean change score of the participants is higher than that of the control group, indicative of a greater increase in differentiation of the image of America. Of these twelve codes, seven show fairly sizeable differences between the two groups: the score for the extent of difference in the respondent's characterization of TV in his own country and in the United States (Code 1); the ratings of range and depth of discussion of the problems faced by American TV (6 and 7); the ratings of range and depth of discussion of the typical American's impression of the respondent's own country (8 and 9); the rating of range of information included in a hypothetical feature program about the United States (13); and the rating of knowledgeability about the American scene (15). For the remaining five of the twelve positive cases, the differences are small but in the expected direction. Finally, there is one case in which the mean change scores are identical for the two groups, and two in which the control group has the higher score, although only by a very small margin. Altogether, this pattern is statistically significant by the sign-test at better than the .01 level of confidence. From the item-by-item comparison, thus, we are clearly justified in concluding that the participants evinced a significantly greater increase in differentiation of their image of America than did the comparison group.

Results for the overall index. To derive a score on the overall index of change in differentiation for each respondent, the following procedure was used: For each of the fifteen codes comprising the index, we noted whether the respondent had changed positively, negatively, or not at all from the before- to the after-questionnaire. The number of positive changes minus the number of negative changes constituted the respond-

Table 9

MEAN BEFORE-, AFTER-, AND CHANGE-SCORES ON EACH OF THE FIFTEEN CODES
CONSTITUTING THE INDEX OF CHANGE IN DIFFERENTIATION OF THE IMAGE OF AMERICA

Codes[a]	Participants				Controls			
	N[b]	Before	After	Change	N[b]	Before	After	Change
1	23	7.00	7.74	.74	15	7.93	7.33	−.60
2	19	2.37	2.37	.00	13	2.08	2.00	−.08
3	19	2.05	2.05	.00	13	2.15	2.15	.00
4	22	2.18	2.00	−.18	15	1.93	1.80	−.13
5	22	2.09	2.14	.05	15	2.27	2.07	−.20
6	13	2.08	2.85	.77	15	2.13	2.07	−.06
7	13	1.85	2.15	.30	15	2.13	1.87	−.26
8	23	2.52	2.61	.09	18	2.50	2.17	−.33
9	23	1.61	1.74	.13	18	1.89	1.67	−.22
10	19	1.47	2.00	.53	13	1.31	1.69	.38
11	15	1.73	2.07	.34	11	1.82	2.27	.45
12	15	1.67	1.87	.20	11	1.91	2.09	.18
13	19	2.00	2.58	.58	16	2.38	2.44	.06
14	19	1.68	1.84	.16	16	1.62	1.62	.00
15	22	1.73	2.23	.50	19	2.16	2.26	.10

[a] See text for description of these fifteen codes.
[b] The Ns represent the number of respondents within a given group (participants or controls) who answered the question on which a particular code is based, both before and after.

ent's score on the index. Thus, a respondent who changed positively on eight codes, negatively on three codes, and not at all on four codes would receive a score of $8 - 3$ or 5. For those respondents who had failed to answer some of the questions and who could therefore not be coded on all fifteen items, the score was corrected accordingly. Thus, a respondent for whom only ten codes were ascertainable, and who changed positively on six, negatively on two, and not at all on two would receive a score of $(6 - 2) \times 15/10$ or 6. In other words, the scores were computed on the assumption that the proportion of positive and negative changes on the missing codes would have been the same as it was on the codes that were available.[2]

The mean score on this overall index for the twenty-seven participants on whom data were available was 2.56. The mean score for the twenty members of the comparison group on whom data were available was −.70. Thus, the participants did show an increase in differentiation. The controls, on the other hand, actually showed a slight decrease on the average.

In order to test the significance of these findings, we first examined the scores of each group separately. Of the twenty-seven participants, seventeen had positive scores (indicating an overall increase in differentiation from before to after), five had scores of zero, and five had negative scores. By the sign-test, this pattern is significant at the .01 level of confidence. Of the twenty controls, only six had positive scores, two had zero scores, and twelve had negative scores. The trend here was obviously in the direction of negative change, though not significantly so.

Again, the most relevant basis for evaluating these results is the comparison between participants and controls. In order to be able to apply the sign-test, we used, for the purposes of this comparison, only those twenty participants for whom we had individual controls. Table 10 presents twenty pairs of scores on the index, each pair consisting of the scores of a participant and of the comparison group member who matched him most closely. In all cases, the comparison group member was from the same country as the participant; and within each country matching was done in terms of nature and level of professional position. The pairs are arranged by continent of residence. Inspection of the table reveals that in sixteen of the twenty pairs, the participant has a higher score than his control; in three pairs the scores are identical; and in only one pair is the

---

[2] In order to make certain that the correction procedure did not produce any systematic biases, all of the comparisons between participants and controls to be reported here were also made with the use of uncorrected scores—that is, scores based on the number of positive changes minus the number of negative changes, regardless of the total number of codes involved. These analyses yielded precisely the same conclusions as those to be reported.

Table 10

SCORES ON THE INDEX OF CHANGE IN DIFFERENTIATION OF THE IMAGE OF
AMERICA FOR INDIVIDUAL PARTICIPANTS AND THEIR MATCHING CONTROLS

Continent of Residence	Participants	Controls
Africa	8	8
	8	−8
	6	−2
	5	−3
	0	−1
	0	−3
	−1	8
Asia	9	6
	8	0
	5	3
	4	3
	4	1
	2	−5
	1	0
	1	−5
	−1	−1
Europe	2	−2
	0	−2
	0	−9
	−2	−2

participant's score lower than that of his control. This pattern of scores
is statistically significant, by the sign-test, at better than the .01 level of
confidence.

In sum, the results suggest very clearly that the participants in the
seminar developed more complex and differentiated images of America
and of American broadcasting. Results from the comparison group permit
us to conclude that these changes in the participants were indeed caused
by their experience in America, which intervened between the first and
second questionnaires.

12

Images of America and the Profession: II. Changes in Content and Evaluation

In addition to the changes in differentiation of the image of America, discussed in the preceding chapter, a number of other findings emerged from the comparison between participants and controls. These additional findings must be viewed cautiously since they represent a relatively small number of systematic differences out of a large number of comparisons. Nevertheless, an examination of these findings can give us at least suggestive evidence about the nature of the changes produced by participation in the seminar.

VIEWS OF AMERICAN BROADCASTING

We examine first changes in the content of respondents' views of

American broadcasting, as revealed by their answers to Questions 2, 4, and 7; and then changes in their evaluation of American broadcasting.

Changes in image content. On Question 2, the overall amount of change in respondents' views of the actual pattern of activities in American TV was greater for participants than it was for controls (means of 4.57 versus 3.56), although the difference between the two groups was not significant by the sign-test. Examination of the individual activities, however, reveals an interesting and consistent trend: For ten out of the thirteen activities, the participants showed a decline in their rating of importance—that is, they were less likely to regard it as a major activity on the after-questionnaire than they had done on the before-questionnaire; for one activity there was no change; and for two the change was in the positive direction. Most of the changes were small, but the trend is highly consistent; a pattern of ten out of twelve changes in the same direction is significant at the .05 level by the sign-test. In contrast, for the comparison group, five changes were negative and six positive—a clearly nonsignificant pattern. If we compare the mean changes on each activity for participants and controls, we find that in eleven out of the thirteen comparisons the participants showed more negative (or less positive) change than the controls—which, again, is significant at the .05 level. The two major exceptions to the participants' tendency to rate activities as less important on the after- than on the before-questionnaire were "providing popular entertainment" and "selling products and services." These were rated as "major activities" on the after-questionnaire by *every* participant (and, for that matter, by every member of the comparison group).

Question 2 also provided information on the respondents' views of the ideal pattern of activities for American TV. Here again, changes were small but consistent: For ten out of the thirteen activities, participants showed positive change—that is, they were more likely to say on the after- than on the before-questionnaire that they thought these activities should receive *more* emphasis; for two activities they showed no change; and for only one activity ("selling products and services") they showed negative change—that is, an increased preference for *less* emphasis. This pattern is significant at the .05 level. By contrast, the comparison group showed five negative, four positive, and four zero changes. If we compare the mean changes on each activity for participants and controls, we find that in twelve out of the thirteen comparisons the participants showed more positive (or less negative) change—which is significant at the .01 level.

In short, judging from their responses to Question 2, participants (more than controls) tended to conclude (1) that most potential TV activities did not receive as much emphasis in the United States as they had originally thought; and (2) that these activities should receive more emphasis than they were in fact receiving. The interpretation of this finding is ambiguous. It certainly suggests an increased familiarity with American TV on the part of the participants, which would be consistent with the earlier finding of increased complexity and differentiation. Whether it also means some increased dissatisfaction with American TV cannot be determined on the basis of these data alone.

Turning to Question 4, we find that the participants showed more overall change than the controls in their views of what broadcasting specialists in their own countries might learn from American experiences in the field. We refer here to the difference in amount of change per se, regardless of its direction—that is, regardless of whether the change represented an increase or a decrease in the respondent's feeling that American broadcasting had positive contributions to offer. (Direction will be discussed below, when we turn to changes in evaluation of American broadcasting.) Responses to Question 4 that described American experiences of potential benefit to the respondent's own country were categorized in terms of ten content areas (for example, "program standards," "technical"). In nine out of these ten areas, participants showed more change from the before- to the after-questionnaire than did controls. Responses describing American experiences that the respondent wanted his own country to avoid were categorized in terms of eight content areas. In seven out of these eight areas, participants showed more change than controls. Both of these differences are significant at the .05 level, permitting us to conclude that the amount of reorganization (of whatever kind) of participants' views of American broadcasting was greater than that of the controls.

This reorganization was particularly marked for two substantive areas: (1) "Presentation style," which includes such matters as program format, announcing techniques, and use of commercials. Of the sixteen participants who responded to the question, ten showed some change within this area, as compared to four out of thirteen controls. (2) "Ownership and control of broadcasting system," which concerns primarily the question of commercial versus public ownership of stations and sponsorship of programs. In this area, eleven out of the sixteen participants showed some change, as compared to two out of the thirteen controls. More than half of these changes, incidentally, took the form of a *decreased* emphasis on the need to avoid American experiences in ownership and control. Many of the participants started with a negative attitude toward commercial broadcasting. It is unlikely that the observed change reflects a newly acquired preference for this type of system, but it probably does reflect the development of a less stereotyped image of it. In short, answers to Question 4 indicate that the seminar produced some reorganization of the participants' views of American broadcasting and of its relevance to their own countries, and possibly some abandonment of stereotyped images insofar as these were present at the beginning.

In response to Question 7, participants showed an increase in the number of separate areas they listed among "the most important problems facing American television today." On the before-questionnaire, the average number of content areas (that is, coding categories) within which participants mentioned problems was 2.31, on the after-questionnaire, 2.92. The mean change, thus, was .61. By contrast, the mean change for controls was −.29 (from 2.50 to 2.21). When we examine the ten content areas individually, we find that the proportion of participants who mentioned problems increased (from before- to after-questionnaires) in six areas, remained unchanged in two, and decreased in two. Comparing participants with controls, we find that the increase in the proportion of participants who mentioned problems in a given area was greater than that of the controls in eight out of the ten cases (a difference that just falls short of significance by the sign-test).

The differences between participants and controls were especially marked in two areas: "program standards" and "educational broadcasting." On the other hand, there was a marked reversal of the general trend in the area of "purpose and function of broadcasting in the society." There was a *decrease* in the proportion of participants who mentioned problems in this area, but not in the proportion of controls.

The tendency among participants to show an increase in the number of problem areas perceived may mean that, as a result of their exposure to American TV, they came to regard it as more problem-ridden than they had before. This, however, is by no means the only interpretation possible. We are more inclined to the view that this change is a consequence of their greater familiarity with American broadcasting, coupled with the fact that the seminar encouraged a more analytical approach to broadcasting and its problems in general. Consistent with this interpretation is the finding, to be reported below, that the participants showed an increase in the number of problem areas perceived, not only with respect to American broadcasting, but also with respect to their own broadcasting systems.

Participants also showed an increase, in response to Question 7, in the number of content areas within which they cited causes of the problems faced by American TV. For seven out of ten areas, the increase in the proportion of participants mentioning causes was greater than the increase in the proportion of controls. The largest difference occurred in the area of "financial limitations": There were a 46 per cent *increase* in the number of participants who mentioned inadequate financial resources as a cause of problems faced by American TV, as compared to a 23 per cent *decrease* in the number of controls who mentioned this cause. This finding is particularly interesting since it represents another change in a commonly held stereotype. Many participants assumed, when they first came to the United States, that American TV operated with unlimited financial resources, but learned that this was far from true—particularly in educational stations and local commercial stations.

Taken together, the findings so far seem to justify the conclusion that the participants experienced a greater reorganization in the content of their views of American broadcasting than did the comparison group. There are several indications that this reorganization was related to greater familiarity with American broadcasting, which led to a filling-in of details and an abandonment of certain stereotyped conceptions. These findings are in line with the observed increase in complexity and differentiation of the image of America and American broadcasting, discussed in the preceding chapter. The increased tendency among participants (as compared to controls) to say that most potential TV activities should receive greater emphasis in America, and to perceive various problems faced by American TV, is consistent with this interpretation. It may also reflect, however, some changes in the *evaluation* of American broadcasting. To explore this possibility, we turn to those data that bear more directly on the evaluative dimensions.

Changes in evaluation. Table 11 presents scores derived from the six codes relevant to the evaluative dimension. The first three of the codes listed in the table are based on answers to Question 4, which called for respondents' views of how American experiences in broadcasting might be instructive to broadcasters in their own countries. We find, first, that participants showed a very slight increase in the number of separate areas in which they felt their own broadcasting systems could benefit from American experiences; controls showed a slight decrease. Participants also showed a small increase in the number of areas in which they believed their own broadcasting systems should avoid American experiences (in which, presumably, they did not want to repeat American mistakes); but the controls showed a larger increase on this code. Thus, both participants and controls changed in the negative direction on this item, but the participants' negative change was smaller. The coders also rated responses to Question 4 on the overall extent to which the respondent perceived American experiences as having a potential contribution to make to broadcasting in his own country. Ratings were done on a four-point scale, ranging from "no contribution" (a rating of 1) to "major contribution" (a rating of 4). On this rating, participants showed a small increase from before- to after-questionnaire, while controls showed a small decrease. Thus, on all

Table 11

Mean Before-, After-, and Change-Scores on Each of Six Codes Relevant to the Evaluation of American Broadcasting

Codes	Participants				Controls			
	N	Before	After	Change	N	Before	After	Change
1. Number of content areas within which respondent feels his own broadcasting system could *benefit* from American experiences (Question 4)	16	2.44	2.50	.06	13	2.08	1.92	−.16
2. Number of content areas within which respondent feels his own broadcasting system should *avoid* American experiences (Question 4)	16	1.06	1.25	.19	13	.23	.77	.54
3. Coder rating of extent of perceived contribution of American broadcasting (Question 4)	17	3.00	3.12	.12	13	3.08	2.92	−.15
4. Coder rating of degree of favorableness of respondent's general attitude toward American TV (Questions 4, 6, and 7)	20	3.05	2.75	−.30	17	2.76	2.65	−.11
5. Respondent rating of extensiveness of coverage of information about his own country by American mass media (Question 10a)	24	2.50	2.17	−.33	17	2.12	2.29	.17
6. Respondent rating of accuracy of coverage of information about his own country by American mass media (Question 10b)	24	3.08	2.79	−.29	17	2.65	2.76	.11

three of the codes relating to the potential contribution of American experiences, the differences between participants and controls were quite small, but consistent in direction: In each case, participants became more positive (or less negative) than controls toward the possibility of contributions from American broadcasting.

In view of the consistency of the trends produced by these three items, we proceeded to combine them into an index of perceived contributions from American broadcasting. A value of +1 was added to a respondent's score on this index for each of the following: an increase in the number of areas in which he mentioned benefits from American experiences, a decrease in the number of areas in which he mentioned that American experiences should be avoided, and an increase in the coder rating of perceived contribution. A value of −1 was added to a respondent's score for a change in the opposite direction on each of these three codes. Mean scores on this index were .06 for participants and −.69 for controls. Thus, it can be said that participants did not show the decline in perceived contribution of American broadcasting evinced by the comparison group. When participants are compared to their matching controls on this index, we find more positive (or less negative) change for the participant in six out of eight pairs.[1] This difference falls short of statistical significance by the sign-test, but there is a definite trend for participants (as compared to controls) to increase their positive evaluation of the potential contributions of American experiences to broadcasting in their own countries.

The other three codes presented in Table 11, however, reveal a rather different picture. One of these codes consists in an overall rating, by the coders, of the degree of favorableness in each respondent's general attitude toward American TV. This rating, based on responses to Questions 4, 6, and 7, was made on a five-point scale ranging from "American TV is viewed in extremely unfavorable terms" (a rating of 1) to "American TV is viewed in extremely favorable terms" (a rating of 5). The remaining two codes are based on precoded questions (10a and 10b) designed to assess respondents' satisfaction with the way American mass media cover information about their own countries. Each item was scored on a five-point scale, with a score of 1 assigned to descriptions of media coverage as "not extensive at all" and "not accurate at all," and a score of 5 assigned to the responses "very extensive" and "very accurate." These two questions were on a rather different level from the others, in that they

---

[1] There are only eight pairs because of frequent failures to respond to Question 4. Whenever *either* member of the matched pair (participant or control) failed to answer a question on *either* of the two questionnaires, that pair had to be omitted from any comparison based on that particular question.

did not call for an evaluation of American broadcasting as such, in terms of its own contributions and accomplishments, but for an evaluation of how well American broadcasting (along with the other mass media) handled a specific task: coverage of information about each respondent's home country. This kind of evaluation represents not merely a professional judgment, but also a highly personal one, insofar as we can assume that the treatment accorded to a visitor's nation carries much personal significance for him.

An examination of Table 11 reveals that on the two codes reflecting the respondent's evaluation of the media coverage of his own country, as well as on the rating of overall favorableness toward American TV, the participants changed in the negative direction. The comparison group also showed a negative mean change on the rating of favorableness, but a smaller one; and small positive changes on the other two codes. Thus, on all three of these measures the participants showed a greater decline in positive evaluation than did the controls. The three codes were combined into an index of change in satisfaction with American broadcasting. For each respondent, a score was computed by assigning +1 for a positive change on any of the three codes and −1 for a negative change. Mean scores on this index were −.71 for participants and .35 for controls. When participants are compared to their matching controls, we find that participants had the lower scores (that is, manifested more negative or less positive change) in ten out of thirteen pairs. This difference just falls short of significance at the .05 level by a two-tailed sign-test. It certainly suggests, however, that there was at least a small tendency for the participants' satisfaction with American media to decline.

None of the findings presented in Table 11 is clear and strong. They do, however, represent some trends with rather interesting implications. It would seem that the participants' evaluation of American broadcasting did not change along a single dimension. The direction of change depended on the particular measure used. On the one hand, they tended to become somewhat less satisfied with American broadcasting; but on the other hand, they tended to become somewhat more inclined to see American broadcasting as a potential source of valuable contributions to their own broadcasting systems. There is certainly no necessary contradiction between these two findings. As a visitor becomes more familiar with American broadcasting, he may find various features with which he is not particularly satisfied. Thus his post-experience reactions may contain more critical comments than his earlier reactions. This would be particularly likely to happen in matters about which he himself is very knowledgeable and in which he is personally involved—such as the information about his own country transmitted by American media. To some extent, the decline in satisfaction may simply reflect a greater willingness to be critical now that he has had the opportunity to make personal observations. Yet, at the same time, the increased familiarity with American broadcasting may increase his awareness of procedures and approaches that might be quite valuable in his own situation. Thus, even though he does not like everything about American broadcasting, he comes to see it as a more useful source of relevant contributions.

It may not be too farfetched to compare this pattern to the experience of an advanced student as he becomes more fully initiated into a specialized field of knowledge: His general satisfaction with the field may decline, because he becomes more aware of its failures and limitations; but at the same time his perception of the potential contributions of the field may increase, because he has a more intimate acquaintance with the accumulated data and the available methods. If this analysis is correct, then it has some definite implications for the evaluation of international exchange programs. It suggests that one can easily draw the wrong conclusion about the effects of a program if one relies on a single measure of "favorableness"; and that a global increase in favorableness is not necessarily the most desirable outcome.

VIEWS OF AMERICA AND AMERICANS

Changes in image content. The major source of information about changes in the content of respondents' views of America was Question 15b, in which they were asked what information might be included in a feature program about the United States. The responses to this question were coded in terms of thirteen content categories. The increase (from before- to after-questionnaires) in the number of content categories covered by their responses tended to be greater among the controls than among the participants. The participants mentioned, on the average, 3.00 areas in the before-questionnaire and 3.33 in the after-questionnaire, an increase of .33. The comparable figures for the controls were 2.86 and 4.00, an increase of 1.14. The difference is not statistically significant, however. The greater increase for the controls held true in only seven out of the thirteen content areas, and in six out of nine matched pairs of participants and controls.

An examination of the specific areas reveals that the largest difference between participants and controls occurred in references to "degree of cultural diversity." Controls mentioned this point more often on the after- than on the before-questionnaire, but this change was not matched by the participants. Differences in the same direction, but of smaller magnitude, were found in three other areas: "degree of national integration," "political life," and "organization of economic life." On the other hand, controls showed a sizeable decrease in references to "cultural aspects," which covered a wide range of features of American society, including education, religion, the arts, the mass media, and well-known personalities.

These findings are very difficult to interpret. They seem inconsistent with the finding reported in the preceding chapter (see Table 9) that the participants showed a greater increase in the range of their responses to Question 15b. It may be that the participants mentioned fewer areas in their after-questionnaire responses than the controls, but that within these areas their responses were more specific and detailed. It must also be kept in mind that we are dealing with a difference that is not statistically significant and could thus represent a chance variation.

It is interesting that a similar pattern was revealed in responses to Question 13, which asked what information should be included in an American feature program about the respondent's own country. These responses were coded in terms of the same thirteen content categories as Question 15b. The participants showed a decline in the number of content categories covered by their responses, from an average of 4.50 before to 3.83 after—thus, a mean change of −.67. (In seventeen out of twenty-two cases, change was in the negative direction.) The controls showed a small increase, from 4.89 to 5.26, or a mean change of .37. Again, the difference is not statistically significant. The greater increase for the controls held true in eight out of the thirteen content areas, and in nine out of fourteen matched pairs of participants and controls. Differences occurred particularly in three areas: "national status," which dealt mainly with the country's international position and activities, "social welfare," and "organization of economic life." Participants were *less* likely to nominate these areas for inclusion in a feature program about their own countries on the after- as compared to the before-questionnaire. Controls, on the other hand, were likely to change in the opposite direction. Again, there seems to be no obvious interpretation of these findings. One possible explanation is suggested by the specific areas that accounted for most of the decline in the participants' mean number of areas: perhaps the participants became more sensitive to aspects of their own countries that might be considered controversial in the United States (for example, any indications of neutralism or socialism) and therefore deemphasized these aspects in the proposed feature program. There is, however, no independent evidence for this interpretation and it represents nothing more than a tentative speculation.

Changes in evaluation. Let us turn now to data bearing on the evaluative dimension of respondents' views of America and Americans. Five codes are relevant to this dimension and mean scores derived from these codes are presented in Table 12. The first three codes are ratings

Table 12

MEAN BEFORE-, AFTER-, AND CHANGE-SCORES ON EACH OF FIVE CODES RELEVANT TO THE EVALUATION OF AMERICA AND AMERICANS

Codes	Participants				Controls			
	N	Before	After	Change	N	Before	After	Change
1. Coder rating of degree to which the "typical American" is described as well-informed and knowledgeable about the respondent's own country (Question 11)	23	2.74	3.09	.35	17	2.53	2.18	−.35
2. Coder rating of degree to which the "typical American" is described as sympathetic to the respondent's own country (Question 11)	23	3.43	3.39	−.04	17	3.00	2.76	−.24
3. Coder rating of degree to which the "typical American" is described as accepting the respondent's own country on equal terms (Question 11)	23	3.00	2.96	−.04	17	2.77	2.71	−.06
4. Coder rating of degree of favorableness of respondent's general attitude toward America (Questions 4, 7, 11, and 15b)	23	3.09	3.26	.17	19	3.11	2.90	−.21
5. Respondent rating of adequacy of coverage of information about the U.S. by the mass media of his own country (Question 15a)	28	2.50	2.71	.21	20	2.15	2.60	.45

based on responses to Question 11, which asked how the typical American would describe the respondent's country. From these responses, it was possible to infer the respondent's attitudes toward Americans in a specific context: Americans as they observe and relate to the respondent's own country. We have no way of knowing to what extent these attitudes can be generalized to other contexts for viewing Americans, but it seems reasonable to assume that a foreign visitor's general attitude toward his hosts is strongly colored by his perception of the hosts' attitude toward the visitor's own country.

Respondents' views of Americans were coded on three five-point scales: the degree to which Americans were seen as well-informed and knowledgeable about the respondent's own country (from 1 for "very ignorant" to 5 for "very well-informed and knowledgeable"), as sympathetic to the respondent's country (from 1 for "very unsympathetic" to 5 for "very sympathetic"), and as prepared to accept the respondent's country on equal terms (from 1 for "low in acceptance, patronizing" to 5 for "high in acceptance"). On the first of these three dimensions, there was a marked difference between participants and controls: participants became more favorable in their evaluation on the after-questionnaire, while the comparison group became less favorable. On the second dimension, the difference was in the same direction but much smaller: controls again changed in the negative direction, but participants showed practically no change. On the third dimension there was no noticeable change for either group. An index combining these three ratings was constructed by adding +1 to a respondent's score for each positive change and −1 for each negative change. The mean score for participants on this index was .09, and for controls −.35. When participants are compared to their matched controls, the participants have larger change scores in ten cases and smaller ones in only three. This difference is significant by the sign-test at the .05 level. We are justified in concluding, then, that on the whole the participants' evaluation of Americans (at least within the context presented by Question 11) became relatively more favorable as a consequence of their American experience.

The fourth code in Table 12 yields similar results. This is an overall rating of the degree to which the respondent's general attitude toward America appeared to be favorable. Ratings were based on answers to Questions 4, 7, 11, and 15b, and were made on a five-point scale ranging from 1 for "America is viewed in extremely unfavorable terms" to 5 for "extremely favorable terms." On the average, participants changed in the direction of a more favorable evaluation, while controls changed in the opposite direction. Compared to their matched controls, participants showed more favorable change in eight pairs, less favorable change in three. This difference is not quite significant by the sign-test, but certainly a strong trend.

The final code presented in Table 12 is based on a precoded question (15a), in which respondents were asked to judge the adequacy of information about the United States provided by their own mass media. The relevance of this question to the evaluative dimension is only indirect. It can be assumed that, other things being equal, a respondent who is more favorably inclined toward America will be less satisfied with the information about America presented by the mass media—that is, will be more likely to feel that the information is incomplete and perhaps distorted. Even though this effect is likely to be overshadowed by other considerations, it is interesting to examine just what results this code has yielded. Responses were scored from 1 for "not too adequate" to 4 for "very adequate." As can be seen from Table 12, both participants and controls changed in the direction of greater satisfaction with the adequacy of information about the United States. However, the mean change of the participants was smaller than that of the controls—that is, their satisfaction did not increase by quite as much. When participants are compared with their matched controls, we find that they have smaller change scores in eight of the pairs and larger ones in four. This difference is not significant by the sign-test. Nevertheless, the direction of the difference is consistent with the other findings of Table 12 in that it suggests that participants became relatively more favorable in their evaluation of America as a consequence of their participation in the seminar.

In sum, whatever information we have on general images of America and Americans seems to suggest that the participants' experience in America led not only to more complex and differentiated images, but also to a generally more favorable evaluation. This, of course, must not be taken to mean that they had no criticisms of American life, but only that they tended, on the whole, to see it in a more positive light.

VIEWS OF BROADCASTING IN HOME COUNTRY

Changes in image content. As might be expected, the content of participants' views of broadcasting in their own countries underwent less change than the content of their views of American broadcasting. There were some changes, however, and they seemed to parallel changes found with respect to American broadcasting.

Answers to Question 1 reveal a slight, though nonsignificant, decline in participants' ratings of the extent to which their own TV systems stressed various activities. Of the thirteen activities listed, participants' ratings decreased in six—that is, they were less likely to regard these as major activities on the after- than on the before-questionnaire—and increased in three; there was no change in the remaining four. For the comparison group, there were four negative, six positive, and three zero changes. When the mean changes of participants and controls on each activity are compared, we find that the participants had lower scores in eight activities and higher ones in four. The specific activity in which the contrast between participants and controls was most marked was "providing information about other countries": Participants were less likely to mention this as a major activity on the after- than on the before-questionnaire; controls changed in the opposite direction. There was also a sizeable difference between the two groups on two other activities: "contributing to the creation and maintenance of national loyalty" and "providing a forum for political discussion."

In sum, it would seem that participation in the seminar may have led some individuals to reexamine their own TV systems and to conclude that some of the potential TV activities did not receive as much emphasis in their own countries as they had originally thought. While the pattern revealed by our findings is not statistically significant, it is of interest because it is similar to the pattern obtained in Question 2, the parallel question dealing with American broadcasting. This allows us to place some of the findings with regard to American broadcasting in perspective by suggesting that they may have derived—at least in part—from a broader process of rethinking professional issues stimulated by the seminar.

Question 8 also yields some results similar to those obtained on the parallel question dealing with American TV. In response to Question 7, as we have seen, participants showed an increase in the number of separate problems facing American TV that they cited. They showed a similar increase in response to Question 8, which referred to the problems faced by TV in their own countries. On the before-questionnaire, the average number of content areas (coding categories) within which participants mentioned problems was 2.64, on the after-questionnaire 3.09. Their mean change, thus, was .45. The comparable figures for the controls were 3.16 and 2.74, yielding a mean change of −.42. When we compare participants and controls, we find that the increase in the proportion of participants who mentioned problems was greater for seven out of eleven content areas. This difference is not significant by the sign-test. The one area in which the difference between participants and controls was especially marked was "public taste," which included all matters pertaining to audience preferences and reactions. Despite the fact that the pattern of change as a whole is not statistically significant, the fact that it yields trends in the same direction as Question 7 is of some interest, as we have already noted. It is at least consistent with our earlier suggestion that the increased perception of problems faced by American TV may be in part a product of the more analytical approach to broadcasting problems *in general* stimulated by participation in the seminar.

Another finding based on Question 8 can be mentioned here. There was a small, but nonsignificant, tendency for participants to show an increase in the number of content areas covered by their proposed solutions to the problems facing TV in their own countries. The number of participants proposing a particular type of solution increased in eight of the eleven content categories in terms of which solutions were coded. The controls showed an increase in only four areas. When participants and controls are compared, we find that the increase in the proportion of participants who proposed a given type of solution was greater than the increase in the proportion of controls in seven out of the eleven content areas. The areas in which the differences were greatest were "national development" and "more capital." That is, participants became relatively more likely to suggest that some general developments in the society as a whole and an increase in available funds were necessary for the solution of problems faced by TV in their own countries. On the other hand, participants became less likely to mention "improved program standards" as a solution, while controls became more likely to do so.[2] This category referred to changes within the broadcasting system itself, such as improving the quality of programs, presenting a wider range of views, or devoting more time to planning. Thus, it would seem that participants became more inclined to seek solutions in the wider social context rather than in the internal operations of their broadcasting systems.

Finally, participants showed an increase in the range of their responses to Question 8, while the comparison group showed a decrease. When participants are compared with their matched controls, we find a greater increase in the rating of range received by participants in nine pairs, a smaller increase in two, and no difference in five. This pattern is significant at the .05 level, and suggests an increase in complexity and differentiation of the participants' views of broadcasting in their own countries. There is no comparable difference between the two groups, however, in the ratings of depth of responses to Question 8.

Changes in evaluation. Let us turn now to data based on Question 3, which have some bearing on respondents' evaluation of broadcasting in their respective countries. Question 3 asked about the experiences in broadcasting in the respondent's own country that might be instructive to broadcasters in other countries. Answers were coded in terms of the

---

[2] It is interesting that the opposite pattern emerged from responses to Question 7: The proportion of participants who proposed "improved program standards" as a solution to problems faced by *American* TV increased; the proportion of controls who offered this solution decreased.

same ten categories used to code responses to Question 4. Participants showed a small decrease in the number of content areas within which they felt other broadcasting systems could benefit from their own countries: The mean number of areas mentioned on the before-questionnaire was 2.32, on the after-questionnaire 2.16, with a mean change of −.16. The controls, on the other hand, showed an increase of .47, from 1.80 to 2.27. When participants are compared with their matched controls, we find smaller change scores (that is, greater decrease or smaller increase in number of areas mentioned) for participants in seven pairs, larger change scores in three pairs, and no difference in three pairs. Similarly, when we compare the two groups area by area, we find that in seven cases there was a smaller increase (or greater decrease) in the proportion of participants mentioning a given area than in the proportion of controls; the reverse was true in two cases; and there was no difference in the tenth case. Neither of these comparisons yields differences that quite reach statistical significance by the sign-test, but a strong trend certainly emerges. It seems that participants, as compared to controls, changed in the direction of perceiving fewer areas in which other broadcasters could benefit from the experiences of their own countries.

This conclusion is also supported by the coder ratings of the overall extent to which the respondent indicated, in his response to Question 3, that his own country had a potential contribution to make to broadcasting in other countries. Ratings were done on a four-point scale, ranging from 1 for "no contribution" to 4 for "major contribution." Participants showed a small decline on this rating, from an average rating of 2.59 on the before-questionnaire to 2.50 on the after-questionnaire—a mean change of −.09. Controls showed a small increase, from 2.33 to 2.53, or a mean change of .20. When participants are compared with their matched controls, we find lower change scores for the participant in seven pairs, higher ones in three pairs, and no difference in three pairs. Again, this difference falls short of significance by the sign-test, but there seemed to be a consistent though small tendency for participants to show a decline in the perceived contribution that their own country's broadcasting experiences could make to others.

It may be of interest to note that the greatest contrast between participants and controls was in the area of "ownership and control of broadcasting system." There was little change altogether in this (or any other) area, and the difference between the two groups was marginal. But controls did tend to become more likely to see this as an area in which other broadcasters could benefit from the experiences of their own countries, while participants did not. We have already seen that, in their responses to Question 4, participants became less likely to emphasize the importance of avoiding American experiences in ownership and control. Another trend, not mentioned before, emerged in participants' responses to Question 8: In contrast to controls, they became more likely to point to "too much government intervention or political interference" as a cause of problems faced by TV in their own countries. Taken together, these different trends suggest that some of the participants may have become less certain of the advantages of public ownership and the disadvantages of private ownership than they had been before. There is no indication here of a major shift in attitude, even on the part of a small proportion of the participants, but simply an indication that they came to see more pros and cons on both sides.

The apparent decline in the participants' perceptions of the potential contributions of their own broadcasting systems probably reflects the shift in "certainty" that we have just noted. There is no indication that participants became generally more dissatisfied with their own systems. Change scores on a coder rating of degree of favorableness of each respondent's general attitude toward his own TV system, for example, showed no differences between participants and controls. Rather, it would seem, the participants became somewhat less *certain* of the advantages of their own systems relative to those of others. They might have come to see some of their own procedures as representing one of a number of possible approaches to broadcasting, each of which had its own assets and liabilities. In particular, they might have concluded that, while their own procedures might be ideally suited to their own circumstances, they might not be equally suited to the circumstances that prevailed in other countries. As a result, they might have become less certain of the benefits that others could derive from the experiences in their own countries—without, however, necessarily becoming less satisfied with their own procedures.

There is one other finding based on Question 3 that appears somewhat paradoxical. On the rating of depth of responses to Question 3, the participants showed a decline from the before- to the after-questionnaire. Their mean change-score was $-.36$, compared to a mean of .07 for the comparison group. When participants are compared with their matched controls, we find lower change scores (a greater decrease in rating of depth) in seven pairs, no difference in six pairs, and a higher score in only one pair. There was no difference between the two groups, however, on the rating of range of response. The only explanation of this finding that suggests itself is that participants' responses to Question 3 might have become less rich and detailed because—in line with our interpretation above —they had become less certain of the contributions their own broadcasting systems could make to others. Thus, they might have been less inclined to dwell and elaborate on the potential contributions; this in turn would have led to a lower rating of depth.

In sum, the pattern of changes in participants' views of broadcasting in their own countries suggests that the seminar had stimulated a certain amount of new thinking about the activities, problems, and values of their own broadcasting systems. In part, this probably reflected a process of examination and analysis of *general* issues in broadcasting, resulting from the observations and discussions in which the participants had engaged. This interpretation is supported by the fact that some of the changes in participants' views of broadcasting in their own countries closely paralleled changes in their views of American broadcasting. In part, changes in participants' views of their own broadcasting systems probably resulted from the opportunity to compare their own systems with those of other countries, including the United States. There is no indication that participants became generally less satisfied with their own systems as a result of such comparisons. They showed no systematic decline in favorable attitudes toward broadcasting at home. Moreover, they became more inclined to seek solutions for the problems of their own systems in the wider context within which these systems operated rather than in their internal procedures. But there is a definite indication that they became less certain of the contributions that their own systems could make to broadcasting in other countries. It would seem that they became more aware of the relative advantages and disadvantages of different approaches, and thus less convinced of the general applicability of some of their own procedures.

PROFESSIONAL ROLE

Changes in definition of the professional role. Question 20 attempted to assess each respondent's definition of his profession by asking him to indicate the other professions to which it was most similar and least similar in various respects. A number of indices were developed to measure the amount of change in role definition revealed by answers to Question 20. No consistent differences on these indices were found between participants and controls, and there is no indication of any major redefinition of their professional roles on the part of participants.

There was some tendency, however, for participants to show more change in their assessment of the importance of various activities that might be involved in their jobs. Question 16 asked respondents to rate each of ten activities as very important, somewhat important, slightly important, or not important to their jobs. A numerical value, ranging from 4 to 1, was assigned to each rating. By comparing the ratings on the before-questionnaire to those on the after-questionnaire, we obtained measures of change (regardless of direction) for each activity. These were then summed, over the ten activities, to yield a total change-score for each individual. The mean change-score on this index was 5.18 for participants and 4.43 for the comparison group. When participants are compared to their matched controls, we find larger scores for the participants in twelve pairs, smaller scores in eight pairs, and no difference in one. When we compare the two groups activity by activity, we find that the participants' mean change-score is higher in six cases, lower in three cases, and the same in one. Neither of these comparisons yields a difference that is statistically significant by the sign-test, but there does seem to be a trend among participants to change more in their perception of the activities associated with their jobs.

The specific activities for which the difference between participants and controls was greatest were "public relations" and "the commercial side of communication." That is, in both of these areas, a large number of participants—relative to the number of controls—manifested some change, assigning either greater or lesser importance to these activities than they had done on the before-questionnaire. Since there were no obvious systematic differences between the two groups in terms of actual changes in the nature of their activities (see Chapter Ten), we can assume that this finding reflects a change in participants' *perception* of their activities. Comparison of their own activities with those of their American counterparts might have led to a change in their definitions of "public relations" and "the commercial side of communication," which in turn could account for the change in their assessment of how much these activities were involved in their own work. Alternatively, comparison with their American counterparts might have led to a change in their evaluation of these activities, which in turn could have caused them to place either more or less emphasis on them in their own work.

There was one other activity on which there was a fairly sizeable difference between participants and controls, although in this case the difference was not in the overall amount of change, but in change in a particular direction. Participants tended to attach increasing importance to "contact with international developments in communications" as an aspect of their job, while controls showed no consistent change in this direction. This change may reflect formal changes in the nature of some participants' jobs, or—more probably—changes in the way in which they carried out their jobs or in their evaluation of the importance of this particular type of activity. In any event, it suggests that there was at least some change in the direction of internationalization of the participants' professional activities.

In sum, there is some evidence of change in participants' views of their professional roles on the descriptive level. They showed somewhat greater change in their perception of the activities involved in their work than did the members of the comparison group, although the differences were by no means marked. Let us now examine evidence of changes on the more personal, affective level.

Changes in satisfaction with the professional role. Of most direct relevance to change on the personal, affective level was Question 17, which concerned respondents' satisfaction with their work. Analysis of responses to this question reveals no consistent differences between participants and controls in their degree of satisfaction with their work, or in the aspects of their work that provided them with the greatest satisfaction, or in the aspects of their work that caused them the most dissatisfaction.

An interesting difference did emerge, however, in responses to Questions 18 and 19. Question 18 asked respondents to indicate what they *hoped* to be doing in five years, under the best of circumstances. Question 19 asked them what they *expected* to be doing in five years, given the circumstances that were likely to prevail. Answers to Question 18 were coded on a three-point scale of level of aspiration, with a rating of 1 representing the low end of the continuum and a rating of 3 the high end. Answers to Question 19 were coded on a similar three-point scale of level of expectation. The congruity of hopes and expectations was also rated on a three-point scale, based on a comparison of answers to the two questions. A rating of 1 was assigned if a respondent's aspirations were much greater than his expectations, a rating of 2 if they were somewhat greater, and a rating of 3 if his aspirations and expectations were very close. Mean scores for participants and controls on these three codes are presented in Table 13. Changes were small, but on all three of these codes participants changed in the positive direction, while the comparison group changed in the negative direction. The three codes were combined into an index of change in positive orientation toward the professional future. A score on this index was computed for each respondent by adding +1 for each of the three codes on which he changed in the positive direction and −1 for each item on which he changed in the negative direction. Mean scores on this index were .35 for the participants and −.12 for the controls. When participants are compared with their matched controls, we find higher scores for participants in eight pairs, lower scores in two pairs, and no difference in four pairs. This pattern barely misses statistical significance at the .05 level by the sign-test.

There seems to be sufficient justification for concluding that participants in the seminar tended to become more positive in their orientation toward their own professional future. They showed some increase

Table 13

MEAN BEFORE-, AFTER-, AND CHANGE-SCORES ON EACH OF THREE CODES RELEVANT TO THE RESPONDENT'S
ORIENTATION TOWARD HIS PROFESSIONAL FUTURE

| | | Participants | | | | Controls | | |
Codes	N	Before	After	Change	N	Before	After	Change
1. Level of aspiration	25	2.36	2.56	.20	17	2.53	2.41	−.12
2. Level of expectation	23	1.87	1.91	.04	16	1.75	1.56	−.19
3. Congruity of aspiration and expectation	23	2.17	2.39	.22	15	2.07	2.00	−.07

(relative to the comparison group) in their level of aspiration, that is, in the professional position that they hoped to achieve and the scope and quality of the operation that they hoped to be in charge of. At the same time, they showed an increase in the congruity of hopes and expectations: They tended not only to increase in their level of aspiration, but also in their confidence that they would be able to achieve this level.

It must be stressed that this effect, like most other effects presented in this chapter, was of relatively small proportions. Only some of the participants changed in the direction indicated, and those who did often changed only to a small degree. When we state, on the basis of a comparison between participants and controls, that there is a statistically significant or near-significant difference, we are only saying that the participants as a group showed a noticeable change on the dimension in question, which is most probably attributable to participation in the seminar rather than to chance fluctuation. A change for the group as a whole can be significant, that is, noticeable and consistent, without being large in absolute terms and without affecting every member of the group. What such a finding tells us, essentially, is that experiences of the type provided by participation in the seminar are *capable* of producing this type of change. And this, it seems to us, is precisely what we need to know for purposes of evaluation. It goes without saying that not everyone was affected to the same degree and in the same way—some individuals changed in some respects, and some in others; and that the questionnaire captured only a small part of the impact of the total experience.

13

High and Low Differentiators

We have seen in Chapter Eleven that the major variable distinguishing participants from controls in their performance on the questionnaire was the degree of change in differentiation of their image of America and American broadcasting. Scores of participants on our index of change in differentiation exceeded scores of the controls at better than the .01 level of confidence. Thus, at least in this instance, participation in an experience that involved exposure to and discussion of American broadcasting and American life in general was associated with an increase in the organized detail with which the participants thought about these phenomena.

This outcome, at first blush, is less than startling. It merely shows that one who has gone to America knows America in more detail than one who has not. On reflection, however, this seemingly obvious result becomes less inevitable. Alternative outcomes would have been plausible too. For example, it is conceivable that broadcasting specialists (and other individuals in relatively high positions within their own societies) would already be so saturated with knowledge about America that an exchange program would add little to their image. If so, we would not have ob-

185

tained the significant increase in differentiation revealed by the question-naires. It is also conceivable that participants, either because of negative preconceptions about America or because of bad experiences during their sojourn, might have avoided genuine exposure to the new information confronting them. They might have viewed America from a distance and in global terms, and thus again they would have failed to manifest a more differentiated image.

If, therefore, this increase in the differentiation with which par-ticipants view America and American broadcasting is *not* an obvious and necessary consequence of the visit, then it becomes an important target for further analysis. What is it about the experience and the individuals undergoing it that accounts for this outcome? What can we discover about the process by which increasing differentiation takes place?

One way of approaching answers to these questions is to compare those individuals who show the most pronounced change on the dimension of differentiation with those who show the least change on this dimension. By examining the characteristics and the interview responses of those who show the change (as compared to those who do not), we can gain some insight into the determinants of this change—into what it is about these individuals, about the nature of their experiences, and about the way in which they responded to these experiences that might account for the effect. Such an analysis also provides some basis for inferences about the process of change, although of necessity these are of a speculative nature.

To find a basis for making the desired comparisons, we ordered the twenty-eight participants in terms of their scores on the index of change in differentiation. Eight participants were then excluded from the ranking because they either had scores too close to the median or had failed to answer enough of the relevant questionnaire items. This left ten individuals with high scores on the index and ten with low scores. For ease of exposition we shall refer to them as *high differentiators* (or *highs*) and *low differentiators* (or *lows*) although it must be kept in mind that the distinction is based not on high versus low differentiation in absolute terms, but on high versus low *change* in differentiation. The mean score of high differentiators on the index is +5.30; the mean score of low dif-ferentiators is −1.30.[1]

The high and low differentiators do not seem to differ from each other in terms of their initial level of differentiation on the questionnaire. For each participant, before-scores on the fifteen codes that are relevant

[1] Scores for the High and Low Differentiators were checked to rule out the possibility that high or low change depended upon unusually low or high scores on the first administration of the questionnaire. Change scores were recalculated for all twenty respondents, eliminating all items for which ceiling effects could be alleged. Use of these alternative scores did not change the composition of the two groups.

to differentiation were summed. The mean score for the high differentiators is almost identical to that for the low differentiators: 31.17 as compared to 31.71. By contrast, mean scores on the after-questionnaire are 38.97 and 29.58, respectively.[2]

PRELIMINARY COMPARISONS

Our major comparisons between high and low differentiators are based on their interview responses. Before proceeding to these data, however, let us examine some of the differences in the compositions of the two groups, in their group behavior as rated by the observer, and in their changes in attitude as assessed by the questionnaires.

Group characteristics. When we compare high and low differentiators in terms of their areas of specialization, we find a somewhat greater tendency for the highs to be in educational broadcasting (six highs versus three lows). With respect to national origin, we were particularly interested in the distribution of Europeans and non-Europeans over the two groups. We shall spell out more fully in the next chapter that we are using the term "Europeans" in the present context not only for individuals who resided in Europe, but also for those who—while residing on other continents—were European in terms of their ethnic and cultural origins. "Non-Europeans," in this context, come from societies that are largely nonwhite and nonindustrialized. Change in differentiation shows no strong relationship to European versus non-European origin, but when we subdivide both Europeans and non-Europeans, an interesting pattern emerges:

	High differentiators	*Low differentiators*
Europeans		
From English-speaking countries	6	0
From non-English-speaking countries	0	4
Non-Europeans		
From African countries	0	4
From other countries	4	2

We can see from this breakdown that all Europeans from English-speaking

---

[2] The differences between before-scores and after-scores are not equivalent to scores on the index of change in differentiation, because scores on the index were computed by adding the number of items (out of the fifteen constituting the index) on which the respondent showed positive change and subtracting the number of items on which he showed negative change. Before- and after-scores, on the other hand, were computed by adding the actual scores the respondent received on each of the fifteen items.

countries (among this group of twenty participants) turned out to be high differentiators. All of the Africans and all of the Europeans from non-English-speaking countries turned out to be low differentiators. The latter four individuals, incidentally, were all people who had at least some difficulty with the English language and expressed serious concern about their English-speaking capacity.

This distribution suggests that increased differentiation may be related to the ease with which a visitor can enter into the give-and-take of a searching interaction with members of the host society. It may well be that marked increases in differentiation require conversations and encounters with Americans that go beyond superficial generalities and thus enable the newcomer to become aware of the wide variety of Americans and of the viewpoints they represent, and to share in the complex picture Americans have of their own culture. Such encounters can occur more easily when visitor and host share the same language and a similar culture; large cultural differences and language barriers—although they can certainly be overcome—may slow down or inhibit these encounters. If so, it is not surprising that the high differentiators included those participants whose native language was English and who, coming from the British orbit, shared much of the culture of the American hosts. The low differentiators, on the other hand, consisted almost entirely of two subsets of individuals: those whose cultural background was most distant from that of the Americans, and those who were somewhat handicapped by language problems.

Observational data. Data based on the ratings by the group observer seem to be consistent with the notion that high differentiators were able to enter into reciprocal interactions with Americans more readily and with greater ease than low differentiators. As was noted in Chapter Three, most of the scheduled group sessions during the university phase of the seminar were attended by a trained observer. Among other things, he made weekly ratings for each individual's behavior in the group along a number of dimensions, listed and defined in Appendix A.

Figure 1 provides a graphic presentation of the differences in group behavior between high and low differentiators on six dimensions, as rated by the group observer. (On the remaining dimensions listed in Appendix A no consistent differences between the groups could be detected.) It is apparent that high differentiators received consistently higher ratings in leadership, participation, and involvement in the group sessions, and usually also in the extent to which they made innovative contributions (for example, by introducing a new topic or approach). Dependent behavior was hardly ever observed; when it was, however, it almost always

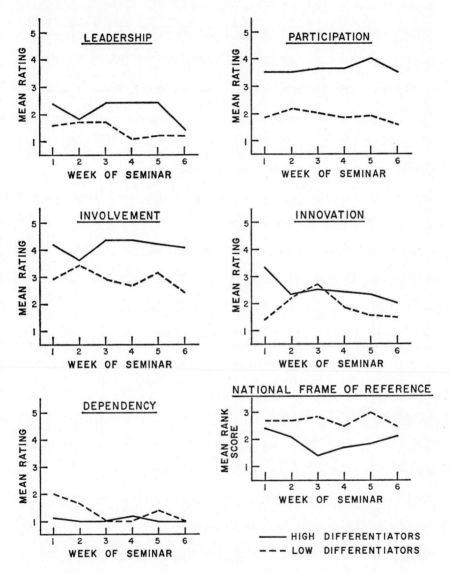

Figure 1. Weekly mean ratings of the behavior of high and low differentiators in scheduled group sessions on each of six dimensions.

occurred among the lows, particularly during the first two weeks of the seminar.

In short, the High Differentiators exhibited a consistently more active and independent pattern of interaction in the group sessions. Most of these interactions, it should be noted, centered around the American staff members or visitors who gave presentations and led the discussions. It is reasonable to suppose that the high differentiators were more ready to engage in such interactions because of the greater cultural familiarity and linguistic facility they brought to them. If they displayed a similar pattern in their interactions outside of the group meetings—during the university phase as well as the travel phase of the seminar—they surely had adequate opportunities for developing an increasingly differentiated image of America and its broadcasting system.

The last graph in Figure 1 requires some explication. The observer ranked three frames of reference—national, professional, and idiosyncratic —in terms of the degree to which they governed each participant's remarks during the group sessions of the preceding week. This ranking, of course, could not be done if a participant did not speak at all during the week, which happened in quite a few cases, particularly among low differentiators. Some of the mean rank scores are, therefore, based on a very small number of cases and are likely to be quite unreliable. Though we must view these findings with caution, it is interesting that lows were most prone to adopt a national frame of reference and least prone to adopt a professional one; highs adopted all three frames of reference with approximately equal frequency. The graph shows mean rank scores for the two groups in use of national frame of reference; curves for professional frame of reference (which are, of course, not independent, being based on the same ranking) show the opposite relationship.

This pattern suggests that lows reacted in the group session with greater caution and less engagement in the issues. They tended to adopt the stance of a national representative, which is the role into which foreign travelers are typically cast by their hosts in superficial interactions and which they can play most comfortably; among other things, it is a role that automatically places them in the position of experts vis-à-vis their hosts, who can report on the way things are done in their own countries. They rarely adopted the role of professional, which would have involved them more fully in discussions around substantive problems and entailed greater risks of exposure. This finding is consistent, then, with the view that the lows were less ready than the highs to engage in reciprocal interactions with the Americans they encountered.

Questionnaire data. The two groups that we are comparing in this chapter were selected on the basis of their different patterns of change in questionnaire responses along one particular dimension. We might be able to gain a fuller understanding of the meaning of high versus low standing on this dimension by examining what other changes in questionnaire responses are correlated with it. To this end, we compared high and low differentiators in terms of the changes they showed on the various codes by which the questionnaire responses had been analyzed (other than those codes, of course, that entered into the differentiation index).

Our most consistent finding is that change in differentiation appears to represent a very general pattern. On every measure that bears a logical relationship to differentiation, the highs showed more change than the lows. Items directly assessing differentiation of the image of America and American broadcasting were, of course, included in the differentiation index. There were, however, several other codes categorizing the content of these images that one would expect to reflect differences in differentiation. Thus, answers to Question 15b enabled us to count the number of content areas that respondents employed in describing the United States. Answers to Question 4 provided measures of the number of areas in which the respondent felt that his own broadcasting system could learn from the American broadcasting experience. Answers to Question 7 yielded counts of the number of different problems facing American television identified by the respondent, the number of causes of these problems that he perceived, and the number of solutions that he offered. On all of these codes, the highs showed greater change than the lows. Though the differences are not always significant, the pattern is completely consistent.

A number of codes measured the degree of differentiation of the respondent's image of his own country's broadcasting system. Thus, Question 8 yielded counts of the number of different problems facing television in his country as identified by the respondent, the number of causes of these problems that he perceived, and the number of solutions to these problems that he offered. Answers to Question 8 were also rated by the coder in terms of their range and depth. Question 3 provided a measure of the number of areas in which the respondent felt other broadcasting systems could learn from the experience of his own country. Again, the range and depth of responses to Question 3 were rated by the coder. On each of these eight codes, the highs showed greater change than the lows, although for the codes based on Question 3 the differences were very small.

All in all, these data show that the increase in differentiation manifested by the highs represents a general and consistent impact that the American sojourn had on their images. The impact was not restricted to the particular set of items that entered into the differentiation index. More importantly, it was not restricted to images of America and American broadcasting, but also extended to their views of broadcasting in their own countries.

In contrast to the rather clearcut differences between highs and lows on cognitive dimensions, results on the evaluative dimensions showed no such consistent relationships. The various items that assessed favorableness to America produced no significant differences between the two groups, nor did changes fall into a discernible pattern. Respondents' evaluations of American broadcasting and of broadcasting in their own countries also failed to yield significant differences and present a somewhat ambiguous picture. Here, however, a consistent pattern of some interest emerges. The coder made two ratings relevant to the respondent's evaluation of American broadcasting, and two parallel ratings relevant to his evaluation of his own country's broadcasting system. Results for these four ratings are presented in Table 14.

None of the differences in mean change-scores between high and low differentiators is significant. The pattern of differences, however, as can be seen in Table 14, is completely consistent. In each case, highs became less positive in their evaluations while lows became more positive. Changes were small, and there is no indication that highs actually came to reject either the American or their own broadcasting systems. Rather, it would seem that high differentiators became more critical in their analysis of broadcasting, and this introduced a somewhat more negative tone into their descriptions of broadcasting in the United States as well as at home. Such a change would be completely in keeping with the increased differentiation in images by which this group is defined.

In sum, the questionnaire data suggest that the differentiation index distinguishes two groups displaying rather general and consistent differences in their patterns of change. High differentiators developed more complex and elaborate views, not only of America and American broadcasting, but also of broadcasting in their own countries. It would seem that their whole approach to the experience—both in relating themselves to the novel environment and in grappling with professional issues—was more analytical and more oriented toward fine nuances and concrete details than that of the low differentiators, leading to the observed increase in the differentiation of their attitudes. These changes in the cognitive structure of the highs' attitudes had no uniform effects on the evaluative dimension. Thus, their images of the United States did not become significantly more favorable than those of the low differentiators; it is likely that, as they filled out and enriched these images, they became more appreciative of some features of American life but more dubious about others. On the other hand, they showed a consistent—though nonsignificant—tendency to become more critical toward broadcasting practices both in the United States and in their own countries; it is likely that these changes resulted from the analytical scrutiny to which they had subjected

Table 14

MEAN BEFORE-, AFTER-, AND CHANGE-SCORES ON EACH OF FOUR CODER RATINGS RELEVANT TO THE RESPONDENT'S EVALUATION OF AMERICAN BROADCASTING AND OF BROADCASTING IN HIS OWN COUNTRY

Codes	High Differentiators				Low Differentiators			
	N	Before	After	Change	N	Before	After	Change
1. Rating (on a 5-point scale) of degree of favorableness of respondent's general attitude toward American TV (Questions 4, 6, and 7)	7	3.00	2.43	−.57	10	2.90	3.00	.10
2. Rating (on a 4-point scale) of extent of perceived contribution of American broadcasting (Question 4)	7	3.14	2.86	−.28	8	2.88	3.12	.24
3. Rating (on a 5-point scale) of degree of favorableness of respondent's general attitude toward TV or its development in his own country (Questions 3, 6, and 8)	9	3.00	2.78	−.22	9	2.78	3.00	.22
4. Rating (on a 4-point scale) of extent of perceived contribution of own broadcasting system (Question 3)	10	2.70	2.30	−.40	8	2.25	2.75	.50

the whole field of broadcasting during their American sojourn and after their return home.

Hypotheses. The data presented so far indicate that high differentiators (1) brought greater cultural familiarity and linguistic facility to their American experience than did low differentiators, (2) were able to enter more easily into intensive and reciprocal interactions with Americans, and (3) generally related themselves to the host society and to professional issues in a more analytical fashion. These points suggest two hypotheses—by no means mutually exclusive—to account for the increased differentiation among the highs.

The first hypothesis very simply proposes that the highs' familiarity with the host culture and language made it easier for them to assimilate new information and to relate it to a preexisting cognitive framework. They were thus able to approach what they saw and heard about American society and broadcasting more analytically and to emerge with more complex and differentiated images.

The second hypothesis is more interesting in that it conceives of the highs' increased differentiation as mediated by a special pattern of social interaction. It proposes that the highs' greater cultural and linguistic communalities with Americans enabled them to establish more readily a pattern of intensive interaction with their hosts and to engage in the give-and-take of probing conversations. This type of interaction, in turn, acquainted them with the diverse viewpoints held by a variety of Americans and with the complex conceptions these Americans had of their own society. Through the process of observing and discussing these American viewpoints and conceptions, their own images became increasingly differentiated.

It seems reasonable to expect that both of these hypothesized effects were operative. Let us keep these two possibilities in mind, then, as we turn to the interview responses of the high and low differentiators. Examination of the interview data may help us trace the processes out of which the different outcomes for the two groups evolved.

INTERVIEW RESPONSES

In the sections that follow we shall present and discuss all of the codes on which there was at least a 30 per cent difference between high and low differentiators. For example, on the basis of responses to some of the questions in the first interview, the coders were asked to check whether a given participant felt that his own special technical skills or knowledge would enable him to make a special contribution to the seminar. It turns out (see Table 15) that the coders checked "yes" for eight of the ten high differentiators and for only five of the ten low differentiators. We

have here, then, a 30 per cent difference between the two groups—just
large enough to meet our criterion for differences we consider worth
noting. Given the extremely small size of our sample, a difference of 30
per cent (which is a frequency difference of three cases) is very unstable
and does not meet the conventional criteria of statistical significance. It
would be a mistake, therefore, to draw any conclusions on the basis of a
single item. Our purpose, however, is to examine clusters of items—within
a given substantive domain—and to see whether they reveal a consistent
pattern. Only if a whole set of items seems to point in the same direction
are we justified in concluding that there is a real difference between the
two groups we are comparing.

   Expectations and goals for the trip. Table 15 presents those items

Table 15

EXPECTATIONS AND GOALS FOR THE TRIP:
COMPARISON OF HIGH AND LOW DIFFERENTIATORS

Items that Discriminate[a]	Number of Respondents to Whom Each Item Applies	
	Highs	*Lows*
1. Professional goals and self-image		
The most important thing the participant hopes to accomplish is to add to his store of professional knowledge and experience	9	6
He previously considered visiting America, to add to his professional knowledge and experience	8	4
He feels that participation in the seminar will result in promotion to a more responsible position	4	1
He feels that he possesses special technical skills or knowledge in broadcasting which could make a unique contribution to the seminar	8	5
He feels that the diversity in professional background, knowledge, and skills of the seminar participants may lower the level of discussion	4	0
2. Preparations and plans for the trip		
He made special preparations for the trip	8	4
To prepare for the trip, he read some of the books about America that were sent to him	4	7

[a] All of these items are taken from the first interview.

Table 15 (Continued)

EXPECTATIONS AND GOALS FOR THE TRIP:
COMPARISON OF HIGH AND LOW DIFFERENTIATORS

Items that Discriminate[a]	Number of Respondents to Whom Each Item Applies	
	Highs	*Lows*
He has a clear idea of the specific itinerary he desires for the travel period	5	2
He intends to contact some of his prior American acquaintances during the trip	10	6
He intends to contact other specific individuals, with whom he is not yet personally acquainted, during the trip	9	6

3. Anticipated new learnings about America

He anticipates that the academic seminars will give him a chance to fill out or revise previous notions about America	6	3
He anticipates that his travels will allow him to get better acquainted with the average American	1	6
One of the impressions of America that he wants to verify is how high its standard of living really is	5	8
The impressions of America that he wants to verify		
cover a broad range	2	6
are not very detailed and elaborated	5	8

4. Anticipated problems and difficulties

He anticipates language difficulties	1	4
He anticipates difficulties in connection with the academic seminars	2	6
. . . because of his poor knowledge of English	1	5
He did not have enough opportunity to prepare for the trip because the final invitation came too late	8	2
He feels that this is not a good time for him to be in America	3	0

[a] All of these items are taken from the first interview.

that show differences in the expectations and goals with which high and low differentiators approached the seminar. All of these items are based on the initial interview, conducted within a few days after participants' arrival at the university.

The first set of items suggests that the high differentiator, as compared to the low, was more likely to have come to America feeling that he was a competent professional in search of a helpful professional experience. The high, we see, had previously wanted to come to the United States specifically in order to add to his professional knowledge. Such professional considerations also constituted his major goal for the present visit. Not only did he hope to increase his professional knowledge and experience, but he also anticipated (more often than the low) that taking part in the seminar would lead to promotion to a more responsible position. The professional self-confidence of the high was shown in his conviction that his skills or knowledge were such that he could make a unique contribution to the seminar, and in his fear that the diversity of the seminar participants might lower the level of discussion—presumably from the level of which he himself would be capable.

As can be seen from the second set of items in Table 15, the highs also had more specific plans for their sojourn. They were more likely to have made special preparations for the trip before leaving home—perhaps by corresponding with people they wanted to see or by preparing samples of their own work that they hoped to demonstrate. In one respect, however, the lows showed greater preparation: They were more likely to report having read the books about America that the director of the seminar had sent to them. This type of preparation probably reflected the lows' comparative unfamiliarity with the American scene and with more specific methods for planning for the trip. In discussing the travel period, the highs communicated a clearer idea of the specific itinerary they wanted to pursue. They were also more likely to mention plans of contacting prior American acquaintances, as well as other specific Americans whose acquaintance they were eager to make.

The two groups also seemed to differ in their anticipations of what they would learn about America in the course of their sojourn. The highs were more likely to imply that they already had a fairly well-developed framework for viewing America which they would be able to fill out, and if necessary revise, with the help of the academic seminars. The lows, on the other hand, had less specific and refined expectations. They anticipated that their travels would allow them to become better acquainted with the average American, and they hoped to check the validity of their impression that America had a high standard of living. In other words, they expected to obtain certain general, basic notions about America, rather than to add detail to an already existing map. Our coders' ratings of the impressions of America that respondents wanted to verify suggest that the new learnings anticipated by the lows covered a broader range than those anticipated by the highs, but that they were less detailed and elaborated—in short, less differentiated.

Finally, the fourth set of items in Table 15 includes one finding that follows directly from what we already know about the characteristics of the two groups: The lows, who included a number of individuals whose English was less than fluent, were more likely to anticipate language difficulties, particularly in the academic seminars. The last two items in the table do not fit into any obvious pattern, but they are consistent with the greater professional self-confidence of the highs that we have already noted. Being more secure in their own status as important and busy professionals whose time is limited and valuable, they may have been more ready to criticize the organizers of the seminar for sending out the invitations too late, and more inclined to feel that they really could not afford the time that they had taken off to come to America. Moreover, since highs—as we have seen above—were more likely to make special preparations for the trip, they were naturally more likely to feel that the short notice limited their opportunity to do so.

In sum, the data presented in Table 15 suggest that the highs arrived in the United States with a greater degree of readiness to enter into intensive interactions with their hosts and to engage in probing conversations, as we have hypothesized. It was to be expected that their greater self-confidence about their professional roles would make them more comfortable in their interactions with professional counterparts; that the greater specificity of their goals and plans would allow them to minimize floundering and to connect more quickly with people and issues; and that their greater linguistic facility and more fully developed framework for viewing America would lower the barriers to productive communication. The readiness to enter into intensive interactions, in turn, would account for the greater increase in differentiation of the highs' images.

The indications that the highs brought to their experience not only a greater linguistic facility, but also a better-articulated framework for viewing America are equally consistent with the first of the two hypotheses with which we entered these data. According to the evidence we have, the highs did not start out with more differentiated images of America and American broadcasting; but, given their more fully developed framework for approaching America, it was to be expected that, once exposed to new information through observation and discussion, they would be able to scan and assimilate it more quickly and to treat it more analytically, which would help to account for their greater tendency to develop more differentiated images.

A further point, though minor, will become important in the context of additional findings: Although the highs came to the seminar primarily with professional goals and expectations for its relevance to their professional careers, they approached also the academic seminars with positive expectations. In particular, they saw them as an opportunity to fill out and revise their ideas about America. There is at least a hint here that the highs may have had multiple agenda—alternative possibilities for turning the experience to their advantage even if it proved to be professionally disappointing.

Satisfactions, perceived accomplishments, and perceived impact of trip. Table 16 presents the large array of items that show differences between highs and lows in their satisfactions with the sojourn and in their perceptions of what they accomplished and what impact the trip had upon them.

The first set of items shows that, by the time of the second interview (that is, toward the end of the university phase of the seminar), highs were less satisfied with their sojourn than lows. Moreover, lows were more likely to report that they had become more satisfied as the seminar proceeded, and highs that they had become less satisfied. Clearly, the highs had found the university phase of the seminar disappointing. The source of this disappointment, as the second set of items suggests, was largely in the professional area. The highs were less likely to locate their most important accomplishments or their most enjoyable experiences in the professional area. They attached less value to the opportunity of listening to the various speakers brought to the professional seminars and to the amount they had learned about mass communications in America. The extent and nature of their dissatisfaction with the professional experience will be presented in considerable detail in the next section, based on Table 17.

It would seem that the lows, who had arrived with a lower level of professional self-confidence and with more diffuse professional goals, found the professional offerings at the university of sufficient quality to engage their interests and meet their needs. If they experiencd any problems, they tended to ascribe them to their own linguistic or professional deficiencies (see the third set of items in Table 16), rather than to the organization of the seminar. They appreciated the new information to which they were exposed, and came away feeling that they had participated in a fruitful and enjoyable professional experience. The highs, on the other hand, who had arrived feeling professionally competent and eager for a productive professional experience, found the professional

Table 16

SATISFACTIONS, PERCEIVED ACCOMPLISHMENTS,
AND PERCEIVED IMPACT OF TRIP:
COMPARISON OF HIGH AND LOW DIFFERENTIATORS

Items that Discriminate	*Number of Respondents to Whom Each Item Applies*	
	Highs	*Lows*
1. Second interview: Level of satisfaction		
The participant's feelings about his visit to America are generally positive	6	9
His feelings, since arrival, have become		
more positive	1	5
less positive	4	1
2. Second interview: Sources of satisfaction and accomplishment during university phase		
He perceives his most important accomplishment as being in an area of specific, direct professional use	2	5
He perceives his most enjoyable experience		
as being in the professional area	0	3
as involving interpersonal aspects of the American environment	6	3
Among his most noteworthy, valuable, or enjoyable experiences he cites		
listening to some of the professional speakers	3	7
exposure to the academic seminars	5	1
He feels that he has learned a great deal about mass communications in America	3	7
The American sojourn has made him more aware of the need for more rapid advancement in education in his home country	0	3
3. Second interview: Problems during university phase		
He feels that his problems have resulted from his own shortcomings, such as deficiencies in background or in language	0	4
Something has come up at home to make him wish he were there	5	1
4. Third interview: Problems during travel phase		
Something has come up at home to make him wish he were there	2	5
. . . more specifically, a problem of a personal nature	1	5

Table 16 (Continued)

SATISFACTIONS, PERCEIVED ACCOMPLISHMENTS, AND PERCEIVED IMPACT OF TRIP: COMPARISON OF HIGH AND LOW DIFFERENTIATORS

Items that Discriminate	Number of Respondents to Whom Each Item Applies	
	Highs	Lows
5. *Third interview: Sources of satisfaction and accomplishment during travel phase*		
He perceives his most important accomplishment during the travel period as being		
in the professional area	9	6
not in the professional area	1	4
Among his most important accomplishments he cites		
learning more about the pattern of mass communication in America	5	8
making new friends	0	3
Among his important and enjoyable experiences he mentions professionally relevant ones, such as visits to broadcasting stations	6	9
He reports that he was able to do everything he planned to do during his professional visits	4	7
He has learned new approaches to programming that will be of direct use to him after return home	0	3
He made many contacts that he plans to maintain	3	6
He feels that he had an adequate opportunity to observe the features of American life he had wanted to observe during his travels	10	6
6. *Fourth interview: Sources of satisfaction and accomplishment during entire sojourn*		
He feels that, in general, the seminar was sufficiently suited to his particular background and interests	8	5
Among his most important accomplishments, he cites		
gaining a greater knowledge about TV in America	3	6
gaining a greater knowledge about America's institutional structure, its political and economic system	5	2
Among his most meaningful or enjoyable experiences he cites		
exposure to new program ideas	3	6
exposure to the academic seminars	4	0

Table 16 (Continued)

SATISFACTIONS, PERCEIVED ACCOMPLISHMENTS,
AND PERCEIVED IMPACT OF TRIP:
COMPARISON OF HIGH AND LOW DIFFERENTIATORS

Items that Discriminate	Number of Respondents to Whom Each Item Applies	
	Highs	*Lows*
He feels that he has gained a greater realization of his communalities with people from other countries and a greater ease in interacting with them	0	4
7. Fourth interview: Anticipated effects of the sojourn		
He anticipates that his experiences in America will have a significant effect on his career	1	4
. . . specifically, that they will increase the probability of his being transferred to a different type of job	0	3
He anticipates that, as a result of his American experiences, he will want to introduce innovations in the approach to educational TV at home	2	5
After returning home, he anticipates maintaining professional contact with American individuals or organizations		
to some extent	4	10
to a great extent	5	0
8. Post-return interview: Satisfactions and accomplishments in retrospect		
In general, he feels that he accomplished neither more nor less than he expected to during the American trip	7	4
Among the most satisfying aspects of the experience he cites		
those seminars that were related to his special interests and experience	3	0
the exchange of ideas with other people (other participants, American broadcasters, and so on)	5	1
9. Post-return interview: Perceived effects of the sojourn		
He feels that his professional activities have been substantially affected by his experience in America	3	6

Table 16 (Continued)

SATISFACTIONS, PERCEIVED ACCOMPLISHMENTS,
AND PERCEIVED IMPACT OF TRIP:
COMPARISON OF HIGH AND LOW DIFFERENTIATORS

Items that Discriminate	Number of Respondents to Whom Each Item Applies	
	Highs	*Lows*
Among the effects of the American experience he cites the enhancement of his professional skills	4	8
On the basis of ideas acquired in America, he is working for the extension of instructional or educational broadcasting in his country	6	3
During the past year, he has had professional contacts with American broadcasting and educational networks, established while he was in America	7	4
The American experience has led him to appreciate more the slower pace of life in his own country	4	0
The trip created special problems, primarily due to his having been away for four months	1	4
10. *Post-return interview: Reported changes since his return home*		
As the basis for changes in his position or responsibilities during the past year he cites		
recognition of his ability	3	6
routinely expectable promotion	0	3
He does not anticipate change in position or duties in the near future	3	6
Among reasons for his increased job satisfaction during the past year he cites		
his increased professional skill and competence	0	3
recognition by others of his ability	0	3
recognition by others of the special relevant experiences he has had	0	4
Innovations at his job that he has considered or has carried out include the increased use of indigenous personnel or materials	0	4
He reports that instructional and educational broadcasting have expanded in his country during the year	7	4
He favors increased emphasis on instructional and educational programs	7	2
His general plans for the future have not changed in any way during the past year	6	3

offerings at the university to be at a lower level than they had anticipated and could not become fully absorbed in them.

Though the university phase of the seminar was disappointing for the highs in the professional area, there are indications that they found satisfactions in other domains. Thus, they were more likely than the lows to locate their most enjoyable experiences in the interpersonal aspects of the American environment, and to attach value to the academic seminars. It may be that their professional disappointment encouraged them to shift their focus of attention from professional concerns to observations of American life and society. We have already seen, in the highs' initial expectations for the academic seminars, a hint that their agenda included an interest in filling out their picture of America. Although this was not their dominant goal, it was available as an alternative to fall back upon, once they realized that their professional goals would not be fully met. In other words, it seems that the high differentiators, experiencing some disappointment in the professional program, revised their goals and expectations—away from an emphasis on professional to one on nonprofessional pursuits—for the remainder of their stay at the university and particularly for the travel period.

Turning to the travel period, we find that the highs' overall satisfaction with their sojourn increased once they were out in the field. The difference in level of satisfaction between highs and lows that we observed in the second interview disappeared in the third interview, conducted during the travel period. As a matter of fact, there is some indirect evidence of a reversal, though admittedly it is based on a highly speculative interpretation. In the second interview, highs were more likely than lows to indicate that something had come up at home to make them wish they were there (see the third set of items in Table 16). In the third interview, by contrast, lows were more likely than highs to express such a wish (see the fourth set of items in the table). If we interpret these items as projective indicators of satisfaction, they suggest that highs were less satisfied than lows during the university phase of the seminar (for which we have other evidence as well), but more satisfied during the travel phase. In any event, at the very least we can say that the relative dissatisfaction with the total experience registered by highs in the second interview had dissipated by the time of the third interview.

Two possible explanations for this rise in satisfaction suggest themselves. It may be that the highs' professional experiences in the field were not as disappointing as those at the university had been, thus removing the major cause of their earlier dissatisfaction. Alternatively, it may be that once the highs redefined their goals and expectations, shifting away from a largely professional emphasis, their overall satisfaction with the sojourn was no longer as dependent on the quality or the specific nature of their professional experience. According to this second explanation, the highs may well have experienced professional disappointments during the travel period, but these no longer carried as much weight in their overall evaluation of the sojourn. The fifth set of items in Table 16, as well as additional data to be presented below, seem to support the second explanation, although there are also indications that the highs had some rewarding professional experiences during their travels.

The first of the items grouped in the fifth set of the table would suggest that the highs did find their travels professionally rewarding. They were, in fact, more likely than the lows to locate their single most important accomplishment during the travel period in the professional area. In all other respects, however, the lows seemed to be more pleased with the professional value of the trip than the highs. Thus, the lows were more likely to value what they learned about mass communications in America; to mention professionally relevant experiences, such as visits to broadcasting stations, among the high points of the trip; to feel that they were able to do everything they had planned to during their professional visits; to believe that they had learned new approaches to programming that would be of direct use to them at home; and to report that they had made many contacts, including professional ones, that they planned to maintain. On balance, then, it seems clear that even during the travel period the highs found their professional activities less absorbing and satisfying than the lows. The first item in the set suggests that they considered at least some of their professional experiences fruitful, but even these probably fell short of their initial expectations—which, we must recall, were higher than those of the lows. Table 18 will provide further support for these conclusions.

The final item in set 5 suggests that the highs derived much of their enjoyment during the travel period from the opportunity to observe American life and American institutions—just as, during the university period, they enjoyed learning about them in the academic seminars. Though they were less likely than the lows to feel that their professional experiences had given them all that they had hoped, they were more likely than the lows to report adequate opportunities to observe the features of American life that they had hoped to observe during their travels. In sum, during the travel period as well as during the university period, the Lows tended to emphasize and find satisfaction in professional pursuits, whereas the highs—after shifting from their initial professional emphasis—derived their primary satisfactions from nonprofessional pursuits. These are, of course, only relative statements. We have already seen that the highs found some of their professional experiences rewarding. Similarly, we should note indications that lows also found satisfaction in nonprofessional areas, particularly in interpersonal relations: They were more likely than highs to include "making new friends" among their most important accomplishments, and to report making many contacts during their travels that they planned to maintain.

The sixth set of items, based on the interview conducted at the end of the seminar and focusing on participants' reactions to the total experience, clearly bears out our interpretation that lows derived their major satisfactions from professional pursuits, whereas highs derived theirs from observing the American scene. Among their most important accomplishments, lows were more likely to mention that they gained a greater knowledge about TV in America, highs that they gained a greater knowledge about America's institutional structure—its political and economic system. Similarly, among their most meaningful or enjoyable experiences, lows were more likely to cite their exposure to new program ideas, highs their exposure to the academic seminars. Interestingly, we find that by the time of the fourth interview, highs felt more often than lows that the seminar was suited to their particular background and interests. We would surmise that they were evaluating the seminar in terms of their revised expectations and goals—with a shift away from purely professional pursuits—rather than in terms of their initial ones. Finally, we again have an indication in this set of items that the lows, though emphasizing professional activities, were also oriented toward their interpersonal encounters.[3] Several lows (but none of the highs) mentioned that the sojourn had helped them realize their communality with people from other countries and become more comfortable in interacting with them. The highs brought, from the very beginning, a greater degree of cultural communality and ease of interaction—at least with their American hosts.

Since the lows found the professional part of the seminar more relevant than the highs, it is not surprising that they expected the trip to have a more significant effect on their careers (see the seventh set of items in Table 16)—in contrast to the first interview, when it was the highs who were more likely to feel that participation in the seminar would result in promotion (see Table 15). Lows were also more likely to anticipate that, as a result of their American experiences, they would want to introduce innovations in the approach to educational TV at home. On the other hand, highs were more likely to anticipate maintaining a great

[3] In this connection we must stress that the data reported in this chapter do not give a complete picture of the attitudes of the two groups, since we are presenting only those items that discriminate between them. Thus, for example, nine lows included first-hand exposure to American life among their most meaningful experiences. This finding is not reported here, however, since a similar statement was made by eight of the highs.

deal of professional contact with American individuals or organizations after their return—this despite our earlier finding in the field interview that lows were more likely to report having made many contacts that they planned to maintain (see the fifth set of items in Table 16). It seems that, when all is said and done, the highs—though they did not feel that they gained much new professional knowledge—were more successful than the lows in establishing professional contacts with the Americans they met. Such an outcome is consistent with the greater professional self-confidence and ease of interaction that they brought to the situation.

In the post-return interview we find, first of all, that the highs felt, in retrospect, that they had accomplished just what they had expected to during their trip, whereas the lows were more likely to feel that they had accomplished either more or less than they had expected (see the eighth set of items in Table 16). This finding is somewhat surprising, in view of the professional disappointment that we know the highs had experienced. Perhaps the best explanation, again, is that they were evaluating their accomplishments in terms of their revised expectations and goals. These expectations, unlike their initial professional orientation, yielded rather general criteria of evaluation, which were indeed met by their actual experiences. By contrast, the lows became, if anything, *more* specific in their expectations and goals, and thus may have had more precise criteria for assessing whether they had accomplished more or less than they had hoped.

Highs were more likely to recall, among the most satisfying aspects of their sojourn, those seminars that were related to their special interests and experience, and the opportunities to exchange ideas with others, such as fellow-participants and American broadcasters. We shall see in the next section, based on Table 17, that the highs were critical of the university phase of the seminar because its sessions were not always at a level commensurate with their own experience, and because there were not enough opportunities to exchange ideas. Yet there were some sessions relevant to their interests and some opportunities for exchange (including those in the travel period), and when these did occur, the highs remembered them with special satisfaction.

The ninth set of items tells us that, after being back home for some months, the lows still felt—more often than the highs—that their experience in America had substantially affected their professional activities and had enhanced their professional skills. In one respect, however, the trip seemed to have had a greater impact on the highs: They were more likely to have maintained professional contacts with American organizations, as they had indeed anticipated in the fourth interview. The highs were also more likely to report that they were using ideas acquired in America in efforts to extend educational TV at home, but here it must be recalled that more of the highs were professionally involved in educational TV.

Finally, the tenth set of items deals with various changes reported by the respondents, which had taken place since their return from the United States but which they did not explicitly link to their sojourn. Several of these items show differences that can be accounted for by the differences in the two groups' countries of origin. For example, several lows—and none of the highs—mentioned the increased use of indigenous personnel or materials because, as we have seen, the lows included a number of African participants, whereas the highs included none. There are, however, several items in this set that probably do reflect differential impacts of the American trip and support our general line of interpretation. In reporting changes in their jobs or responsibilities, lows were more likely to ascribe these to recognition of their abilities (as well as to routinely expectable promotions). In citing reasons for their increased job satisfaction during the preceding year, several lows—but none of the highs—mentioned their increased professional skill and competence, the recognition of their abilities by others, and the recognition by others of the special relevant experiences they had had. Thus, it seems that the trip enhanced the lows' professional self-confidence and sense of competence. They felt that they had acquired new skills and relevant experiences and that these were recognized by others in their professional environment.

In sum, Table 16 reveals two distinct patterns of satisfaction with the sojourn and perceived accomplishment for the high and low differentiators. The highs arrived with high professional expectations, but were disappointed by the professional part of their experience, particularly during the university phase. They proceeded to revise their expectations and goals, shifting away from an emphasis on professional pursuits to one on observation of American society and American life. They took an active interest in learning about America and its institutions through academic seminars, personal visits, and conversations with Americans. They brought to their visit a readiness to engage in intensive interactions with Americans and a cognitive framework to which new information about America could be assimilated, as well as an agenda that seemed to include—though initially not in a central position—an interest in general observations of America. Thus, when the professional experience turned out to be somewhat disappointing, they were ready to shift their emphasis to these nonprofessional pursuits. Once they had redefined their goals in this fashion, they derived considerable satisfaction from the experience. It should be noted that, despite their emphasis on observations of America, they also found some of their professional experiences rewarding. For example, they seemed to enjoy their interactions with American colleagues and, in fact, succeeded in establishing professional contacts that they continued to maintain after returning home.

The lows arrived with lesser professional self-confidence and with more diffuse goals. Under the circumstances, they found themselves satisfied with the professional activities that had been made available to them and became fully absorbed in professional pursuits. Throughout the sojourn, they appreciated the professional information and experience they were able to acquire and considered them relevant to their own work. After they had been back home for some time, they felt that their American visit had indeed affected their professional activities and increased their skills, and they communicated an increased sense of competence and professional self-confidence. Despite their emphasis on professional accomplishments, they also seemed to derive other satisfactions from the experience, particularly in the personal relationships they had been able to establish.

These two patterns are of interest in their own right, in that they suggest that there is more than one way in which an exchange experience may prove satisfying and valuable to its participants. The highs seemed to find it satisfying despite their disappointment with its professional side; the lows seemed to benefit from it despite the relatively diffuse goals and expectations they brought to it. This is not to say that participants will be satisfied with exchange experiences regardless of what happens, but simply that a variety of experiences might offer satisfaction. An experience that is unsatisfactory for one participant may be highly satisfactory for another; and an experience that is unsatisfactory in one respect, may be highly satisfactory in another. In organizing exchange programs, we ought not to search for a single model that will be totally satisfactory to all. Rather, we should attempt to devise each program in a way that takes account of the specific needs and interests of its participants, and build into the program enough options so that those who find some features irrelevant to their interests can fruitfully turn to other pursuits.

Aside from these general considerations, what do the data presented in this section tell us about the process that leads to increase in differentiation in the image of America? We have seen that the highs placed a greater emphasis on observations of American society and American life. Given this orientation, it is not surprising that they emerged with more highly differentiated images. What is not clear, however—and cannot be clearly established from the present data—is the nature of the causal relationship and the precise role of professional disappointment in the process. One could posit a direct causal connection between the highs' professional disappointment and the increased differentiation of their images. The highs, having come with great expectations and been disappointed, may have been especially motivated to find some compensation—some way of making the best of a bad situation; thus, they may have taken a strong interest in learning about American society which, in turn—given their readiness to interact with Americans easily and a cognitive framework capable of assimilating the new information—would have led to greater differentiation. Alternatively, one could explain the results without assigning any causal function at all to the highs' professional disappointment. The highs may have brought to their experience a predisposition to develop more differentiated images; in fact, the very factors that predisposed them to develop more differentiated images may also have predisposed them to come with greater expectations and hence to experience disappointment. According to this view, the highs would have developed more differentiated images even if their professional experience had been fully satisfactory; the disappointment did not interfere with the differentiation process, but it also did not spur it on.

We are inclined to a formulation bridging the two positions that have just been presented. We assume that the highs were, indeed, predisposed to develop more differentiated images and might have done so regardless of their professional disappointment, but that the disappointment served to reinforce the process. Given the highs' readiness for intensive interactions and their receptive cognitive framework, they could have focused their attention equally well on professional pursuits and on observations of America. Since the professional part of the experience was disappointing to them, however, they placed greater emphasis on observations of America, which in turn led to marked changes on the differentiation dimension. Thus, if this view is correct, the professional disappointment contributed to the effect, not so much by creating the motivation for compensatory satisfactions, as by giving relatively greater weight to one of the interests that was already on the high differentiators' agenda.

Reactions to the university phase of the seminar. Central to our account, in the preceding section, of highs' and lows' satisfactions and perceived accomplishments was the assumption that highs were largely disappointed with their professional experiences at the university, whereas lows were largely satisfied with them. The present section, which examines the reactions of the two groups to the various aspects of the university phase of the seminar, will allow us to check on the validity of this assumption. The data on which this section is based are presented in Table 17.

The first four sets of items in the table, all taken from the second interview, demonstrate graphically and at length the highs' dissatisfaction with the university phase of the experience. The highs were consistently—with only four exceptions on this long list of items—more critical or less

Table 17

REACTIONS TO THE UNIVERSITY PHASE OF THE SEMINAR:
COMPARISON OF HIGH AND LOW DIFFERENTIATORS

Items that Discriminate	*Number of Respondents to Whom Each Item Applies*	
	Highs	*Lows*

1. *Second interview: Reactions to the seminar program*

	Highs	*Lows*
The participant found more than three quarters of the program at least indirectly relevant to his interests	8	4
Among his disappointments he mentions that		
the exchange of professional views among participants has been carried out at a lower level than he had anticipated	4	0
there have been administrative failures of organization, such as the lack of planning to present videotape material	7	1
He feels that the schedule has been unnecessarily long, that it could have been condensed	3	0
He feels that the program has been too rigid	6	1
He feels that the professional seminars had an excessive number of speakers	3	0
Among aspects of the seminar that were especially well planned he cites		
the provision of highly skilled broadcasting people as speakers	2	5
the excursions to mass media facilities	0	4
Among the field trips he found valuable he cites the weekend in New Hampshire	6	9

2. *Second interview: Reactions to the group composition*

	Highs	*Lows*
He generally feels that the multinational composition of the group was beneficial	1	9
Among the values of the group's multinational composition he mentions that it permits an interchange of professional skills and ideas	5	8
Among reasons for adverse effects of the group's multinational composition he cites		
diversity of professional backgrounds, positions, and interests	7	4
diversity in level of professional knowledge	3	0
diversity in ideology or cultural background that caused conflict or hampered effective group functioning	4	0

Table 17 (Continued)

REACTIONS TO THE UNIVERSITY PHASE OF THE SEMINAR:
COMPARISON OF HIGH AND LOW DIFFERENTIATORS

Items that Discriminate	Number of Respondents to Whom Each Item Applies	
	Highs	Lows
He cites unevenness in choice of participants as a source of dissatisfaction with the seminar	4	1
Among aspects of the seminar that seemed poorly planned he mentions that the composition of the group is too heterogeneous	5	0
He feels that the participants functioned as a very congenial group	1	8
As sources of friction among participants he cites		
lack of common interests	3	0
personal idiosyncrasies	6	0
conflict of ideologies	3	0
He has a generally high estimate of the value that contributions by other participants have had for him	5	10
Among contributions he found especially valuable he cites the technically superior presentations made by representatives from "advanced countries"	3	6
3. Second interview: Satisfaction with own role and with role of participants in general in the seminar		
He feels largely satisfied with his own contribution to the seminar	5	2
In discussing his inability to make sufficient contributions to the professional seminars he cites		
personal reasons (language difficulty; lack of professional knowledge)	1	5
external reasons (schedule provided insufficient opportunity for presentations by participants; some participants monopolized the discussion)	4	0
Among aspects of the seminar that seemed poorly planned he cites failure to provide adequate audiovisual facilities for participants' special programs	4	0
He feels that he was personally inconvenienced by the inadequate audiovisual facilities for showing films or slides	4	0

Table 17 (Continued)

REACTIONS TO THE UNIVERSITY PHASE OF THE SEMINAR:
COMPARISON OF HIGH AND LOW DIFFERENTIATORS

Items that Discriminate	*Number of Respondents to Whom Each Item Applies*	
	Highs	*Lows*
He feels that the participants did not have enough opportunity to determine the course of the seminar	5	0
He has a generally negative evaluation of the Fellows' Committee	3	0
Among the reasons for dissatisfaction with the Fellows' Committee he mentions that it does not carry out its function effectively	4	1
The functions of the Fellows' Committee as he perceives them include transmission of participants' personal complaints to the directorate	6	2

4. *Second interview: Reactions to living arrangements and leisure-time activities*

	Highs	Lows
Among aspects of the seminar that seemed poorly planned he cites		
insufficiently mature administrative personnel	3	0
inefficiency in small administrative details (for example, posting of schedule changes, repair of TV sets)	6	3
He feels that he was personally inconvenienced by		
inadequate provision for personal transportation	9	6
inadequate provisions for leisure activities	5	1
Among criticisms of the living arrangements he cites the failure to supply current newspapers	4	1
He feels that the seminar did not provide enough opportunity for spontaneous socializing	6	2
Among aspects of the seminar that were especially well planned he cites the weekend visit with an American family in New Hampshire	4	7
Among activities that he found particularly interesting he cites visits to cultural sights	3	0
Among activities that he found uninteresting he cites recreational trips, such as the Fourth of July outing	0	3
His activities outside the seminar have included visits to theaters and concerts	7	4

Table 17 (Continued)

REACTIONS TO THE UNIVERSITY PHASE OF THE SEMINAR:
COMPARISON OF HIGH AND LOW DIFFERENTIATORS

Items that Discriminate	Number of Respondents to Whom Each Item Applies	
	Highs	*Lows*
5. *Fourth interview: Predeparture reactions to the university phase of the seminar*		
He feels that he gained more from the period at the university than he did from the travel period	0	3
He feels that some of the seminar goals were inappropriate for this kind of group	3	0
He feels that the seminar did, in general, provide enough opportunity for the exchange of ideas among the participants	4	7
He feels that future seminars could improve the exchange of ideas by providing for more planned discussions among participants	5	1
He feels that a future seminar should include the same kind of participants	6	1
He suggests that selection criteria be changed for the future in order to increase the specialization of the seminar (for example, by focusing on technical aspects of TV or on school TV)	2	6
He feels that he was presented with a reasonably well-balanced picture, that both sides of issues received enough attention	7	4
6. *Post-return interview: Retrospective reactions to the university phase of the seminar*		
He feels that the seminar could be improved by reducing the amount of time given to lectures and seminars	1	5

laudatory of various features of the seminar than the lows. Their major criticisms focused on the professional aspects of the experience, though they were also more prone to complain about administrative details.

The very first item in the table provides one of the small handful of exceptions. Despite their criticisms, the highs were more likely to state that a large proportion of the program at the university was relevant to their interests. It must be recalled that they were assessing a program which included not only professional seminars, presentations by visiting broadcasters, and trips to broadcasting facilities, but also academic seminars and visiting speakers on topics other than broadcasting. We have already seen that highs were interested in the academic seminars and in opportunities to learn about America; they were also interested in the whole range of professional topics, even though (as we shall see) they were not always happy with the way in which these were presented. The lows, on the other hand, were more oriented towards specific professional concerns; thus, they had less interest in the academic seminars and were also more likely to assess the professional sessions in terms of relevance to their specific professional concerns. Overall, then, the highs—with their wider agenda—saw relevance in a larger proportion of the offerings and, in that respect, we can assume that they were more satisfied. It is important to keep this in mind as we review the many criticisms expressed by the highs, since it puts these reactions into a more balanced perspective.

The remaining items in the first set demonstrate the nature of the highs' criticisms of the seminar program. They expressed two disappointments: that the exchange of professional views among participants was carried out at a lower level than they had anticipated; and that there had been certain administrative failures, including the failure to provide equipment for videotape presentations. These two points anticipate two major sources of dissatisfaction among highs that are illustrated more fully in the second and third sets of items in this table: their relative dissatisfaction with the group composition and with opportunities for participation by seminar members. Highs were also more likely to feel that the schedule had been too long, the program too rigid, and the professional seminars marked by an excessive number of speakers. They were less likely to praise the organizers of the seminar for the array of highly skilled broadcasters whom they had brought in as speakers and for the excursions to various mass media facilities that they had planned. They were even less enthusiastic about the generally popular weekend in New Hampshire, which included a visit to a small university-based radio station and private hospitality with American families. In short, their less than total satisfaction with the professional side of the seminar was quite apparent.

The second set of items points to one of the two major sources of the highs' professional disappointment: the composition of the group, which, in their view, lowered the level at which professional discourse among participants was carried on. The highs, unlike the lows, spontaneously mentioned unevenness in choice of participants and heterogeneity in group composition as criticisms of the seminar. In sharp contrast to the lows, they did not regard the multinational composition of the seminar as clearly beneficial. (Of *all* comparisons between the two groups, this item yielded the largest difference.) They were less inclined to value the opportunities for professional interchange that it provided, and more inclined to feel that the diversity in professional background, in level of professional knowledge, and in ideological or cultural orientation characterizing a multinational seminar might have adverse effects. Under the circumstances, it is not surprising that they did not share the lows' view of the seminar participants as a highly congenial group. Some of them cited lack of common interests, personal idiosyncrasies, or conflict of ideologies as limitations on group cohesiveness. It is also not surprising that the lows found the contributions by other participants more valuable, particularly the presentations by representatives from "advanced countries."

The third set of items points to the other major source of the highs' professional disappointment: the limited opportunity for personal participation and for making the specialized contributions that they had come prepared to make. Highs—whose greater professional self-confidence we already know about—were more satisfied with their own contributions to the seminar. They were more inclined to feel, however, that the structure of the seminar prevented these contributions from attaining their maximum. In explaining their inability to make sufficient contributions, lows were more likely to cite personal failings, whereas highs were more likely to point to external obstacles. Several highs (but none of the lows) complained about the inadequate audiovisual facilities at the university, which made it difficult or impossible for them to present the samples of their own work that they had brought along. The participants' opportunity to make their own presentations was further limited by the excessive number of scheduled speakers, of which several highs complained (see the first set of items). Half of the highs (but none of the lows) felt that participants had insufficient opportunity to determine the course of the seminar. This is consistent with the earlier finding that highs considered the program too rigid (see first set of items). Also, not surprisingly, the highs were more critical of the Fellows' Committee—the one mechanism for formalizing member participation that had been set up.

In short, it seems that some of the highs were disappointed in the first phase of the seminar largely because they were unable to play a role congruent with their capacities, and because they felt that the lesser competence and experience of some of their fellow-participants forced the seminar into a professionally less-challenging and productive mold. Their expectations for an experience in which the professional knowledge that they had to offer would be eagerly sought and in which, at the same time, they would be able to raise even further their own level of competence and be involved in enriching exchanges were clearly not met. It is reasonable to suppose that, in the face of this disappointment, they would turn their attention into other directions. The lows, on the other land, found the level of the professional offerings appropriate to their needs, and greatly valued the multinational composition of the seminar. They felt that they had much to learn from the American speakers and from other participants, particularly those from countries with more highly developed broadcasting systems, and they appreciated the opportunity to have contact with these top-flight specialists. Moreover, it seems clear that the lows had not come with an expectation to make active personal contributions to the program, and they were, therefore, not disturbed by the limited opportunity for member participation.

A final set of items taken from the second interview concerns participants' reactions to the living arrangements at the university, to leisure-time activities, and to various adminstrative details. Again we find, on most of these items, a more critical attitude on the part of the highs. They were more likely to complain that administrative personnel were not sufficiently mature and that some administrative details had been handled inefficiently. With regard to "extracurricular" activities, they complained more often than lows that there was inadequate provision for leisure activities, that there was not enough opportunity for spontaneous socializing, that they were inconvenienced by the inadequate transportation arrangements, and that the supply of current newspapers was insufficient. The lows were more enthusiastic about the weekend in New Hampshire; but, on the other hand, they showed less interest than the highs in some of the other recreational trips and in visits to cultural sights, and they attended theaters and concerts less frequently. This is consistent with earlier indications that highs were more oriented toward observing American life and culture, while lows (aside from their professional interests) were more oriented toward meeting average Americans and becoming acquainted with them.

The more critical attitude conveyed by the highs in the fourth set of items may represent a generalization from their dissatisfaction with the professional part of the program. Since they were already criticizing the seminar administration for shortcomings in the professional activities, they may have been more inclined to complain about other failures in planning and organization as well. It is also possible that the highs—in view of their greater self-confidence and their greater freedom from linguistic and cultural barriers—felt more comfortable about expressing criticism than the lows. While this may well be true, the total pattern of findings—particularly the consistent differences relating to group composition and personal participation—suggests that we are not dealing merely with a stylistic difference, but with a difference in the nature and quality of the professional experience perceived by the two groups.

The fifth set of items lists reactions of the two groups to the university phase of the seminar culled from the interviews conducted at the very end of the sojourn. Not surprisingly, none of the highs was prepared to say that he had found the university period more beneficial than the travel period. Highs were more likely to feel that they had been presented with a reasonably well-balanced picture; this may reflect their satisfaction with the academic seminars. On the professional side, however, they still felt that the seminar did not provide enough opportunity for the exchange of ideas among participants, and recommended that future seminars provide for more planned discussions within the group.

Several highs (but none of the lows) felt that some of the seminar goals were inappropriate for the kind of group that had been brought to it. Yet, surprisingly—particularly in view of the highs' earlier complaints about the group composition—they were more likely to suggest that a future seminar should include the same kind of participants. Perhaps they were no longer disturbed by the heterogeneity of the group, having shifted their emphasis away from the pursuit of specific professional goals. Even those who considered some of the seminar goals inappropriate for this group of participants may have favored, not a change in participants, but a change in goals—comparable to the change in goals that they themselves had undergone. By contrast, the lows called for a change in the criteria of selecting participants, suggesting a group that would be more homogeneous with respect to area of specialization. This is consistent with our general impression that they had become more, rather than less, oriented to the professional possibilities of the experience. They probably felt, therefore, that it would be better to have a more specialized seminar that could focus on concrete issues, directly related to the participants' work situations back home. The one relevant item taken from the post-return interview (see the sixth set of items) points in a similar direction. Perhaps lows were more likely to feel that it would be best to reduce the time given to lectures and seminars, not only because they had relatively little interest in the academic seminars, but also because—even on the professional side—they had developed a preference for workshop-like experiences.

Reactions to the travel phase of the seminar. The first set of items in Table 18 is drawn from the second interview and deals with participants' anticipations for the travel period, shortly before embarking upon it. We see, first of all, a reversal from the first interview, consistent with the data we have already reviewed. In thinking about the impending trip, it was the lows rather than the highs who displayed greater expectations for the professional value of the experience and who were more fully absorbed in professional interests. In particular, some of the lows were looking forward to opportunities to obtain practical professional experi-

Table 18

REACTIONS TO THE TRAVEL PHASE OF THE SEMINAR:
COMPARISON OF HIGH AND LOW DIFFERENTIATORS

Items that Discriminate	Number of Respondents to Whom Each Item Applies	
	Highs	*Lows*
1. *Second interview: Anticipations for the travel period*		
Most of the things that the participant is looking forward to during the trip concern professional activities	4	8
Among the experiences he looks forward to he cites the opportunity to obtain some practical professional experience (by actually working at an American broadcasting station) or specific professional training	1	4
Among problems he anticipates during the travel period he cites language difficulties	0	3
Among features of American life about which he wants more information he cites the American educational system	2	5
He anticipates that two months of travel will not give him all the experiences he would like to have	3	0
His travel arrangements are not yet completed	4	1
2. *Third interview: Satisfaction with itinerary and travel experiences*		
He is, in general, satisfied with his itinerary	3	6
He found some of the places he visited professionally inappropriate because activities were curtailed for the summer and it was thus impossible to observe certain kinds of programs or operations	4	0
Among reasons for considering certain places on the itinerary unrewarding he cites their lack of professional relevance	3	0
Among reasons for considering certain places particularly interesting he cites their scenic beauty	3	0
Among the sources of satisfaction with the professional aspects of the travel period he cites the opportunity to obtain new ideas for programs	5	2

Table 18 (Continued)

REACTIONS TO THE TRAVEL PHASE OF THE SEMINAR:
COMPARISON OF HIGH AND LOW DIFFERENTIATORS

Items that Discriminate	Number of Respondents to Whom Each Item Applies	
	Highs	Lows
the opportunity to work at stations or to observe in detail facilities, techniques, or programs that have possible future professional relevance	4	7
3. *Third interview: Satisfaction with travel arrangements*		
He found the per diem allowance inadequate	5	2
He found the transportation arrangements inadequate	4	1
He found the hotel arrangements adequate	5	2
Among the reasons for the inadequacy of some hotels he cites		
their poor location	0	3
their lack of personal comforts	1	4
4. *Third interview: Interaction experiences*		
He found the interaction with broadcasters in the field more valuable than at the university	0	3
The new acquaintances that he formed with Americans during the travel period were often the result of		
meetings that had been prearranged by the seminar staff	7	10
social contacts he made spontaneously after his arrival in a new community	4	8

ence or specific professional training. These findings are in line with the lows' increased professional orientation that we have already noted, and especially with their interest in concrete learnings applicable to their job situations. By contrast, we have postulated a shift in the highs' goals and expectations, which would reduce their concentration on professional activities in looking forward to the travel period. This does not betoken a general lack of enthusiasm for the trip among the highs. Their feeling that two months of travel would not give them all the experiences they would like to have suggests an eagerness for a rich and varied array of activities, but these were not necessarily of a professional nature.

The finding that the travel arrangements were still incomplete for more highs than lows by the time of the second interview is somewhat surprising, since highs had a clearer idea from the beginning of the specific itinerary they desired to follow (see Table 15). Perhaps it took longer to arrange their trip because they had more specific idiosyncratic plans and a longer list of people whom they hoped to contact (as recorded, again, in Table 15). The anticipated language difficulties among several lows merely serve as a reminder that this group included a number of individuals whose English was less than fluent.

The second set of items supports our earlier statement that, even during the travel period, the highs found their professional activities less absorbing and in some respects less satisfying than the lows, although they did derive some benefits from them. Highs were, in general, less satisfied with their itineraries than lows. Thus, several highs (but none of the lows) mentioned that several places they visited were professionally inappropriate because activities were curtailed for the summer and they were unable, therefore, to observe the programs or operations they were interested in. It should be recalled that a larger proportion of the highs were in educational broadcasting and thus particularly affected by the summer schedule. Also, several highs (but none of the lows) cited lack of professional relevance in explaining why some places on their itineraries had been unrewarding. The lows, furthermore, were likely to report—among their sources of professional satisfaction—the opportunity to have the kinds of concrete, practical, job-relevant experiences to which they had looked forward. On the other hand, the highs were more likely to report satisfaction derived from the opportunity to obtain new ideas for programs, based, presumably, on their observations of American life and institutions. Thus, even though the highs were less oriented toward the professional part of their experience, it seems that they saw possibilities of turning their general observations of America to specific professional use.

We have argued, of course, that highs were especially interested in learning about American life and institutions, so that the opportunity to make general observations of America was inherently satisfying for them. In Table 16 (fifth set of items) we saw that highs uniformly felt that they indeed had adequate opportunities to observe the features of American life that they had wanted to observe during their travels. In the present table we also find an indication that the highs were more oriented to the scenic beauty of the places they visited than the lows. In short, then, the highs were oriented toward and derived satisfactions from the extraprofessional aspects of the trip—from observing the country, the society, and the people of the United States. Their professional experiences were also rewarding in some respects, though on the whole they found them less rewarding and certainly less relevant to their own work than did the lows. But the highs were not as dependent on the professional usefulness of the trip for their overall satisfaction, in view of their broader agenda and their shift in emphasis from professional pursuits to general observations. All in all, then, they found the experience no less satisfying than did the lows.

The third set of items in Table 18 suggests that highs were less prone to criticize administrative details and arrangements during the travel phase than they were at the university (see Table 17, especially the fourth set of items). Differences are small and inconsistent. Thus, highs were more critical of the per diem allowance that they were receiving during the travel period and of the transportation arrangements that had been made for them. On the other hand, they were less likely than the lows to complain about the adequacy of the hotel arrangements. This pattern is consistent with our impression that, by the time of the travel period, highs had adjusted their goals and expectations and any disappointment they might still have felt with their professional experiences did not influence their general mood.

In the final set of items of Table 18 we find, first, that several lows (but none of the highs) found interaction with broadcasters in the field more valuable than at the university. The broadcasters who came to speak at the university were usually leaders in the field, and we know that the lows were particularly appreciative of their quality. However, they probably found them relatively inaccessible and their presentations on a rather general level. In the field, on the other hand, they had more opportunities to interact with American colleagues who—being less prestigious— were also more accessible, in the actual setting in which these colleagues were doing their professional work, and around more concrete job-related issues. Given the lows' interest in workshop-type experiences, directly related to their own work, it is not surprising that they found these interactions of greater value. Finally we find, in the fourth set of items, that that the new American acquaintances that the lows made during the travel period were more often the result of prearrangement of the seminar staff or of spontaneous social contacts than the acquaintances made by the highs. Perhaps this was because highs, as we have already seen (Table 15), were more likely to have come prepared with names of individuals whose acquaintance they wanted to make. In any event, the finding that most lows made spontaneous social contacts shows, once again, that they were interested in personal interactions with Americans and, moreover, that they had no particular difficulty in arranging these—at least on a casual level.

Perceptions and evaluations of America and Americans. Items that yielded differences in the two groups' perceptions and evaluations of America and Americans are presented in Table 19.

The first set of items, taken from the first interview, indicates that the highs, as we have already seen (Table 15), arrived on the scene with a greater degree of familiarity with America than did the lows. Prior to the present trip, they had had—more often than the lows—special reasons for obtaining information about America, and close American friends. They were also more likely than the lows to have kept in touch with their American contacts on their own initiative. In one respect, the lows had closer contact with America: They were more likely to report that they had close friends or relatives who had lived in America. These contacts, however, were funneled through fellow-nationals of their own countries, rather than through Americans.

The highs' first impressions of America, as we see in set 2 of Table 19, were less uniformly positive than those of the lows, but they were more detailed and elaborated.[4] Thus, even in the first interview, we find some indication of the greater differentiation of highs' images of America. This is consistent with our earlier statement that highs arrived with a better-articulated framework for viewing America to which they could fit new information. They were thus able to treat this information more analytically and recognize its more far-reaching implications, emerging with an increasingly complex and differentiated cognitive structure. The lows, on the other hand, had a less-organized framework, and thus their new learning more often took the form of adding new fragments of knowledge to the collection of fragments they had brought with them.

By the time of the third interview, there were no systematic differences between the two groups in their evaluations of America, but there were a very few differences in the features of America that they selected for positive or negative comment. The relevant items are collected as set 3 in Table 19. As the table shows, the lows were more likely to locate their major disappointments in nonprofessional areas. Specifically, half of them cited the handling of the racial problem among their major disappointments with the United States. The latter finding is almost entirely accounted for by the four Africans included among the lows. As for features of America that had pleased them most, lows were more likely to cite its democratic atmosphere—its general openness and toleration for differences of opinion.

The fourth set of items deals with the observations and insights reported by the two groups in the third interview. Most of the reported observations of American life fell into one of six content categories. Three

---

[4] We have no obvious explanation for the third item in the set.

Table 19

PERCEPTIONS AND EVALUATIONS OF AMERICA AND AMERICANS:
COMPARISON OF HIGH AND LOW DIFFERENTIATORS

Items that Discriminate	Number of Respondents to Whom Each Item Applies	
	Highs	*Lows*
1. First interview: Prior contacts with America		
The participant had special reasons for obtaining information about America prior to this trip	10	7
His prior contacts with Americans have included close American friends	8	5
He has kept in touch with his American contacts on his own initiative	6	2
People from his own country who have lived in America include		
close friends	6	9
relatives	2	5
2. First interview: First impressions of America		
His first impressions of America are quite positive in tone, rather than mixed	7	10
His first impressions of America are at least moderately detailed and elaborated	10	7
One focus of his first salient impressions is the high cost of living	5	1
3. Third interview: Evaluations of America		
His major disappointments with America tend to be in nonprofessional areas	6	10
Among his major disappointments he cites the handling of the Negro problem	2	5
Among the things that have pleased him most about America he cites its democratic atmosphere (its general openness, the toleration for differences of opinion, and so on)	1	5
4. Third interview: Reported observations and insights		
During his travels, his observations of American life have focused, among others, on		
the state of broadcasting	5	2
the American political system	3	0
the religious aspects of American life	7	4
Most of the major new insights into American life that he reports having gained from the trip concern		

Table 19 (Continued)

PERCEPTIONS AND EVALUATIONS OF AMERICA AND AMERICANS:
COMPARISON OF HIGH AND LOW DIFFERENTIATORS

Items that Discriminate	*Number of Respondents to Whom Each Item Applies*	
	Highs	*Lows*
qualities of the American people	5	2
the political or economic institutional structure of America	2	6
His new insights include an understanding of the importance of diversity and variety in America (for example, the role regional differences play)	5	1
His new insights into American life cover only a narrow range	3	6
5. *Third interview: Perceived differences within America*		
Among regional differences he noted in America he cites differences		
in the ease with which one can get to know people	4	1
in political attitudes	3	0
in weather	1	4
The regional differences he perceives cover a broad range	3	0
Among other differences within the population that contributed to his understanding of American society he cites racial and ethnic differences	6	2
When asked about religious differences, he indicates that they do not play an important role in America	5	2
When asked about socioeconomic differences in America, he indicates that they play an important role	4	8
. . . particularly in domestic policy	3	6
Among differences that have affected the development of American broadcasting he cites		
racial and ethnic differences	2	5
socioeconomic differences	1	5
6. *Fourth interview: Predeparture attitudes toward America*		
He is not sorry to be leaving America	3	7
He expects to broadcast programs, write articles, or otherwise report publicly about his trip upon his return	9	6

Table 19 (Continued)

PERCEPTIONS AND EVALUATIONS OF AMERICA AND AMERICANS:
COMPARISON OF HIGH AND LOW DIFFERENTIATORS

Items that Discriminate	Number of Respondents to Whom Each Item Applies	
	Highs	Lows
In general, he expects to praise America when discussing it after his return	7	4
Among new insights about America that he acquired he mentions greater awareness of how high the standard of living is in America	1	4

7. *Post-return interview: Evaluations of America*

	Highs	Lows
Among ways in which his trip to America exceeded his expectations he cites the hospitality and friendliness of the people	3	0
Among things that impressed him favorably about America he cites		
the generosity and hospitality of the people	3	7
the friendliness and informality of the people	1	8
the beauty of the country	4	0
the size, complexity, and variety of the country	4	0
Among things that impressed him unfavorably about America he cites the extent and severity of the race problem	1	4

8. *Post-return interview: Perceptions of America*

	Highs	Lows
His visit to America confirmed more of his expectations than it disconfirmed	6	3
When asked whether there is such a thing as an "American attitude or point of view" he replies that		
there is no such thing as an American point of view	1	0
one cannot speak of a single American point of view because of America's complexity and diversity	5	2
there is a general point of view but that one must be aware of America's complexity and diversity	2	5
there is a general American point of view	1	2

Table 19 (Continued)

PERCEPTIONS AND EVALUATIONS OF AMERICA AND AMERICANS:
COMPARISON OF HIGH AND LOW DIFFERENTIATORS

Items that Discriminate	Number of Respondents to Whom Each Item Applies	
	Highs	Lows
Among the components of the American point of view he cites preoccupation with communism	0	3
He can identify subgroups within the population that differ from each other in their basic point of view	9	6
. . . including racial, ethnic, or religious groups	6	2
. . . and geographic or regional groups	4	0
When asked which groups of Americans have different (nonmodal) views of his own country, he mentions those who have had direct contact with the country	6	2

9. *Post-return interview: Communications about America*

	Highs	Lows
Among programs about America that he has presented or is likely to present he cites		
instructional programs about American life, history, geography	4	0
documentaries or special feature programs	6	9
newscasts, editorials, or commentaries	1	4
Among the contents of such programs he lists information about		
places and personalities of special interest	6	3
American communications media	0	3
When asked whether, in America, he came across any specific materials that could be used to give a realistic picture of life in America, he mentions		
materials that would tend to broaden the perspective about America	4	7
materials that depict American social and economic institutions, such as private enterprise, social welfare, and the educational system	0	3
Among the points he tried to get across in reports about his trip he cites the wealth, the high standard of living, and the advanced technical development of America	1	5

of these—the state of broadcasting, the political system, and religious aspects of American life—were more often cited as foci for observation by the highs than by the lows. On the other three there were no differences between the groups. The next item yielded somewhat surprising results. When asked to mention the most important new insights the trip had given them into American life, the highs were more likely to speak of qualities of the American people, whereas the lows were more likely to speak of the political or economic institutional structure.[5] This would seem to contradict our earlier impression (see Table 16, sixth set of items) that highs were more interested in learning about America's institutional structure than lows. One possible way of reconciling these contradictory findings is to assume that, although highs may have been interested in learning about American institutions, this learning was more likely to yield further details and elaborations of their already well-articulated framework, rather than totally new insights. Lows may have been less interested in learning about American institutions, but more likely to make entirely new discoveries in this area.

The remaining two items in the fourth set indicate that, during the travel period, highs were indeed engaging in a process of differentiation to a greater extent than lows. First, we find that highs were more likely to mention, among their new insights, an understanding of the importance of diversity and variety in America—as reflected, for example, in the role played by regional differences, to which we shall return shortly. Thus, their image of America was becoming increasingly complex and differentiated. Second, according to the ratings of our coders, the highs' insights into American life covered a broader range than those of the lows.

The next set of items, focusing on differences within America perceived by the respondents, also tends to point to a more active process of differentiation among the highs. When asked about the nature of the differences among different regions of America that they had found, highs more often than lows cited differences in political attitudes and in the ease with which one can get to know people. The only category noted by lows more often than by highs involved the rather obvious differences in weather. According to our coders' ratings, the regional differences perceived by the highs covered a broader range than those perceived by the lows. Highs were also more likely to mention racial and ethnic differences

---

[5] These codes were mutually exclusive. That is, the coder had to pick the one category into which most of a given respondent's major new insights had fallen. Thus, if *most* of a respondent's insights concerned qualities of the American people, his response was coded only under that category, even though *some* of his insights might have related to the American institutional structure.

in response to a general question that probed which differences, in addition to regional ones, they had found important to their understanding of American society. When asked specifically about religious differences and about socioeconomic differences, however, highs were more likely than lows to say that these did *not* play an important role in American society. They were also less likely to cite racial and ethnic differences or socioeconomic differences as having affected the development of American broadcasting. Thus, there appears to be no general tendency among highs to attach greater importance, in this set of questions, to differences within the American population; highs seem to be more impressed by some differences, lows by others. Highs showed their greater degree of differentiation, however, in the specific content of the regional differences that they perceived, and in *spontaneously* bringing up racial and ethnic differences as contributing to their understanding of American society.

The fourth interview yielded only four differences between the two groups in their attitudes toward America. These are collected as set 6 in Table 19. One interesting finding emerges from this set of items. The highs, as we have seen (second set of items in the table), started out *less* positive than the lows in their first impressions of America. By the time of the third interview, their level of satisfaction seemed to be equal to that of the lows; and by the time they were ready to leave the United States, as the present set of items suggests, they had actually become *more* positive in their feelings than the lows. They were more likely to feel sorry that they were leaving America, and more likely to predict that, in discussing America after their return, they would generally praise it. We have no indication here of sharp or extensive differences between the two groups or of disaffection among the lows. What the data seem to imply is that the highs, as they continued to interact with Americans and to observe American life, developed increasing degrees of positive affect, which reached its highest point as they contemplated the end of the sojourn.

In the post-return interview we again find no consistent difference between the two groups in their overall evaluation of America. What we do find, as displayed in the seventh set of items, are differences in some of the features of America that the two groups pick out for favorable or unfavorable comment. First, we see that several highs (but none of the lows) indicated that the hospitality and friendliness of Americans exceeded their original expectations. This does not mean that they were more favorably impressed than the lows with the hospitality and friendliness of their hosts; the second item in the set shows clearly that, in fact, the opposite was true. What it must mean, then, is that their original expectations were rather low and that they were pleasantly surprised by

what they actually experienced. We have already had some indication of
such surprise in the third interview (see the fourth set of items in this
table): the highs, more often than the lows, reported that the major new
insights into American life that they had gained from their trip concerned
qualities of the American people. It may be that the highs were more
likely to bring to their sojourn a slightly skeptical attitude, which their
travels and interactions with Americans helped to counteract. Such an
attenuation of initial skepticism may also account for the increasingly
positive affect toward America displayed by the highs. It would seem that
they had some surprisingly cordial interpersonal encounters with their
American hosts, which left them rather sentimental about the whole experience.

Though none of the lows indicated that the hospitality and friendliness of Americans exceeded their expectations, they were considerably
more likely than the highs to cite these qualities of the people among the
things that impressed them favorably about America. The highs, on the
other hand, were more often favorably impressed with the beauty of the
country—in keeping with their greater orientation toward observing
America and indulging in touristic pleasures; and with the size, complexity, and variety of the country—in keeping with the increased differentiation of their images. The final item in this set shows, once more, that
the lows reacted more negatively to the extent and severity of the race
problem in the United States; this finding, again, is mostly accounted for
by the African participants.

The eighth set of items provides further evidence of the more
highly differentiated images held by the highs. They were more likely to
insist that one cannot speak of a general American point of view. Also,
they were more often able to identify subgroups within the American
population that differed from each other in their basic point of view.
Specifically, they were more likely to mention racial, ethnic, or religious
groups in this connection, as well as geographic or regional groups. These
items, it must be recalled, come from the post-return interview, which was
conducted at about the same time that participants filled out their after-
questionnaires. Thus, the finding of greater differentiation among the
highs essentially serves to validate the criterion by which the two groups
were initially distinguished. The first item in this set, incidentally, suggests
again that the highs brought to their sojourn a greater familiarity with
America and a better-articulated framework for viewing it.

Finally, the ninth set of items in Table 19 deals with the communications about America that participants had presented after their
return or had thought of presenting. These items do not fall into any
obvious single pattern. The first item is probably a reflection of the fact

that a larger proportion of the highs were involved in instructional broadcasting. The second item is consistent with our general finding that highs were more oriented toward observations of America and touristic pursuits, lows toward the professional side of the trip; not surprisingly, these orientations affected the contents of the programs they presented. The third item seems to go against the general pattern. The only explanation that suggests itself is that the highs approached the question differently from the lows; five of them (but none of the lows) answered in a way that gave the coders no basis for assessing the image of America that the materials conveyed. Thus, the differences may simply be due to the fact that the highs less often specified the content of the materials they had come across. The last item in set 9 simply reflects the fact that more of the lows came from developing countries and were therefore more impressed with American affluence and technology; the five lows who tried to get this point across in their reports included the four Africans in this group.

In sum, Table 19 shows that the highs brought to the sojourn a greater familiarity with America and a more fully developed cognitive framework to which new information could be assimilated; that, in the course of the sojourn, they engaged in a process of differentiation to a greater extent than did the lows; and that, a year after their return, they had more differentiated images (as would, of course, be expected from the criterion by which participants were assigned to the two groups). There is also some support for our earlier formulation that highs were more oriented toward general observations of America and touristic pursuits. Finally, there are indications that highs were initially somewhat less favorable toward America than lows—perhaps because of a mild degree of skepticism about the qualities of American people—but that they developed increasingly positive affect, tinged with a touch of sentimentality.

Perceptions and evaluations of American broadcasting. The participants' perceptions of American mass media, after they had been at the university for several weeks, yielded an intriguing finding, displayed in set 1 of Table 20. In rating participants' descriptions of changes in their picture of American mass media, our coders judged those of the lows to be more broad-ranging, and particularly more detailed and elaborated than those of the highs. This may be surprising in that the high differentiators, in this case, responded in a less differentiated manner. It must be recalled, however, that the highs had been quite disappointed in the professional part of their experience at the university and that the second interview was replete with criticisms on this score (see Tables 16 and 17). The lows, on the other hand, found the university phase professionally rewarding; in particular, they indicated that they had learned a

Table 20

PERCEPTIONS AND EVALUATIONS OF AMERICAN BROADCASTING:
COMPARISON OF HIGH AND LOW DIFFERENTIATORS

Items that Discriminate	Number of Respondents to Whom Each Item Applies	
	Highs	*Lows*
1. *Second interview: Perceptions of American mass media*		
The participant's description of changes in his picture of American mass media		
covers a moderate to broad range	5	8
is at least moderately detailed and elaborated	3	9
2. *Third interview: Evaluations of ownership and control patterns in American broadcasting*		
He feels that private ownership of broadcasting offers		
no advantage	7	2
some advantage for America, but not for his own country	0	4
some advantage in general	2	4
Among the advantages of private ownership he mentions that		
it is especially suited to the conditions of American society	1	5
it makes for competition between stations	1	4
Among the disadvantages of private ownership he cites the neglect of specialized audiences interested in high-quality programming	2	5
Among the difficulties faced by American broadcasters he mentions that they are overly constrained by pressures of advertisers	6	3
Among the major problems of American broadcasting he cites the fear of government control (for example, of giving more power to the FCC)	3	0
He feels that Americans are aware of the problems associated with private ownership of the broadcasting media		
but do little to solve the problems	7	4
and are making real efforts to solve the problems	1	4

Table 20 (Continued)

PERCEPTIONS AND EVALUATIONS OF AMERICAN BROADCASTING:
COMPARISON OF HIGH AND LOW DIFFERENTIATORS

Items that Discriminate	Number of Respondents to Whom Each Item Applies	
	Highs	*Lows*
3. *Third interview: Evaluations of programming in American broadcasting*		
Among features of American broadcasting that could be profitably adopted in his country he cites the use of closed circuit TV in educational programming	3	0
Among features of American broadcasting that should be avoided in his country he cites the Westerns	0	3
Among features of broadcasting in his country that could be profitably adopted in the U.S. he cites the high level of public service and educational programming on radio	0	4
4. *Post-return interview: Evaluations of American broadcasters and broadcasting*		
His evaluation of American broadcasters is largely favorable (rather than mixed)	4	7
Among negative features of American broadcasting he mentions that there is too much commercial interference	3	0
Among the points he tried to get across in reports about his trip he cites		
the importance of avoiding the commercialism of American TV	3	0
the effective use that Americans make of TV for instructional and educational purposes	9	4

great deal about mass communications in America. In this context, it is understandable that the lows would give a more extensive and detailed description of what they had learned. The highs had not only learned less—thus having fewer changes to report—but they also felt keenly that the professional part of the experience was not very valuable and they used the second interview to express this feeling. The coders' ratings no doubt reflected the lack of enthusiasm conveyed in the highs' responses.

The third interview probed in some detail into participants' evaluations of American broadcasting. The highs were generally more critical of American broadcasting, directing most of their criticisms to the pattern of private ownership and control. The second set of items in Table 20 clearly conveys the extent and consistency of this reaction. Most of the highs could see no advantage at all in private ownership of broadcasting, even within the context of American society. The majority of lows also rejected private ownership for their own societies, but they were more likely to consider it suited to American conditions. Highs were more likely to mention pressures from advertisers and the fear of government control among the problems of American broadcasting, and to feel that Americans were doing little to solve the problems associated with private ownership of the media. There is only one exception in this set of items: Lows were more likely to cite the neglect of specialized audiences among the disadvantages of private ownership. The highs' more critical attitude was probably a reflection of their greater professional self-confidence and of their more analytic orientation. It must also be recalled that the highs were more interested in observing America—including its broadcasting system. The lows, being more oriented toward specific professional learnings, were more concerned with the practices of American broadcasting than with the pattern of ownership and control.

There were very few differences between highs and lows in their evaluations of programming features in American broadcasting, and these do not form a general pattern. The lows were, if anything, slightly less positive on these items than the highs, but there is certainly no indication of an overall negative attitude on their part. As can be seen in set 3 of Table 20, several lows (but none of the highs) criticized the Westerns on American TV and clearly implied disappointment with the level of programming on American radio. Several highs (but none of the lows) spoke favorably of the use of closed-circuit TV in American educational programming; this is probably a reflection of the larger proportion of instructional broadcasters in this group.

In the post-return interview (see the fourth set of items in the table), we find confirmation of the highs' more critical attitude toward American broadcasting and particularly toward the commercial system. Highs were less favorable in their evaluations of American broadcasters, more critical of commercial interference in American broadcasting, and more emphatic about the importance of avoiding the commercialism of American TV in their own societies. On the other hand, highs were considerably more likely to stress the effective use being made of TV for instructional and educational purposes in the United States.

Views on international exchange. Table 21 lists items relating

Table 21

VIEWS ON INTERNATIONAL EXCHANGE:
COMPARISON OF HIGH AND LOW DIFFERENTIATORS

Items that Discriminate	Number of Respondents to Whom Each Item Applies	
	Highs	Lows
1. *Fourth interview: Attitudes toward international exchange and participant's own contributions*		
The seminar has made him feel more positive about international exchanges	1	4
Among values of such exchanges of which he has become aware he mentions that		
they make possible a mutually beneficial exchange of professional information	1	4
they promote understanding among peoples, help to reduce cold war tensions	1	5
Among the potential contributions that he could personally make to international exchanges he mentions that he could communicate his own professional knowledge in a given area	6	1
2. *Post-return interview: Attitudes toward and participation in international exchange*		
As a result of his American experience he has become more convinced of the value of international exchange	5	8
The types of exchange that he considers valuable include		
exchange of program material	9	3
exchange of information about developments in communication media	8	3
Among the benefits of international exchange he mentions that it may		
introduce participants to new ideas that can be applied to their own situations	4	1
increase participants' technical knowledge of broadcasting	6	1
Among the contributions that other countries could make to the development of broadcasting in his own country he cites the exchange of personnel	6	2

Table 21 (Continued)

VIEWS ON INTERNATIONAL EXCHANGE:
COMPARISON OF HIGH AND LOW DIFFERENTIATORS

Items that Discriminate	*Number of Respondents to Whom Each Item Applies*	
	Highs	*Lows*
Among the contributions that his country could make to the development of broadcasting elsewhere or to international exchanges he cites its special experiences in instructional or educational broadcasting (for example, literacy training, community education)	4	0
During the past year, his professional contacts with America have included communication with the seminar directors	5	2
During the past year, his professional contacts with other countries have included meetings with visiting broadcasters	6	2
He has some fairly definite plans for participating in further international exchange	8	5

to international exchange that yielded differences between high and low differentiators.

At the end of the seminar (see the first set of items in the table), lows were more likely to report that the experience had made them feel more positive about international exchanges. They had become aware of the value of such endeavors in facilitating mutually beneficial exchange of professional information and in promoting international understanding. These responses are consistent with our impression that the lows came to the seminar with relatively vague goals and expectations, but that they soon found the experience professionally useful and became fully absorbed in it. It is not surprising that this general attitude to international exchange and its potential benefits became more enthusiastic.

Although the highs did not show this *increase* in enthusiasm, we have no reason to believe that, in absolute terms, they were any less positive toward international exchange than the lows. In fact, there are indications that the highs were more geared to active and continuing participation in such exchanges. The last item in set 1 shows that the highs—in keeping with their greater professional self-confidence and their often greater experience—were more likely to feel that they could personally contribute to international exchanges by communicating their own professional knowledge. Also, we have seen earlier (Table 16, seventh set of items) that the highs were more likely to anticipate maintaining a great deal of professional contact with American individuals or organizations. Thus, it seems that, among the lows, the sojourn led to an increase in generalized approval of international exchange with a greater, but mostly undifferentiated awareness of its potential benefits. Among the highs, on the other hand, it further increased the prospects of active involvement in an international network of fellow-broadcasters, to which they were already more likely to belong from the beginning.

The post-return interview, as can be seen in the second set of items in Table 21, seemed to confirm this general pattern. Again, lows more often than highs indicated that, as a result of their American experience, they had become more convinced of the value of international exchange. Highs, on the other hand, were more concrete in spelling out the values of international exchange and more actively involved in actual exchange activities. Thus, while a majority of both groups felt that multinational seminars were highly valuable, many more highs than lows mentioned additional types of exchange—specifically, exchange of program materials and of information about new developments in the media—as potentially valuable. More highs than lows specify such benefits of international exchange as exposure to new ideas that might prove applicable to one's own situation, and increase in technical broadcasting knowledge. More highs than lows felt that others could contribute to the development of broadcasting in their own countries through the exchange of personnel, and that they could contribute to the development of broadcasting elsewhere through their special experiences in educational programs. Finally, highs reported more contacts during the preceding year with the directors of the seminar and with visiting broadcasters from other countries, and they more often had definite plans for participating in further international exchange.

In sum, data from the fourth as well as from the post-return interviews suggest that highs had a greater professional involvement in international exchange than lows and a more elaborated conception of it. Lows, on the other hand, were more inclined to report an increase in global approval of such activities, with relatively little attention to their specific values and only a limited degree of personal involvement in them.

SUMMARY

Our preliminary comparisons of the high and low differentiators indicated that highs brought greater cultural familiarity and linguistic facility to their American experience, that they were able to enter more easily into intensive and reciprocal interactions with Americans, and that they generally related themselves to the host society and to professional issues in a more analytical fashion. These findings suggested two inter-related hypotheses to account for the highs' increased differentiation: (1) Their familiarity with the host culture and language made it easier for them to assimilate new information and to relate it to a preexisting cognitive framework. They were thus able to approach what they saw and heard about American society and broadcasting more analytically and to emerge with more complex and differentiated images. (2) Their greater cultural and linguistic communalities with Americans enabled them to establish more readily a pattern of intensive interaction with their hosts and to engage in the give-and-take of probing conversations. This type of interaction, in turn, acquainted them with the diverse viewpoints held by a variety of Americans and with the complex conceptions these Americans had of their own society. Through the process of observing and discussing these American viewpoints and conceptions, their own images became increasingly differentiated.

The interview data are consistent with both of these hypotheses. We find that the highs did indeed bring to their sojourn a greater degree of familiarity with America and a better-articulated framework for viewing American life and society. They had more prior contacts with Americans and came with more specific plans to make further contacts. Unlike several of the lows, they had no linguistic obstacles to overcome. Thus, they were better equipped—as our hypotheses assume—to enter into intensive interactions with Americans and to integrate new information about America. Furthermore, the interviews show that the highs in fact made many contacts with Americans (maintaining these after they returned home), that they enjoyed exchanging ideas with American colleagues, that they made extensive and detailed observations of American life, and that they approached what they saw and heard more analytically than did the lows. One qualification is necessary here: The lows were also interested in interacting with their hosts—particularly in getting to know many "average Americans"—and showed themselves completely capable of making new acquaintances. Both groups apparently had some enjoyable and warm interpersonal encounters. It seems, however, that the interactions of the lows tended to be more superficially social in nature, tending to bring out the broad human communality between their hosts and themselves. The interactions in which the highs engaged, on the other hand, tended to be focused more on the exchange of ideas—both general and professional—and on the intensive exploration of issues of common concern.

The interview data, thus, tend to support the hypothesis that the increased differentiation manifested by the highs was a product of the more receptive cognitive framework and the greater readiness for intensive interaction with Americans that these individuals brought with them. There are several additional differences between the highs and the lows, however, that stand out from the array of interview data presented in this chapter, and that can help us understand more fully the dispositions with which the two groups came to their American sojourn and the dynamics of the changes they underwent.

First, we find clear indications, at the beginning of the seminar and at several points throughout the sojourn, that the highs came to the American experience with considerable self-confidence about their professional competence and their ability to make the contacts and gain the information they wanted. This self-confidence was no doubt bolstered by their linguistic and cultural proximity to the host society, but it also reflected the reality that a larger proportion of the highs were broadcasters with long professional experience and with involvement in an international network of specialists. In short, the highs more often saw themselves as accomplished professionals, whereas the lows were more inclined to see themselves as apprentices and learners. In line with these self-orientations, highs came with more specific professional goals and expectations, lows with more diffuse ones. The highs' self-confidence about their professional roles and the specificity of their expectations—coupled with the linguistic and cultural familiarity they brought to America—made it possible for them to connect quickly and easily with the Americans they met and to enter into the intensive give-and-take interactions that we hypothesized as mediating their increased differentiation.

Second, we find that the highs—partly because of their professional self-confidence and their initially high expectations—were greatly disappointed in the professional part of their experience, particularly during the university phase of the seminar. They felt, above all, that the level of discussion was lower than they had expected and that they did not have the opportunity to make the personal contributions to the seminar that they had come prepared to make. This professional disappointment most probably accounts for their shift from a largely professional orientation in the first interview to a largely nonprofessional one in the second and subsequent interviews. Even in the first interview, there were indications that the highs were interested in learning about America and filling out their picture of American life and society—for example, through the academic seminars—though this interest constituted only a secondary part of their agenda for the sojourn. When the professional experience turned out to be disappointing, however, they deemphasized specific professional pursuits and gave greater weight to these more general interests. Thus, they focused their attention on learning about America through academic seminars, personal observations, and discussions with Americans, and on such touristic pleasures as meeting people, seeing sights, and taking in the country's scenic beauties.

This does not mean that the highs lost all interest in professional matters. They did find some of their professional experiences rewarding, particularly during the travel period. For example, they seemed to enjoy their encounters with American colleagues and established professional contacts that they maintained after returning home. In short, they acted like the accomplished professionals that they felt themselves to be and they used the trip to expand their network of professional relations. They were no longer dependent on specific professional accomplishments, however, for deriving a sense of satisfaction from the sojourn. Indeed, the indications are that, once they revised their goals in response to the initial disappointment, their overall satisfaction with the experience was quite high.

The highs' professional disappointment and their shift, apparently in response to this disappointment, to nonprofessional pursuits add a new element to our understanding of their increased differentiation. We propose that, since the highs' experience was relatively unrewarding from a professional point of view, they turned their attention to alternative sources of satisfaction. Having had some interest, to begin with, in observing American life and deepening their knowledge of American institutions, they now proceeded to concentrate on this part of their agenda. The professional disappointment did not, in our view, *create* the interest in general learning about America, but it gave greater weight to it than it might otherwise have received. This greater interest in general observations, coupled with the highs' capacity to engage in intensive interactions with Americans and to integrate new information about America into a fairly well-articulated cognitive framework, led to the marked increase in differentiation of images manifested by this group. Thus, the highs' professional disappointment helped to trigger off a process to which they were already predisposed. Given their predispositions and their multiple agenda, it is quite possible that they would have come away with more highly differentiated images even if their professional experience had been entirely satisfactory. The disappointment, however, reinforced and intensified the process by providing additional motivation to engage in it.

The data do not imply that disappointment is a necessary condition for the development of differentiated images. What they do suggest is that the capacity for such change is not a sufficient condition to bring it about; there must also be some situational motivation to set the process into motion. In the present case it happened to be the highs' professional disappointment that provided this motivation. It ought to be possible, however, to find other—and less risky—ways of building such motivations into exchange programs.

The low differentiators, according to our original hypotheses— supported by the interview data—did not have the highs' *capacity* to develop highly differentiated images: Because of their greater cultural and linguistic barriers, they were not as ready to establish intensive interactions with Americans or to assimilate new information into a preexisting cognitive framework. We can now add that the lows also did not have the highs' *motivation* to concentrate on general observations of America, since they found the professional part of the experience not at all disappointing. The lows had come with more diffuse professional goals and saw themselves primarily, as we have already noted, as learners and apprentices. They were, therefore, very satisfied with the professional activities that had been lined up for them and with the composition of the seminar. They considered the level of the discussion, as well as of their personal participation, quite appropriate to their needs and their perceived capacities. Unlike the highs, they became—if anything—*more* professionally oriented as the seminar proceeded and more absorbed in professional activities (though they also derived some pleasure from their personal encounters with Americans). Having started out with rather vague expectations, they became eager for workshop-like experiences, focusing on specific problems relevant to their work situations at home. After they had been back home for some time, they seemed to feel that the seminar had indeed been relevant. They reported that the American sojourn had affected their professional activities and enhanced their skills, and they exuded a sense of greater competence and professional self-confidence.

It was, perhaps, fortunate that the highs rather than the lows experienced professional disappointment. The highs, because of their dispositions and interests, were able to fall back on nonprofessional activities without difficulty and to derive satisfaction from them. Moreover, though the professional experience was not quite what they had hoped it would be, they were able to use it to some professional advantage by making new contacts and expanding their international network. Thus, despite their professional disappointment, the overall experience was rewarding and, in fact, conducive to meaningful changes. By contrast, if the experience had been professionally disappointing for the lows, one wonders if they would have as readily found compensatory satisfactions. The fact that they did not bring to the sojourn the same capacity or desire to fill out an already well-articulated framework for viewing America as the highs suggests that at least this alternative avenue of deriving satisfaction from the experience would not have been available to them. On the other hand, the lows did express an interest in meeting "average Americans" and making personal acquaintances. Insofar as the trip provided opportunities for such encounters, they might have found it enjoyable and enriching even in the absence of high professional rewards. There is no question that the lows, though they were at some disadvantage in this strange situation, had many personal resources to draw upon, but we have no way of knowing how well these would have served them in the face of professional disappointment.

The different reactions of the highs and lows to the professional experience illustrate the dangers of devising a single program for a heterogeneous group. Clearly there is a need to match programs with the specific needs and interests of each participant or subgroup of participants. Yet our data also suggest that a less than perfect matching is not totally devastating, provided there is enough variety and flexibility built into the program. There is more than one way in which an exchange experience may prove satisfying and valuable to its participants, and different individuals may draw their rewards from different features of the experience. Even a disappointment on a central dimension does not preclude satisfaction and meaningful change on other dimensions. What is essential, however, is that the total experience allow for a range of options and a variety of satisfactions—as the present seminar did, particularly in the way in which the travel period was organized. No matter how carefully a program is tailored to the specific needs of its participants (and we consider such tailoring crucial despite the resilience of many participants in the face of disappointment), one cannot assume that it will prove satisfactory to all concerned in all respects. There must, therefore, be room for movement—for pursuing different goals, indulging different interests, deriving different benefits—within the overall framework.

In much of the discussion in this chapter, the focus has been primarily on the high differentiators, rather than the lows. This was a direct consequence of the definition of the two groups in terms of the presence or absence of differentiation change. Insofar as we were interested in understanding the dynamics of this type of change, we tended to concentrate on the group that manifested it and treated the lows, essentially, as a control group. There were some indications, however, that the lows may be an interesting group in its own right, marked not merely by the absence of change in differentiation, but by the presence of some other syndrome which could not emerge clearly from the present data. Perhaps another way of forming groups for comparison may pick up this syndrome more adequately. One possibility that readily suggests itself in this connection is a comparison between Europeans and non-Europeans. We have already seen that there is some correlation, though not a strong one, between high versus low differentiation and European versus non-European origin. Moreover, some of the differences that we have noted between high and low differentiators are quite reminiscent of differences one might expect to find between Europeans and non-Europeans participating in the present type of seminar. To explore this possibility, we have divided our sample into Europeans and non-Europeans and shall proceed, in the next chapter, to present comparisons between these two groups—comparisons that partially overlap those made in the present chapter.

14

Europeans and Non-Europeans

In Chapter Thirteen we compared two subgroups of participants that had been selected on the basis of an outcome variable. One group—the high differentiators—consisted of individuals about whom we knew that their image of America and American broadcasting had become more complex and differentiated in the course of the year that included their American sojourn; the other group—the low differentiators—consisted of individuals who had not shown this change. Our task then was to explore the factors distinguishing these two groups—the personal characteristics, experiences, and reactions to these experiences that seemed to be related to increased differentiation.

In the present chapter, we are again comparing two subgroups of participants, selected, however, on an entirely different basis—namely, on the basis of a difference in certain of their defining characteristics. Any visitor brings with him certain personal characteristics that help to shape the nature of his experience in the host country. These may include his store of knowledge, his goals, his personal agenda for the visit, his pre-existing conceptions of the host, and his capacity to speak casually and

244

intimately with citizens of the host nation. These characteristics guide his perceptions, determine his modes of coping with his experiences, and evoke particular responses from those who meet him. They therefore play an important role—in interaction with the situation in which the visitor actually finds himself and with the experiences that he undergoes—in determining his reactions to the sojourn and the impact it has upon him. Each visitor, of course, has a unique set of such personal characteristics. There are certain characteristics, however, shared within various subgroups of visitors, that may affect their ways of relating themselves to the experience with some degree of consistency. It thus becomes possible to identify distinct patterns of reaction for such groups. On the basis of earlier research and perusal of our own data, we suspected that European versus non-European origin of the seminar participants might be such a distinguishing characteristic. The present chapter is devoted, therefore, to a comparison between the European and non-European members of the seminar.

We are using the term *European* here as the best approximation of the distinguishing characteristic that we have in mind. We classified as European, for our purposes, not only those participants who resided on the European continent, but all those whose cultural origin was essentially European and who (regardless of where they were living) were identified with the industrialized sector of the world. Thus, we included as European in our classification not only the British, Italian, Swedish, and Yugoslav participants, but also those from Australia, Cyprus, and Israel, and the Englishmen working in Africa. Participants from Iran, the Philippines, Thailand, and Jamaica, as well as the seven African participants, we classified as non-Europeans. The Japanese participants were difficult to classify in terms of the scheme we had in mind, since they came from a culture that is non-European in origin, yet in terms of level of industrial development is clearly closer to Europe than it is to Africa and much of Asia. We decided, therefore, to omit the Japanese participants from the present comparison. We were left with twenty-six cases, of whom thirteen were classified as Europeans and thirteen as non-Europeans.

PRELIMINARY COMPARISONS

As in Chapter Thirteen, our major comparisons in the present chapter are based on the interview responses of the two groups. First, however, we shall present some of the differences in the group characteristics of the Europeans and non-Europeans, in their group behavior as rated by the observer, and in their changes in attitude as assessed by the questionnaires.

Group characteristics. By definition, the cultural background of the Europeans was more similar to American culture than that of the non-Europeans. (This does not mean that all of the Europeans, as individuals, were necessarily more familiar with American culture than the non-Europeans.) The Europeans were all white-skinned; twelve of the thirteen non-Europeans were black or Oriental. The Europeans were identified with the industrialized part of the world (even if they lived in a relatively undeveloped area), the non-Europeans with the developing part of the world. The Europeans were generally associated with experienced and sophisticated broadcasting systems or received their basic training within such systems, the non-Europeans less so.

So much for the defining characteristics of the two groups. In terms of areas of professional specialization, they distributed as follows:

	Europeans	Non-Europeans
Educational broadcasting	4	4
News and current events	5	2
General programming	4	7

Thus, a somewhat larger proportion of the Europeans was concerned with news broadcasting and documentaries; a somewhat larger proportion of non-Europeans was concerned with general programming. In the light of findings we reported in earlier chapters, there thus ought to be a somewhat greater tendency for the Europeans to be interested in general American affairs, since political or cultural insights far removed from the seminar would still be grist for the professional mill of the newscaster.

Observational data. Figure 2 provides a graphic presentation of the differences in group behavior between Europeans and non-Europeans, based on the weekly ratings by the group observer. The group behavior of each participant, it will be recalled, was rated along a number of dimensions, which are listed and defined in Appendix A. Figure 2 presents mean ratings for those nine dimensions on which consistent differences between the two groups emerged.

The pattern of differences is, in some respects, reminiscent of that found for the comparison between high and low differentiators (see Figure 1 in the last chapter). The Europeans, like the high differentiators, received higher ratings on participation and involvement. But the differences between the Europeans and non-Europeans on these two dimensions, though fairly consistent, are very small. On the other hand, ratings of the *nature* of the two groups' contributions—as distinguished from the *amount* of involvement or interest—separate the Europeans and non-Europeans quite clearly. Europeans were rated higher in the extent to which they made contributions in the form of innovation (for example, introducing new topics or approaches), exposition (for example, giving information or explanations), and clarification (for example, making distinctions or focusing the discussion). In other words, it seems that the Europeans differed from the non-Europeans, not so much in the degree to which they dominated the group discussions in general, but in the degree to which they adopted a didactic or expert role in these discussions.

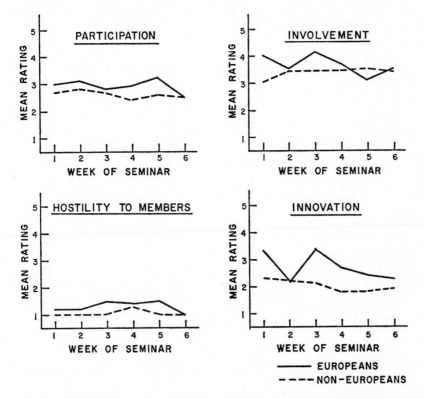

Figure 2. Weekly mean ratings of the behavior of Europeans and non-Europeans in scheduled group sessions on each of nine dimensions. (*Continued on next page.*)

Hostile behavior toward other members was very rarely observed in the group sessions; when it did occur, however, it was almost always among Europeans. Nurturant behavior toward other members was also quite rare; when it did occur, however, it was generally among the non-Europeans. Furthermore, non-Europeans were somewhat more likely to

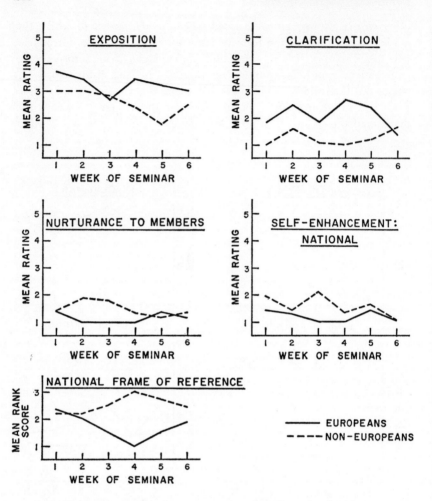

Figure 2 (cont.). Weekly mean ratings of behavior of Europeans and non-Europeans in scheduled group sessions on each of nine dimensions.

seek self-enhancement by presenting their countries' accomplishments and experiences in a positive light. Finally, non-Europeans were more likely than Europeans to adopt a national frame of reference in their group remarks (as shown in the graph) and less likely to adopt a professional frame of reference. These findings concerning frame of reference, however, as we mentioned in the last chapter, must be viewed with caution, since some of the mean ranks are based on a smaller than usual number of cases. All in all, the differences on the dimensions of hostility, nurturance, self-enhancement, and frame of reference are not very strong, but they are at least consistent with the view that the non-Europeans felt less secure about their status in the group. They seemed somewhat more concerned about maintaining personal relationships at a friendly level and were more inclined to adopt the national role, which was less threatening in that context than the professional role.

In sum, the observational data suggest that the Europeans were more prone than the non-Europeans to present themselves as established, knowledgeable specialists, confident about their professional contributions to the proceedings. Their average level of participation was only slightly higher than that of the non-Europeans—probably because five of the Europeans, but none of the non-Europeans, had some language difficulties. Europeans were more likely, however, to make contributions in a didactic or expert capacity, and showed less concern with interpersonal harmony or national status.

Questionnaire data. In comparing Europeans and non-Europeans on attitude changes, as manifested in their before- and after-questionnaire responses, we turn first to the differentiation index. For a rough indication of the relationship between cultural origin and change in differentiation, we can compare the number of Europeans with the number of non-Europeans who were classified as high versus low differentiators by the criteria described in Chapter Thirteen. If we cross-tabulate the participants who show up in both breakdowns we obtain the following distribution:

	Europeans	*Non-Europeans*
High Differentiators	6	3
Low Differentiators	4	5

It can be seen that Europeans were somewhat more likely to be classified among the highs than non-Europeans, but the relationship between these two dimensions is not particularly strong. This is not surprising when we recall, for example, that the low differentiator group included four Europeans from non-English-speaking countries. To be sure, as we saw in the last chapter, one subset of Europeans—the participants from English-speaking countries—were all classified as highs, and one subset of non-Europeans—the participants from African countries—were all classified as lows. When we draw on the total group of Europeans and non-Europeans, however, the overlap between the two bases of classification is far from perfect.

To obtain a more refined indication of the relationship between cultural origin and change in differentiation, we compared scores on the index of change in differentiation for Europeans and non-Europeans. For this comparison we used the twelve Europeans and nine non-Europeans for whom stable scores on the index were available.[1] The mean score for Europeans was 2.33, the mean for non-Europeans 1.22. The same relationship holds when we examine separately the scores on the set of index items measuring change in differentiation in the image of America and Americans, and on the set dealing with the image of American broadcasting. Though the difference thus appears to be consistent, it does not attain statistical significance by the usual standards.

In short, it can be concluded that Europeans tended to show a greater increase in differentiation than non-Europeans, but the difference between the two groups is small and nonsignificant. Insofar as there is a relationship between the two variables, we can expect to find some parallels between the European versus non-European and the high versus low comparisons. That is, we can expect the reactions of Europeans to resemble those of the high differentiators, as described in Chapter Thirteen, and the reactions of non-Europeans to resemble those of the low differentiators. Since, however, the relationship between the two variables and the overlap between the two classificatory schemes are relatively slight, it may well be that Europeans and non-Europeans will differ from each other along rather different dimensions than those we found to be important in distinguishing between high and low differentiators.

Turning now to other questionnaire items, we find only two differences between Europeans and non-Europeans that are worthy of note. First, there is some indication that non-Europeans showed a greater increase than Europeans in favorable attitudes toward America and Americans. Table 22 lists five codes based on questionnaire responses that we considered relevant to respondents' evaluations of America and Americans in general (see Chapter Twelve, particularly the discussion of Table 12). On four of these five codes—that is, all but code (2)—non-Europeans showed more change in a favorable direction than did Europeans.[2]

---

[1] In assigning individuals to the high and low differentiator groups, we had excluded some participants because they had scores too close to the median and some because they had answered too few of the questions on which the change index was based. The former individuals were used in the present comparison, since they did have stable scores; the latter were omitted.

[2] For code 5, a *negative* change implies a more favorable attitude toward America, on the assumption that the more favorable his attitude, the less satisfied a respondent will be with the information about America presented by the mass media. Needless to say, a negative change does not necessarily reflect a more favorable evaluation of America; it may simply indicate that, having become more familiar with America, the respondent came to realize that his country's mass media did not adequately cover information about America.

Table 22

MEAN BEFORE-, AFTER-, AND CHANGE-SCORES ON EACH OF FIVE CODES RELEVANT TO THE EVALUATION OF AMERICA AND AMERICANS

Codes	Europeans				Non-Europeans			
	N	Before	After	Change	N	Before	After	Change
1. Coder rating (on a 5-point scale) of degree to which the "typical American" is described as well-informed and knowledgeable about the respondent's own country (Question 11)	12	2.92	3.00	.08	9	2.22	2.89	.67
2. Coder rating (on a 5-point scale) of degree to which the "typical American" is described as sympathetic to the respondent's own country (Question 11)	12	3.42	3.42	.00	9	3.22	2.89	-.33
3. Coder rating (on a 5-point scale) of degree to which the "typical American" is described as accepting the respondent's own country on equal terms (Question 11)	12	3.33	3.08	-.25	9	2.33	2.56	.23
4. Coder rating (on a 5-point scale) of degree of favorableness of respondent's general attitude toward America (Questions 4, 7, 11, and 15b)	13	3.00	3.15	.15	8	3.00	3.25	.25
5. Respondent rating (on a 4-point scale) of adequacy of coverage of information about the U.S. by the mass media of his own country (Question 15a)	13	2.38	3.08	.70	13	2.54	2.38	-.16

We combined the five codes into an index and computed an index score for each respondent. Again, non-Europeans showed more favorable change than Europeans on the combined score, but the difference between the two groups was not quite significant by the Mann-Whitney U test.

Secondly, there are some indications that non-Europeans became more aware of the limitations of the broadcasting systems in their own countries. Question 3 asked about the experiences in the respondent's own country from which broadcasters in other countries could potentially benefit. Europeans showed a small increase in the number of content areas within which they felt others could benefit from their own broadcasting systems, but non-Europeans showed a decrease. The difference between the two groups on this item was significant at the .05 level by the Mann-Whitney U test. Question 8 asked about problems facing TV in the respondent's own country. Non-Europeans showed a greater increase than Europeans in the number of content areas within which they cited problems in response to this question (though Europeans showed a greater increase in the number of areas within which they cited causes and solutions for such problems). The difference falls short of statistical significance, but it is especially interesting because it goes counter to the general tendency of increased differentiation among Europeans. Taken together, these two items suggest that the non-Europeans developed a more critical approach toward their own broadcasting systems, although there is no indication that they became generally less favorable toward them.

In sum, the questionnaire data tell us (1) that the Europeans tended to show a greater increase in the differentiation of their images of America and American broadcasting than the non-Europeans—a nonsignificant difference, which is probably accounted for to a large extent by the European participants from English-speaking countries (all of whom were high differentiators) and the African participants (most of whom were low differentiators, none highs) ; (2) that the non-Europeans tended to show a greater increase in favorable attitudes toward America and Americans than the Europeans; and (3) that the non-Europeans tended to show a greater increase in the critical awareness of limitations and problems of their own broadcasting systems.

Hypotheses. Our problem in the present chapter is different from that in Chapter Thirteen. There we were comparing two groups defined in terms of an outcome variable and we explored conditions and processes that would help us account for the differences in outcome between the two groups. Here, however, we are comparing two groups defined in terms of an important set of characteristics that they brought to their exchange experience and we are concerned with the effects of these different "inputs" on their reactions to the experience and its impact upon them.

We have not drawn up a set of specific predictions about differential reactions and impacts for the two groups. The preliminary comparisons presented so far, however, suggest some mediating variables that may help us organize the main data of this study, that is, the data based on the five interviews.

By definition, the European participants came from cultures more similar to the host culture, from technologically more advanced societies, and from more highly developed broadcasting systems. These differences, no doubt, help to account for the differences in group behavior suggested by our observational data. The Europeans seemed to be more secure about their national and particularly their professional status than the non-Europeans. They were more likely to present themselves as established, knowledgeable specialists, confident about their professional contributions to the group's proceedings. We would hypothesize that this difference in self-image and self-presentation played a major role in determining the two groups' approaches to the experience and hence the ways in which it affected them.

The Europeans, in this view, were more likely to see themselves as professional colleagues to their American counterparts, equal to them in every respect, and capable of making expert contributions out of their own knowledge and experience, not only in the seminar sessions, but also in their visits to broadcasting facilities and in their interaction with American broadcasters. The non-Europeans, on the other hand, were more likely to see themselves as learners, concerned with acquiring new information and skills that they would be able to apply in their home situations and eager to benefit from the greater experience of American and European broadcasters. We would expect, accordingly, certain systematic differences in the agenda of the two groups. Europeans would be expected to take a greater interest in observing American broadcasting, in obtaining general information about it, in comparing it to their own systems, in examining it critically—in short, in focusing upon it as an object of interest in its own right. Non-Europeans, by contrast, would be expected to focus more heavily on their own professional situations and problems and to look to American broadcasting for more specific information about practices and procedures that might be relevant to these concerns. These differences in agenda, furthermore, might affect the orientation of the two groups, not only to American broadcasting, but also to American society in general.

The few differences between the two groups that we found in the questionnaire data are consistent with this general hypothesis. The Europeans tended to develop a somewhat more differentiated view of American broadcasting and American society, as one might expect from the broader agenda that we postulated for them. They also seemed to be somewhat more critical of America than the non-Europeans; we would have expected them to be more critical of American broadcasting as well, but the differences on this dimension were very slight. The non-Europeans tended to develop a more critical awareness of the limitations and problems of their own broadcasting systems, which is consistent with the focus on the back-home situation that we postulated for them. While the questionnaire data are, thus, consistent with our hypothesis, they are very limited in scope and can, moreover, be easily interpreted in other terms. To gain a fuller picture of the extent to which the hypothesized differences in self-presentation and agenda help us organize the differential reactions of Europeans and non-Europeans, we must turn to the interview responses of the two groups.

INTERVIEW RESPONSES

As in Chapter Thirteen, we shall present and discuss all of the codes on which there was at least a 30 per cent difference between the two groups. Since each of the two groups contains thirteen respondents, a 30 per cent difference in the present comparisons corresponds to a frequency difference of four cases. For example, in analyzing the first interview, coders were asked to check whether or not a given participant anticipated language difficulties in connection with the academic seminars. As can be seen in Table 23, they checked "yes" for eight of the thirteen Europeans (62 per cent) and for four of the thirteen non-Europeans (31 per cent). We have thus a frequency difference of four cases between the two groups—the minimum required to meet the 30 per cent criterion for inclusion in the tables that follow. In reading these tables, it must be kept in mind that, with Ns of thirteen per group, a 30 per cent difference is small and unstable. As we pointed out in Chapter Thirteen, therefore, we cannot draw meaningful conclusions on the basis of a single item, but must search instead for clusters of items that reveal a consistent pattern.

Expectations and goals for the trip. Items from the initial interview that show differences in the expectations and goals with which Europeans and non-Europeans approached the experience are listed in Table 23.

The first set of items tends to support the distinction in the professional self-images and self-presentations of the two groups that we have proposed. On the one hand, the non-Europeans seemed to see themselves as learners, concerned with the applicability of their American experiences to their situations back home. Thus, they were more likely than the Europeans to indicate that they had wanted to come to America on previous occasions in order to add to their educational background, and that they

Table 23

EXPECTATIONS AND GOALS FOR THE TRIP:
COMPARISON OF EUROPEANS AND NON-EUROPEANS

Items that Discriminate[a]	*Number of Respondents to Whom Each Item Applies*	
	Europeans	*Non-Europeans*
1. Professional goals and self-image		
The participant previously considered visiting America to add to his educational background	0	4
He expects to set up permanent professional contacts in the United States	8	13
He believes that he was selected as a seminar participant because of the quality of his past work	5	1
He feels that the diversity in professional background, knowledge, and skills of the seminar participants may lower the level of discussion	5	0
He is not clear about the criteria for the composition of the group	1	6
2. Preparations and plans for the trip		
To prepare for the trip, he read at least some of the books about America that were sent to him	11	4
He reports that the books or other materials needed to prepare for the trip arrived too late or not at all	2	6
He feels that, in general, the agencies involved planned the trip adequately	13	8
3. Anticipated new learnings about America		
He anticipates that the academic seminars will provide information that he can put to specific nonprofessional use (for example, general lecturing, writing, social conversation)	8	2
He includes general sight-seeing among the accomplishments he anticipates from his travels	11	5
The impressions of America that he wants to verify are not very detailed and elaborated	6	11

[a] All of these items are taken from the first interview.

Table 23 (Continued)

EXPECTATIONS AND GOALS FOR THE TRIP:
COMPARISON OF EUROPEANS AND NON-EUROPEANS

Items that Discriminate[a]	Number of Respondents to Whom Each Item Applies	
	Europeans	Non-Europeans
4. Anticipated problems and difficulties		
He anticipates difficulties in connection with the academic seminars	8	4
. . . because of his poor knowledge of English	6	1
He anticipates difficulties in connection with the professional seminars	8	3
. . . because of his poor knowledge of English	5	1

[a] All of these items are taken from the first interview.

expected to establish professional contacts in America on which they could draw in their future work. It must be noted, however, that these two items provide only indirect support for our formulation and will have to be reinforced by findings from later tables before we can conclude that non-Europeans were indeed more concerned with specific learning and application. The Europeans, on the other hand, clearly displayed a high degree of professional self-confidence and presented themselves as knowledgeable and skilled specialists. Thus, they were more likely than the non-Europeans to believe that they had been selected for participation in the seminar because of the quality of their past work, and to express concern that—because of the diversity of the participants—seminar discussions might not be quite up to their own level. The final item in the first set can be interpreted as a generalized indication of the uncertainty of non-Europeans—in contrast to Europeans—about their own status within the group.

The second set of items yields little of special importance to our formulation. We see that non-Europeans were more likely to report that the books and other materials needed to prepare for the trip arrived too late or not at all, and less likely to feel that the agencies involved in planning their trip did an adequate job. Both of these items probably reflect the reality that facilities for communication of Americans with non-European countries are poorer than those with European countries: Mail deliveries are slower and agencies charged with making travel arrangements are less fully informed and equipped to handle the necessary details. We also find that, even allowing for the fact that fewer non-Europeans received the books about America or received them in time, a larger proportion of Europeans read at least some of them. It may be that the greater similarity between European and American culture made it easier for the Europeans to grapple with these books.

The third set of items also shows one difference that is probably attributable to the Europeans' greater cultural familiarity with the host country. The impressions of America that non-Europeans wanted to verify contained less detail and elaboration than those of the Europeans. The Europeans, it seems, came with an image of America that was already more differentiated and better structured. The other two items in this set are particularly germane to our hypothesis that the two groups—in view of their different self-images and self-presentations—would show differences in agenda that might affect their orientations, not only to American broadcasting, but also to America in general. Indeed, the Europeans were more likely to express an interest in the academic seminars and their potential nonprofessional uses, and in general sightseeing. We suspect that the non-Europeans were too heavily focused on the specific professional relevance of the seminar to emphasize extraprofessional goals. We shall find further evidence for this distinction in subsequent tables.

The final set of items in Table 23 shows that Europeans were more likely to anticipate difficulties in both academic and professional seminars than non-Europeans. This difference is entirely accounted for by the greater concern among Europeans with their poor knowledge of English. Thus, these items merely remind us of something we already know: that the Europeans included a subgroup of participants from non-English-speaking countries who had varying degrees of difficulty with the English language. It will be recalled from Chapter Thirteen that these Europeans (in contrast to those from English-speaking countries) had low scores on the index of change in differentiation.

In sum, Table 23 suggests that Europeans brought to their sojourn a relatively high degree of professional self-confidence and an image of themselves as accomplished specialists, capable of making useful contributions to a professional exchange. At the same time, they came with a relatively broad agenda, which included an interest in learning about America and seeing the country. The non-Europeans, on the other hand, were less confident about their status and more likely to see themselves as learners. Moreover, they seemed to have a narrower agenda, being oriented toward acquiring specific professional information and skills of potential relevance to their work situations back home.

Satisfactions, perceived accomplishments, and perceived impact of trip. Table 24 presents the items that distinguish between the two groups in terms of their satisfactions with the sojourn, their perceived accomplishments, and the impact they felt the experience had upon them.

We see, first of all, that the Europeans expressed greater satisfaction with their visit at the time of the second interview than did the non-Europeans. This difference in overall satisfaction can, we think, be accounted for by the differences in the agenda of the two groups. The Europeans, with their broader agenda, found larger portions of the program relevant to their interests (as can be seen in Table 25, first set of items) and were thus generally more satisfied with the experience. The non-Europeans, on the other hand, tended to focus more narrowly on those activities that were directly germane to their professional concerns. Though they were quite satisfied with those portions of the program—in fact, considerably more so than the Europeans (as can be seen, again, in Table 25, first set of items)—they probably felt that not enough time was devoted to them. Thus, since they judged the program as a whole to be relatively lacking in relevance, their overall satisfaction tended to be lower.

The second set of items in Table 24 deals with the perceived sources of satisfaction and accomplishment during the university phase of the seminar. Europeans, we find, were more likely to cite the academic seminars and the tours of communication facilities among their most valuable experiences. This is in keeping with our hypothesis that Europeans were more interested in learning about America and American broadcasting. In the professional as well as the nonprofessional domain, they tended to take the stance of the observer. Thus, unlike the non-Europeans, they found the academic seminars and the tours of facilities useful as ends in themselves, giving them the opportunity to observe American practices, to gather facts about them, to analyze them, and to compare them to their own.

Somewhat surprising is the finding that non-Europeans—more so than Europeans—described their most enjoyable experiences as ones involving interpersonal aspects of the American environment. We would have expected them, in line with our hypothesis, to emphasize professionally relevant experiences. The present finding suggests that the non-Europeans were not totally caught up in their professional pursuits, but also enjoyed meeting and interacting with people. Such experiences, however, constituted pleasant by-products for them, rather than part of their "official" agenda. The non-Europeans probably made sharper distinctions than the Europeans between what was useful and what was enjoyable. As

Table 24

SATISFACTIONS, PERCEIVED ACCOMPLISHMENTS, AND
PERCEIVED IMPACT OF TRIP:
COMPARISON OF EUROPEANS AND NON-EUROPEANS

Items that Discriminate	*Number of Respondents to Whom Each Item Applies*	
	Europeans	Non-Europeans
1. *Second interview: Level of satisfaction during university phase*		
The participant has been very satisfied or quite satisfied with his visit thus far	12	8
2. *Second interview: Sources of satisfaction and accomplishment during university phase*		
He perceives his most enjoyable experiences as involving interpersonal aspects of the American environment	4	9
Among his most noteworthy, valuable, or enjoyable experiences he cites		
exposure to the academic seminars	7	3
the tours of different communication facilities	9	5
The American sojourn has made him more aware of the need for more rapid advancement in education in his home country	0	4
The American sojourn has made him more aware of his home country's potential for growth and progress	1	5
3. *Third interview: Level of satisfaction during travel phase*		
He has been very satisfied with the travel phase of his visit	11	7
He describes his present feelings about the visit largely in positive terms	11	7
His feelings about the visit have become more positive since he left the university	9	5
4. *Third interview: Problems during travel phase*		
Something has come up at home to make him wish he were there	1	8
. . . more specifically, a problem of a professional nature	0	6

Table 24 (Continued)

SATISFACTIONS, PERCEIVED ACCOMPLISHMENTS, AND
PERCEIVED IMPACT OF TRIP:
COMPARISON OF EUROPEANS AND NON-EUROPEANS

	Number of Respondents to Whom Each Item Applies	
Items that Discriminate	Europeans	Non-Europeans
5. *Third interview: Sources of satisfaction and accomplishment during travel phase*		
Among his important and enjoyable experiences he mentions aspects of the physical environment (natural and man-made)	12	8
He has learned new approaches to programming that will be of direct use to him after return home	1	5
6. *Fourth interview: Sources of satisfaction and accomplishment during entire sojourn*		
Looking back over the entire four-month period, he perceives his most meaningful and/or enjoyable experiences to have been in nonprofessional rather than professional areas	9	5
Among his most meaningful or enjoyable experiences he cites		
exposure to new program ideas	3	8
observation of local broadcasting facilities and activities	10	4
firsthand exposure to American life	12	8
observations of the physical environment (natural and man-made)	7	3
Among his most important accomplishments he cites		
gaining a greater understanding of the American way of life, of American values	12	8
establishing new relationships with fellow professionals	4	8
Among original goals for the trip that he feels he has achieved he cites the acquisition of a firsthand knowledge of the United States	13	9

Table 24 (Continued)

SATISFACTIONS, PERCEIVED ACCOMPLISHMENTS, AND
PERCEIVED IMPACT OF TRIP:
COMPARISON OF EUROPEANS AND NON-EUROPEANS

Items that Discriminate	Number of Respondents to Whom Each Item Applies	
	Europeans	Non-Europeans
Among things that he now feels he should have handled differently, to make the experience more rewarding, he cites the advance preparation for the seminar in his own country	11	7
7. *Fourth interview: Changes in perspective attributed to the sojourn*		
He feels that he has changed his perspective about America, American institutions, the American people	12	7
He feels that his experiences in America have given him a new perspective on his own country	8	12
. . . specifically, he now has a greater appreciation of his country's potential for economic and political development	0	5
He feels that his experiences in America have given him a new perspective on his professional role	4	8
He feels that his view of the role of broadcasting in his own country has changed	8	4
8. *Post-return interview: Satisfactions and accomplishments in retrospect*		
Among ways in which the trip exceeded his expectations he cites		
the opportunity to travel throughout the country	10	6
the opportunity to learn about educational TV	0	5
Among the most satisfying aspects of the experience he cites		
the opportunity to travel around the country and meet average Americans	6	2
the opportunity to see the beauty of the American landscape	4	0

Table 24 (Continued)

SATISFACTIONS, PERCEIVED ACCOMPLISHMENTS, AND
PERCEIVED IMPACT OF TRIP:
COMPARISON OF EUROPEANS AND NON-EUROPEANS

Items that Discriminate	Number of Respondents to Whom Each Item Applies	
	Europeans	Non-Europeans
While in America he established many professional contacts with American individuals or organizations	6	1
9. *Post-return interview: Perceived effects of the sojourn*		
He has made attempts to apply specific ideas or procedures acquired in America to his professional activities, and the outcome of these attempts		
was unsuccessful	1	0
was partially successful and partially unsuccessful	3	0
was successful	5	3
is still uncertain at this time	0	7
Among the ideas acquired in America that he introduced in his own system he cites new types of programs (for example, audience participation, documentaries, quizzes)	5	0
During the past year, he has had professional contacts with American broadcasting and educational networks, established while he was in America	10	5
People he met in America with whom he has maintained some personal contact include		
American broadcasters	5	1
other seminar participants	9	5
The American experience has made him more aware of his country's limitations	0	6
The trip created some special problems for him	2	7
. . . which were of a nonprofessional nature	0	5
10. *Post-return interview: Reported changes since his return home*		
He reports no change in position or responsibilities during the past year	7	3

Table 24 (Continued)

SATISFACTIONS, PERCEIVED ACCOMPLISHMENTS, AND
PERCEIVED IMPACT OF TRIP:
COMPARISON OF EUROPEANS AND NON-EUROPEANS

Items that Discriminate	*Number of Respondents to Whom Each Item Applies*	
	Europeans	*Non-Europeans*
. . . nor had he expected such changes to occur	7	1
As a basis for changes in his position or responsibilities during the past year he cites personal career considerations	0	4
He anticipates a change in his position or responsibilities in the near future	3	8
He reports that he feels more satisfied with his job now than he did last year	2	7
Among the reasons for his increased job satisfaction during the past year he cites recognition by others of his ability	0	5
He has not introduced any innovations or changes in his work situation	5	1
Innovations at his job that he has considered or has carried out include changes of a technical nature	4	0
Among the directions in which he would like to see his own country's broadcasting system develop he cites		
technical advances	5	1
expansion of services (for example, increasing the number of channels)	7	2
His plans for the future have changed during the past year	4	10
He considers a future visit to the United States very likely	6	10

far as their enjoyment of interpersonal contacts is concerned, it should be noted that we are not dealing with an isolated finding here. We will find further indications, in subsequent tables, that non-Europeans tended to involve themselves more fully in interpersonal relationships than Europeans, particularly in nonprofessional contexts. The Europeans were very interested in American life, but they were perhaps more likely to maintain their distance, in keeping with their stance as observers.

Two of the items included in the second set indicate that non-Europeans were more likely to report new insights about the needs and potentials of their own countries. This may be due to their greater tendency, as we have proposed, to focus on the situation back home and to relate their experiences to problems in their own societies. It may also be due to the fact that they came from societies that were undergoing dramatic change and development and thus offered greater opportunities for reassessment than the stabler European societies.

Turning to the travel period, we find again, in the third set of items, a higher level of overall satisfaction among the Europeans. They were more likely to report being very satisfied with the travel phase of the visit and to describe their feelings at the time of the third interview in largely positive terms. They were also more likely than the non-Europeans to indicate that their feelings about the visit had become more positive since leaving the university. The fourth set of items provides some indirect corroboration of the Europeans' higher level of satisfaction. Eight non-Europeans—compared to only one European—reported during the third interview that something (in most cases a problem of a professional nature) had come up at home to make them wish they were there. If we interpret this item as a projective indicator of satisfaction (see Chapter Thirteen, discussion of Table 16), we have further evidence of a relatively high level of overall satisfaction among Europeans, as compared to non-Europeans, during the travel phase. The explanation we can offer here is similar to the one offered above for the Europeans' greater satisfaction with the university phase of the seminar: Given their broader agenda, the Europeans found almost all of their travel experiences rewarding and were thus generally satisfied with the trip. The non-Europeans, on the other hand, being oriented toward activities directly relevant to their professional concerns, may have been less satisfied because only a relatively small proportion of their experiences met these specific needs.

The fifth set of items is consistent with the different orientations that we postulated for the two groups. The Europeans, in keeping with their interest in general observations, were more likely to mention aspects of the physical environment (for example, landscapes or architecture) among their most important and enjoyable experiences. The non-Europeans, in keeping with their interest in specifically applicable information and skills, were more likely to mention that they had learned, during their travels, new approaches to programming that would be of direct use to them after their return home. Further data on the different sources of satisfaction and accomplishment for the two groups during the travel period will be found in Table 26.

The different orientations of the two groups emerged even more clearly when the participants reviewed their satisfactions and accomplishments during the entire sojourn shortly before their departure (see sixth set of items). Thus, the Europeans were more likely to perceive their most meaningful and enjoyable experiences to have been in nonprofessional areas. Among such experiences, they were more likely than non-Europeans to cite observations of local broadcasting facilities and activities, firsthand exposure to American life, and observations of the physical environment. Among their most important accomplishments, they were more likely to mention that they had gained a greater understanding of the American way of life and of American values. They were also more likely to feel that, in acquiring firsthand knowledge of the United States, they had achieved one of their original goals for the trip. In short, it is clear that the Europeans had a relatively broad agenda, which included such non-professional interests as learning about American life and observing America as a country and as a society at first hand. Their agenda also included a strong interest in professional matters, but here again they appreciated the opportunity to observe American broadcasting facilities and activities; they were satisfied with the role of the professional spectator, seeing what was happening in broadcasting in America, meeting American colleagues and comparing notes with them.

The non-Europeans, by contrast, were more likely to cite exposure to new program ideas among their most meaningful or enjoyable experiences. In other words, they seemed to seek specific professional information that they could apply directly in their own work situations. Somewhat more ambiguous is their greater tendency to cite the establishment of new professional relationships among their most important accomplishments. It is reasonable to suppose, however, that here again they were expressing their interest in outcomes that would be of concrete benefit to them in their future professional activities.

The seventh set of items groups a number of changes in perspective that the participants, in the fourth interview, attributed to their American sojourn. Not surprisingly, Europeans were more likely to feel that they had changed their perspective about America, American institutions, or the American people. This is fully consistent with their interest in observing American life and gaining a greater understanding of it. Non-Europeans, on the other hand, were more likely to report that their American experiences had given them a new perspective on their own countries. As we pointed out above (see discussion of second set of items in Table 24), this may be due to their greater tendency to focus on the back-home situation and to relate their experiences to problems in their own societies, or it may be due to the greater fluidity of the societies from which they came and hence the greater likelihood of seeking and finding new perspectives.

Non-Europeans were more likely to feel that their experiences in America had given them a new perspective on their professional roles. Here too it must be kept in mind that they tended to come from more fluid, less established broadcasting systems, in which their own roles were still undergoing definition and reassessment. This finding is also consistent, however, with the view that the non-Europeans were more actively involved in a professional learning process, relating their American experiences directly to their own work situations. They used the experience not only to acquire information that they could apply back home, but also to think through their personal positions in the professional settings in which they were employed. It is interesting that the Europeans were more likely than the non-Europeans to report that their views of the role of broadcasting in their own countries had undergone change. We did not particularly expect such a change, but it is important to underline the difference between this change and the one observed among non-Europeans. The Europeans changed their views of the role of broadcasting, while the non-Europeans changed their views of their own professional roles. The change among Europeans, in other words, was an impersonal one, consistent with their interest in learning about American broadcasting and comparing it (often, we would presume, in the course of discussions with American colleagues) to their own systems. The change among non-Europeans, on the other hand, was a personal one, consistent with their interest in a more specific and intensive professional learning experience.

In the post-return interview, when participants discussed their satisfactions and accomplishments in retrospect, the difference in orientation was still evident. As can be seen in the eighth set of items, Europeans were more likely to cite the opportunity to travel around the country and meet Americans and the opportunity to see the beauty of the American landscape among their major satisfactions. Non-Europeans, on the other hand, were more likely than Europeans to cite the opportunity to learn about educational TV—a specific professional accomplishment—as an unanticipated source of satisfaction.

The picture changes, however, when we examine the actual effects that the sojourn had on participants' professional activities, as reported by them in the post-return interview (see ninth set of items). There is no difference between the two groups in reported attempts to apply specific ideas or procedures acquired in America to their professional activities. For the Europeans, however, most of these attempts had been successful or at least partially successful, while for the non-Europeans, the outcome of these attempts was still uncertain at the time of the interview. Europeans were more likely to report the introduction of new types of programs, based on ideas acquired in America—although it was the non-Europeans who had stressed new program ideas in the interviews conducted during the American sojourn. Europeans were also more likely to report continuing contacts with professional organizations and colleagues encountered in America—although, again, it was the non-Europeans who had expressed strongest interest in establishing new professional relationships during the earlier interviews. Most probably these findings reflect the differences in the professional status, self-confidence, and experience of the two groups and in the degree of development of their respective broadcasting systems. Thus, the Europeans expressed greater certainty about the outcomes of any innovations they had introduced (even when they did not regard them entirely successful), while the non-Europeans were more reluctant to make a final judgment. The Europeans, though less eager for new program ideas, were in a better position to implement whatever ideas they acquired abroad. Similarly, though they were less eager to develop new professional contacts, the Europeans—being more established, more experienced, and more integrated in an international network—were in a better position to maintain whatever contacts they had developed.

Of the remaining two items in set 9, the first is completely consistent with what we know about the non-Europeans: In reporting that the American experience had made them more aware of the limitations of their own countries, they are reflecting both the reality of their own countries' less advanced level of technology and their own emphasis, while abroad, on relating their experiences to the situation back home. The final item, indicating a greater tendency among non-Europeans to report that the trip had created some special problems—of a nonprofessional nature—for them, does not readily fit into any discernible pattern. Perhaps non-Europeans, because of the greater disparity between the cultures of host and home societies, experienced some difficulties in readjustment during the first few months after their return.

The final set of items in Table 24 lists various changes, reported by the respondent, that had taken place during the year since his return but that he did not explicitly ascribe to the sojourn. Most of these items reflect differences in the professional situations of the two groups: The Europeans returned to well-established and rather stable broadcasting systems, while the non-Europeans were more likely to find themselves in fluid situations, undergoing change and development. Thus, the Europeans were more likely to report that they had neither expected nor experienced changes in their positions or responsibilities and that they had not introduced innovations or changes in their work situations. In general, one presumes, they simply returned to their established roles and procedures within their stable organizations. Understandably, they showed a greater interest than non-Europeans in technical advances and expansion of services within their broadcasting systems—that is, in further improvement and diversification of systems that were already highly developed. The one area in which they were more likely than non-Europeans to report innovations were changes of a technical nature.

The non-Europeans, one presumes, were preoccupied with the more basic requirements of developing relatively new systems and making them fully operational. The fluidity of their broadcasting systems (and of their societies in general) also affected their personal positions within them. Thus, they were not only more likely to report changes in their own positions during the preceding year (changes that several of them, but none of the Europeans who reported changes, ascribed to personal career considerations), but they were also more likely to anticipate such changes in the near future and to report that their plans for the future had changed during the past year. Interestingly, plans for the future included a visit to the United States for more non-Europeans than Europeans, perhaps because the non-Europeans attached greater value to the specific professional experience that such a trip could provide. Though the reported and anticipated changes in positions and plans were no doubt related to the fluidity of the non-Europeans' professional situations, their American experience may well have contributed both to the occurrence and to the nature of such changes. They were, after all, foreshadowed in the fourth interview, when non-Europeans—more often than Europeans —reported that their experiences in America had given them a new perspective on their professional roles (see seventh set of items, Table 24).

The most interesting items in the tenth set are the two concerned with job satisfaction, which probably do represent changes attributable to the American sojourn. Non-Europeans were more likely to report that they felt more satisfied with their jobs than they did the year before, and to ascribe this increased job satisfaction to recognition of their abilities by others. It may be that their experience abroad had indeed increased their professional competencies to a noticeable degree; alternatively, this experience may have enhanced their prestige among their colleagues who were now more inclined to respect and acknowledge the abilities they had had all along. We suspect that both of these processes were operating and mutually reinforcing each other. In any event, what is important is that, a year after the seminar, the non-Europeans reported increases in job satisfaction and in feeling of recognition, which were probably mediated by their increased professional self-confidence.

In sum, Table 24 demonstrates that the two groups related themselves quite differently to their American experience. On the professional side, the Europeans were primarily interested in observing American broadcasting, in learning about its operations, and in comparing notes with their American counterparts. The non-Europeans, on the other hand, were primarily interested in specific professional information and skills that would be of direct use to them in their work situations back home. Furthermore, the Europeans' agenda extended beyond professional concerns. They wanted to see the country, to meet Americans, and to deepen their understanding of American life and American values. It was in nonprofessional areas, in fact, that they had their most meaningful and enjoyable experiences; in particular, they considered their new understanding of the United States among their most important accomplishments and felt that it gave them a new perspective on American institutions and the American people. The non-Europeans' agenda, by contrast, focused more narrowly on professional activities as these related to the back-home situation. Even in their general observations of America, they tended to stress implications for the situations in their own countries. Thus, they considered exposure to new program ideas that would be of direct professional use to them, and establishment of new professional contacts, among their major accomplishments; and they reported that the trip had given them a new perspective on their own professional roles and on their own countries. This is not to say that the non-Europeans had only professional interests in mind and remained aloof from their immediate environment. In fact, they seemed to find greater enjoyment in meeting and interacting with Americans than did the Europeans, who took the more distant stance of the observer. The non-Europeans, however, made sharper distinctions between enjoyable and useful experiences; among the latter they tended to count only those activities that had direct professional relevance.

Both in the second interview, conducted at the university, and in the third interview, conducted in the field, the Europeans expressed greater overall satisfaction with their experience. This was probably a result of their broader agenda, which meant that they found a wider range of their experiences relevant to their interests. The non-Europeans were quite satisfied with the professional aspects of the program—more so than the Europeans—but they felt that these were not given sufficient emphasis, which may account for their lower level of overall satisfaction. These differences in level of satisfaction, however, disappeared by the time of the fourth interview, conducted just prior to the participants' departure from the United States.

It is interesting that, in the first year after their return home, the Europeans seemed to make greater professional use of their American experience than did the non-Europeans. The Europeans were more likely to report the introduction of American-inspired programs and the continuation of professional contacts with American organizations and individuals, even though it was clearly the non-Europeans who had been more interested in acquiring new program ideas and establishing new professional contacts during the American sojourn. No doubt the Europeans, because of their greater professional status and experience and greater involvement in international networks were in a better position to implement new ideas and maintain new contacts, even though they may have been less eager to do so. On the other hand, the non-Europeans were more likely to report changes in their professional positions or responsibilities during their first year back home, or to anticipate such changes for the future. While these changes were probably due to the fluidity of their less-established broadcasting systems, they may also have been influenced by the new perspectives on their professional roles that the non-Europeans felt they gained in the course of the seminar. More importantly, non-Europeans—more so than Europeans—reported that their job satisfaction had increased during the past year, and attributed this increase to the greater recognition by others of their own abilities. It would seem that the experience abroad increased their professional self-confidence, either because it helped to enhance their professional knowledge and skills or because it enhanced their prestige among colleagues or both.

Reactions to the university phase of the seminar. Our formulation of the differences in the level and nature of satisfaction derived from the seminar by the two groups is further amplified by the data in Table 25, which presents items tapping reactions to the university phase of the seminar.

In the first set of items, we see that Europeans—in keeping with the broader agenda that we postulated for them—found a larger proportion of the seminar relevant to their interests, which probably accounts for their high level of overall satisfaction (see Table 24, first set of items). They were not particularly satisfied with the professional seminars, feeling that they did not have much useful information to offer them. They also expressed disappointment in the level of professional exchange among the participants. There were other activities, however, including the visits to broadcasting facilities and the academic seminars, that they found relevant and interesting (see Table 24, second set of items). The non-Europeans, on the other hand—in keeping with the more narrowly professional

Table 25

REACTIONS TO THE UNIVERSITY PHASE OF THE SEMINAR:
COMPARISON OF EUROPEANS AND NON-EUROPEANS

	Number of Respondents to Whom Each Item Applies	
Items that Discriminate	Europeans	Non-Europeans
1. Second interview: Reactions to the seminar program		
The participant found more than three quarters of the program at least indirectly relevant to his interests	9	5
He feels that the professional seminars were both useful and relevant to his specific professional concerns	7	13
Among the reasons for his satisfaction with the professional seminars he cites the presentation of large amounts of information (for example, about programs or production) that will help him in his own work	3	11
He found the visits to communication facilities to be uninteresting	0	4
Among his disappointments he mentions that the exchange of professional views among participants has been carried out at a lower level than he had anticipated	5	0
Among aspects of the seminar that seemed poorly planned he mentions that activities were overscheduled, with too little time left free for recreation or reflection	6	10
2. Second interview: Reactions to the group composition		
He cites unevenness in choice of participants as a source of dissatisfaction with the seminar	6	1
Among reasons for adverse effects of the group's multinational composition he cites diversity of professional backgrounds, positions, and interests	9	3
He feels that the participants functioned as a very congenial group	3	8
As a source of friction among participants he cites personal idiosyncrasies	6	2

Table 25 (Continued)

REACTIONS TO THE UNIVERSITY PHASE OF THE SEMINAR: COMPARISON OF EUROPEANS AND NON-EUROPEANS

Items that Discriminate	Number of Respondents to Whom Each Item Applies	
	Europeans	Non-Europeans
Among contributions by other participants that he found especially valuable he cites the technically superior presentations made by representatives from "advanced countries"	5	11
3. *Second interview: Satisfaction with own role and with role of participants in general in the seminar*		
He feels largely satisfied with his own contribution to the seminar	7	2
He presented a special program to the group	7	2
Among aspects of the seminar that seemed poorly planned he cites failure to provide adequate audiovisual facilities for participants' special programs	4	0
He feels that he was personally inconvenienced by the inadequate audiovisual facilities for showing films or slides	4	0
4. *Second interview: Reactions to leisure-time activities*		
Among aspects of the seminar that were especially well planned he cites the weekend visit with an American family in New Hampshire	5	9
His activities outside the seminar have included visits to American families	9	1
5. *Fourth interview: Predeparture reactions to the university phase of the seminar*		
He feels that the individual talents of the participants were utilized		
to a great extent	5	1
to a moderate extent	5	6
to a small extent or not at all	1	5
Among modifications for the university phase of the seminar he suggests the use of more mature administrative personnel	4	0

Table 25 *(Continued)*

REACTIONS TO THE UNIVERSITY PHASE OF THE SEMINAR:
COMPARISON OF EUROPEANS AND NON-EUROPEANS

	Number of Respondents to Whom	
Items that Discriminate	*Each Item Applies*	
	Europeans	*Non-Europeans*
6. *Post-return interview: Retrospective reactions to the university phase of the seminar*		
He feels that the seminar could be improved by		
reducing the amount of time given to lectures and seminars	2	7
improving the professional part of the program	5	1
changing the selection procedure to insure greater homogeneity	9	2
clarifying the definition of its aims	6	1
Among the kinds of people to whom he would recommend a similar seminar he lists working broadcasters (in contrast to those in policy or administrative positions)	0	4

agenda and the focus on directly applicable professional experiences that we postulated for them—were very satisfied with the professional seminars, but did not consider many of the other activities particularly relevant to their interests. All of the non-Europeans felt that the professional seminars were both useful and relevant to their specific professional concerns. Most of them expressed satisfaction with the large amounts of information presented in these seminars that would help them in their own work; by contrast, only three Europeans expressed this view, presumably because most of the Europeans came with greater professional experience and considered much of the information transmitted at the seminars at too low a level to add to their own knowledge. The non-Europeans were more likely to find the visits to communication facilities—which afforded opportunities to observe broadcast stations and newspaper offices, but not to acquire applicable information and skills—as lacking in interest. They were also more likely to complain that too many activities were scheduled, making it more difficult for them to absorb those aspects of the seminar that were of real concern to them.

The second set of items elaborates further on the Europeans' dissatisfaction with the professional part of the seminar. Europeans, more often than non-Europeans, were critical of the unevenness in choice of participants and the diversity in their professional backgrounds, positions, and interests. In the light of some of the items already discussed, they probably felt that the composition of the group made for a lower level of professional seminars and discussions than they had anticipated. The non-Europeans, by contrast, were satisfied with the composition of the group, found it very congenial, and were particularly appreciative of the contributions made by some of their fellow-participants from "advanced countries." In short, the Europeans, who saw themselves as accomplished specialists and had anticipated a high-level professional exchange of views, were somewhat disappointed in the group; the non-Europeans, on the other hand, who came with a lower degree of professional self-confidence and saw themselves as learners, were happy with the composition of the group and valued the opportunity of learning from more experienced colleagues that it offered them.

The self-image of the Europeans as accomplished specialists is also reflected in the third set of items. Europeans were more likely to feel satisfied with their own contributions to the seminar. Presumably they felt more confident about the quality and value of what they had to say. Their greater satisfaction, however, can also be traced to the fact that the Europeans had greater opportunities to make personal contributions to the group: As the second item in the set shows, more Europeans than non-Europeans presented special programs to the group, demonstrating their own work. That satisfaction with one's own contribution is related to the opportunity to make such presentations is evidenced by the overlap between these two items: Six of the nine participants who presented a special program (five Europeans and one non-European) were among those who expressed general satisfaction with their contributions. Since more Europeans had presented programs or had wanted to do so, they also felt more critical of and personally more inconvenienced by the lack of adequate audiovisual facilities. Four Europeans, but no non-Europeans, expressed these criticisms. Of the four, three had in fact presented programs, but felt that the facilities for doing so were not as good as they would have liked; the fourth was unable to present the program he had brought because the appropriate facilities were unavailable and he felt deeply disappointed. In short, the Europeans—in keeping with their self-images of active contributors to an exchange—were eager to present their work; they were, in fact, more likely to do so than the non-Europeans; to the extent that such presentations were possible, they were satisfied with their own contributions, but they were also more critical of technical failures that interfered with their presentations.

As for leisure-time activities during the university phase of the seminar, we find in set 4 that Europeans much more often received personal invitations to visit American families. In some cases, these invitations came from people whom participants had known before or with whom they shared mutual acquaintances, but the data to be presented in Table 27 (first set of items) suggest that such prior contacts could not account for the difference between Europeans and non-Europeans. Perhaps the Europeans—because of their professional status and their cultural similarities to Americans or to certain subgroups of Americans—fit more readily into the pattern of invitations common among the people they met at the university. The non-Europeans more often than the Europeans expressed enthusiasm about the weekend visit with American families in New Hampshire. In fact, no doubt, this weekend meant more to the non-Europeans since most of them had not had prior opportunities to visit American homes. In addition, however, their enthusiasm is consistent with several other indications in the tables presented in this chapter that non-Europeans were more likely to enjoy informal, spontaneous interactions with Americans. Some of the Europeans were put off by the "arranged hospitality" characterizing the New Hampshire weekend; they probably preferred the more individualized invitations to American homes, which gave due recognition to their status. Most of the non-Europeans, however, appreciated the opportunity the New Hampshire visit offered them for interacting with Americans in a relaxed, informal, homey atmosphere.

In the fourth interview, we found two discriminating items relating to the university phase of the seminar (see fifth set of items). First, Europeans were more likely to feel that the individual talents of the participants were utilized to a great extent, while non-Europeans were more likely to state that talents were underutilized. These responses reflect, to a considerable extent, participants' satisfaction with their own contribution to the seminar. Thus, of the six participants who felt that individual talents were utilized to a great exent, four had been largely satisfied with their own contributions during the second interview; also, four had reported in the second interview that they had presented a special program to the group (see third set of items in Table 25). On the other hand, of the six participants who felt that individual talents were underutilized, none had expressed satisfaction with his own contribution in the second interview and none had presented a special program. It is quite possible that the non-Europeans who spoke of the underutilization of participants' talents may have had in mind the talents of some of their highly experienced European colleagues rather than their own talents. The pattern of results suggests, however, that they were at least in part referring to their own talents. This item is, thus, important to keep in mind, lest we assume

—in the light of our formulation of the non-Europeans' orientation—that all non-Europeans were fully satisfied with the role of learner at all times. At least some non-Europeans felt that they had personal contributions to make to the seminar and were disappointed at the lack of opportunity to do so.

The second item in the fifth set is consistent with our general impression that Europeans were somewhat more concerned with proper recognition of their status. This may be one explanation—though by no means the only one—of the feeling among several Europeans that the seminar's administrative personnel should have been more mature.

Finally, the participants' retrospective reactions to the university phase of the seminar in the post-return interview (see sixth set of items) reviewed some of the central themes that emerged from the earlier interviews. The Europeans expressed their reservations about the professional part of the seminar. They recommended changes in the procedure of selecting participants to insure greater homogeneity—and thus, presumably, raise the level of professional discourse. They felt a need for a clearer definition of the aims of the seminar, having in mind, quite probably, a choice between a training seminar and a high-level exchange among accomplished professionals. The non-Europeans, on the other hand, felt that the seminar could be improved by reducing the amount of time given to lectures and seminars. They probably wanted more time to absorb what they were learning, as we already noted earlier (see first set of items in Table 25). More importantly, they probably wanted a greater emphasis on workshop-type experiences, focusing on specific problems relevant to their professional activities. Their view of the seminar along the model of a workshop is also reflected in the final item: Several non-Europeans (but none of the Europeans) mentioned that they would recommend this kind of seminar to "working" broadcasters, in contrast to those in policy or administrative positions.

Reactions to the travel phase of the seminar. Table 26 provides some further elaboration of the differential reactions of the two groups to the travel experience. In particular, it illustrates nicely the Europeans' emphasis on observations of America, in both professional and nonprofessional spheres.

The first set of items is based on the second interview, conducted shortly before the beginning of the travel period. We see that Europeans were more likely to express an interest in sight-seeing, in keeping with the broader agenda that we postulated for them. They also seemed to have an explicit interest in gaining information about the state of broadcasting in America—not so much because of the professional usefulness of such information, but as an end in itself and as part of their general interest

Table 26

REACTIONS TO THE TRAVEL PHASE OF THE SEMINAR:
COMPARISON OF EUROPEANS AND NON-EUROPEANS

Items that Discriminate	Number of Respondents to Whom Each Item Applies	
	Europeans	Non-Europeans
1. Second interview: *Anticipations for the travel period*		
Among the experiences the participant looks forward to during the trip he cites the opportunity to do sight-seeing	10	6
The features of American life about which he particularly wants more information		
have a good deal of professional relevance	8	3
have little professional relevance	3	10
Among features of American life about which he wants more information he cites the state of professional broadcasting	5	1
2. Third interview: *Satisfaction with itinerary and travel experiences*		
He found some of the places he visited professionally inappropriate because activities were curtailed for the summer and it was thus impossible to observe certain kinds of programs or operations	5	1
Among the sources of satisfaction with the professional aspects of the travel period he cites		
the opportunity to obtain a good overall picture of the great variety and range of programs, facilities, and approaches in American broadcasting	11	5
the opportunity to meet fellow-professionals who were very helpful	5	12
3. Third interview: *Satisfaction with travel arrangements*		
He reports difficulties in cashing his checks from the university	7	3

Table 26 (Continued)

REACTIONS TO THE TRAVEL PHASE OF THE SEMINAR:
COMPARISON OF EUROPEANS AND NON-EUROPEANS

Items that Discriminate	*Number of Respondents to Whom Each Item Applies*	
	Europeans	*Non-Europeans*
4. *Third interview: Interaction experiences*		
In general, he traveled with another person	8	4
. . . and was satisfied with this arrangement	8	3
The new acquaintances that he formed with Americans during the travel period were often the result of social contacts that he made spontaneously after his arrival in a new community	6	11
He has made some nonprofessional contacts during the trip that he intends to maintain	2	8

in rounding out their picture of American society. Non-Europeans had much less interest in detailed information about American broadcasting per se, except insofar as such information had direct relevance to their own work.

During the travel period itself, Europeans were more likely to complain that curtailment of activities for the summer at some of the professional sites they visited kept them from observing some of the programs or operations they had been interested in (second set of items). The inability to make these particular observations, however, did not interfere with their generally high level of satisfaction with the travel experience (see Table 24, third set of items). Clearly, they found many other satisfactions—not only in enjoyment of the physical environment (see Table 24, fifth, sixth, and eighth sets of items) and in learning about American life (see Table 24, sixth set of items), but also in observing broadcasting facilities. Most of the Europeans cited the opportunity to obtain a good overall picture of the great variety and range of programs, facilities, and approaches in American broadcasting as a major source of satisfaction with the professional side of the travel period. By contrast, most of the non-Europeans cited the opportunity to meet fellow-broadcasters who were very helpful as a major source of professional satisfaction. We have already seen (Table 24, fifth set of items) that non-Europeans were more likely to mention that they had learned new approaches to programming during their travels that would be of direct use to them after returning home. In short, for the Europeans the professional value of the travel period lay in the opportunity to observe and gain insight into American broadcasting, for the non-European in the opportunity to meet people and learn approaches that they found helpful in their specific professional tasks.

Set 3 contains only a single item which is not particularly informative. Set 4 tells us, first, that more Europeans than non-Europeans traveled with a companion; the difference is largely accounted for by the fact that four Europeans, but none of the non-Europeans, had brought along their wives. The remaining two items in Set 4 are of greater interest, since they point to the non-Europeans' propensity to enter into interactions with Americans, which we have already noted earlier. Thus, non-Europeans, more often than Europeans, spontaneously established social contacts after arriving in a new community. It may be that Europeans had more prearranged contacts and thus less need and time for spontaneous ones. It is probably also true, however, that non-Europeans were somewhat more informal and expressive in forming new relationships, while Europeans may have been more constrained by considerations of status and protocol. The final item in the table, which shows more non-Europeans reporting new nonprofessional contacts that they intended to maintain, would seem to be consistent with this interpretation.

Perceptions and evaluations of America and Americans. The major finding in Table 27, which shows up repeatedly, is that Europeans developed a more differentiated image and a more complex understanding of America than did non-Europeans. This is a predictable consequence of their greater interest in observing American society and understanding its character.

In examining the table in more detail, we find a somewhat surprising pattern in the first set of items. Non-Europeans, in the first interview, reported more personal contacts with America prior to their trip than did Europeans. They had met more Americans, had formed close professional relationships with them, had learned about America from them. They also had more close friends, relatives, and acquaintances who had lived in America. The most reasonable explanation would seem to be in terms of a selection factor. It may be that in the European countries the local committees played a larger role in selection of participants, while in the non-European countries selection was more influenced by Americans—by the director of the seminar and the representative of the Bureau of Educational and Cultural Affairs, who visited each country to set the

Table 27

PERCEPTIONS AND EVALUATIONS OF AMERICA AND AMERICANS:
COMPARISON OF EUROPEANS AND NON-EUROPEANS

Items that Discriminate	*Number of Respondents to Whom Each Item Applies*	
	Europeans	*Non-Europeans*
1. First interview: Prior contacts with America		
The participant has had personal contact with many Americans prior to the present trip	5	9
His prior contacts have included close professional working relationships with Americans	3	8
Among his major sources of prior information about America he cites meeting Americans	9	13
People from his own country who have lived in America include		
close friends	8	12
relatives	0	8
acquaintances	6	10
2. Second interview: Impressions of America		
Since the time of his arrival, his impressions of America		
have become more positive	7	1
have become less positive	4	2
have become more positive in some respects, less in others	0	2
have remained unchanged	2	8
3. Third interview: Evaluations of America		
Among his major disappointments with America he cites the handling of the Negro problem	2	7
4. Third interview: Reported observations and insights		
During his travels, his observations of American life have focused, among others, on economic aspects	11	4
His observations of American life		
cover a broad range	8	1
are very detailed and elaborated	7	3
Among the new insights into American life that he reports having gained from the trip he mentions		
a better understanding of the underlying character and philosophy of America as a country	9	5

Table 27 (Continued)

PERCEPTIONS AND EVALUATIONS OF AMERICA AND AMERICANS:
COMPARISON OF EUROPEANS AND NON-EUROPEANS

Items that Discriminate	Number of Respondents to Whom Each Item Applies	
	Europeans	Non-Europeans
an understanding of the importance of diversity and variety in America (for example, the role regional differences play)	6	2
5. Third interview: Perceived differences within America		
Among regional differences he noted in America he cites differences in social customs (for example, in the role of tradition in people's behavior)	6	2
The regional differences he perceives		
cover a broad range	4	0
are moderately or very detailed and elaborated	8	2
When asked about regional differences in America, he indicates that they play an important role	9	5
. . . particularly in domestic policy	9	4
In his discussion of other differences (aside from regional ones) within the population that contributed to his understanding of American society, he indicates that these have been largely new discoveries for him, rather than confirmations of things he already knew	10	4
The other population differences he perceives		
cover a broad range	8	2
are moderately or very detailed and elaborated	11	6
Among differences that have affected the development of American broadcasting he cites		
regional differences	4	0
religious differences	4	0
socioeconomic differences	7	2
6. Post-return interview: Evaluations of America		
Among things that impressed him favorably about America he cites the country's wealth, high standard of living, and advanced technology	6	10

Table 27 (Continued)

PERCEPTIONS AND EVALUATIONS OF AMERICA AND AMERICANS:
COMPARISON OF EUROPEANS AND NON-EUROPEANS

Items that Discriminate	Number of Respondents to Whom Each Item Applies	
	Europeans	Non-Europeans
Among things that impressed him unfavorably about America he cites		
the extent and severity of the race problem	2	9
instances of inefficiency and poor organization	5	0
7. *Post-return interview: Perceptions of America*		
He can identify subgroups within the American population that differ from each other in their point of view and state the bases on which they differ	9	5
The subgroups differing in point of view that he identifies include		
groups varying in educational level	8	4
geographic or regional groups	6	0
When asked which groups of Americans have different (nonmodal) views of his own country, he mentions those who are at a higher level of education and sophistication	6	2
8. *Post-return interview: Communications about America*		
Among programs about America that he has presented or is likely to present he cites newscasts, editorials, or commentaries	2	6
Among the contents of such programs he lists information about		
places and personalities of special interest	7	3
the racial situation in America	7	3
Among the main themes emphasized in such programs he cites		
the diversity and heterogeneity of America	7	2
the inaccuracy of popular images of America and Americans	0	4
Among the points he tried to get across in reports about his trip he cites the wealth, the high standard of living, and the advanced technical development of America	1	6

selection process into motion, or by the representative of the American Embassy to the selection panel.[3] Since individuals who had considerable personal contact with America would be better known and more visible to Americans, they would stand a better chance of being selected if Americans were centrally involved in the selection process. On the other hand, contact with America was probably unrelated to the probability of selection by local committees. It is also possible that in non-European countries most broadcasters—a small group, drawn from a relatively small segment of the population—have extensive foreign, including American contacts; such contacts play a role in their professional training and practice and, in general, characterize the elites of most developing countries. In European countries, on the other hand, broadcasting systems are more self-contained and it is quite possible to find accomplished specialists whose contacts are almost entirely within their own countries or within the European continent. If this is true, then even a chance selection process would yield more non-Europeans than Europeans with extensive links to America.[4] Whatever the explanation of this finding, it does not change the fact that Europeans—even if they had less prior contact with America—came to the sojourn with a higher degree of cultural similarity to the host country.

Set 2 contains one item from the second interview. Europeans were more likely to report that their impressions of America had become more positive since their arrival, while non-Europeans more often reported that their impressions had remained unchanged. It may be that Europeans had started out with a more negative image and thus had more room for change; or perhaps their greater interest in observing American life and in the contents of the academic seminars provided them with more opportunities for revising earlier impressions. In any event, this item is the only indication in the entire set of interviews of a difference (in either direction) between Europeans and non-Europeans in their overall evaluation of America. The questionnaire results, in fact, point to a small trend in a direction opposite to that found here, though these results are based, of course, on a different time period: On their after-questionnaires, non-Europeans showed a slightly greater increase than Europeans in favorable attitudes toward America and Americans

[3] See Chapter Two for a description of the selection procedure.

[4] The second explanation appears to be inconsistent with the indications, reported elsewhere in this chapter, that the Europeans were more fully integrated into an international professional network than the non-Europeans. Actually, there is no necessary contradiction since the international networks in which Europeans are involved may include various European countries, but not extend to America. Nevertheless, we would favor the first explanation, since it fits less ambiguously into our general formulation.

(see Table 22). All told, then, it would be hazardous to draw any general conclusion from the present item.

While there are no consistent differences between the two groups in their overall evaluations of America, there are differences in their evaluations of specific features of American life. One such difference, which showed up more than once, is presented in set 3. Non-Europeans, more often than Europeans, cited the handling of "the Negro problem" among their major disappointments with America. It is understandable, of course, that non-Europeans—particularly Africans—would be more sensitive to this issue.

The fourth set of items speaks to the Europeans' greater emphasis on observations of American life during their travels, which resulted in a greater degree of differentiation and understanding. Europeans, more often than non-Europeans, focused their observations on economic aspects of American life. In evaluating participants' responses in this general area, our raters felt that the observations of Europeans covered a broader range and were more detailed and elaborated than those of non-Europeans. In their own assessments of the new insights they had gained from the trip, Europeans were more likely than non-Europeans to report that they had achieved a better understanding of the underlying character and philosophy of America. They also reported, more often than non-Europeans, an increased understanding of the importance of diversity and variety in America—for example, of the role that regional differences play in American life.

The fifth set of items demonstrates that the Europeans did indeed gain an increased understanding of American diversity and variety, as they claimed. This set includes a varied array of items, all of which add up to the conclusion that Europeans were more cognizant of differences within American society than non-Europeans. They were more likely to mention regional and other differences and to attach importance to them. Moreover, according to our raters' assessments, the regional and other population differences perceived by Europeans covered a broader range and were more detailed and elaborated than those perceived by non-Europeans. In short, the Europeans, being more interested in observing and learning about America, did indeed manifest a higher degree of differentiation when interviewed in the course of their travels.

In the post-return interview, we find, first, some quite understandable differences between the two groups in their evaluations of specific features of American life (see sixth set of items). Non-Europeans were more favorably impressed than Europeans with America's wealth, high standard of living, and advanced technology. They were more unfavorably impressed, as they had already mentioned in the third interview, with the extent and severity of America's race problem. Europeans were more likely to cite instances of inefficiency and poor organization among the things that impressed them unfavorably about America. No doubt they had higher expectations than the non-Europeans in this sphere and were disappointed to find that America did not quite live up to its popular image.

In the seventh set of items we find that the more highly differentiated view of American society among Europeans continued to manifest itself a year after they had returned home. In several ways, the Europeans showed themselves to be more attentive than non-Europeans to subgroup differences within the American population. Also, in programs about America that they had presented or were planning to present (see eighth set of items), they were more likely to emphasize the diversity and heterogeneity of America than were the non-Europeans. The non-Europeans, in turn, were more likely to emphasize the inaccuracy of certain popular images of America and Americans—a dimension that is not as subtle as the one stressed by the Europeans, though it certainly reflects a significant outcome of any international exchange program.

In reports about their trip, non-Europeans were more likely than Europeans to discuss the wealth, living standard, and advanced technology of America; we have already seen (sixth set of items) that this was one of the features of America with which they were favorably impressed. Set 8 lists several other differences between the two groups in their communications about America that do not show any obvious relationships to the patterns we have been drawing. It is interesting to note, however, that Europeans were more likely to include information about the racial situation in their programs about America, even though non-Europeans were obviously more concerned about this issue.

Perceptions and evaluations of American broadcasting. Items showing differences between the two groups in perception and evaluation of American broadcasting are listed in Table 28. Set 1, based on the second interview, suggests that the non-Europeans' images of American mass media was less differentiated than that of the Europeans: Our raters judged their descriptions of changes these images had undergone to cover a narrower range and to be less detailed and elaborated than those of the Europeans.

In the third interview, we had two indications that the non-Europeans' evaluations of American broadcasters were generally more favorable than those of the Europeans (see second set of items). Non-Europeans were more likely to state that American broadcasters compared favorably with the best in the world, and that they were meeting their responsibilities well. On the other hand, non-Europeans were more likely to feel that

Table 28

PERCEPTIONS AND EVALUATIONS OF AMERICAN BROADCASTING:
COMPARISON OF EUROPEANS AND NON-EUROPEANS

Items that Discriminate	Number of Respondents to Whom Each Item Applies	
	Europeans	Non-Europeans
1. Second interview: Perceptions of American mass media		
The participant's description of changes in his picture of American mass media		
covers a narrow to moderate range	7	11
lacks detail and elaboration	4	8
2. Third interview: Evaluations of American broadcasters		
He feels that American broadcasters, in general, compare favorably with the best in the world	1	5
He feels that American broadcasters are meeting their responsibilities well	0	4
He feels that most American broadcasters are aware of the major problems confronting American broadcasting		
and that they are making an effort to solve them	4	0
but that they are making no real effort to solve them	5	9
3. Third interview: Evaluations of ownership and control patterns in American broadcasting		
He sees a clear and basic conflict between the requirements of making a profit and providing public service in American broadcasting	8	4
Among the difficulties faced by American broadcasters he mentions that they are overly constrained by pressures of advertisers	7	3
Among the major problems of American broadcasting he cites the fear of government control (for example, of giving more power to the FCC)	5	1
Among the advantages of private ownership of broadcasting he mentions that it provides a greater degree of freedom in choosing and organizing programs	1	5
4. Third interview: Evaluations of programming and facilities in American broadcasting		
Among the major problems of American broadcasting he cites the lack of balance in programming	9	3

Table 28 (Continued)

PERCEPTIONS AND EVALUATIONS OF AMERICAN BROADCASTING:
COMPARISON OF EUROPEANS AND NON-EUROPEANS

Items that Discriminate	*Number of Respondents to Whom Each Item Applies*	
	Europeans	*Non-Europeans*
Among the major successes of American broadcasting he cites the documentaries and experimental programs produced by the large networks	6	1
One of the features of American broadcasting that he feels should be avoided in his own country is the custom of breaking up news programs with commercials	4	9
He feels that radio in his own country offers more high-quality drama programs than radio in America	4	0
Among the advantages of radio over TV he mentions that		
it is more economical to run (production costs are lower)	3	8
it is more economical to receive (sets are cheaper)	3	8
He feels that the conditions under which American broadcasters work are not always very good	12	8
He found during his professional visits that some stations worked with poorer technical facilities than he had expected	4	0
5. *Fourth interview: Evaluations of American broadcasting*		
In describing the reports that he expects to present after returning home he indicates that		
in general, he will probably praise American broadcasting	0	8
he will probably say some good things and some bad things about American broadcasting	10	0
6. *Post-return interview: Evaluation of American broadcasters and broadcasting*		
His evaluation of American broadcasters is largely favorable (rather than mixed)	6	11
Among the points he tried to get across in reports about his trip he cites the advantages of certain American broadcasting techniques, such as documentaries and newscasts	9	2

American broadcasters, though aware of the major problems confronting American broadcasting, were making no real effort to solve them; Europeans more often felt that they *were* making an effort to solve these problems. This last item is an exception to the general trend, found in the present table, of the more favorable evaluations of American broadcasters and broadcasting on the part of non-Europeans. We have no ready explanation for this exception. There is, incidentally, no systematic relationship between responses to this item and to the preceding one about the way in which American broadcasters were meeting their obligations.

The third set of items deals with participants' evaluations of one aspect of American broadcasting: the pattern of ownership and control. The Europeans were consistently more negative than the non-Europeans in their evaluations of the American system of private ownership in broadcasting. They were more likely to perceive a basic conflict between the requirements of making a profit and providing public service in American broadcasting; to consider the pressures of advertisers a source of excessive constraint on American broadcasters; and to cite the fear of government control as a major problem of American broadcasting. Non-Europeans were more likely to feel that private ownership had some advantage in providing a greater degree of freedom to choose and organize programs. There is no reason to believe that non-Europeans had any greater preference for private ownership in broadcasting, but they felt less strongly about the issue and, what is more, were not particularly interested in the structure of broadcasting in America. Such an interest was in keeping with the Europeans' orientation toward studying the American broadcasting system per se and comparing it to their own, but not with the non-Europeans' orientation toward specific new learnings relevant to the working broadcaster. Thus, it is understandable that, in responding to questions about the structure of American broadcasting, non-Europeans simply allowed their generally favorable attitudes to prevail.

In evaluations of programming and facilities in American broadcasting (fourth set of items), we again find a generally more critical stance among the Europeans. One very specific criticism was more often raised by non-Europeans: They were more likely to mention disapprovingly the practice of breaking up news programs with commercials. On several other, more general issues, however, the Europeans were more likely to be critical. More Europeans than non-Europeans expressed the feeling that there was a lack of balance in programming on American media; that the quality of radio drama was lower in America than in their own countries; that the working conditions of American broadcasters were not always very good; and that some broadcast stations worked with disappointingly poor technical facilities. The Europeans' critical attitude, however, was by no means unrelieved. There was one feature of American broadcasting that more Europeans than non-Europeans singled out for praise: the documentaries and experimental programs produced by the major networks. Thus, though the Europeans had some serious criticisms, they were certainly not totally negative toward American broadcasting. They were, however, considerably more selective in their approval than were the non-Europeans.

This difference shows up with perfect clarity in the one item from the fourth interivew recorded in set 5. Participants were asked to describe the reports of their trip that they expected to present after returning home. Most of the non-Europeans (but not a single European) anticipated that these reports, in general, would probably praise American broadcasting, with little or no qualification. By contrast, most of the Europeans (but not a single non-European) anticipated that they would probably present mixed evaluations in their reports, saying some good things and some bad things about American broadcasting. Thus, it seems evident that, at the end of the sojourn, the non-Europeans viewed American broadcasting with an attitude of global approval, while the Europeans' view was marked by a greater degree of differentiation and an attitude of selective approval.

There are indications in the sixth set of items that this difference between the two groups persisted into the post-return interview, conducted a year later. This time the difference showed up in discussions of American broadcasters: Most of the non-Europeans evaluated them in largely favorable terms, while the Europeans were more prone to give them mixed evaluations. That this represented not merely a more negative attitude but a more selective one on the part of the Europeans is evident from the next item. Europeans, far more often than non-Europeans, told us that, in their reports about the trip, they had stressed the advantages of certain American broadcasting techniques, such as those used in documentaries and newscasts. Thus, while the non-Europeans were higher in their global approval, the Europeans singled out for praise certain specific features of American broadcasting that they considered particularly successful or effective.

In sum, the array of items presented in Table 28 shows a tendency toward global approval of American broadcasting and broadcasters on the part of non-Europeans, though they were of course critical of certain specific features. The Europeans, on the other hand, reacted in a more differentiated and selective fashion. They had some serious criticisms and reservations about the structure, the programming, and the facilities of American broadcasting, and the quality of American broadcasters. They had high praise, however, for certain types of American programs and broadcasting techniques, such as the TV documentaries, and for some of the experimental work being carried out.

Views on international exchange. Table 29 lists the items concerning international exchange to which the two groups responded differentially. Set 1 presents the single item in this area that emerged from the fourth interview. In keeping with their greater professional self-confidence, Europeans were more likely to feel that they could personally contribute to international exchanges by communicating their own professional knowledge. This finding is consistent with data presented earlier, in Tables 23 and 25, which showed that Europeans, more often than non-Europeans, felt competent and eager to make personal contributions to the seminar.

The second set of items brings together all the relevant information from the post-return interview. The first item is surprising: Non-Europeans were more likely than Europeans to cite increased information about broadcasting media in other countries among the benefits of international exchange. This is the type of response we would have expected from the Europeans in view of their earlier emphasis on observing and learning about American broadcasting. Perhaps the non-Europeans had in mind information about broadcasting media in other countries that they could apply directly to their own situations, but we have no way of checking out this possibility.

The remaining items are consistent with earlier findings. When asked about contributions that other countries could make to the development of broadcasting in their own countries, Europeans were more likely to mention program ideas. We have seen earlier (Table 24, ninth set of items) that Europeans, more often than non-Europeans, actually introduced new program ideas acquired in America after returning home. Non-Europeans, on the other hand, were more likely to mention active contributions that other countries could make to the development of broadcasting in their own countries. Others could provide direct assistance to them in making programs available and in contributing to the training of their personnel. These answers reflect the reality that many of the non-Europeans came from broadcasting systems in a relatively early stage of development, and are consistent with the practical orientation that the non-Europeans brought to their own exchange experience. The differences in stage of development between European and non-European systems are also reflected in the next item: A number of Europeans felt that their countries could contribute to the development of broadcasting elsewhere or to international exchanges out of their own special experiences in in-

Table 29

VIEWS ON INTERNATIONAL EXCHANGE:
COMPARISON OF EUROPEANS AND NON-EUROPEANS

Items that Discriminate	Number of Respondents to Whom Each Item Applies	
	Europeans	Non-Europeans
1. *Fourth interview: Perception of participant's own contributions to international exchange*		
Among the potential contributions that the participant could personally make to international exchanges he mentions that he could communicate his own professional knowledge in a given area	5	1
2. *Post-return interview: Attitudes toward and participation in international exchange*		
Among the benefits of international exchange he mentions that it may increase participants' information about broadcasting media in other countries	3	8
Among the contributions that other countries could make to the development of broadcasting in his own country he cites		
program ideas	5	1
the exchange of programs	5	10
the training of personnel	5	9
Among the contributions that his country could make to the development of broadcasting elsewhere or to international exchanges he cites its special experiences in instructional or educational broadcasting (for example, literacy training, community education)	5	0
During the past year, he has had a considerable amount of professional contact with American individuals or organizations	7	1
His professional relations with America have included contact with American broadcasting and educational networks	11	4
During the past year, he has had a considerable amount of professional contact with individuals or organizations from other countries	6	1

structional or educational broadcasting; none of the non-Europeans mentioned this possibility.

The remaining three items in Table 29 elaborate on an earlier finding, presented in Table 24 (ninth set of items). In the earlier table we noted that the Europeans were more likely to have maintained the professional contacts they had established in America, both with individual broadcasters and with broadcasting organizations. In the present table we find that this is part of a more general pattern of involvement in international professional activities. Europeans, more often than non-Europeans, reported that they had had a considerable amount of professional contact with American individuals or organizations (contacts that may or may not have been established in the course of the sojourn). Furthermore, more Europeans than non-Europeans reported a considerable amount of contact with individuals or organizations from other countries. In short, it seems the Europeans were more integrated in an international professional network than were the non-Europeans, as we proposed in the discussion of Table 24.

In sum, the differences in views on international exchange between Europeans and non-Europeans can mostly be traced to differences in the degree of professional establishment of the two groups and of their broadcasting systems. Europeans were more certain of the contributions that their broadcasting systems and they personally could make to international exchanges; they were more likely to perceive the contributions of such exchanges to their own broadcasting activities in terms of the stimulation of new program ideas; and they were more fully integrated into an international professional network. Non-Europeans were more likely to stress that international exchanges could be of direct help in the development of their own broadcasting systems by supplying programs and contributing to the training of personnel. The groups did not differ in their overall evaluations of international exchange.

SUMMARY

In comparing two groups, there is always the danger of overlooking the enormous amount of variation within each group and overlap between the two. There is a tendency to equate the profiles of the *groups,* which emerge from differences in the patterns by which responses on various dimensions are distributed in each, with profiles of the *individuals* who make up the groups. At best, the group profile approximates the profile of some of its members. For each individual, a different and partial combination of group characteristics is likely to apply, and some individuals in the group may share none of its characteristics. It is particularly important to keep this caveat in mind here, since many of the differences between Europeans and non-Europeans that we noted were based on a small proportion of the cases. Nevertheless, the data clearly suggest a distinct European pattern and a distinct non-European one, although it is equally clear that not all of our participants fit their respective patterns, and that none of them fits the pattern entirely.

The differences between the two groups can ultimately be traced to the differences in the backgrounds from which they came to the sojourn. The Europeans came to America from more similar cultures, from technologically more advanced societies, and from more highly developed broadcasting systems than did the non-Europeans. They were more secure about their national and—what was most important in the context of the seminar—their professional status than the non-Europeans. They were, by and large, professionals with high status and long experience, coming from organizations that themselves had high status and long experience. The non-Europeans were generally less experienced and, even when they had high status within their own organizations, these organizations themselves were not well established.

These background differences led to differences in the self-images, the goals, and the agenda that the two groups brought to their sojourn. The Europeans tended to present themselves as accomplished specialists, confident about their professional knowledge and abilities. They felt capable of making useful contributions to high-level professional exchanges, both at the university and in the field, out of their own experience and expertise, and they were very much interested in making such contributions. The non-Europeans, on the other hand, were less confident about their own ability to contribute to the exchange and more eager to benefit from the contributions of others and from the seminar as a whole. They tended to present themselves as learners, interested in acquiring new information and skills that they would be able to apply upon returning to their own organizations. Perhaps the difference in the self-images and goals of the two groups can best be characterized in terms of a distinction between two aspects of self-actualization: self-utilization and self-development.[5] The Europeans saw the trip primarily as an opportunity for self-utilization, for exercising skills and expressing talents that they already possessed. The non-Europeans saw it primarily as an opportunity for self-development, for acquiring new knowledge, improving their skills, and achieving a higher level of competence. The distinction must not be overdrawn; we have evidence of an interest in self-development among Euro-

[5] See J. R. P. French, Jr., and R. L. Kahn, "A Programmatic Approach to Studying the Industrial Environment and Mental Health," *Journal of Social Issues*, 1962, *18* (3), 1–47.

peans and in self-utilization among non-Europeans. It does, however, capture the primary emphases of the two groups.

Along with the differences in self-images and goals, the two groups brought different agenda to the sojourn. The Europeans came with a broader agenda, including an interest, not only in professional experiences, but also in seeing America, in meeting people, and in deepening their understanding of American life and American society. On the professional side, they were interested in observing American broadcasting, in learning about its operations, and in comparing notes with their American counterparts. Thus, in both the professional and the nonprofessional spheres, they considered observation and critical examination of American institutions and practices as ends in themselves. The non-Europeans, on the other hand, came with a narrower agenda. They were more oriented toward their own professional situations and problems and were interested in acquiring specific information and skills that would be directly applicable in their own work upon returning home. American practices and procedures were of interest to them, not as objects of general curiosity, but as potential sources of relevant information.

Given their different self-images, goals, and agenda, the two groups related themselves quite differently to the American experience. The Europeans were largely oriented toward observation and, in keeping with their broader agenda, this interest extended considerably beyond the professional sphere. Thus, among their most meaningful and enjoyable experiences, they counted both observations of broadcasting facilities and activities, and observations of the physical environment. In fact, they considered the bulk of their most important experiences to have been in nonprofessional rather than professional areas. Their greatest accomplishments consisted in acquiring firsthand knowledge of the United States and gaining a greater understanding of the American society and way of life.

The Europeans were highly satisfied (more so than the non-Europeans) with the university phase of the seminar, even though they did not find it very useful from a professional point of view. They apparently decided, very soon after arrival, that the way in which the seminar was set up and the participants were selected was not conducive to a professional exchange at the level they had expected and considered themselves qualified for. They did have occasions (more often than the non-Europeans) to present samples of their own work and were, by and large, satisfied with their own contributions to the seminar. Nevertheless, they probably found the opportunities for self-utilization too limited and were, to that extent, disappointed with the professional experience. The disappointment, however, was not very deep, since there were other aspects of the seminar that clearly met their interests. Thus, they enjoyed the visits to broadcasting and other communication facilities, as well as the academic seminars, which allowed them to learn about American society. All in all, they found a large proportion of the university program relevant to their broad interests, which no doubt accounts for their high level of overall satisfaction.

The Europeans were also highly satisfied with the travel phase of the trip, although here again the professional aspects of the experience were not the ones that stood out as accomplishments and sources of enjoyment for them. They did enjoy the opportunity of making professional observations in the course of their travels, and of thus obtaining a good overall picture of the great variety and range of programs, facilities, and approaches in American broadcasting. But they particularly appreciated the nonprofessional side of the trip—the opportunity to travel around the country, to meet Americans, and to enjoy the physical environment.

In contrast to the Europeans, the non-Europeans were largely task-oriented. Not only did they focus heavily on professional concerns in general, but they sought out professional exchanges around *specific* problems that would be of direct utility in their own work. They saw relatively little value in observing what Americans were doing and hearing descriptions of it, unless such experiences were applicable to the situations in their own countries. Even in their observations of American society in general, they tended to dwell on the implications for their own societies. Among their most important experiences they counted exposure to new program ideas and establishment of new relationships with other broadcasters—both of which were potentially useful in their future professional work. They also valued the opportunity to learn about educational TV. Despite their professional task-orientation, the non-Europeans were by no means impervious to their immediate environment. They particularly enjoyed opportunities for informal interactions with Americans, such as those provided by the New Hampshire weekend, and spontaneously made many social contacts during their travels. They seemed to be less concerned about proper recognition of their status and thus found it easier, perhaps, to enter into such relationships. These were, however, the *enjoyable* aspects of the trip, as distinguished from the *useful* ones, which clearly centered around the acquisition of applicable professional information.

The non-Europeans were considerably more satisfied with the professional part of the program at the university than were the Europeans. They found the professional seminars relevant to their interests and felt that they presented large amounts of information that would help them in their own work. They were happy with the composition of the group and found the contributions of some of the other participants useful. Though most of them were not entirely satisfied with their own contributions to the seminar and some apparently felt that their talents were underutilized, the non-Europeans by and large seemed to be quite comfortable in the roles of learners. Their main source of dissatisfaction was that the program did not provide as much opportunity as they would have liked for workshop-type experiences, focusing in concrete and task-oriented fashion on specific professional concerns. They would have preferred to have fewer other activities—such as lectures, tours of facilities, and academic seminars—so that they could fully concentrate on exchanges around professional problems and absorb the new information to which they were exposed. If they were less satisfied with the university phase of the seminar than the Europeans, it was mostly because they felt that not enough of the program was relevant to their more narrowly defined agenda.

During the travel period, again, the lower level of the overall satisfaction among the non-Europeans, as compared to the Europeans, may have resulted from their narrower, more task-oriented agenda. Since they were looking for more specific, potentially applicable information and experiences, they probably found a smaller proportion of their activities in the field to be relevant to their specific interests. What they particularly appreciated during the trip was the opportunity to meet fellow-broadcasters who were very helpful to them and to learn new approaches to programming that would be of direct use to them after their return home.

By the end of the sojourn, the earlier differences between the two groups in their overall levels of satisfaction had completely disappeared. It is clear that, on balance, both groups found the trip satisfying, though each in a somewhat different way. The Europeans had reservations about the professional value of some of their experiences, but they derived satisfactions from the many other experiences—some professional, many nonprofessional—that were relevant to their broad agenda. The non-Europeans would have preferred a greater concentration on exchanges around specific professional problems, but they found at least some experiences that were relevant to their interests and that they expected to be useful to them in their own professional situations. Both groups attributed to the sojourn certain changes in their views and perspectives. The Europeans felt that they had changed their perspectives about America, its institutions, and its people, as well as their views of the role of broadcasting in their own countries. The non-Europeans reported that their experiences in America had given them a new perspective on their own countries and on their professional roles.

We have argued so far that the different backgrounds of our two groups led to differences in the self-images, goals, and agenda that they brought to the sojourn; and that these, in turn, account for differences in the ways in which they related themselves to the American experience, in the satisfactions they derived from it, and in the reassessments of attitudes that it set into motion. We turn, finally, to the question of whether the trip actually had a different impact on the Europeans and the non-Europeans, in line with their different expectations and goals and their different ways of relating themselves to the experience. Our data indicate that, indeed, there were some interesting differences in the impact of the trip on the two groups' views of America and American broadcasting, and on their professional activities.

The groups showed no systematic differences in their overall evaluations of America, although there were some minor differences in their reactions to specific features of American society. For example, the non-Europeans, quite understandably, were more impressed with America's high standard of living and advanced technology, and more disturbed by the state of American race relations. The major difference between the two groups, however, was registered on cognitive rather than evaluative dimensions. The Europeans developed a more differentiated image and a more complex understanding of American society than did the non-Europeans. They not only placed a greater emphasis on the diversity and heterogeneity of America, but they also showed a more wide-ranging and detailed awareness of the ways in which regional and other differences functioned in American life. No doubt these differences can be attributed in part to the greater cultural similarity with which the Europeans started their sojourn. The major determining factor, however, seems to be the Europeans' greater interest in observing American life and understanding its institutions and the special weight they gave to such observations and insights throughout their stay.

In their attitudes toward American broadcasting, non-Europeans came away with considerably more favorable evaluations than did Europeans. Though critical of certain of its specific features, the non-Europeans tended to regard American broadcasting with global approval. The Europeans were more differentiated and much more selective in their approval. They had some serious criticisms of the structure, the programming, and the facilities of American broadcasting and of the quality of some of their American colleagues. At the same time, they had high praise for certain types of American programs and broadcasting techniques, such as those used in TV documentaries, and for some of the experimental work being carried out. The more critical attitude of the Europeans can probably be accounted for by two factors: (1) since they themselves came from more highly developed broadcasting systems, they had both more severe standards against which to measure American broadcasting and more definite ideas about the way things ought to be done; and (2) they were more interested in examining American broadcasting critically and comparing it to other approaches, while the non-Europeans were much more interested in extracting from American broadcasting specific procedures and practices that might be applicable to their own systems.

As far as professional activities are concerned, it is interesting that more Europeans than non-Europeans gave evidence of having put their American experience to concrete use within the first year after their return home. They reported more often that they had introduced American-inspired programs and that they had maintained professional contacts with individuals and organizations established while they were in the United States. This despite the fact that, during the sojourn, the non-Europeans expressed greater interest in learning new approaches to programming and in establishing new professional contacts. Most probably, the Europeans—in view of their own and their organizations' higher degree of professional establishment—found it easier to implement new program ideas and to maintain cross-national contacts. They were more accustomed to looking toward international exchange as a source of stimulation of new program ideas and they were more fully integrated into an international professional network. Thus, it seems that the Europeans' greater readiness to make use of ideas and contacts acquired in America more than compensated for their lesser motivation to do so.

Nevertheless, the indications are that the sojourn had a more far-reaching impact on the professional activities of the non-Europeans. They felt that the experience gave them, not only new information relevant to their own work, but a new perspective on their professional roles. More non-Europeans than Europeans reported changes in their professional positions or responsibilities in the year following upon their return home or anticipated such changes for the near future. No doubt these changes were due to the greater fluidity of their broadcasting systems, which were undergoing a process of rapid development. Their own participation in this process, however, may have been greatly affected by the new knowledge, the new perspective, and the new prestige they acquired as a result of their trip abroad. Of special significance is our finding that non-Europeans reported (more often than Europeans) that their job satisfaction had increased in the year since their return home, and ascribed this increase to the recognition that others gave to their abilities. It may be that the trip to America had noticeably increased their professional competencies, or that it had increased their prestige so that colleagues were now more inclined to acknowledge their abilities. In either event, the new recognition of their abilities, occasioned by their trip abroad, enhanced their professional self-confidence, which certainly ought to facilitate their professional development over a period of years.

The array of data presented in this chapter suggests that the seminar did not fully meet either the Europeans' need for self-utilization or the non-Europeans' need for self-development. Yet it seemed to meet them sufficiently to make the experience, on the whole, a satisfying and meaningful one, and to produce an impact that still manifested itself a year later. What is important to note, in the present context, is that there are different ways in which an international exchange experience of this sort can have value for its participants. The Europeans and non-Europeans differed in the expectations and agenda they brought to the sojourn, in the ways they went about meeting their respective goals, and in their final achievements. Nevertheless, both groups seemed to be at least moderately satisfied with their experience and both manifested significant effects—each in its own way.

15

Conclusions

The evaluation of the multinational seminar for broadcasters, described in the preceding chapters, had a twofold purpose. It was designed (1) to assess the effectiveness of the seminar in achieving its goals; and (2) to identify the specific features of the seminar that were most successful and those that created difficulties, so that we might be able to recommend arrangements and procedures that would enhance the effectiveness of similar seminars in the future. What have we learned from our findings that is relevant to these two research objectives?

Information relevant to the second objective was derived primarily from the interviews held with participants while the seminar was in progress (Chapters Four and Six); this information was validated by data from the retrospective interviews (Chapter Seven) and supplemented by group observations and reactions of the seminar staff (Chapter Five). This information has yielded a series of conclusions about the conditions for a satisfying experience in a multinational seminar. After presenting these conclusions, we shall turn to those of our findings that can help us assess the effectiveness of the present seminar in achieving its goals (Chapters Eight through Twelve). Finally, we shall draw out the implications that these findings, as well as our findings about the differential reactions of different subgroups (Chapter Thirteen and Fourteen), have for international exchange experiences.

SATISFYING EXCHANGE

Our analysis has suggested several conclusions that ought to be applicable to a variety of situations involving international exchange. Each situation, of course, has some unique features and some special problems that have to be handled in terms of its own requirements. Much depends, for example, on the professional field with which a particular program is concerned, on the professional positions of the participants, on the range of countries represented, and on the setting in which the program is conducted. Nevertheless, there are certain general principles that should be relevant to most of these situations, even though they might take a different specific form in each case. We shall attempt to summarize some of these principles, as they emerge from our data and from the interpretations we have placed upon them.

From the reactions of the participants to their experiences, one can draw some inferences about the major conditions that are likely to enhance their satisfaction. We have identified seven such conditions on the basis of our analysis of the first three interviews, which focused (in part) on participants' reactions to the seminar while it was still in progress. Analysis of the subsequent interviews confirmed our earlier conclusions and gave added weight to one point that had not emerged quite as sharply out of the first three interviews: As participants reflected on their experience retrospectively, they stressed even more emphatically than before the importance of active participation and direct involvement in professional activities as a major component of an exchange program.

The seven conditions we have identified appear to have general applicability to multinational programs. It would be important, in our view, to take them into account in planning and conducting such programs and to structure exchange situations with an eye to maximizing these conditions. In presenting each of the conditions, we shall both refer to the aspects of the present seminar that have suggested its importance and try to draw out its implications for the organization of multinational exchange programs in general.[1]

---

[1] The data presented in Chapters Thirteen and Fourteen suggest that some of the points to be listed here are more applicable to high differentiators than to low differentiators, or to Europeans than to non-Europeans. It must be kept in mind, however, that Chapters Thirteen and Fourteen dealt with the *relative* standings of different subgroups on the various issues. Thus, for example, although Europeans placed *less* emphasis on the relevance of the experience to their specific professional concerns than did non-Europeans, they were not necessarily indifferent to this issue. Obviously, every one of the points is more important to some individuals than it is to others, but they have all come up sufficiently often in our interviews to constitute general trends for the sample as a whole.

1. Relevance of the experience to the participant's professional concerns. Perhaps the key factor in satisfying a mature professional with his experience abroad is how much value it has from the point of view of his specific professional concerns. His whole attitude to the experience is likely to be shaped by the extent to which it gives him an opportunity to exchange ideas and explore problems that are directly relevant to his work; the extent to which it provides him with new information that he can apply to his own professional situation; and the extent to which it enables him to establish contacts with colleagues in other countries who have similar interests, and thus to lay the groundwork for future exchanges. A seminar participant may be interested in many things. He may enjoy learning about America in general and, in particular, about the American developments in his own professional field. In the final analysis, however, his satisfaction with the experience will depend to a considerable extent on its relevance to his specific professional concerns.

The participants in the present seminar enjoyed listening to American leaders in the field of broadcasting, and were particularly appreciative of the high quality of the invited speakers who were presented to them. Yet, some participants were not entirely satisfied because the organization of the professional seminars made it difficult to focus on specific issues of common concern, to delve more deeply into them, and to discuss them in detail. The presentation of what was happening in American broadcasting was interesting to them up to a point, but they also would have liked to use it as a springboard for detailed exploration of concrete professional problems of their own. Similarly, some participants were not entirely satisfied with their experiences in the field, because they saw too many stations for too short a period of time, without sufficient opportunity to observe their operations in detail. They were less interested in seeing facilities than they were in discussing specific problems in programming. They would have liked an opportunity to be attached to a station for a longer period of time, and actually to work there alongside the regular staff or to study its operations at close range. Participants who had this kind of opportunity were highly satisfied with their field experiences.

It would seem, then, that in organizing an exchange program it is usually not enough to ask: What can we show and tell the participants that would be of interest to them? The primary question ought to be: What can we enable the participants *to do* that would have concrete professional value for them? The problem is not merely one of selecting lecturers they would like to hear and facilities they would like to see, but also one of deliberately and systematically structuring the program so that participants would have the opportunity to address themselves actively, along with American colleagues, to central issues in their work. What they

can see and learn about American activities in their field is certainly
valuable, but it should be more than a mere description of current
practices and a display of local facilities. It should be part of a more
active process of exploration and exchange of common problems. The
participants should be viewed not as professional sightseers, but as colleagues engaged in a professionally relevant enterprise.

If direct professional relevance is to serve as the guiding principle
in organizing a seminar, a number of more specific steps can be recommended:

a. Participants should be so selected that the group will be relatively homogeneous in terms of a focal problem with which all members
are professionally concerned. This criterion is not incompatible with having some diversity in background, experience, positions, and specific activities, as long as, at some level, there is a shared problem on which all
participants can come together.

b. The professional part of the seminar should be organized in
terms of an integrating framework, built around issues related to the focal
area of concern. This framework should be communicated to the participants in advance, so that they will know what to expect and what is expected of them, and will be able to prepare accordingly.

c. Deliberate attempts should be made to match activities with the
specific interests and needs of the participants. During their stay at the
university, this would mean providing opportunities for alternative activities on the part of different subgroups in line with their special interests. For the field trip, it would mean finding out exactly what kinds of
activities each participant would like to engage in and then selecting
facilities that will make these activities available.

d. Both at the university and in the field, it is necessary to make
some sacrifice in the number of offerings—the number of speakers invited,
the number of facilities visited—in order to allow for longer and deeper
exposure to each. This need not be an absolute rule, of course. On some
occasions it may be valuable to bring in an outstanding speaker or to visit
an outstanding facility even though only a limited amount of time is
available.

e. Exposure to American speakers and facilities should be of such
a nature that participants will have ample opportunity to explore procedures and approaches in detail and to relate them to their own specific
interests, problems, and experiences. During the stay at the university,
this means that there should be time and encouragement to follow up each
presentation with extended discussion and exchange, going beyond questions and answers into an actual sharing of experiences. During the field
trip, it means that each participant should, if possible, be attached to at

least one facility for a longer period of time and directly involved in its ongoing activities. He may take either the role of a temporary staff member or of an observer who can explore the operations of the facility in detail.

f. Even in the planning of those activities that are not specifically professional, it may be worthwhile to consider their possible professional relevance. Some participants may be interested in numerous aspects of American life; others, however, may be interested only in those aspects that touch on their professional specialties. In developing academic seminars and in arranging the nonprofessional side of the travel period, therefore, it would be important to keep in mind which aspects of American life are likely to interest the participants, given their particular professional concerns. Insofar as possible, it would be desirable to offer participants alternative academic seminars from which each can select those that are of the greatest interest to him.

We have dwelt at such length on the professional relevance of the experience because we consider it a key to the participant's reaction to the experience as a whole. We would venture to predict that the extent to which the trip turned out to be a meaningful professional experience would affect not only the person's satisfaction with it at the moment, but also its longer-range impact on him. This should be so for several reasons. First of all, a satisfying experience is more conducive to a process of re-examination of one's assumptions and approaches. Thus, anything that has a marked effect on satisfaction should also have a marked effect on impact. Secondly, to the extent that the person is engaged in a meaningful professional experience, he will *ipso facto* be involved in an active process of thinking through his professional role and professional activities. The results of this process should then continue to manifest themselves when he comes back to his home situation. Finally, to the extent that he has been involved in a meaningful professional experience, he will have established actual links with colleagues from America and from other countries who participated in the experience with him. He would thus become part of a wider network of fellow-professionals, with whom he maintains contact and engages in exchange. Thus, the effects of the experience would enter directly into his subsequent professional life.

2. The participant's opportunity to establish reciprocal relationships with colleagues in the host country. As we have already noted, most of the participants in the present seminar wanted a relationship with their American colleagues that would go beyond listening to them speak, or asking them questions, or being shown their facilities. Certainly, the kind of professional experience they desired—an experience directly germane to their own specific professional concerns—presupposes a greater degree of discussion and exchange of ideas and experiences than the one-sided relationship of speaker to listener or guide to tourist makes possible.

Although the participants did not often mention this point directly, there are good theoretical reasons for believing that more reciprocal, give-and-take relationships are valued, not only because they allow for a more intensive problem-orientation, but also because they are inherently more satisfying. Sometimes, the presence or absence of reciprocal relationships is linked to considerations of status: Where such relationships do not occur, the visitor may feel that his host does not really regard him as an equal with whom he can engage in a mutually beneficial exchange. From all indications, however, this feeling did not prevail among the specialists whom we interviewed. They were generally accorded very high status by the organizers of the seminar, and by the colleagues they met both at the university and in the field. Moreover, they did not seem to mind being in the role of learner or observer. Nevertheless, it seems reasonable to suppose that there is a limit to how long one can sustain these passive roles. Quite aside from status considerations, it is frustrating to remain for a long time in the role of spectator rather than participant, the role of recipient rather than contributor. A more active, give-and-take relationship with colleagues from the host country would make the interaction intellectually more stimulating and interpersonally more rewarding. It would allow the participant to use his own potentialities to a greater extent and to experience the satisfaction that comes from establishing a personal contact. It is quite likely that our respondents' desire for more discussion after lectures and for greater involvement in the facilities they visited reflects, at least in part, a desire for more participatory relationships with their American counterparts.

The recommendations that we have already offered for making encounters with American colleagues (both at the university and in the field) longer and more intensive would go a long way toward facilitating this type of relationship. We would go further, however, in recommending a more deliberate and more complete introduction of reciprocal relationships with members of the host society into the exchange program. Thus, for programs such as the one under study, we would recommend the inclusion of several Americans as regular participants during the period at the university. Ideally, they would remain with the seminar during the entire period, but there would be value in having them come even for a period of one or two weeks. The essential point is that they would come not as invited speakers, but as regular participants, who see themselves as involved in an exchange activity, rather than in mere information-giving. This is not meant to replace the procedure of bringing in American experts for short periods as speakers and resource persons, but rather to supplement it with another—more participatory—type of relationship with American colleagues.

During the field period, we would recommend that participants be encouraged, whenever possible, to become participant observers in at least one of the facilities they visit. If they can serve as temporary staff members, who are intimately involved in the ongoing operations of the organization, then the experience is likely to be most rewarding. This type of participation is not always feasible, but an attempt should be made to approximate it.

3. The participant's opportunity to make personal contributions. A major source of satisfaction is the opportunity to be an active contributor, rather than just a recipient. Being able to make a contribution enhances a person's self-esteem. It gives him the reassurance that he has something of value to give to others and that they are interested in what he has to offer. Moreover, it strengthens his feeling that his participation in the program is worthwhile in that his own talents and relevant experiences are not being wasted. Finally, as the participant contributes personally, the experience becomes more enriching for himself. He is able to relate what he hears to his own situation, he is stimulated to develop and formulate his ideas, and he is given the opportunity to try them out on others. On the practical side, when participants make personal contributions, others can become acquainted with their work, and a basis for future interaction can thus be provided.

Some of our respondents mentioned that during their stay at the university their own contributions and the contributions of other participants were not being used as fully as possible. They were often prepared to contribute more than they were asked or encouraged to contribute. There was a general feeling that not enough exchange occurred among the participants themselves. The fact that opportunities for personal contributions by the participants were not built into the program to any great extent was disappointing, not only because the participants were not able to contribute as much as they would have liked to, but also because they were not able to benefit as much from the contributions of other participants. In the field interviews, respondents did not express any feeling that their contributions were being underutilized. It is quite possible, however, that this is part of the reason for the less than total satisfaction with short, touring-type visits, and for the generally high degree of satisfaction found among those individuals who were attached to facilities for longer periods of time and more directly involved in their operations—and who, presumably, had greater opportunity to make personal contributions.

Again, the recommendations that we have already made for a more problem-oriented organization of the professional seminars and a more intensive involvement in facilities during the travel period are also designed to enhance the participants' opportunity to make personal contributions. During the period at the university, if lectures are followed by opportunities for extensive discussion around concrete problems, participants are able to bring in their own relevant experiences, to learn more about what each of them is doing and thinking, and to hear reactions from one another. We would further recommend that the program be so structured that participants whose experience is particularly relevant to the problem under study can be called upon to lead discussions, make presentations, or give demonstrations. It might also be a good idea to invite each participant to describe to the group the relevant professional developments in his own country. In this way, one could take fuller advantage both of the personal contributions of individual participants and of the multinational character of the seminar for the transmission of useful information.

Longer and more intensive involvement of the participants in the facilities they visit during the travel period would, of course, increase their opportunities for making personal contributions, especially if they were actually working alongside their American counterparts. The organization to which the participant is to be attached should be informed early and fully of his background and qualifications to give his colleagues an idea of the potential contributions that he could make to their program, and enable them to invite him to make these contributions.

4. Availability of choice in the activities and arrangements offered to the participant. Satisfaction is likely to be greatest if the person's activities and arrangements are not entirely predetermined, but if he is given some freedom of movement so that he can pursue his own interests and maximize his own values. We have already mentioned the importance of providing the participant, insofar as possible, with choices in his professional and academic activities and in the facilities he visits during the travel period. The same considerations hold true for social, cultural, and recreational activities.

The participant's choice of activities can be enhanced in three interrelated ways:

a. The range of opportunities made available to the individual can be generally broadened. This does not necessarily mean *organizing* a large variety of activities. It does mean, first of all, acquainting the participants with as many ongoing activities as possible (for example, various cultural and recreational events at the university and the neighboring community, and in the cities they will be visiting during the travel period), so that they can select the particular ones that are of interest to them. Second, it means facilitating arrangements for engaging in these activities, for example, by obtaining tickets and providing transportation.

b. Wherever possible, activities ought to be planned in such a way that the group can be broken down into smaller subgroups, in line with their diverse interests. There are, of course, occasions when activities involving the total group are completely appropriate, but it must be kept in mind that the total group is not always the most meaningful basis for organizing the program. If this principle is followed, participants will have genuine alternatives among which they can choose. Thus, in professsional activities there should be some mechanisms for the formation of special interest groups around specific issues. Academic activities should consist of a series of offerings within which participants can make selections. Organized social and recreational activities should be of different types, reflecting the differences in preference among the participants.

c. Finally, one can enhance choice by ensuring that "saying no" always remains an available alternative. It is important to watch out that an opportunity does not degenerate into an obligation. This can happen, for example, during the travel period if a heavy program of social activities is prearranged for a participant who would rather rest, or have privacy, or pursue his own interests.

The problem of choice also enters into some of the practical arrangements. It is important to keep in mind that meals, accommodations, transportation, and the like involve competing values to which different participants may assign different weights. One should not assume, therefore, that all participants would prefer the same arrangement. Rather, one should try to individualize arrangements as much as possible, and allow each participant to choose in terms of his own preference.

5. *Arrangement of the participant's schedule and facilities in line with his desired pattern of activities.* It is obvious that a participant's satisfaction depends on his ability to do the things that he wants to do— or perhaps has to do. In working out a schedule and in arranging facilities, it is essential to take this criterion into account in a very deliberate way. Thus, it is not enough to think in terms of giving him certain blocks of time. One must consider in detail the kinds of activities in which he would want to engage during that time. The time is not very valuable unless it comes at a point at which he needs it and at which he can use it to maximum advantage, given the activities in which he wishes to engage. Thus, in scheduling free time during the stay at the university, one must consider at what point this time could be used most effectively in the context of the overall program. For example, at what point do the participants need time for absorbing new material, for reflection, or for relaxa-

tion? One must also consider the specific activities in which participants would want to engage—such as visiting the library or setting appointments for individual consultations—in order to determine what blocks of time would be required and during which parts of the day. Similarly, in scheduling time in different cities during the travel period, one must make sure that the amount of time and the points at which it is introduced are such as to make the desired activities possible and convenient. Similar considerations pertain to the arrangement of facilities. It is essential not only to provide facilities that participants require for their desired activities, but also to provide them in a form and at a time that they can be used to maximum advantage.

6. *The participant's opportunity for informal social contacts with nationals of the host society.* For many visitors, informal social contacts, which permit some degree of personal interaction, are a major source of satisfaction. Some of our respondents indicated that, although they enjoyed the more formal occasions organized for the group as a whole, these did not completely satisfy all of their social needs. In the light of this experience, it would seem to be important to supplement the more formal gatherings with other types of experiences that allow for informal interactions. One way of meeting this need would be to encourage staff members, such as the leaders of the academic seminars, to spend more time in informal contacts with the participants, to be present at some of the meals, or to invite the participants to their homes. Another way of meeting this need would be to arrange informal gatherings at the university, to which members of the community—from different walks of life—are invited. Small gatherings in private homes also can be arranged, to which several participants along with several members of the community are invited. At such gatherings, individual participants would be able to strike up acquaintances with individual Americans. This, in turn, is likely to lead to subsequent contacts and to spontaneous invitations to American homes.

Although there is a special value in spontaneous invitations, we found that even the organized private hospitality seemed to be highly successful. The participants reacted very favorably to their experiences of private hospitality, both during their period at the university and during their travel period. These were often mentioned as highlights of their visit. Participants saw these invitations to private homes as opportunities to meet Americans as individuals, in the context of their families, and in an informal and relaxing atmosphere. They enjoyed the personalized nature of the relationship, the conversations that it engendered, and the chance to participate in the regular activities of an American family. They were impressed by the generosity, frankness, openness, and the amount of interest in the outside world shown by their American hosts.

Visits to private homes can, on occasion, be quite unpleasant, if the encounters turn out to be patronizing, ritualistic, and impersonal. In our interviews, however, we had practically no indication of any negative reactions to these experiences. We would recommend that arrangements for private hospitality continue to be included in future exchange programs, both during the period at the university and during the travel period. In the selection and orientation of families participating in these arrangements, one must pay deliberate attention to the possible ways in which private hospitality might backfire. In arranging an itinerary for the travel period, it may be a good idea to encourage those participants who are likely to find it difficult to make their own social arrangements to visit, other things being equal, communities that are smaller and less inundated with foreign visitors. In such communities, they are more likely to receive individualized attention.

The opportunity for informal social contacts with nationals of the host society is likely to be a major factor in determining the visitor's general reaction to the experience as a whole. The personal relationships formed in such contacts often represent the most warmly remembered aspect of a trip abroad. Not only do they provide the visitor with satisfying experiences while he is in the foreign country, but they may also lead to the establishment of lasting personal ties.

7. *Enhancement of the participant's national and personal status.* The question of whether they are being accorded the status they are due is likely to arise in the minds of participants in any group situation. It is, however, particularly likely to come up in a multinational setting. Here, national status tends to be tied in with personal status: Participants may become sensitive about the status accorded their own national group. Such sensitivities have often been noted among representatives from African and Asian nations who may feel (sometimes with justification) that Americans and Europeans are undervaluing their countries and are patronizing them. The reverse reaction has also been noted. Some Europeans may feel that they are taken for granted and representatives from developing countries are given more attention. Asian participants, in particular, may experience a feeling of status deprivation. They may feel that they are neither assigned equal status to the extent of the Europeans, nor given the special attention that is accorded to the Africans.

A participant's satisfaction with his experience as a whole is likely to depend, to a large extent, on the degree to which it helps to enhance his status and thus also his self-esteem. The recommendations that we have already made for increasing the participants' opportunities for colleague-type relationships with their counterparts in the host country and their opportunities to make personal contributions to the program are clearly designed to provide status enhancement. A participant's sense of personal as well as national status is likely to increase when he finds that others regard his professional contributions of interest to them, or when he is asked to report about his own work and about the activities in his country. Our respondents also appreciated the fact that very prominent people came to speak to them at the university or arranged social gatherings for them at their homes. One can assume that they found such gestures satisfying, at least in part because they contributed to their sense of status enhancement. Private invitations to American homes, in general, can serve to enhance the participant's status—provided that the American hosts are genuinely interested in the visitor and not patronizing toward him.

Of at least equal importance is the other side of the coin: In organizing an exchange program, one must be actively concerned with *avoiding* experiences that represent *status deprivation*. Organizers of such programs must be aware of the various points at which participants may potentially experience status deprivation:

a. It is possible for the professional staff of an exchange program to define the role of the participant in such a way that it would lower his status. This would happen, for example, if he is personally treated as a student, or as a representative from a backward country. This kind of definition can too easily be built into the structure of a seminar and produce a patronizing attitude on the part of the staff. Fortunately, such a definition of the participants' role was completely absent in the seminar under study. The participants were clearly treated as high-status professionals, which probably helps to account for their generally high level of satisfaction with the experience.

b. There are also various ways in which the administrative staff, both at the university and in the field, can inadvertently contribute to experiences of status deprivation. Thus, differential treatment of the participants by the administrative staff, particularly where this can be interpreted in terms of nationality, may have this effect, and may produce resentment. Similarly, when a participant does not receive individualized treatment—when arrangements for him are made entirely in the context of arrangements for the group as a whole—he may feel that he has not been accorded the attention that his status warrants.

c. We have already mentioned that in their social and professional contacts outside the seminar, participants may experience status deprivation if they are ignored, or if they are treated in a patronizing way. We find no indication that this happened to our respondents to any noticeable degree, which probably helps to account for their high satisfaction with their experiences of private hospitality and the travel period in general.

d. Finally, status deprivation can be experienced in the course of contacts with officials and service personnel unconnected with the exchange program. For example, participants may be subjected to bureaucratic indignities or to racial prejudice. The organizers of an exchange program are, of course, unable to control completely the occurrence of such experiences. What they can do, however, is to anticipate the possibility that participants might be faced with such situations, to prepare them for these, to give them some explanation of the relevant context, and to provide them with information that would help them deal with the situations if they did arise.

Conclusion. Creating the conditions for a truly satisfying exchange experience requires careful planning and coordination, attention to many details, and probably considerable expense. There is every reason to believe, however, that these are investments worth making. International exchanges have an enormous potential for enriching the professional lives of the participants; for developing fuller, more refined, and more differentiated views of other nations; and for establishing networks of professional communication and exchange that cut across national boundaries. The more satisfying the experience as the person participates in it, the greater the likelihood that its longe-range potential will be realized.

IMPACT OF THE SEMINAR

The importance of providing an experience that will be satisfying to its participants certainly requires no justification. It is an end in itself, both from the point of view of the responsibility that the organizers of exchange activities have toward those whom they invite to participate in these activities, and from the point of view of maintaining a positive relationship between organizers and participants, in the short run as well as in the long run. We have gone beyond these obvious desiderata, however, and suggested, in the preceding paragraphs, that the more satisfying an exchange experience is for those who participate in it, the more likely it is to have a significant and positive impact on them—on their professional activities and attitudes, on their views of other nations, and on their involvement in international networks of professional communication and exchange.

Granting the relationship between satisfaction and impact, it is of course possible that an experience that has been satisfying in many respects has failed to produce significant effects in certain areas, or that an experience that was unsatisfactory in many ways has nonetheless had an important impact on many of the participants. Moreover, there are many instances in which short-run discomfort may be necessary if long-run effects are to take place. For example, new learning may require the often painful re-examination of preconceived ideas; insight into a foreign culture may require an immersion into it that is sufficiently intense to carry with it certain risks of "culture shock" and personal misunderstanding. Thus, one can certainly not expect a perfect correlation between satisfaction and impact, and one may in fact find that the relationships are quite different, depending on whether impact is assessed in the short run or in the long run.

We would assume, furthermore, that the relationship between satisfaction and impact is often of a very subtle and detailed nature— that certain kinds of satisfaction are most likely to facilitate certain kinds of impact. Our data (especially those reported in Chapters Thirteen and Fourteen) offer some hints about these more subtle relationships, to which we shall return below. For the moment, however, we want to ask a far grosser question. We have seen that the seminar under study was, on the whole, a very satisfying experience for those who participated in it, although certainly many participants had some criticisms of it, and some participants had many criticisms. Do we have any evidence that this satisfying experience had an impact on the participants?

Impact on attitudes toward America and American broadcasting. The most striking finding of impact concerns the participants' images of America and American broadcasting, and specifically the degree of complexity and differentiation of these images. The data that are most directly relevant to this point come from the before- and after-questionnaires. Scores on an overall index of change in degree of differentiation of the image of America and American broadcasting were computed for each participant and each member of the comparison group, on the basis of their questionnaire responses. When the scores of participants were compared to those of their controls, a very clear finding emerged: Participants showed an increase in differentiation, whereas comparison group members actually showed a slight decrease. The difference between the two groups is statistically significant, and suggests very strongly that the participants in the seminar did indeed develop more complex and differentiated images of America and of American broadcasting as a result of their American experience. Their responses on the after-questionnaire tended to become more concrete and specific; they evidenced an awareness of a greater number of aspects of American society and of differences within it, a better understanding of American institutions in their own terms, and a picture that was generally more detailed and elaborate.

Thus, we are justified in concluding that the seminar participants' experience in America did produce measurable changes in their attitudes toward American broadcasting and America in general on what we would regard as the most crucial dimension: the complexity and differentiation of their images. Changes on these cognitive dimensions, we submit, are far more important and meaningful than global increases in overall favorableness, which are often based on incomplete understanding and are likely to be quite ephemeral. The increased complexity and differentiation that we found in our data are particularly significant in view of the fact that our respondents were quite sophisticated and already relatively knowledgeable about America and American broadcasting. Thus, it seems reasonable to generalize these findings to other exchange experiences and to conclude that such experiences are indeed capable of producing significant changes on the cognitive dimensions of attitudes toward the host country and some of its institutions.

Our major finding was registered on these cognitive dimensions, but we were also able to identify other (though weaker) effects of the trip on participants' images of America and American broadcasting. The images they held of America, after completion of the sojourn, varied greatly, although certain common themes emerged again and again. Some of these were positive in tone, some negative, and some cannot really be placed on a favorable-unfavorable dimension. On the whole, the participants' view of America and of Americans was clearly more positive than it was negative, but it was by no means wholly uncritical. The point that came up most frequently and most emphatically was the participants' awareness of the complexity and diversity of America—which is in keeping with our evidence that their images of America had indeed become more differentiated.

When we compare the responses of participants and controls, a year after the seminar's completion, we find several differences between them. Aside from the participants' greater tendency to stress the complexity and diversity of America, they were also more likely to dwell on certain of the human qualities of Americans, on the importance of socioeconomic differences within American society, and on the commitment of Americans to democratic values. These are features of America whose full implications, it would seem, could only be understood through firsthand contact. Questionnaire responses also reveal a change on the evaluative dimension, though not as marked a change as that found on the dimension of differentiation: All the information from the questionnaire that relates to respondents' general images of America and Americans suggests that the seminar participants (relative to the comparison group) became more favorable in their evaluations as a result of their experience in America. This finding does not imply that they had no criticisms of American life, but simply that, by and large, they tended to see it in a more positive light.

What about participants' images of American broadcasting and broadcasters? With American broadcasters, as individuals, many of the participants seemed to have developed a sense of colleagueship and of identity in interests and values. They had generally high regard for them, and certainly evaluated them more favorably than unfavorably. They did have criticisms, particularly about the way in which American broadcasters met their responsibilities toward their audiences. They tended to ascribe the shortcomings of their American colleagues in this area to the conditions under which they worked, which, in turn, they saw as related to the structure of American broadcasting. Their descriptions of American broadcasters actually did not differ markedly from those given by comparison-group members, but what differences did emerge reflected the participants' greater familiarity with American colleagues—with their strengths, as well as their weaknesses.

As for American broadcasting, the participants seemed to be impressed with its potential for high-quality programming and with some of the products that had been achieved, but they felt that the structure of broadcasting was not set up so as to maximize this potential. They were critical of the limited allocation of resources to such high-quality programming relative to more strictly commercial pursuits. They saw commercial considerations as a major source of the problem, although they could also point to certain advantages of private ownership of broadcasting media, particularly within the context of American society. The differences in broadcasting structure and the low quality of some of the American products limited, in their view, the applicability of American approaches to their own countries, but some of the creative ideas—particularly in educational and public affairs broadcasting—clearly seemed of value to them. Certain features of American broadcasting—such as the extensive use of commercials and the low repute of radio—should, they felt, be systematically avoided. In fact, in these areas it would be best for American broadcasters to learn from their counterparts abroad.

When we compare the questionnaire responses of participants with those of their controls, we find two changes in their evaluation of American broadcasting which, though small, are consistent with the composite image we have just presented. On the one hand, participants tended to become somewhat less satisfied with American broadcasting—particularly with its coverage of information about their own countries, which was of course a matter of personal significance to them. On the other hand, they tended to become somewhat more inclined (relative to the comparison group) to see American broadcasting as a potential source of valuable contributions to their own broadcasting systems. It seems reasonable to suggest that increased familiarity with American broadcasting may lead to a tendency to become both more critical of certain aspects of it, and more aware of specific approaches and procedures that can fruitfully be applied to one's own situation. In other words, having observed American broadcasting in some detail, the participants seemed to like it less, but at the same time they were more cognizant of valuable lessons that they could learn from it.

The last pair of findings, taken together with some of the other findings summarized here, reminds us again of the limitations in using favorableness toward the host country and its institutions as a criterion for evaluating international exchange programs. These limitations can be illustrated most effectively by juxtaposing changes from the before- to the after-questionnaires on four of the dimensions discussed above. To make the dimensions comparable, Table 30 simply presents the percentage of participants and the percentage of controls who have shown changes on each dimension. We see, first of all, that there is a very large difference between participants and controls on the cognitive dimension: Participants showed a much greater increase in the differentiation of their images of America and American broadcasting. Changes on the evaluative dimensions are considerably smaller and inconsistent in direction. Thus, participants, as compared to controls, did become more favorable in their general attitude toward America, but they actually became less favorable (whereas the controls showed no net change) in their general attitude toward American TV. Finally, it is clear that favorableness toward American broadcasting itself is not a unitary dimension: Though participants became less favorable toward American TV in general, they became more favorable in their view of the potential contributions that American experiences could make to broadcasting in their own countries.

This pattern of results suggests quite clearly some of the subtleties that must be kept in mind as one assesses the impact of an international exchange experience on participants' attitudes toward the host society. Specifically, our conclusions are likely to be misleading (1) if we assess change solely on the evaluative dimension, rather than assigning an important place in the analysis to the cognitive dimensions of attitudes; (2) if we treat the host society as a unitary object, rather than taking into account the likelihood that different patterns and institutions of the society may be evaluated quite differently; and (3) if we treat the evaluation of the society or even of a specific pattern or institution within it as a unitary dimension, rather than exploring the possibility that it may be evaluated favorably along one dimension and unfavorably along another.

Personal and professional impact. So far, we have been speaking about the impact of the sojourn on the participants' views of what they found in America—of American society and its members, of American

Table 30

CHANGES ON FOUR DIMENSIONS OF ATTITUDE TOWARD AMERICA AND AMERICAN BROADCASTING: COMPARISON OF PARTICIPANTS AND CONTROLS

Dimensions	Participants			Controls		
	Percentage Showing Increase	Percentage Showing Decrease	Net Change	Percentage Showing Increase	Percentage Showing Decrease	Net Change
Differentiation of the image of America and American broadcasting	63	19	44	30	55	−25
Favorableness of general attitude toward America	35	17	18	10	26	−16
Favorableness of general attitude toward American television	20	40	−20	29	29	0
Perception of potential contribution of American experiences to broadcasting in respondent's own country	35	18	17	23	38	−15

broadcasting and its practitioners. There is also some evidence of the personal and professional impact that the sojourn had on the participants.

In their own evaluations of the significance that the experience had for them, a large proportion of the participants indicated that they succeeded in learning many of the things that they had hoped to learn when they first arrived. First and foremost, they gained new professional knowledge and insight, which were relevant to their professional activities at home. In addition, they acquired new knowledge about American broadcasting specifically and about American society, which was, indeed, an important part of the agenda that many participants had brought with them. An impact of a different sort was the sense of enjoyment that they derived from traveling throughout the United States and interacting with Americans. Such enjoyment is often a part of the traveler's experience that is even more highly valued in retrospect, when he reflects on the trip and speaks about it, than it is while the trip is in progress. Many participants also reported that their American sojourn produced some changes in their perspectives on their own countries, or in their orientations toward international exchanges and their involvement in international contacts.

All of these reports suggest that, at least subjectively and at least in small ways, many participants had become different persons as a consequence of their trip. For different participants the impact had been in different areas. For some the trip may have been responsible, in part, for a reorganization of their professional ideas and plans, with substantial consequences for their careers. For others, its significance may largely have rested in the warm memories and the tidbits of new knowledge that it had produced. In either event, however, these were effects that the person carried with him at the end of the sojourn and that, in some sense, made themselves felt in his life back home.

Comparisons between participants and controls yield further information about the professional impact of the experience. Although both participants and controls often reported changes in their positions or responsibilities during the year following the seminar, the participants were more likely to ascribe these changes to the recognition of their own abilities. One might speculate that the experience abroad had enhanced their self-confidence and sense of professional competence. Further evidence along these lines can be found in the questionnaires. Between the first and the second questionnaires, participants tended to become more positive in their orientation toward their own professional future. Unlike the controls, they showed some increase in their level of aspiration, that is, in the professional position they hoped to achieve and the scope and quality of the operation they hoped to oversee. At the same time, they showed an increase in the congruity of hopes and aspirations: They tended not only to increase in their level of aspiration, but also in their confidence that they would be able to achieve this level.

In discussing their general views about broadcasting in the post-return interviews, participants were more likely to report that these had undergone some changes. Comparisons between participants and controls, however, yield rather little information about the specific nature of these changes; one point that did emerge more often among participants than among controls was a renewed or increased commitment to the importance of radio. There is some indication in the questionnaire data that the participants did indeed reorganize their views about broadcasting—at home as well as in the United States—to a somewhat greater extent than the controls. The questionnaire data also revealed a change with interesting evaluative implications among the participants: They tended to reduce the number of areas in which they felt broadcasters in other countries could benefit from their own experiences. This change probably reflected an increased awareness of the relative advantages and disadvantages of their own broadcasting procedures and approaches as compared to those of other countries. In general, this greater awareness did not make the seminar participants dissatisfied with their own procedures, but it did seem to make them less certain of the applicability of these procedures to the situations prevailing in other countries.

There is also some evidence that the reverse effect occurred—that participants became less certain of the applicability of procedures used in other countries to their own professional situations. Participants tended to express greater reservations than controls about the training value of international exchanges for their own broadcasters. These reservations seemed to be based precisely on the feeling that adaptation of the procedures used in one country to the conditions of another country is often a difficult and hazardous task. This does not mean that participants came to reject the value of international exchanges. As a matter of fact, according to their own reports, they became more positive about such exchanges as a result of their experience. What apparently happened, however, was that they had become more realistic about the potential contributions of such exchanges. They found exchange valuable, but also became aware of its limitations and thus tended to assign to it a more modest role than did the controls.

As for international communication, many participants seemed to have established and maintained a considerable number of contacts with American individuals and organizations. A much smaller number, however, had maintained their contacts with fellow-participants. One wonders whether this very limited success in building continuing connections among the participants was related to the limited place accorded to professional exchange among the participants themselves in the overall design of the seminar.

Conclusion. It is quite apparent from the data we have just reviewed that the seminar had a major impact on participants' views of America and American broadcasting, and one that is likely to be lasting because it involved not merely a change in the favorableness of images held, but a change in their complexity, differentiation, and richness of detail. The seminar's impact on the participants' professional attitudes and activities was less marked, but there certainly is some evidence of changes in these respects too. The seminar seemed to be least effective in generating an international network of professional communication and exchange, although it produced a stepped-up level of interaction of the participants with American individuals and organizations.

These findings suggest the kinds of changes that an international exchange of the type that we have investigated is capable of producing in some of the participants. This does not mean, of course, that such changes will occur in every program of this type and certainly not in every individual participant in such a program. It is obvious that in the present study, too, not every participant was affected to the same degree and in the same way. Let us turn, therefore, to some conclusions about the differential reactions manifested by different subgroups within the seminar, and some of the possible implications of such differences.

SUBGROUP DIFFERENCES

In order to explore possible differences in reaction within the total group of participants, we divided our population into subgroups, using two bases of division. One involved comparison between two subgroups differing in terms of demonstrated impact. We used, for this purpose, our index of change in degree of differentiation of the image of America and American broadcasting, which is the measure that yielded our major finding of impact. The comparison, then, is between those who showed the greatest amount of change on this index and those who showed the least —in other words, between high and low differentiators (Chapter Thirteen). Our second approach involved comparison between two subgroups differing in certain defining characteristics that were likely to have a bearing on their reactions to the situation and its impact upon them. For this purpose, we divided our population into Europeans and non-Europeans and examined the differences between these two groups in their patterns of reaction (Chapter Fourteen).

High versus Low Differentiators. The comparison between high and low differentiators affords us some insight into the processes that led to the development of more highly differentiated images among some of the seminar participants. The highs, as compared to the lows, were more familiar with America before the present trip, had more prior contacts with Americans, and had a better-articulated framework for viewing American life and society. Unlike some of the lows, they had no linguistic obstacles with which they had to contend. Furthermore, the highs more often came to the American sojourn with considerable self-confidence about their professional competence—a self-confidence bolstered by their linguistic and cultural proximity to the host society. They saw themselves as accomplished specialists, with a long history of involvement in their professional field and in an international network of fellow-professionals. In contrast to the lows, they had rather specific professional goals and expectations upon arrival and, in line with their self-orientation, they anticipated little difficulty in making the contacts and participating in the professionally stimulating discussions they were interested in.

Central to the highs' experience, however, was the fact that these expectations were not met. They were greatly disappointed in the professional part of the seminar, particularly during its university phase. They felt that the level of discussion was lower than they had hoped it would be, in part because of the heterogeneous composition of the group. They were dissatisfied with the limited opportunity they had for making personal contributions and exchanging ideas. In the interview conducted toward the end of the university phase, the highs expressed numerous criticisms of the professional program and of various other features of the seminar. Their dissatisfaction seemed to abate, however, as they shifted from a professional to a nonprofessional orientation. They had had some interest, from the beginning, in learning about America as a society, as evidenced by their positive expectations of the academic seminars. Thus, when they found the professional program disappointing, they were able to turn to these other pursuits with some enthusiasm. They gave increasing emphasis to extensive and detailed observations of American life, to sight-seeing and the enjoyment of scenic beauty, and to exchanging ideas with Americans. They expressed a high degree of satisfaction with all of these activities and apparently found them sufficiently enjoyable to compensate for their initial disappointment.

Given their emphasis on observations of American life and on interactions with Americans (focusing these interactions on an intensive exchange of ideas), it is not surprising that the highs developed more differentiated images of the host society and its institutions. Three factors, in interaction with each other, can probably account for the increased differentiation manifested by this subgroup of participants: (1) their readiness—due to their freedom from cultural and linguistic barriers, their professional self-confidence, and the specificity of their expectations—to enter quickly and easily into intensive interactions with the Americans they met, and thus to become exposed to the variety and complexity of Americans and their views; (2) their possession of a fairly well-articulated cognitive framework about the United States, which helped them scan new information more quickly and integrate new insights more readily; and (3) their disappointment in the professional experience, which may have caused them to give greater weight to the interest in learning about America—an interest they had brought with them but that might, under other circumstances, have remained more latent. The disappointment may or may not be causally related to the changes manifested by the highs. We are inclined to the view that the highs' professional disappointment helped to trigger off a process to which they were already predisposed and to intensify this process by providing additional motivation to engage in it. In any event, whether or not the disappointment intensified or even caused the process of differentiation, it is clear that at the very least it did not interfere with it. This result does not mean, of course, that such disappointments would never interfere with significant change. It is quite conceivable that, for some individuals, disappointment in the professional sphere may have rather devastating effects. The highs in the present study, however, given their dispositions and interests, were able to look for and find their satisfactions in other pursuits, and to come away from the experience with a major impact on their attitudes.

The trip also had an important impact on the lows, though an impact of a rather different nature than that manifested by the highs, in keeping with the different patterns represented by these two groups. The lows, because of their greater cultural and linguistic barriers, were not as ready to enter into intensive interactions with Americans, focusing on the exchange of ideas, or to assimilate new information into a preexisting cognitive framework for viewing the United States. Thus, they did not have the highs' capacity for developing highly differentiated images; nor did they have the highs' motivation for doing so, since they were not at all disappointed in the professional part of the experience. They had come to the sojourn with less professional self-confidence than the highs, with a greater tendency to see themselves as learners and apprentices, and with more diffuse professional goals and expectations. They were, therefore, highly satisfied with the professional activities that had been made available to them, and with the composition of the group. They considered the level of the discussion and of their personal participation quite appropriate to their needs and their perceived capacities. In contrast to the highs, they tended to become more professionally oriented as the seminar proceeded and more absorbed in professional pursuits. Having started out with rather vague expectations, they became eager for workshop-like experiences, focusing on specific problems relevant to their own work situations. A year after returning home, they seemed to feel that the seminar had indeed affected their professional activities and increased their skills, and they communicated an increased sense of competence and professional self-confidence. Thus, though the trip had a less marked impact on their images of America and American broadcasting, it had a greater impact on their professional activities than it did for the highs.

It would be a mistake to exaggerate the difference between the two groups—to assume that for the highs the satisfactions and impact of the sojourn were entirely in the nonprofessional domain and for the lows entirely in the professional domain. We have evidence that the highs found some of their professional experiences rewarding, particularly during the travel period. For example, they seemed to enjoy their professional encounters with American colleagues and were more likely than the lows to establish professional contacts that they maintained after returning home. In keeping with their self-images as accomplished professionals, they used the trip to expand their network of professional relations. Similarly, we have evidence that the lows found some of their nonprofessional experiences rewarding. They seemed to be more interested than the highs in meeting average Americans and they enjoyed making friends and discovering commonality with people from other countries. Whereas the highs became more absorbed in interactions focusing on exchange of ideas, the lows were more oriented toward personal, social interactions with Americans.

Thus, for both highs and lows, the sojourn had professional as well as nonprofessional components. For the highs, however, it was the nonprofessional experiences that constituted the highlights of the trip and affected them most profoundly; some of their professional encounters were very valuable, but—after their initial disappointment—they no longer depended upon them as a primary source of satisfaction. For the lows, on the other hand, saw the professional experiences as their major source of accomplishment and were influenced by them in important ways; they greatly enjoyed their personal encounters and remembered them warmly, but these represented a pleasant by-product rather than a primary purpose of the sojourn.

Europeans versus non-Europeans. The comparison between Europeans and non-Europeans allows us to trace some of the effects of differences in background, goals, and agenda on the quality and impact of an exchange experience.

In a number of respects, the differences between Europeans and non-Europeans parallel those between high and low differentiators. The Europeans brought to the experience a greater degree of professional self-

confidence and of cultural similarity to the host society than did the
non-Europeans; they were less satisfied with the professional part of the
program; they were more interested in deepening their understanding of
American life and society; and they were less affected than the non-Europeans by the experience in the professional sphere, but more affected in
their conceptions of the host society. In all of these ways, the Europeans
resembled the high differentiators, and the non-Europeans the lows. Perhaps these similarities can best be accounted for by the overlap between
the two comparisons. The English-speaking Europeans form a subgroup
of the highs as well as of the Europeans; the African participants form a
subgroup of the lows as well as of the non-Europeans. Thus, any consistent differences between these two subgroups would be reflected in both
sets of comparisons.

In addition to these parallels, there are also some important differences between the two sets of comparisons. A dominant feature of the
high-low comparison was the highs' professional disappointment. They
started out with high expectations for a useful professional experience;
only when they found these expectations frustrated did they shift to an emphasis on observing American life. The lows, by contrast, started out with
more diffuse professional expectations; they were highly satisfied with
what they found and, if anything, became more professionally oriented as
the seminar proceeded. In the comparison between Europeans and non-
Europeans, on the other hand, professional disappointment and shifts in
orientation did not seem to play a major role. Rather, the differences between the two groups in their orientations, their satisfactions, and the impact the experience had upon them can be traced to differences in the
initial agenda that they brought to the sojourn.

The Europeans tended to come to the seminar with a broader and
less specific agenda, which included not only professional concerns, but
also an interest in seeing the country, in meeting people, and in deepening
their understanding of American society. They concluded, shortly after
their arrival, that the structure of the seminar and the composition of the
group would not permit a professional exchange at the level they desired.
They readily adopted, therefore, the stance of observers. Both in professional and nonprofessional spheres, they took observation and critical examination of American institutions and practices as ends in themselves.
Both at the university and during the travel period they were interested
in everything they could learn about America; they appreciated the opportunity to travel and enjoyed the physical environment; they regarded
the acquisition of firsthand knowledge of the United States and of a
greater understanding of its institutions as their most important accomplishment. On the professional side, too, they enjoyed visiting broad-

casting facilities, observing their activities, meeting American broadcasters, and comparing notes with them. Their opportunity for professional self-utilization was probably more limited than they would have liked, but they found a large proportion of their experiences—of a professional and particularly of an extraprofessional nature—to be relevant to their interests and rewarding. As a result, their overall level of satisfaction, with both the university and the travel phases of the seminar, was very high.

The non-Europeans, by contrast, came with a more limited and specific agenda. They were concerned with increasing their professional skills and learning about broadcasting procedures that could be applied to their home situations. They were more interested in professional self-development than in self-utilization. As a result, they were highly task-oriented during both phases of the seminar. Not only did they focus primarily on professional pursuits, but even within the professional domain they sought out exchanges around specific problems that promised to be directly useful to their own work. They were not particularly interested in observing and hearing about the practices and procedures of American broadcasting, except insofar as these were potentially applicable in their own broadcasting systems. Unlike the Europeans, they found many of the professional exchanges at the university highly useful and at a level appropriate to their needs. They were eager to benefit from the experience of the American speakers and of other seminar participants, particularly those from highly developed broadcasting systems; they regarded the contributions of these colleagues as sources of relevant information. During the travel period, too, the non-Europeans appreciated the opportunity of meeting helpful colleagues and of learning new approaches to programming. If their overall satisfaction—with both the university and the travel phases of the seminar—was lower than that of the Europeans, it was probably because too small a proportion of the total program was directly relevant to their more narrowly defined agenda. They would have preferred fewer lectures, academic seminars, and tours of facilities, and more workshop-like experiences. By the end of the sojourn, however, the non-Europeans' overall level of satisfaction was as high as that of the Europeans, although the sources of satisfaction differed for the two groups.

The impact of the trip on the two groups' views of America and American broadcasting and on their professional activities differed in ways consistent with their different backgrounds, agenda, orientations, and sources of satisfaction. The most striking effect of the trip on the Europeans was in the cognitive structure of their images of American society. They developed a more differentiated view and a more complex understanding of America than did the non-Europeans. They not only placed a greater emphasis on the diversity and heterogeneity of America, but also showed a more detailed awareness of the ways in which internal differences functioned in American life. This effect is in keeping with the agenda that the Europeans had set for themselves—with their emphasis, throughout the sojourn, on observing American life and understanding its institutions.

In their attitudes toward American broadcasting, non-Europeans tended to be highly favorable, in rather global terms. The Europeans, by contrast, were more differentiated and much more selective in their approval. They praised certain specific approaches and techniques of American broadcasting, but had some serious criticisms of its overall structure and quality. The more critical attitude of the Europeans probably reflects, at least in part, their greater interest in examining American broadcasting and comparing it to other approaches—in contrast to the non-Europeans, who were much more interested in extracting from American broadcasting specific procedures that might be applicable to their own situations.

Interestingly, more Europeans than non-Europeans seemed to have put their American experience to concrete use within the first year after returning home. Though the non-Europeans had expressed, during the sojourn, greater interest in learning new approaches to programming and in establishing new professional contacts, the Europeans more often reported that they had in fact introduced American-inspired programs and maintained professional contacts with American individuals and organizations. It seems that the Europeans—being professionally more experienced and working in more established organizations—found it easier to implement ideas and to maintain contacts acquired in America, and that this more than compensated for their lesser motivation to do so. Nevertheless, the sojourn did seem to have a more far-reaching impact on the professional activities of the non-Europeans, in keeping with the particular agenda that they had brought to it. They felt that the experience gave them, not only new information relevant to their work, but a new perspective on their professional roles. They reported, more often than Europeans, that their professional positions or responsibilities had changed in the year since their return or would soon change; although these changes probably resulted from the rapid development that their broadcasting systems were undergoing, their own participation in this process may have been greatly affected by the new knowledge, perspective, and prestige that they acquired as a result of their trip. Finally, non-Europeans reported, more often than Europeans, that their job satisfaction had increased, and ascribed this increase to the recognition others gave to their abilities. These reactions are indicative of an increased professional self-confidence among the non-Europeans, which can be expected to facilitate their professional development over a period of years.

The portraits of the European and the non-European that we have drawn do not apply to every member of these groups within our sample; they are even less representative of Europeans and non-Europeans in general. What is important about these portraits is not so much what they tell us about Europeans and non-Europeans, but what they tell us about two different patterns of reaction to an international exchange experience of the kind that we have investigated. They illustrate some of the differences in goals and expectations, in orientations and agenda, that different participants might bring to such an experience, and the effects these have on their reactions to the experience and the impact it has upon them.

Conclusion. The two sets of subgroup comparisons that have been presented contribute to our theoretical understanding of attitude change in general, and of change in a cross-national context in particular. They demonstrate the interactions between predispositions, goals, and experiences in the determination of change. Moreover, they help us conceptualize the change process not merely in quantitative but also in qualitative terms. That is, they suggest relationships between the specific form of change-inducing variables and the type of change they are likely to yield.

Aside from these theoretical considerations, what implications do the two sets of comparisons have for the conduct of cross-national exchange programs? One thing that is quite clear from our data is that such programs may be of benefit to a wide variety of participants. It would not make sense to draw up *general* qualifications for participants in international exchange—to propose, for example, that participants in such programs ought to be young, or experienced, or politically moderate, or what have you. Many different types of individuals may find the experience satisfying and meaningful, providing the particular program in which they are involved is relevant to their particular interests and needs. By the same token, it is clear that different types of programs may be rewarding and beneficial. It would not make sense to draw up rigid criteria for the structure and content of exchange programs in general, without regard to the particular participants they are designed to serve—to search for a single model that would meet everyone's needs. The specific requirements of a program that will be satisfying and useful for one participant may be quite different from the requirements for another.

These considerations underline the importance of careful matching of participants and programs. Given a particular group of participants, one must devise a program that meets their particular needs and interests most adequately. For example, the shape of the program will have to depend on the extent to which participants' interests are focused on professional concerns or include a strong extraprofessional component as well; and—within the professional domain—on the extent to which they are looking for self-utilization or for self-development. Given a particular program, one must select participants to whose goals and interests it is most likely to be suited. For example, the type of participants selected will have to depend on the extent to which the program is designed to include workshop experiences that provide training in basic skills, or is oriented primarily toward observations and demonstrations.

The matching between programs and participants cannot be done blindly. Thus, it would be unfortunate if one were to conclude, on the basis of our analysis, that Europeans as a group need one kind of experience and non-Europeans another. Our analysis suggests that European versus non-European in this context is an important variable, but we must keep in mind that (a) it is only one of many variables, and (b) it is a variable that itself consists of many variables—that is, it reflects a number of factors that need not always go together. Our hope, then, is that the two patterns we have identified will be considered in the matching of participants and programs, but on an individual rather than on a group basis—that they will help organizers of exchange programs assess whether the fit between a given program and a given *individual* is right, in view of the needs and expectations of that individual.

Our two sets of comparisons suggest that not only can different types of programs be beneficial for different participants, but even within the same program it is possible for different participants to derive different kinds of satisfaction and to manifest different kinds of change. Thus, one ought not assume that a particular program can serve only one purpose and must therefore be restricted to one type of participant. Our comparison between Europeans and non-Europeans demonstrates, for example, that, despite their different orientations, both of these groups were able to derive some degree of satisfaction and benefit from the same seminar. While the seminar did not fully meet the special needs of either type of participant, it seemed to meet them sufficiently to make the experience, on the whole, a satisfying and meaningful one for each, and to produce an impact that still manifested itself a year later. In short, the same program can have different meanings and uses for different participants; there are alternative ways in which it may turn out to be successful.

As a matter of fact, as the high-low comparison demonstrates, even participants who find the program greatly disappointing—who find that it is not what they had expected and hoped it to be—may be able to turn the sojourn into a satisfying and meaningful experience by reorienting themselves and shifting their emphases. In other words, a less than perfect match between participant and program need not be totally devastating. There is often more than one way in which an exchange experience may prove satisfying and valuable to its participants, and different individuals may derive their rewards from different features of the experience. Even a disappointment on a central dimension does not preclude satisfaction and meaningful change on other dimensions.

It does not follow, of course, that participants will be satisfied with the experience regardless of what happens. A favorable outcome in the face of disappointment, such as manifested by the high differentiators in the present study, presupposes that the individual's interests are sufficiently broad and flexible so that he can change direction with a fair degree of equanimity. Furthermore, it presupposes that the program itself is sufficiently varied and flexible so that it has something worthwhile to offer to different kinds of participants and so that it can be adjusted once it becomes clear that some participants' needs are not being adequately met.

This brings us to another important implication for the conduct of exchange programs. It is essential to build into each program a variety of options so that participants can find at least some activities that are suited to their particular needs and interests. If enough alternatives are available, individuals who regard the main lines of the program irrelevant to their interests, or those whose interests change as they go along, can fruitfully turn to other pursuits. Along with variety, the program must also build in flexibility, not only to allow different individuals to follow different pursuits, but also to allow the program itself to be modified as it proceeds if it appears to be unsuited to the needs of most or some of its participants.

The need for building a range of options into the program becomes evident once we recognize that, even under the best of circumstances, we cannot achieve a perfect match between participants and programs, since neither is completely predictable. We have already pointed out that the needs and interests of an individual participant cannot be reliably predicted from the categories into which he falls. Knowing that he is European or non-European, young or old, experienced or inexperienced, does not tell us to what extent his personal needs and interests deviate from those that might be modal for his group. Even if his personal needs and interests are carefully assessed before his program is planned, the possibilities of providing him with a perfect fit are limited; his needs may not become fully crystallized until he arrives on the scene, and his interests may change as the sojourn progresses. Similarly, programs are not fully predictable. Unanticipated changes in personnel or facilities or available resources may drastically affect the quality of the experience. Moreover, as a program unfolds, it takes on a life of its own and often turns out differently than expected.

In planning an exchange program, we should not count on the resilience of the participants in the face of disappointment. All efforts must be made to select participants whose interests match the available opportunities and to tailor programs to the specific needs of those who have been selected. No matter how conscientiously this is done, however, organizers of exchange programs cannot assume that the outcome will prove satisfactory to all concerned in all respects, or that it will remain satisfactory throughout the life of the program. They must also, therefore, prepare for the possibility that some of the matchings between participant and program will be less than perfect or will become so with time. The only way to prepare for such eventualities is to build enough options into the program so that participants can choose among alternative activities, can pursue some of their specialized interests, and can redirect their goals and orientations within the overall framework.

In sum, two major general implications can be drawn from our subgroup analysis: (a) that different individuals, in keeping with their different goals and orientations, need different kinds of experiences if an exchange program is to be satisfying to them and have an impact upon them; and (b) that there is more than one way in which a given program can provide satisfaction and have an impact. Thus, the same program can be satisfying and effective for different individuals in different ways, despite differences in their goals and orientations, as long as it offers alternative paths for meeting their special needs.

Appendix A

Dimensions Used by the Group Observer to Make Weekly Ratings of Individual Behavior in the Group[1]

Dimension	Definition
1. Leadership	Degree to which individual has guided direction of discussion and shaping of opinion

[1] Ratings on dimensions 1 through 11b were made on a five-point scale, with a rating of 1 representing a low level of leadership, participation, and so on, and a rating of 5 representing a high level. Dimensions 12a, 12b, and 12c were ranked in terms of the relative dominance of each of the three frames of reference in the participant's behavior during the week; the highest ranked frame of reference was assigned a score of 3, the lowest ranked a score of 1.

Dimension	Definition
2. Participation	Degree to which individual has dominated discussion and interaction (independent of the impact this had)
3. Involvement	Amount of interest—animation, attentiveness—shown in group sessions (independent of leadership and participation)
4a. Hostility, aggression toward members	Amount of behavior aimed at belittling, harming, blaming, accusing, or ridiculing other members of the group
4b. Hostility, aggression toward leader	Amount of behavior aimed at belittling, harming, blaming, accusing, or ridiculing the formal group leader
5. Novelty, innovation	Degree to which individual acts differently from other members, holds unique views, introduces new topics or approaches
6. Cognizance	Proportion of individual's activity directed to seeking information and raising questions
7. Exposition	Degree to which individual points out, demonstrates, relates facts, gives information, explains, interprets
8. Clarification	Degree to which individual makes distinctions, points to similarities, addresses himself to the course of the discussion
9a. Nurturance toward members	Amount of behavior aimed at enhancing, encouraging, supporting, or offering sympathy to other members of the group
9b. Nurturance toward leader	Amount of behavior aimed at enhancing, encouraging, supporting, or offering sympathy to the formal group leader
10. Dependency	Degree to which individual seeks enhancement, support, or protection from degradation by others

11a.	Effort at national self-enhancement	Ratio of positive to negative statements individual makes about his country's accomplishments and experiences
11b.	Effort at personal self-enhancement	Ratio of positive to negative statements individual makes about his own accomplishments and experiences
12a.	National frame of reference	Degree to which individual tends to speak in a national capacity
12b.	Professional frame of reference	Degree to which individual tends to speak in a professional capacity
12c.	Idiosyncratic frame of reference	Degree to which individual tends to invoke roles other than national or professional ones

Appendix B

Questionnaire for Specialists in Broadcasting

1. Below is a list of activities in which television might be engaged. To what extent are these activities involved in television (as it is practiced or planned) *in your country?* For each item, please check whether it represents (or will represent) a major activity, a minor activity, or one which is hardly ever engaged in.

	Major activity	*Minor activity*	*Hardly ever done*
a. Providing specific information, such as news, to the public	....	....	....
b. Providing education to the public	....	....	....
c. Providing popular entertainment	....	....	....
d. Providing high-level entertainment for those groups within the population that are interested	....	....	....

334

e. Giving the general public contact with good literature, art, and music

f. Contributing to the improvement of artistic and literary taste

g. Providing programs of interest to special groups within the population, such as religious, ethnic, or occupational groups

h. Providing a forum for political discussion

i. Communicating the goals of the government to the citizens of the country

j. Selling products and services

k. Creating common ties in the country

l. Contributing to the creation and maintenance of national loyalty

m. Providing information about other countries

Which of the above activities do you think should receive *more* emphasis by television in your country (as it is practiced or planned) than they do now? Please list them by letter below:

Which of the above activities do you think should receive *less* emphasis by television in your country (as it is practiced or planned) than they do now? Please list them by letter below:

2. The list of activities in which television might be engaged is repeated below. This time, consider the extent to which these activities are involved in television *in the United States.* For each item, please check whether it represents a major activity, a minor activity, or one which is hardly ever engaged in.

	Major activity	*Minor activity*	*Hardly ever done*
a. Providing specific information, such as news, to the public			
b. Providing education to the public			
c. Providing popular entertainment			
d. Providing high-level entertain-			

ment for those groups within the
population that are interested ....

e. Giving the general public contact with good literature, art,
and music ....

f. Contributing to the improvement
of artistic and literary taste ....

g. Providing programs of interest to
special groups within the population, such as religious, ethnic,
or occupational groups ....

h. Providing a forum for political
discussion ....

i. Communicating the goals of the
government to the citizens of the
country ....

j. Selling products and services ....

k. Creating common ties in the
country ....

l. Contributing to the creation
and maintenance of national
loyalty ....

m. Providing information about
other countries ....

Which of the above activities do you think should receive *more* emphasis by American television than they do now? Please list them by letter below:

Which of the above activities do you think should receive *less* emphasis by American television than they do now? Please list them by letter below:

3. It may be helpful to broadcasting specialists in other countries to learn about the experiences that your country has had in this field. Can you mention some of the experiences in your country that may be particularly instructive to broadcasters in other countries?

4. Similarly, it may be helpful to broadcasting specialists in your country to learn about the experiences that the United States has had in this field. Can you mention some of the experiences in the United States that may be particularly instructive to broadcasters in your country? (This may include experiences that you would want to adapt to your own situation, as well as experiences that you would want to avoid.)

5. How similar should the functions of television in your country be to the functions of television in the United States? Please check the item below that seems most descriptive of your position.

.... Very similar
.... Similar, but different in some respects
.... Different, but similar in some respects
.... Very different

6. *In what ways* (if any) should the functions of television be different in your country from the United States?

7. Specialists in mass communications in the United States are, at present, engaged in a critical examination of the state of television in their country. Because of their direct involvement in the situation, they may have some difficulty in seeing all of the problems. From your position of greater distance, what would *you* say are the most important problems facing *American* television today?

a. First problem:
What do you think is the major cause of this problem?
Can you suggest any measures that might alleviate this problem?
b. Second problem:
What do you think is the major cause of this problem?
Can you suggest any measures that might alleviate this problem?
c. Third problem:
What do you think is the major cause of this problem?
Can you suggest any measures that might alleviate this problem?

Other problems:

8. Although to a certain extent television faces the same problems in every country, situations do arise that are unique to a particular country. What are some of the major problems that television (or the development of television) faces *in your country?*

a. First problem:
What do you think is the major cause of this problem?
Can you suggest any measures that might alleviate this problem?
b. Second problem:
What do you think is the major cause of this problem?
Can you suggest any measures that might alleviate this problem?
c. Third problem:
What do you think is the major cause of this problem?
Can you suggest any measures that might alleviate this problem?
Other problems:

9. By what means do you think Americans obtain information about your country?

10. Do you think American mass media provide adequate information about your country?

   a. How extensive is the coverage?   b. How accurate is the coverage?

   .... Very extensive   .... Very accurate
   .... Quite extensive   .... Quite accurate
   .... Fairly extensive   .... Fairly accurate
   .... Not too extensive   .... Not too accurate
   .... Not extensive at all   .... Not accurate at all

11. What impressions of your country do you think Americans have? That is, if a typical American were asked to describe your country, what characteristics would he be likely to mention?

12. Can you think of any groups of Americans whose impressions of your country differ from the ones you just described?

   Group:
   In what ways do their impressions differ?
   Group:
   In what ways do their impressions differ?
   Group:
   In what ways do their impressions differ?

13. If an American television network were planning a feature program about your country, what would you recommend that they include in order to help the American public gain a better understanding of your country?

14. By what means do most people in your country obtain information about the United States?

15. a. Do you think the mass media in your country provide adequate information about the United States?

   .... Very adequate
   .... Quite adequate
   .... Fairly adequate
   .... Not too adequate

   b. In what ways do you think the coverage might be extended? For example, what information might be included in a feature program about the United States?

16. How important is each of the following in your kind of job? For each item, please check whether it is very important, somewhat important, slightly important, or not important in your kind of job.

	Very important	*Somewhat important*	*Slightly important*	*Not important*
a. Administration and management	....	....	....	....
b. The engineering and technical side of communications	....	....	....	....
c. Public relations (interpreting your organization to the public)	....	....	....	....
d. Collaboration with others within and outside your organization	....	....	....	....
e. The artistic side of communications	....	....	....	....
f. Research	....	....	....	....
g. Contact with developments in the field of education	....	....	....	....
h. Contact with the government of your own country	....	....	....	....
i. The commercial side of communication	....	....	....	....
j. Contact with international developments in communications	....	....	....	....

Please describe the *specific activities* involved in your job:

17. a. In general, how satisfied are you with your work?

.... Very satisfied
.... Satisfied
.... More satisfied than dissatisfied
.... More dissatisfied than satisfied
.... Dissatisfied
.... Very dissatisfied

b. Which aspects of your work provide you with the greatest satisfaction?
c. In contrast, which aspects of your work cause you the most dissatisfaction?

18. If there were no obstacles in your path, what would you *hope* to be doing in five years? Please be as optimistic as you can in your description.

19. Now, taking into account the circumstances that are likely to prevail, describe what you *expect* to be doing in five years.

20. If people working in broadcasting were asked to name the professions that were most similar to their own, they might name the following ones:

> advertising executive   newspaper editor
> artist   politician
> businessman   teacher
> civil servant   theatrical director
> electrical engineer   university professor
> film producer   writer

   a. In general, which one of the professions listed above do you consider to be:

> Most similar to your own? ....
> Next most similar?   ....
> *Least* similar?   ....

   b. Taking only the *social status* of the professions into consideration, which one would you say is:

> Most similar to your own? ....
> Next most similar?   ....
> *Least* similar?   ....

   c. Now consider only the *skills* required for your work. Which of the professions is:

> Most similar to your own? ....
> Next most similar?   ....
> *Least* similar?   ....

   d. Finally, consider the *activities* involved in your work and name the profession:

> Most similar to your own? ....
> Next most similar?   ....
> *Least* similar?   ....

Index

341